Preface to the fourth edition

The style and structure of *Introductory Economics* remain largely unchanged.

The modifications incorporated in this new edition are:

a the inclusion of some new material,
b a revised treatment of certain topics,
c a very necessary updating of the factual content, data and tables.

The introductory section now includes an explanation of the production possibility curve and a revision of the material on scarcity and choice.

The chapters on business organisation, the finance of industry and regional policy have been revised and updated, and the chapter on population has been substantially modified.

New material is included in the chapters on prices and markets while the section on the control of monopoly has been largely rewritten. This is also true of the material on trade unions.

Recent important changes in the structure and practice of banking are now included in the text and the treatment of monetarism has been given rather more prominence. The chapters on the international sector have been brought up to date with a major revision of the section on the IMF.

In addition to the updating of the statistics, the chapter on public finance has been subject to some rearrangement of the material and a considerable amount of rewriting. The recent fundamental changes in the performance of the UK economy and in government economic policy have been incorporated in the text in the appropriate chapters.

G.F.S.

Contents

Part Six: The National Income and Its Distribution

Part Seven: Money and Banking

Part Eight: Changes in the Value of Money

Part Nine: International Trade, Finance, and Co-operation

Part Ten: Public Finance

Part Eleven: Managing The Economy

Part One: Introduction

1 The Nature, Scope, and Methods of Economics

The economic problem

The individual and society

Most introductory textbooks of Economics begin by posing the question, 'What is Economics about?' Although Economics is a vast subject and precise definitions are usually very complex, it is not a difficult matter to give a simple and sensible answer to this basic question. Economics is essentially a study of the ways in which humankind provides for its material wellbeing. Economists are concerned with the ways in which people apply their knowledge, skills, and efforts to the gifts of nature in order to satisfy their material wants.

Economics limits itself to the study of the material aspects of life, and while it is true that man cannot live by bread alone, it is equally true that he cannot live without it. An underlying problem in economics is that of survival and we must examine how people have solved or are trying to solve this problem. In the more advanced countries this may seem a very remote problem – few people, if any, are conscious of a life or death struggle for existence. In many other countries however, the continuity of human existence is by no means assured – starvation is a very real prospect for millions of human beings.

Even in the prosperous, economically advanced countries there is an aspect of survival which attracts little or no attention from those of us fortunate enough to live in these areas. This is our relative helplessness as 'economic' individuals. The Indian peasant and the South American peón have an extremely low standard of living, yet, left completely to their own devices, they can survive. Such people have the abilities to sustain life without outside assistance. A large percentage of the human race still lives in very small self-sufficient peasant communities. These people experience great poverty, but they can provide, on an individual basis, for their own survival. They have a degree of *economic independence*.

If we now turn to the inhabitants of New York, London, or any other great metropolitan area we must observe the opposite situation – a high standard of living together with an extreme *economic dependence*. The inhabitants of cities are totally incapable of providing for themselves, directly, the means of their survival. They could not feed themselves, clothe themselves, or build their own houses. The richer the nation, the greater is the inability of its citizens to survive unaided and alone. Such people depend, each and every day of their lives, on the efforts and cooperation of many thousands of specialist workers. The production of the simplest of our daily needs, a loaf of bread for example, requires the cooperative activities of hundreds of specialists. The recent experience of prolonged major strikes has shown us that the failure to perform its functions by any single group of specialists could so easily cripple an industrialised society. In these societies a high standard of living is possible only if the organised cooperation of large numbers of people can be guaranteed. Underneath the affluence there is a very real vulnerability. In the economically developed countries we are rich, not as individuals, but only as members of a complex economic organisation.

Scarcity and choice

Economics, then, is about the satisfaction of material wants. It is necessary to be quite clear about this; it is people's *wants* rather than their *needs* which provide the motive for economic activity. We go to work in order to obtain an income which will buy us the things we want rather than the things we need. It is not possible to define 'need' in terms of any particular quantity of a commodity, because this would imply that a certain level of consumption is 'right' for an individual. Economists tend to avoid this kind of *value judgement* which tries to specify how much people *ought* to consume. It is assumed that individuals wish to enjoy as much well-being as possible, and if their consumption of food, clothing, entertainment, and other goods and services is less than the amount required to give them complete satisfaction they will want to have more of them.

If the resources available to people are insufficient to satisfy all their wants, we say that such resources are scarce. Scarcity is a relative concept; it relates the extent of people's wants to their ability to satisfy those wants. Neither people's wants nor their ability to produce goods and services are constant. Their productive potential is increasing all the time, but so is their appetite for material things. If all the British people were content to live at the level of an Indian peasant, all our wants could be easily satisfied with one or two hour's labour each day; we would not experience scarcity. In fact we find that scarcity is a feature of all societies from the richest to the poorest. In both affluent societies and those afflicted by general poverty we find the great majority of people demanding higher living standards. The achievement of some desired goal of material satisfaction seems to do little more than raise people's expectations of something even better. Whether this perpetual increase in the demands for more and better material satisfactions is in the nature of humankind or whether it is artificially stimulated by modern advertising is a subject much disputed at the present time.

Whatever the reason, the fact is that we find ourselves in a situation of scarcity. We cannot have all the things we want. The resources available to satisfy our wants are, at any time, limited in supply. Our wants, however, appear to be unlimited. Thus, we are all in a position of having to make choices; we can only have more of X by having less of Y. Our incomes are insufficient for us to buy all the things we would like to have. The individual with a limited income and unlimited wants is forced to exercise choice when he or she spends that income. Society as a whole faces a similar problem.

There is a limit to a country's productive capacity because the available supply of land, factories, machines, labour and other economic resources is limited. These economic resources have alternative uses; they can be used to produce many different kinds of goods and services. If some of these resources are committed to the production of one thing then society must forego the outputs of the other things which it might have produced. For example, if we commit resources to the building of houses then the real cost of these houses is the potential output of schools, shops, office blocks or theatres which has been sacrificed in order to produce houses.

Production possibilities and opportunity cost

The problems of scarcity and choice can be illustrated by making use of a production possibility curve. This is a curve which shows what a society *could* produce with its existing supplies of land, labour, capital, and technical knowledge. With this limited supply of economic resources, a society has a wide variety of options as to the quantities and varieties of goods and services it may produce. It might produce fewer ships and more aircraft, less wheat and more barley, fewer tanks and more motor cars and so on. In an advanced economy capable of producing thousands of different commodities the range of choices is clearly enormous, but the basic problem can be illustrated by greatly simplifying the situation and assuming that the economy can only produce two types of good, say agricultural products and manufactured products. Table 1 illustrates such a situation.

The extreme possibilities are (i) the economy devotes all its resources to agriculture and produces 6 million tonnes of food and no manufactured goods and (ii) all the resources are put to work in manufacturing industry and no food is produced. These are very unrealistic possibilities. The economy will choose to produce some combination of the two commodities.

Columns 3 and 4 illustrate the very important point mentioned earlier, that is, the production of one thing involves the sacrifice of another thing. In column 3 we can see the 'cost' of producing one more

Table 1 Production possibilities

Agricultural products (millions of tonnes)	Manufactured products (millions of units)	Opportunity cost of one tonne of agricultural products (expressed in units of manufactured products)	Opportunity cost of one unit of manufactured products (expressed in tonnes of agricultural products)
0	60		
		2	$\frac{1}{2}$
1	58		
		3	$\frac{1}{3}$
2	55		
		5	$\frac{1}{5}$
3	50		
		8	$\frac{1}{8}$
4	42		
		12	$\frac{1}{12}$
5	30		
		30	$\frac{1}{30}$
6	0		

tonne of agricultural produce measured in terms of manufactured products. The quantity of manufactured products which has to be foregone in order to produce one more tonne of agricultural products (food) is described as the *opportunity cost* of that tonne of food. If this community increases its food production from 3 million tonnes to 4 million tonnes, the opportunity cost of the additional output is 8 million units of manufactured goods. Column 4 shows the opportunity cost of manufactured products measured in terms of the output of agricultural products which have to be foregone when more resources are allocated to manufacturing. Figure 1 is based on the information contained in Table 1.

Notice that as the production of food increases so does the opportunity cost of the food. This is partly because some resources will be more suited to agriculture and some more suited to manufacturing.[1] As food production increases, the resources being moved into the industry will be less and less suited to agriculture. The same reasoning can be applied to attempts to increase the output of the manufacturing industries; as resources are transferred from agriculture to manufacturing, the cost, in terms of the foregone agricultural output, will steadily increase.

---

[1] It is also due to the operation of the Law of Diminishing Returns (see page 52).

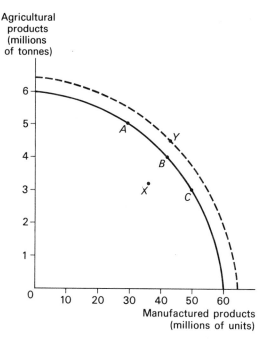

Fig. 1 Production possibility curve

Points on the production possibility curve such as *A*, *B*, and *C* show the maximum possible combined outputs of the two commodities. The economy can produce any combination *inside* the curve, but this would mean that some resources are unemployed. Point *X* illustrates this type of situation. In this case the economy could produce more of *both* goods by moving to a point such as *B*. Points outside the production possibility curve (such as *Y*) are not attainable with the country's present productive capacity. Output *Y* will only become a production possibility if the country's ability to produce increases and the production possibility curve moves outwards as shown by the dotted line.

A country's ability to produce more goods and services of all types depends upon changes such as an increase in the labour force, an increase in the stock of capital goods (factories, power stations, transport networks, machinery etc.) and/or an increase in technical knowledge.

Three basic problems

People have limited means to satisfy unlimited wants so they are forced to choose. The problems of choice are essentially problems of *allocation*. People must decide how to allocate resources to different uses

5

and then how to allocate the goods and services produced to the individual members of society. There are three fundamental choices to be made.

1 Which goods shall be produced and in what quantities? This problem concerns the composition of total output. The community must decide which goods it is going to produce and hence which goods it is *not* going to produce. Having decided the range of goods to be produced, the community must then decide how much of each good should be produced. In reality the choices before a community are rarely of the 'all or nothing' variety. They usually take the form: more of one thing and less of another. The first and major function of any economic system is to determine in some way the actual quantities and varieties of goods and services which will best meet the wants of its citizens.

2 How should the various goods and services be produced? Most goods can be produced by a variety of methods. Wheat can be grown by making use of much labour and little capital, or by using vast amounts of capital and very little labour. Electrical appliances can be made by using large and complex machines operated by relatively few semi- or unskilled workers. Alternatively they might be produced in hosts of small workshops by highly skilled technicians using relatively little machinery. Different methods of production can be distinguished from one another by the differences in the quantities of resources used in producing them. Economists use the terms capital-intensive and labour-intensive to describe the alternative methods just outlined. The total output of the community depends not only on the total supply of resources available but on the ways in which these resources are combined together. A community must make decisions on the methods of production to be adopted.

3 How should the goods and services be distributed? This is the third function which an economic system has to perform. The total output has to be shared out among the members of the community. The economic system has to determine the relative sizes of the shares going to each household. Should everyone be given an equal share? Should the division depend upon the individual's contribution to production? Should the output be shared out in accordance with people's ability to pay the price, or should the shares be decided according to tradition and custom?

These basic problems are common to all societies no matter what level of economic development they have reached. The methods of solving them will be different from one society to another – the USA and the USSR adopt very different methods – but the problems are common to all societies.

Economics as a social science

Normative and positive statements

It may be useful to begin this section on the scientific approach by distinguishing between positive and normative statements. An understanding of the difference between these two types of statement will help us to appreciate the scope and limitations of economics. *Positive statements* are those which deal only with facts. 'Britain is an island', 'British Leyland employ x thousand workers', 'Jane Smith obtained a grade A in Economics', are all positive statements. If a disagreement arises over a positive statement it can be settled by looking to the facts and seeing whether or not they support the statement. Positive statements must be either true or false, where the word 'true' is taken to mean 'consistent with the facts'.

Normative statements usually include or imply the words 'ought' or 'should'. They reflect people's moral attitudes and are expressions of what some individual or group thinks ought to be done. 'Britain should leave the Common Market', 'We ought to give more aid to under-developed countries', 'Income should be distributed more equally', are all normative statements. These statements are based on value judgements and express views of what is 'good' or 'bad', 'right' and 'wrong'. Unlike positive statements, normative statements cannot be verified by looking at the facts. Disagreements about such statements are usually settled by voting on them.

Scientific method

Scientific enquiry, as the term is generally understood, is confined to positive questions. It deals with those questions which can be verified or falsified by actual observations of the real world (i.e. by checking the facts).

One major objective of science is to develop theories. These are general statements or unifying principles which describe and explain the relationships between things we observe in the world around us. Theories are developed in an attempt to answer the question 'Why?'. Tides rise and fall at regular intervals of time, a city is afflicted by smog at certain times of the year, the price of strawberries falls sharply during the summer months. When some definite regular pattern is observed in the relationships between two or more things, and someone asks why this should be so, the search for a theory has begun.

In trying to produce an explanation of observed phenomena, scientific enquiry makes use of procedures which are common to all sciences. These procedures are called scientific method.

7

1 The first step is to define the concepts to be used in such a way that they can be measured. This is necessary if we are to test the theory against facts. If the task is to discover a relationship between 'income' and 'consumption', these terms must be defined in a clearly understood manner.

2 The next step is to formulate a *hypothesis*. This is a tentative untested statement which attempts to explain how one thing is related to another. For example, an economist asked to say why prices vary over time, might offer the hypothesis that changes in prices are caused by changes in the quantity of money. Hypotheses will be based on observation and upon certain assumptions about the way the world behaves. These assumptions may themselves be based upon existing theories which have proved to have a high degree of reliability. In economics, for example, many theories are based upon the assumption that people will behave in such a manner as to maximise their material welfare. Using observed facts and making use of certain assumptions, a process of logical reasoning leads to the formulation of a hypothesis. This must be framed in a manner which enables scientists to test its validity.

3 It is now necessary to think out what would happen if the hypothesis is correct. In other words, the hypothesis is used to make predictions (or the hypothesis itself may be framed as a prediction). If the hypothesis is correct, then if certain things are done, certain other things will happen. If the general level of prices is causally related to the supply of money, we might deduce that an expansion of bank deposits would be followed by an increase in prices.

4 The hypothesis must now be tested – are the predictions of the hypothesis supported by the facts? In the natural sciences the testing of hypotheses can be carried out by controlled experiments in the laboratory, but this, as explained later, is not possible for the social scientist. If the hypothesis is supported by the factual evidence we have a successful theory which may be formulated in the form of a scientific 'law'. It must be noted, however, that, since the number of tests which can be carried out is limited, we can never say that a theory is true for all times and in all places. A successful theory is one which *up to now* has not been proved false. If, at some future time facts emerge which confound the theory and its predictions become unreliable, it will be discarded and a search for a better theory will begin. A successful theory is extremely useful because it helps us to predict with a high degree of probability the outcome of certain events.

Is economics a science?

Economic analysis is based upon the procedures described above, and, to the extent that the economist makes use of scientific method, economics may be described as a science. The subject matter of economics, however, is human behaviour and this is much more difficult to predict than the reactions of inanimate matter. Economists, like other social scientists, cannot achieve the precision of the natural scientists and they are denied the use of many of their techniques. Many people argue that these differences are so fundamental that economics cannot be regarded as a 'true' science. Others would say that the differences are not fundamental but merely differences in the degree of accuracy attainable.

The most obvious limitation experienced by the social scientist is that he cannot test his hypotheses by laboratory experiment. His laboratory is human society; he cannot put a group of human beings into a controlled situation and then see what happens. The predictions of economic theory must be tested against developments in the real world. Economic activities must be observed and recorded and the mass of resulting data subjected to statistical analysis. Modern statistical techniques help the economist determine the probability that certain events had certain causes. He can assess from recorded data, for example, the probability that some given increase in consumption was caused by an increase in income.

The fact that 'all people are different' is not such a handicap to the social scientist as might appear at first sight. The economist is interested in group behaviour. He is concerned with the total demand for butter rather than the amount purchased by any one individual. While the behaviour of any one person may be unpredictable, this is not necessarily true of the large group. When Arsenal score a goal at Highbury we can predict with a high degree of certainty that there will be a roar from the crowd, although we cannot forecast how this or that individual will react. The economist is able to make generalisations about economic groups (consumers, workers, shareholders) which are quite dependable guides to their expected behaviour.

Another problem facing economists is the complexity of the world they are studying – so many things are changing simultaneously. Natural scientists in their laboratories can 'hold other things constant' while they study the effects which changes in X have on Y. Economists cannot do this. They cannot vary the quantity of money in the economy, hold everything else constant, and then see what happens. What they have to do is to *assume* that other things remain constant. Many propositions in economics begin with the phrase 'If other things remain equal' (or the Latin equivalent *ceteris paribus*).

From the vast array of facts observed, economists (and other scientists) must isolate those things which are important and study them in isolation. They have to *abstract* from reality in order to build a simplified model of a small part of the real world which will help them to see how things are related one to another. In fact, the influences surrounding real-life situations are so many and so varied that we cannot take them all into account. All that economists can do is to try to get close to the real world by extending their model to include more and more 'other influences' – but no one can construct or understand a model which includes everything. What we are saying is that economic theories as such do not describe the real world as we see it. They attempt to show, one by one, the forces that operate within that real world. We proceed step by step from very simple models of economic reality to more and more sophisticated ones, introducing at each stage more and more of the facts of life which we can observe and experience.

Why economists disagree

It is often said that economics cannot be a science because no two economists agree on any economic problem. This is an exaggeration, but it is certainly true that economists disagree. Disputes among economists often arise from problems of definition and from the inadequacy of statistical data. For example, the statement 'The unemployment rate in the USA is much higher than that in the UK' may be based upon the official figures issued by the authorities in these countries, but that does not mean that the statement cannot be disputed.

The numbers unemployed may refer to those people who actually register themselves as available for work, or it may represent all those who would take a job if one became available. This latter group would include a large number of people (e.g. married women) who do not normally register themselves as unemployed. In fact, the figures for the UK and the USA are collected on these very different bases so that *official* unemployment rates are not strictly comparable and the real differences between them may be disputed.

Although statistical information on economic affairs is now available to a far greater extent than ever before, there are still many deficiencies. Such information often takes a long time to become available in processed form, and often it is too late to be used in current analysis. It may often be presented in a form which is not very convenient for analysis, as the example above demonstrates. These deficiencies therefore leave room for disagreement among economists.

Economics is a very young science, and although economic analysis has made great strides in recent years, there is still a great deal about the workings of the economic system which is imperfectly understood. There are many implications of existing theories which have not yet been tested, either because insufficient time has elapsed to provide adequate data, or because no one has found a satisfactory way of testing them. Technical and economic changes also bring about changes in economic behaviour so that assumptions about human behaviour which served as useful bases for predictions at one period of time may become increasingly unreliable as the social and economic environment changes. Economists, then, will be in dispute over the adequacy of certain existing theories – but it is these very disputes which lead to improvements in existing theories and the development of new ones.

The main area of disagreement among economists is on matters of economic policy. This is exactly what one would expect because policy statements are normative statements. They are value judgements. The determination of policies lies in the province of politics; it is the politician's function to decide policy matters. The economist's role in policy making is to act as an adviser, using specialist knowledge to provide policy makers with an analysis of the likely economic effects of the policy proposals. The economist, as such, has no more right to decide policies than the lorry driver, the shop assistant, or the artist. We must recognise, however, that economists, like everyone else, will have their own personal viewpoints on what is 'best' and we must, therefore, expect them to disagree on policy questions such as the desirability of Britain's membership of the Common Market, or the likely effectiveness of an incomes policy. What we have to recognise, however, is that when economists pronounce on the desirability of any economic policy they have moved out of the field of economic analysis – they are making a value judgement.

2 Economic Systems

To an economist, economic society presents itself as a mechanism for survival – a means whereby people are able to carry out the tasks of production and distribution. If we look at the very different political and social structures which exist in the world today, and the way in which these systems have developed over the years, we are tempted to say that people have made use of, and are making use of, a very great variety of economic systems. In fact, in spite of the appearance of great variety, it is possible to group these different economic structures into three broad categories. These basic types of economic organisation are usually described as Traditional economies, Market economies and Command economies.

Traditional economies

The oldest and until fairly recent times by far the most common way of solving economic problems was that of tradition. In traditional societies, people use methods of production and distribution that were devised in the distant past and which have become the accepted ways of doing things by a long process of trial and error. The strong attachment to *custom and habit* is often reinforced by superstition and religious beliefs. People may hold on to traditional ways of life because they believe that some misfortune will befall them if they deviate from the accepted patterns of life and work.

In these societies we find that the division of land among the families in the village or tribe, the methods and times of planting and harvesting, the selection of crops, and the way in which the produce is distributed among the different groups are all based upon custom. Year by year little is changed; indeed, a change in working procedures may well be regarded as an affront to the memory of one's ancestors or as an offence against the gods.

The basic economic problems do not arise as problems to be discussed and argued about. They have all been decided long ago. One follows the path that one was born to follow; a son follows in the footsteps of his father and uses the same skills and tools. A caste system such as obtained in India until quite recent times provides a good example of the rigidity of a traditional society. The production problems (i.e. What? and How?) are solved by using land as it has always been used and by the worker carrying out the traditional skills according to his or her fixed place in the social structure. The distribution problem (i.e. For Whom?) is solved in a similar manner. There will be time-honoured methods of sharing out the produce of the harvest and the hunt. The elders, the heads of families, the women, and the children will receive shares according to ancient custom.

Traditional solutions to the economic problems of production and distribution are encountered in primitive agricultural and pastoral communities. The economies of the Burmese village or Bedouin tribe will be much the same today as they were a thousand years ago. But, even in advanced countries, tradition still plays some part in determining how the economy works. We are all familiar with industries in which it is customary for the son to follow his father into a trade or profession, and in Britain equal pay for women did not obtain legal sanction until the 1970s.

Market economies

A society may attempt to deal with the basic economic problems by allowing free play to what are known as *market forces*. The state plays little or no part in economic activity. Most of the people in the non-communist world earn and spend in societies which are still fundamentally market economies.

The market system of economic organisation is also commonly described as a *free enterprise* or *laissez-faire*, or *capitalist system*. We shall use all these terms to stand for a market economy. Strictly speaking the pure market or laissez-faire system has never existed. Whenever there has been some form of political organisation, the political authority has exercised some economic functions (e.g. controlling prices or levying taxation). It is useful, however, to consider the way in which a true market system would operate because it provides us with a simplified model, and by making modifications to the model we can approach the more realistic situations step by step.

The framework of a market or capitalist system contains six essential features. They are:

1 private property
2 freedom of choice and enterprise
3 self-interest as the dominating motive
4 competition
5 a reliance on the price system
6 a very limited role for government

1 Private property

The institution of private property is a major feature of capitalism. It means that individuals have the right to own, control, and dispose of land, buildings, machinery, and other natural and man-made resources.

13

Man-made aids to production such as machines, factories, docks, oil refineries and road networks are known as capital. Personal private wealth, of course, can also be held in the form of money, but money should be regarded as a *claim to wealth*. For an individual, money owned is part of personal wealth because it represents the ability to purchase property owned by others. The *whole community's* stock of money, however, is not part of its wealth; we cannot count both the claims to wealth *and* the wealth itself. A society cannot make itself richer by creating more claims to wealth (i.e. money) if the quantity of things on which that money can be spent is not increasing.

Private property not only confers the right to own and dispose of real assets, it provides the owners of property with the right to the income from that property in the form of rent, interest, and profits.

Although all non-human resources can be privately owned, labour cannot be bought and sold in the same way. Except in slave societies, every labourer belongs to him or herself, whilst land, buildings, and machinery are owned by others. Owners of land and capital purchase *the services of labour* in order to operate their factories, farms, shops, and so on.

2 Freedom of choice and enterprise

Freedom of enterprise means that individuals are free to buy and hire economic resources, to organise these resources for production, and to sell their products in markets of their own choice. Persons who undertake these activities are known as *entrepreneurs* and such people are free to enter and leave any industry.

Freedom of choice means, as we have seen, that owners of land and capital may use these resources as they see fit. It also means that workers are free to enter (and leave) any occupations for which they are qualified.[1] Finally it means that consumers are free to spend their incomes in any way they wish. This freedom of consumer choice is usually held to be the most important of these economic 'freedoms'. The consumer is regarded as being sovereign since it is the way in which he chooses to spend his income which determines the ways in which society uses its economic resources. In the model of capitalism, producers respond to consumers' preferences – they produce whatever consumers demand. This feature of capitalism is discussed more fully in the section on Prices.

[1] This is a rather meaningless freedom, of course, when there is large-scale unemployment.

3 Self-interest

Since capitalism is based on the principle that individuals should be free to do as they wish, it is not surprising to find that the motive for economic activity is *self-interest*. Each unit in the economy attempts to do what is best for itself. Firms will act in ways which, they believe, will lead to maximum profits (or minimum losses). Owners of land and capital will employ these assets so as to obtain the highest possible rewards. Workers will tend to move to those occupations and locations which offer the highest wages. Consumers will spend their incomes on those things which yield the maximum satisfaction.

Advocates of the market system such as Adam Smith argued that the individual pursuit of self-interest would lead to the maximum public good. 'By pursuing his own interest he [the individual] frequently promotes that of society more effectually than when he really intends to promote it'.[1]

4 Competition

Economic rivalry or competition is another essential feature of a free enterprise economy. Competition, as economists see it, is essentially *price competition*. The model of the market economy envisages a situation where, in the market for each commodity, there are large numbers of buyers and sellers. Each buyer and seller accounts for an insignificant share of the business transacted and hence has no influence on the market demand or market supply. It is the forces of total demand and total supply which determine the market price, and each participant, whether buyer or seller, must take this price as given since it is beyond her influence or control. In theory at least, competition is the regulatory mechanism of capitalism. It limits the use of economic power since no single firm or individual is large enough or strong enough to control a market and exploit the other buyers or sellers.

5 Markets and Prices

Perhaps the most basic feature of the market economy is the use of the *price mechanism* for allocating resources to various uses. The price system is an elaborate system of communications in which innumerable free choices are aggregated and balanced against each other. The decisions of producers determine the supply of a commodity; the decisions of buyers determine the demand. The interactions of demand and supply determine the price. Changes in demand and supply cause

---

[1] Adam Smith, *The Wealth of Nations*.

changes in market prices and it is these movements in market prices which bring about the changes in the ways in which society uses its economic resources.

Let us take a simple example. A particular product proves to be increasingly popular with consumers. Increasing demand outstrips supply at the existing price, a shortage develops and price increases. This rise in price makes production more profitable. Existing firms will tend to expand their outputs and new firms will be attracted to this industry. More and more resources will move into the industry because the greater profitability will enable firms to offer higher rewards in order to bid labour and capital away from other uses. The opposite process will apply when the demand for a commodity is declining. Price movements act as indicators and provide an essential link between consumers' preferences and producers' profit-seeking decisions.

In a free enterprise society, price has another important function – it acts as a rationing device. We have seen that economic goods are scarce goods. Price serves to ration these scarce goods among the people who are demanding them. Where the supply of a good or service is insufficient to meet the demands of prospective buyers at the existing price, the market price will rise and continue to rise until the quantity demanded is just equal to the existing supply. Those unable to pay the higher prices will be eliminated from the market. Price rations scarce goods to those who can afford to pay the price. If supply exceeds demand, the price will fall bringing in more buyers (and expanding the purchases of existing buyers) until a price is established which equates the quantities being demanded and supplied. Note that price rations goods and services, not on any basis of need or want, but on the basis of the ability to pay the price.

The price mechanism allocates resources to different uses on the basis of consumer 'votes'. The act of purchasing a commodity is, in effect, a vote for the production of that commodity. Under this system those with the greater purchasing power have more votes. This might be regarded as an inequitable system especially where there is great inequality in the distribution of income.

Command economies

Another method of solving the economic problems is also one which has a long history. This is the method of economic command where the solutions to the economic problems are worked out by some all-powerful authority which imposes its solutions on the population.

This authoritarian method of economic control may be superimposed, as it usually was in the past, on a traditional society. Thus the Pharoahs, while not changing the customary agricultural practices of Ancient Egypt, were able to command vast resources of labour and materials for the building of the pyramids. But the command type of economy is an equally important feature of the modern world. The communist regimes in Russia and China can be described as command economies, although this type of economic structure is not peculiar to communism. It is applicable wherever the economic resources of a nation are directly controlled by some centralised authority. The UK became very much a command economy during the years of the Second World War when the government took control of all important economic affairs.

It is more usual to refer to the present-day command economies as *planned* economies although, strictly speaking, leaving the economy to run itself (i.e. laissez-faire) may be described as a kind of economic 'plan'. Nevertheless, in line with general usage, we shall use the term 'planned economy' to refer to an economy which is subject to a high degree of direct centralised control.

It is important to note that no modern economy is without some elements of command, just as none is devoid of elements of tradition. In all developed and most underdeveloped countries, even those described as capitalist, there is a large measure of government control. In the UK, for example, the government is the biggest business in the country.

Ownership and control of economic resources

Although economic planning may be employed in societies where property is privately owned, it seems realistic to assume that a fully planned economy means one in which all the important means of production are publicly owned. In communist and socialist societies (which are the most important examples of planned economies) all land, housing, factories, power stations, transport systems, and so on are usually owned by the state.

The logic of public ownership in these societies is based upon the desire for a more equitable distribution of income and wealth. Private ownership of property leads to great inequalities of wealth, and this, in turn, means that the wealthier groups are able to exercise great economic power. Such a situation implies great inequalities of opportunity. The better-off members of society are able to use their greater wealth to obtain superior education, better health services, more effective training, and better business opportunities. The elimination, or severe limitation, of private ownership is seen, therefore, as the most effective way of removing these inequalities of opportunity. It is also argued by the supporters of the planned economy that only the direct ownership of the means of production can give the state the full control which it needs in order to carry out its economic plan.

Although land and capital may be owned *collectively* rather than individually, it does not follow that control of these resources must be centralised. In some planned economies the state keeps a tight control on the use of economic resources and all important economic decisions are taken by powerful central committees. They decide what should be produced, how and where production should take place, and how the output should be shared out among the people. This is described as *bureaucratic* organisation, because the running of such an economy will require large numbers of planners and administrators to draw up and operate the national plan.

Alternatively, although the ultimate ownership of resources may be vested in the state, the control and day-to-day running of the farms, factories, and shops may be handed over to cooperative groups of workers and consumers. These organisations are usually described as *workers' collectives*, as opposed to the state enterprises which are controlled directly by the government.

One important feature of a society in which property is publicly owned is that there will be no form of personal income which is derived from the ownership of property. In the capitalist system incomes take the form of wages, interest, rent, and profits – the latter three of which arise from the ownership of various types of property.

Planning by direction

1 Production In a planned or command economy, the profit motive and the free play of self-interest are not allowed to determine what is produced and how it is produced. These matters are decided by some elected or appointed planning group. Production is said to be *for use* rather than *for profit* (although it is a matter of personal judgement as to which best meets the wishes of consumers).

The administrators in a planned society face a most complex task. They must begin by making a survey of the productive potential of the economy. Assessments must be prepared showing the outputs which might be produced by the mines, farms, factories, etc., together with some estimates of the carrying capacities of the transport networks and the capacities of the other service industries. The decisions on the quantities and varieties of goods to be produced must then be made and each unit of production (e.g. farm or factory) will be given a target output for the period of the plan – normally five years. The next task will be to allocate the necessary supplies of materials, equipment, and labour to the various units of production.

A modern economic system is exceedingly complex. The output of any one factory is dependent upon supplies from many different sources. The fitting together of all these planned outputs into one huge national plan is a formidable task. In fact it is virtually impossible for central planners to fix targets and resource allocations for every single farm, factory, and shop. The planners are more likely to set targets for whole industries and the ways in which these targets are met may be left to local decisions at the industry and factory levels. Even so it is most probable that the allocations to various industries of the more vital resources (e.g. new capital) will be centrally controlled.

2 Distribution. While it is possible, although very difficult, to subject the outputs of goods and services to complete control by planners, it is much more difficult to use these methods in the markets for labour and consumer goods. In respect of industrial investment (i.e. capital goods), defence requirements, and social investment (e.g. schools, hospitals, housing) the necessary allocations of resources can be directly controlled and the outputs firmly determined. In the case of consumer goods, however, there are restraints on the planners' ability to use direct controls.

Ideally, the complete planning of production should be accompanied by the complete planning of distribution. What had been produced could then be allocated to consumers by some kind of physical rationing scheme. Workers could be paid in kind, receiving vouchers which entitled them to various quantities of different goods and services. In this manner the pattern and volume of consumption could be matched exactly to the planned output. Such a system might operate perfectly well in a poor country where all resources are committed to the bare necessities of life. In a more developed economy, however, consumers are likely to demand a large measure of freedom of choice in the disposal of their income. Allowing for freedom of choice in the consumers' market makes the planners' problems much more difficult. It is very unlikely that the spending plans of consumers will exactly match the production targets of the planners. This does not mean that direct planning will not work; it means that the plan must contain some flexibility so that production can respond to the various surpluses and shortages as they appear in the consumer markets.

There are various ways in which planners can test consumer demand – assuming, that is, that they wish to respond to it. They might conduct a continuous poll of public attitudes and preferences. Alternatively they could allow the goods to be sold in free markets. Goods which are in short supply will rise in price while those in surplus will fall in price. These price movements could then be used as indicators to producers as to which industries should expand their outputs and which should contract output. Planners may, however, regard such price movements as an inequitable means of testing the market (e.g. a shortage of bread might cause its price to rise beyond the means of the poor). The state may, therefore, fix prices, and where shortages arise the good may be physically rationed. In this case it would be the movements in retail stocks which act as indicators to the planners.

3 Labour. There are similar problems to be dealt with in the market for labour. Whilst iron ore, wool, machines, lorries and so on can be distributed directly to the different industries, workers will not usually continue to accept such direction. They will demand some degree of freedom in choosing their jobs and the part of the country in which they wish to work. Getting the right amounts of labour in the right places to meet the production targets cannot normally be achieved by the direction of labour; it must be done by inducement. As is the case with consumer goods, it means that some limited use must be made of the price mechanism.

Plants which are short of labour will have to be given permission to offer higher wages in order to attract labour from other sources. In the longer run the state can influence the supplies of the different types of labour by providing more and better training facilities for those skills which are in short supply and reducing the intake of trainees for occupations where demand is declining.

Mixed economies

We have seen that there is some use of the market mechanism in planned economies. Likewise there is some measure of state control in free market economies. Here the term mixed economy is used; it describes most of the economies in the non-communist world. These countries are basically market economies, but all contain elements of state enterprise and governments in all of them intervene to modify the operation of market forces. They are mixtures of command and market economies.

In these mixed economies private property is an important institution. Supporters of the mixed system hold the view that private property provides an important incentive for people to work, save, and invest. They oppose the abolition of private property and argue that it is possible to prevent great inequalities of wealth from arising by the appropriate government measures (e.g. heavy taxation of income and wealth).

The mixed economy has come into being as a result of increasing government intervention and control in capitalist societies. This development has been particularly extensive during the 20th century. There are many reasons for this increasing activity of governments.

The unacceptable features of Laissez-faire

1 Instability. The laissez-faire or market economy has been judged inadequate in meeting many of the demands of a democratic society. One unacceptable feature of the capitalist system is its instability. The early history of industrial capitalism was characterised by a series of booms and slumps and this cyclical pattern of economic activity seems to be endemic to a free market economy. The dissatisfactions which arise from this state of affairs have forced governments to control their economies so as to create more stable conditions.

2 Monopolies. It is a feature of the market economy, especially in more recent times, that firms tend to increase in size and power. Modern technology has made it possible for large-scale producers to obtain great advantages in the form of lower production costs. This tendency towards market domination by giant firms reduces, or removes, the limiting role of competition and gives the large firm power to exploit the consumer by charging prices well above costs. It does not follow, of course, that such exploitation will take place, but governments have been obliged to take precautions against such a possibility.

This tendency towards monopoly in business has been accompanied by a corresponding development in the organisation of labour. Large and powerful trade unions have arisen to balance the power of large companies. Clearly the system has moved a long way from the model of capitalism in which exploitation is effectively limited by the forces of competition.

3 Inequalities. The ability of some individuals and firms to acquire excessive market power has led to great inequalities in the distribution of income and wealth. Such developments are increasingly unacceptable in a political democracy.

4 Economic change. The market economy is subject to severe criticism on the grounds that it does not provide an equitable basis for sharing the burdens of economic change. Technological progress produces a stream of new products, new materials, and new methods of production. The demands for the older products decline and the demands for the new ones expand, although some new products open up entirely new markets. Tastes and fashion are always changing especially when incomes are rising. Political changes and changes in world trade also call for adjustments in the economic system. Economic change means that some industries will expand while others decline. But workers trained in particular skills, and capital equipment designed for particular uses, cannot be moved quickly and easily from declining to expanding industries. Under pure capitalism, these workers would be redundant; their means of livelihood would disappear. Owners of capital would find themselves with assets which cannot earn an income. The burdens of change would fall almost entirely on the unlucky ones who worked in, or had invested in, those industries whose products were no longer in demand. It has now become an accepted view that the burdens of economic change should be borne by the community as a whole, and only the state can ensure that this is so.

5 Social and private values. One criticism of the private enterprise economy that has attracted increasing attention in recent years is the fact that the prices established in a free market do not fully take into account *social costs* and *social benefits*. In a competitive system market prices reflect the costs of production incurred by those actually producing the goods, and the satisfactions obtained by those purchasing them. We assume that the price which people are prepared to pay provides an indication of the satisfaction or utility derived from the product, while competition will ensure that these prices are kept down to levels very near to producers' costs.

For some goods and services, however, market price does not provide a good measure of the benefits and costs *to society as a whole*. Take, for example, a factory which emits some kind of pollution or obnoxious smells. These nuisances impose costs on the community, but the firm operating the factory does not have to bear these social costs. The total costs to society are greater than the private costs.

There are also cases where the total benefits to society exceed the private benefits derived by the purchasers. For example, the private benefit to the individual who safeguards himself from a dangerous disease by submitting to an innoculation, are greatly exceeded by the benefits to society as a whole in the form of a reduced risk of an epidemic. Market prices, therefore, may give a misleading indication of social costs and social benefits, and, in certain cases, governments may be obliged to intervene to change the allocation of resources from that which market forces would bring about. For example, the private benefits (i.e. revenues) from a railway line may not cover the private costs, but the government may believe that the social benefits of keeping the line open may be great enough to justify a subsidy.

The role of government

It is useful to classify the economic activities of government in a mixed economy according to their function.

1 Creating a framework of rules. Most of the rules and regulations under this heading are designed to see that there is 'fair play' in the competition between producers and in the relations between producers and consumers. Most of the regulations are necessary if the freedom to compete is not to be abused. There are laws which protect property rights, and which enforce contractual obligations (e.g. people are legally obliged to pay their debts). The public is protected from fraud by regulations such as those which oblige firms to publish adequate financial information so that investors will not be misled, and which prevent the dishonest labelling of goods. Regulations which insist on adequate standards of hygiene and on minimum safety standards in manufacture protect the public from unnecessary dangers and health hazards. To ensure a reasonable degree of competition the state may make laws forbidding restrictive trade agreements between producers (e.g. agreements between firms to limit output so as to maintain high prices). Workers are protected by regulations which govern the conditions of work in factories, offices, and shops. In most modern economies, industrial and commercial behaviour is closely regulated by the state.

2 Supplementing and modifying the price system. It has long been recognised that certain services, regarded as essential to civilised existence, will not be provided by private enterprise, or, if provided, will not be made available on a scale which society thinks desirable. Such things as defence, internal law and order, education, roads, and health services, are typical of the kind of services which have become accepted as suitable subjects for public enterprise. These services may be purchased by the state but provided by private firms. In most cases however the state takes over the full responsibility for the supply of such services. The government may also influence the pattern of production by making use of taxes and subsidies. The output of goods subject to taxation is likely to fall, while subsidies generally lead to an increase in output.

3 Redistribution of income. It is now a major objective of governments to promote the general economic welfare of the citizen. One means towards this end is a more equitable distribution of income and wealth. Governments may aim to achieve this by a system of taxation which bears more heavily on the richer members of society, together with the provision of benefits for the needier groups. These benefits may take the form of money grants such as child benefit and unemployment benefit, but in other cases the government may attempt to ensure greater equality by providing the services directly at zero market prices. Education and health services are the best examples of the universal provision of essential services financed from taxation.

4 Stabilising the economy. The Great Depression of the inter-war years and the prolonged nature of the large-scale unemployment during that period forced governments in almost every country to accept the responsibility for the maintenance of a high and stable level of employment. This responsibility has obliged governments to take wider powers to influence the level of economic activity. We shall see later in this book that governments in mixed economies now have policy instruments which enable them to influence the volume of money, the level of spending, the amount of investment, the location of industry, the levels of imports and exports, and most of the important economic variables. Quite apart from using its powers to influence the private sector, the government may feel that it is also necessary to take important sectors of the economy into public ownership (i.e. nationalisation).

The economic role of government is discussed in some detail in Chapter 12 (Government and Industry) and Chapter 30 (Income and Expenditure of Public Authorities).

Part Two: The Factors of Production

3 The Economic Resources

The meaning of production

The purpose of economic activity is the satisfaction of wants, and any activity which helps to satisfy wants is defined as production. This is a wider meaning of the term than it carries in everyday speech where it is usually taken to mean the making of some physical object or the growing of produce. It is still common practice to talk of 'productive' and 'non-productive' workers. Productive workers are generally understood to be those who work directly on the goods being made. Turners and grinders in an engineering factory, coalminers, brick-layers, farmers, and potters would be classified as productive workers. On the other hand, teachers, bank-clerks, shop assistants, and entertainers would be described as non-productive workers, because they do not 'make anything'.

The economist does not restrict the meaning of production in this manner. All those activities which assist towards the satisfaction of material wants must be considered to be productive. If the public are prepared to pay for the services of teachers, accountants, surveyors, and clerical workers, these people must be satisfying wants. They are not producing goods; they are producing *services*. As a nation grows richer it tends to spend more and more of its income on services rather than goods. About half the working population of the UK is engaged in producing services.

Production must be understood therefore as comprising all those activities which provide the goods and services which people want and for which they are prepared to pay a price. The complete cycle of production in a modern society can be a very long drawn-out process. It is a process which is not complete until the commodity is in the hands of the final consumer. The production of a shirt may begin in the cotton fields of Alabama, but it will not be complete until a consumer makes a purchase in a retail store. The making of a shirt will engage the efforts of thousands of workers in fields, factories, offices, ships, docks, railways, road transport, banks, insurance companies, warehouses, and shops.

The output

Economic activity results in the output of an enormous variety of goods and services. In economics we are obliged, for purposes of analysis, to resort to some kind of classification of the great variety of things dealt with. The composition of total output is usefully classified into consumer goods, producer goods, and services.

Consumer goods are those commodities which satisfy our wants directly – we want them for their own sake. This group of commodities is usefully sub-divided into non-durable and durable consumer goods.

Non-durable consumer goods are items such as food, heating, lighting, cigarettes, etc. They are consumed or destroyed in the very act of being used. Some of them are good only for a single use while others, such as soap, can be used up a bit at a time.

Durable consumer goods include such things as books, furniture, television sets, motor cars, and domestic electrical appliances. Such goods produce a steady stream of satisfaction while their values diminish relatively slowly through age and use.

Producer goods do not satisfy wants directly. They are not wanted for their own sake, but for the contribution they make to the production of other goods (both consumer and producer goods). Lathes, lorries, bulldozers, cranes, factory buildings, and blast furnaces are examples of producer goods. The term *capital* is normally used to describe these producer goods.

Services might be defined as intangible economic 'goods'. A large part of the total output of a developed economy consists of the kinds of services mentioned in the first section of this chapter.

The structure of production

The make up of economic activity may be appreciated a little more clearly if we subdivide production into certain broad categories. The production of physical things begins with the extraction of some basic material such as wood, mineral ores, oil, or fibres. The *extractive industries*, therefore, will consist of farming, forestry, fishing, mining, and quarrying. The products of such industries are often described as primary products. There follows a series of operations in the process or *manufacturing* industries such as engineering, vehicle manufacture, chemicals, and food processing. The final stage in production is carried out by the *distribution industries* which embrace the activities of wholesaling and retailing.

All these stages of production make use of the *service industries*. Production in developed countries cannot be carried on effectively without the services rendered by banking, insurance, advertising, administration, etc. Some idea of the relative sizes of these broad divisions of the productive process is provided by Fig. 2 which shows the proportions of the employed population engaged in each type of activity in the UK economy. The diagram understates the proportion of the labour force working in the service trades since quite a number of

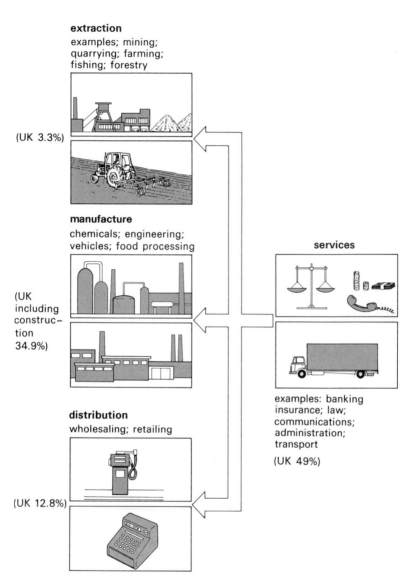

extraction
examples; mining;
quarrying; farming;
fishing; forestry

(UK 3.3%)

manufacture
chemicals; engineering;
vehicles; food processing

(UK
including
construc-
tion
34.9%)

services

examples: banking
insurance; law;
communications;
administration;
transport

(UK 49%)

distribution
wholesaling; retailing

(UK 12.8%)

Source: Department of Employment Gazette May 1982

Fig. 2 Distribution of employed population December 1981 Department of Employment Gazette Table 1.2

those employed in the extractive and manufacturing industries will be clerks, surveyors, accountants, and so on.

The factors of production

Production cannot take place unless the necessary resources are available. We are all familiar with these resources. Factories, railways, farms, mines, human skills, offices, and shops – these are the kind of things we identify as economic resources. Again, for purposes of analysis, economists resort to a broad classification of these resources or *factors of production* as they are usually called.

The factors of production are usually divided into three main types, land, labour, and capital. Land is the term used to stand for natural resources; labour represents all human resources; and capital is the term used for all man-made resources. Economists often identify a fourth factor – enterprise. This is discussed later.

This classification is not completely satisfactory because it is sometimes difficult to allocate the real-world resources into these neat categories. For example, land which has been fertilised, drained, and fenced is really a combination of land and capital. We shall also find that within each broad category there are very wide divergencies. Nevertheless the classification is still the one most commonly used and it does serve to assist analysis.

Land (natural resources)

The term 'land' is used to describe all those natural resources over which people have the power of disposal and which may be used to yield an income. It includes, therefore, farming and building land, forests, mineral deposits, fisheries, rivers, lakes – all those resources freely supplied by nature which aid people in producing the things they want.

The supply of land

Economists have always emphasised one particular aspect of land – the fact that its supply is strictly limited. Now this is true of the total supply of land in the world in the sense of the surface area available to man. Although reclamation work has tended to increase the supply in some areas, this is offset by erosion of various kinds so that changes in the total area are probably relatively insignificant.

If, however, we are considering the supply of land for some *particular use*, this strict limitation on supply is not applicable. The amount of land used for growing wheat can be increased by growing less of some other crop (e.g. barley). The supply of building land can be increased at the expense of farmland, and the area of *cultivated* land may be increased by drainage, irrigation, and the use of fertilisers.

There is, however, one very important application of the principle of a fixed supply in the case of the *site value* of land, especially in urban areas. The area of land in a given location cannot be changed. No matter how high the price may rise for sites fronting the High Street, the supply cannot be increased. This particular feature of land has important economic implications which are discussed later in the section on Rent.

Conservation

In recent years we have become dramatically aware of the fact that the supply of many natural resources is strictly limited. This is most obviously true of the mineral resources and especially of those which man relies upon for his sources of energy. Present-day civilisation is based upon a massive utilisation of non-replaceable minerals and fuels. Some raw materials such as cotton, wool, timber, and foodstuffs are replenishable, but others such as coal, iron ore, oil, and natural gas cannot be replaced. In the case of oil, we are already faced with a prospect of the complete exhaustion of known reserves within a matter of a few decades.

A rapidly rising world population together with insistent demands for higher standards of living have led to a growing awareness of this problem. It has been calculated that the American standard of living requires an annual consumption per head of about 20 tons of fuels, metals, other minerals, and non-metallic building materials – most of it coming from non-replaceable resources. The more obvious consequences of present trends are rising prices as these things become more scarce and a more energetic search for substitutes.

The most pressing immediate requirement is for an effective policy for the *conservation* of natural resources. This does not mean that we should refrain from using them, but that we should use them much more efficiently and less wastefully. Every effort must be made to get a greater value of output per unit of input of these depletable resources, and more attention must be paid to schemes for the recovery of such materials for future use – recycling as it is called. While such resources are abundant and cheap there is little financial incentive to embark upon relatively costly projects of research and recovery, but as fuels and minerals become more scarce and more expensive such projects become more profitable and hence more attractive to profit-seeking enterprises. It is doubtful, however, if conservation can be left entirely to market forces and governments will increasingly become involved in this matter.

Costs of production

A further characteristic of land is that it has no costs of production. It is already in existence – there are no costs involved in creating it. In this respect it differs from labour and capital. Labour has to be reared, educated, and trained. Capital has to be created by using labour and other scarce resources. From this it follows that any increase in the value of natural resources due to rising populations and rising incomes accrues to the owners of these resources as a windfall gain – it does not arise from any efforts on their part.

Labour

Labour is human effort – physical and mental – which is directed to the production of goods and services. But labour is not only a factor of production, it is also the reason why economic activity takes place. The people who take part in production are also consumers, the sum of whose individual demands provides the business person with the incentive to undertake production. For this reason when we are considering real-world economic problems it is necessary to treat labour somewhat differently from the other factors. There are social and political problems which have to be taken into account. For example, the question of how many hours per day a machine should be operated will be judged solely in terms of efficiency, output, and costs. The same question applied to labour would raise additional considerations of individual freedom and human rights.

It must be borne in mind that it is the *services of labour* which are bought and sold, and not labour itself. The firm cannot buy and own labour in the same way that capital and land can be bought and owned.

The supply of labour

The supply of labour available to an economy is not the same thing as the number of people in that community. The labour supply is a measure of the number of hours of work which is offered at given wage rates over some given period of time. It is determined, therefore, by the number of workers and the average number of hours each worker is prepared to offer. Both of these features are subject to change and, at any moment of time, they will depend upon a number of things.

1 The size of the total population. This is obviously very important because the size of the total population sets an upper limit to the supply of labour.

2 The age composition of the population. The age composition of a population takes account of the proportions in the different age groups. Two countries might have the same total populations, but very different age compositions and hence very different numbers in the working age groups.

3 The working population. In many countries the minimum age at which a person may engage in full-time employment is legally controlled. In the UK this is now 16 years and the normal age for retirement is 65 years (60 in the case of women). The age range 16 to 65 years (or 60 years) covers the working age groups, but this does not mean that the total working population embraces all the people in these age groups. Many people now continue in full-time education well beyond the age of 16. Another large group which must be excluded consists of people who do not engage in paid employment outside the home. A number of people also retire early.

The working population may be defined as the number of people who are eligible for work and offer themselves for employment. As a proportion of the total population it will differ widely from country to country, especially where the levels of economic development are substantially different. In the UK the working population is rather less than one half the total population; about 26 million out of a total of 56 million.

4 The working week and holidays. The number of people who work (or are available for work) is an important determinant of the supply of labour, but so is the average number of hours each person works. The supply of labour provided by 20 people working for 40 hours is the same as that provided by 40 people working for 20 hours. The recognised working week in most developed countries has been progressively reduced and the 40-hour week has become a general pattern. Other things being equal, the shorter the working week, the smaller the supply of labour.

The gradual reduction in the working week has been accompanied by an extension of the annual holiday period. Again this amounts to a reduction in the supply of labour.

It must not be assumed, however, that a fall in the supply of labour implies a reduction in the output of goods and services. In spite of the decline in the average number of hours worked by each person, output per worker has continued to rise because of improved technology.

5 Remuneration. The relationship between quantity supplied and price is discussed at length later in the book, but for the time being it should be apparent that there will be a relationship between the amount of work offered and the price paid for that work. Generally speaking, when wage rates are relatively low, increases in wages will tend to lead to an increase in the supply of labour, but there comes a point when higher incomes make leisure more attractive. When incomes are relatively high, therefore, higher wage rates may reduce the amount of labour offered by the individual worker.

The efficiency of labour

Production, of course, is not only affected by the size of the labour force and the number of hours worked, but also by the quality and effective utilisation of the working population. Workers may not be working at their most efficient level, and many workers may fail to reach their full potential because of lack of education and training.

Improving the efficiency of labour is a matter of concern to all countries. When the number of hours worked per head of the population is tending to fall, rising living standards can only be achieved by a greater output per hour of work. In other words, it is the productivity of labour which becomes the critical factor. Productivity refers to the output per worker per unit of time, and the unit of measurement is invariably output-per-man-hour. The efficiency of labour is dependent upon a number of factors.

1 Education and training. An educated labour force which has the benefit of a sound technical training is more effective than one which lacks these benefits. Modern industrial techniques require highly skilled scientists, engineers, economists, accountants, managers, administrators, and so on. Economic progress is dependent upon the institutions which provide such skills and knowledge. Training is provided in the universities, colleges, and by industry itself, but these establishments can only do their jobs really well if there is a well established system of general education provided by the schools.

2 Working conditions. A dark, cold, and cheerless workshop will not encourage industrious and careful effort. The efficiency of labour is very much influenced by the conditions under which it is carried out. During the present century there has been, in most countries, continuous improvement in the conditions under which labour performs its daily tasks. Great attention is now paid in places of employment, to such matters as ventilation, lighting, temperature, decor, and working positions. Many of these things are now carefully regulated by the state through an official inspectorate.

3 Welfare services. In the UK and many other countries, the state provides a national health service which makes medical attention available to all, irrespective of the ability to pay. National insurance schemes provide unemployment pay, sickness benefits, and supplementary benefits which are designed to see that misfortune does not deprive people of some minimum level of income. These services are based upon current ideas of social justice, but, in helping to maintain the health and morale of the people, they also make a positive contribution to the efficiency of the labour force. Many larger firms also provide welfare services for their employees. Playing fields, social and recreational facilities, works canteens, and factory medical facilities are fairly common features of the larger industrial and commercial enterprises. Such provisions all contribute towards a happier, healthier, and hence more efficient labour force.

4 The cooperating factors. It is often said that the superior productivity of American workers is due to the fact that they have more and better power at their elbows. While this is not the only explanation, it cannot be denied that the worker using better equipment will produce a greater output. The quality of the factors (land and capital) with which labour has to work is an important determinant of labour's productivity. But it is not only a matter of providing labour with bigger and better machinery and more fertile land; organisation and motivation are also important.

One important development in recent times has been the increasing utilisation of the techniques of Work Study and Method Study. These are procedures which are designed to increase output by careful and systematic analysis of the methods of production. The individual movements of the operative, the layout of the machinery, the movement of materials, the positioning of the working tools, and the sequence of operations, are photographed, measured, timed, and carefully analysed. The result of this type of investigation may be a completely new layout and a fundamental change in working methods. Even when the amount of machinery and labour employed is not changed such a reorganisation can often lead to very substantial improvements in productivity.

5 Motivation. This is obviously a very important determinant of productivity. As specialisation and mass production techniques are extended in their applications, it becomes increasingly difficult for management to provide that most important feature of motivation – a high degree of job-satisfaction. Methods of payment involving various incentive and bonus schemes where monetary reward is more closely related to effort, are widely used as a means of stimulating output. Some firms try to associate the workers more closely with the objectives of the firm by including their employees in profit-sharing schemes. But the most difficult aspect of this problem, and one which will undoubtedly become increasingly important in the near future, is that of bringing the workers more prominently into the decision-making processes. Those who work in industry and commerce will continue to demand more say in the important decisions on what is produced, how it should be produced, and for whom it is produced.

33

Capital

Capital is a man-made resource. Any product of labour-and-land which is reserved for use in further production is capital. We have already identified the things described as capital in the earlier discussion of producer goods.

Capital was created when people began to make simple tools and implements to assist them in the production of food, the hunting of animals, and in the transportation of their possessions. Even in the least developed societies some capital is used. Members of these societies use simple ploughs, axes, bows and arrows, and water bags.

It might be helpful at this stage to deal with the confusion which commonly arises over the meanings of three important terms: capital, money, and wealth.

Capital, as already indicated, means any produced means of production.

Wealth is quite simply the stock of all those goods which have a money value. Capital, therefore, is an important part of the community's wealth.

Money is a claim to wealth. From the standpoint of the community as a whole, money is not wealth, since we cannot count both the value of real assets *and* the value of the money claims to those assets. From the point of view of the individual citizen, however, money represents a part of his *personal* wealth since he sees it as a claim on assets held by other people. To the individual business person, therefore, any money he possesses he regards as capital since it gives him a claim on resources now possessed by others. We must be quite clear, however, that money is not part of the *national* wealth.

Working capital and fixed capital

Capital is usually divided into two types; that which is used up in the course of production and that which is not.

Working capital consists of the stocks of raw materials, partly finished goods, and finished goods held by producers. These stocks are just as important to efficient production as are the machines and buildings. Stocks are held so that production can proceed smoothly when deliveries are interrupted, and so that unexpected additional orders for finished goods can be met without changing production schedules. This kind of capital is sometimes called *circulating capital* because it keeps moving and changing. Materials are changed into finished goods which are then exchanged for money and this in turn is used to buy more materials.

Fixed capital consists of the equipment used in production – build-

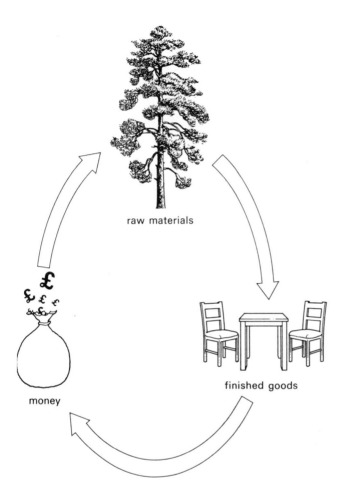

raw materials

finished goods

money

Fig. 3 Circulating capital

ings, machinery, railways, and so on. This type of capital does not change its form in the course of production and move from one stage to the next – it is 'fixed'.

A large part of a nation's stock of capital, particularly its fixed capital, consists of houses, schools, hospitals, public baths, and other types of property which is not *directly* concerned with the production of goods. The term *social capital* is used to describe this type of asset. Such property is part of the capital stock because it assists people in the production of their material wants, but it does so indirectly. We can verify this by asking ourselves the question, 'Would the nation be more or less productive if it did not have its present stock of houses, schools, hospitals, and so on?'

Capital accumulation

People use capital not to satisfy any personal craving, but to produce goods with less effort and lower costs than would be the case if labour were unassisted by capital. But in order to use capital goods people must first produce them and this calls for a sacrifice. While it is producing capital goods, labour cannot also be producing consumer goods. The opportunity cost of the capital goods is the potential output of consumer goods which has to be forgone in order to produce that capital. The production of capital demands *abstinence* from consumption.

A castaway might survive by catching fish with his bare hands. He is able, perhaps, to catch 6 fish each day by this simple method. A net would enable him to catch the same number in half an hour, leaving him valuable time to devote to other activities. But the net might take 2 days to construct. Our castaway can only obtain his capital equipment by sacrificing consumption in the form of 12 fish.

The creation of capital means forgoing some *present* consumption for the prospect of a much higher level of *future* consumption. People are prepared to make this sacrifice because the use of capital equipment greatly increases labour's productivity. This is the reality of capital accumulation and it is as true of the complex society as it is of the less developed society. The machines, factories, houses, and roads we are building today involve the use of resources which could be used to make more consumer goods.

Two things make possible the creation of capital: (*a*) saving, and (*b*) a diversion of resources. *Saving* is the act of forgoing consumption. It means that a claim on the resources required to produce consumer goods is not being exercised. By choosing not to buy consumer goods with some part of our income, we refrain from buying the services of the factors of production required to make those goods. The factors of production might, therefore, remain unemployed. But these savings might be borrowed (by entrepreneurs) and used to finance the construction of capital goods. This is the second step – the *diversion of resources* from the production of consumer goods to the production of producer goods. Saving makes possible capital accumulation – it does not *cause* it.

Capital consumption

A modern economy produces a large output of capital every year, but all of this does not add to the national stock of capital. Capital goods are continually wearing out or becoming obsolete. Repairs and replacements are required as capital depreciates. In any one year some proportion of the total output of producer goods is required for replacement. The value of this part of the total output is known as *depreciation.* The total production of capital is termed *gross investment,* and any addition to the capital stock is *net investment.* Hence,

Gross Investment − Depreciation = Net Investment

It could happen that the rate of depreciation exceeds the total output of capital so that net investment is a minus quantity. A nation which finds itself in this position is said to be consuming capital; it is not making good the wear and tear and obsolescence of its capital stock. If this should continue, output in the future is bound to decline. Capital consumption is most likely to occur during a war when a country is obliged to devote a large part of its economic resources to the production of military equipment.

The entrepreneur

As mentioned earlier, economists sometimes identify a fourth factor of production – enterprise. It is held that, left to themselves, land, labour, and capital will not produce anything. There must be some person or persons, who will organise these three factors so that production can take place. Someone must take the decisions (*a*) what to produce (i.e. the type of good or service and the quantity); (*b*) how to produce (i.e. the methods of production); (*c*) where to produce (i.e. the location of the enterprise).

Whoever takes the decisions, and the consequent risks, is known as the *entrepreneur.* There is no really suitable English word to describe such a person; perhaps 'enterpriser' is the nearest we can get. The entrepreneur is the person who undertakes production with a view to profit. In a capitalist society, production would not take place unless someone was prepared to buy and organise economic resources for production on the basis of expected profits.

The entrepreneur is a *risk-bearer.* Most production is undertaken in anticipation of demand. Firms will produce those things which they *believe* will yield a profit – they do not *know* that they will do so, because the future is unknown. Entrepreneurs must bear the costs involved during the time which elapses between the decision to produce and the eventual marketing of the commodity. They must pay rent for their land, interest on the money borrowed, wages to labour, and meet the costs of materials. These payments must be made without any certainty that such costs will be covered by receipts. If the sales revenue exceeds their expenses, the entrepreneurs will make a profit – if not, they must bear the loss. The risks borne by entrepreneurs arise from uncertainty. Economic conditions are always changing and past experience is not necessarily any good guide to future prospects.

Organisation, management and risk-bearing – these are the entrepreneurial functions. In the one-person business they are clearly all carried out by the sole proprietor. In the large company, the functions of the entrepreneur are shared; riskbearing is the role of the shareholders; management is the function of the directors.

Many economists do not accept that the functions just described represent those of a factor of production which is clearly distinguishable from labour. They argue that the entrepreneurial function is no more than that of a particular and specialised form of labour. They point out that risk-bearing is not peculiar to the entrepreneur. Many types of labour take risks – the steeplejack and the miner run the risk of personal injury, and most forms of labour cannot avoid the risk of unemployment.

4 Specialisation and Mobility

The division of labour

By far the most striking feature of production in a developed economy is the fact that a worker almost never makes a complete product. By the time a product reaches the retail store nobody can say 'I made that'. People's daily work does not consist of providing for their own wants directly. The food we eat, the clothes we wear, the furniture we use, are all made by hands other than our own.

All this emphasises the fact that workers *specialise*. They contribute but a small part to the production of some article or the provision of some service. Labour is *divided* in the sense that the production process is split into a very large number of individual operations and each operation is the special task of one worker. This principle of the division of labour is now carried to remarkable lengths and the production of relatively simple things may be broken down into hundreds of separate operations.

At a very early stage in human development, people realised the gains to be obtained by applying this most important principle. The earliest people must have attempted to provide all their daily wants by their own efforts. They would have been obliged to provide food, clothing, shelter, and protection for themselves. In doing so they could have produced little more than the barest essentials for survival. By living in communities where some degree of specialisation was practised they learned that the total output of any group was much greater than the sum of the individual outputs of independent producers. One person might specialise in hunting, another in making cloth, another in making tools, and so on. Each would exchange his or her surplus for the goods made by other specialists. From these earliest times the principle of the division of labour has been progressively extended. The process is still going on, and a visit to any modern factory making motor cars, television sets, or clothing gives a vivid picture of the extent to which production is now specialised.

Adam Smith, writing in the latter part of the eighteenth century, provided what has now become the most celebrated account of specialisation. On a visit to a factory engaged in making pins he observed: 'One man draws out the wire, another straightens it, a third cuts it, a fourth points it, a fifth grinds the top to receive the head; to make the head requires two or three distinct operations; to put it on is a peculiar business; to whiten it is another; it is even a trade in itself to put them into paper. The important business of making pins is, in this manner, divided into about 18 distinct operations.'

He estimated that production per day in this factory was about 5 000 pins per person employed. If the whole operation had been carried out from start to finish by each employee, Smith estimated that he would have been able to make only a few dozen each day.

Advantages of the division of labour

Why should specialisation lead to such great increases in productivity? Smith followed up his description by an analysis which attempted to discover the reasons for the improved performance.

1 A person who spends his or her time performing one relatively simple task becomes extremely proficient at that particular operation. Constant repetition leads to great dexterity, or, as most people would say, 'practice makes perfect'.

2 No time is wasted in moving from one job to another. The necessity of moving from station to station, putting down one set of tools and picking up another is eliminated.

3 There is a saving of time in the training of operatives. A man or woman can be trained very quickly for the performance of a single operation.

4 There is a saving of skill. Specialisation means that many different occupations are created, each one of which calls for some particular aptitude. It is possible, therefore, for each worker to specialise in the job for which he or she is best suited.

5 One of the most important advantages of the division of labour is that it makes possible a much greater use of machinery. When a complex process has been broken down into a series of separate, simple processes it is possible to devise machinery to carry out each individual operation. It would be extremely difficult, for example, to construct a machine which would carry out the whole business of making a chair, but, once this has been reduced to a series of separate operations, it becomes possible to use electric saws, planing machines, power-driven lathes, etc.

With regard to the fourth point, it might be objected that one person might be more efficient in all tasks than another person. In such a case it can be shown that specialisation of labour might still be advantageous. A simple arithmetical example will make this point clear. Let us suppose that there are two leather workers, A and B, each producing shoes and handbags.

In 1 week A can make *either* 10 pairs of shoes, *or* 10 handbags
In 1 week B can make *either* 8 pairs of shoes, *or* 4 handbags

In the absence of any specialisation we will suppose that each week,

A makes 5 pairs of shoes *and* 5 handbags
B makes 4 pairs of shoes *and* 2 handbags

Total: 9 pairs of shoes *and* 7 handbags

A is more efficient in both activities, but the fact that he is *relatively* more efficient in producing handbags (10:4) than in producing shoes (10:8) means that specialisation will result in a greater total output. We can assume that B specialises completely in shoes while A partially specialises in handbags. Thus each week,

A makes 2 pairs of shoes and 8 handbags
B makes 8 pairs of shoes and 0 handbags

Total: 10 pairs of shoes and 8 handbags

This is a very simple account of the important principle of *comparative advantage* which is discussed in detail on pp. 351–353.

The disadvantages of the division of labour

There are a number of reasons why the development of specialised production has not been an unmixed blessing. The drawbacks of the system are mainly concerned with the loss of 'job satisfaction' which results from the constant repetition of simple operations.

Monotony

A cycle of simple movements which is repeated every few minutes is all that is demanded of large number of workers in factories. This undoubtedly makes for monotony and boredom; there is no opportunity for the worker to exercise initiative, judgement, manual skills, or responsibility. Whilst there are operatives who may prefer to have daily tasks which make very limited calls upon them and who do not wish to have a job which carries any great responsibility, it must be the case that large numbers of workers do find such jobs rather frustrating.

Loss of craftsmanship

The extension of specialisation has been accompanied by a great increase in the use of machinery which, in turn, has tended to become more and more automatic. Basic skills have been transferred from the hands of the worker to the machine; it is the machine which now controls the design, the quality, and the quantity of the product, and not the person tending the machine. All this has led to a marked decline in the degree of craftsmanship required of the average industrial worker. The satisfaction to be derived from 'making something' – the pride in creation – is denied to the machine minder.

While much of this criticism is well founded, we must not overlook the fact that mechanisation has produced many new types of craftsmen – the designers and creators of the machines themselves – and many new occupations which call for a high degree of skill and applied knowledge (e.g. the computer has created a demand for systems analysts). The use of machines has also abolished much of the heavy manual labour associated with hand methods of production. Imagine the work involved in reducing the trunk of a tree to a dining table without the use of power-driven tools.

Increased risk of unemployment

Specialisation means that workers do not have the wide industrial training which would make them adaptable to changes in the techniques of production. Their specialised functions can become obsolete when new machines are invented, and their particular skills will be useless elsewhere. Such workers, it is held, are especially liable to unemployment in a rapidly changing world.

In answer to this argument it has been pointed out that the division of labour, by simplifying tasks, makes jobs in one industry very similar to those in another. Since the operation is easy to learn, retraining is easily and quickly accomplished and workers can, without great difficulty, move from one job to another.

Interdependence

A specialised system of production increases the extent to which different sectors of the economy depend upon one another. It is not simply a question of workers specialising, factories, firms and even whole industries specialise. Many modern industries consist of a large number of firms each concentrating on the production of one, or very few, components which are brought together in what is in effect a large assembly plant. This is most clearly typified by the motor car industry where many hundreds of different parts are manufactured by relatively small specialist firms. These components are brought together on the assembly line. This is a very efficient, low-cost method of production, but it is extremely vulnerable to a breakdown in any one of the large number of links in the chain. Delays in the supply of any one component may cause massive hold-ups throughout the industry.

Modern technology allied to the extensive use of the division of labour has made possible enormous increases in the output of goods and services. It has transformed the living standards of millions of people, removed much of the back-breaking toil from people's daily labour, made possible a great reduction in working hours, and, by providing for more leisure, has given people the opportunity to lead fuller and richer lives.

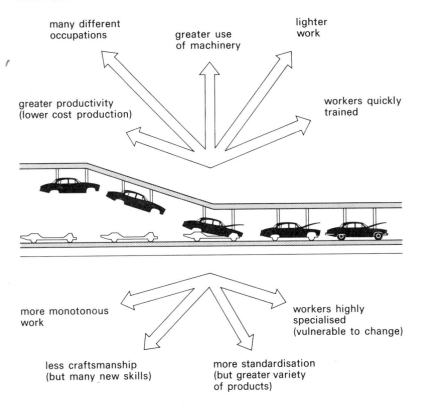

Fig. 4 The division of labour

Nevertheless the loss of job satisfaction, particularly in manufacturing industries, is raising some serious social problems. In many industrial countries, managers are seriously considering various projects aimed at 'job enrichment'. These are attempts to reverse recent trends by enlarging the role and responsibilities of the workers. Several factories have tried to abolish the assembly line by reorganising production so that teams of workers are responsible for assembling the entire product (or a major component of it). Each team is free to decide how the various tasks will be allocated and the speed with which the job is carried out. Within each team the jobs may be rotated so as to increase the element of variety in the work.

43

Specialisation and exchange

A system of specialised production, no matter how simple, cannot exist without exchange. When people become specialists they are dependent upon some system of exchange to provide them with the variety of goods and services required to satisfy their wants. Without some means of exchange, the farmers would have too much corn for their personal needs, but would have no coal, oil, electricity, or machinery. There must be some means whereby the outputs of specialist producers can be exchanged.

In addition to this need for a highly developed mechanism for carrying out exchanges, there is another important factor governing the degree of specialisation. The principle of the division of labour can only be applied extensively when there is a large market for a standardised product. Automatic and semi-automatic machinery and highly specialised workers are equipped to produce large outputs of identical products. Specialisation, therefore, is limited by the extent of the market.

Specialisation and the size of the market

The work of engineers and scientists continues to provide increasing scope for wider applications of the principle of the division of labour. The most striking evidence of this fact is the increasing use being made of robots in mass production industries. These methods of production are only worthwhile if there is a market (i.e. a potential demand) large enough to keep this expensive capital equipment fully employed. The size of the market, therefore is an *economic* limit to the degree of specialisation.

On a more simple level, a person in a remote village could not earn a living by becoming a specialist cabinet maker or tailor. The size of the market would be too small to provide such a highly specialised worker with an adequate income. The great expansion in the size of markets for most consumer goods and services, made possible by rising real incomes, increasing populations and by improvements in transport and communications, has been a major factor in the development of specialisation in the methods of production.

Specialisation and economic change

We live in a world of specialists. Many people are trained for highly specialised roles in the economic system. Doctors, lawyers, accountants, physicists, chemists, surveyors, civil engineers – the list of specialised occupations seems endless. All of these people may be extremely productive in their particular fields, but the fact that each of them concentrates on a narrow range of skills makes them *occupationally immobile*. They can do one thing very well, but they cannot do much else. A shortage of labour in one profession cannot be overcome by moving people from another profession; a chemist cannot do the work of an accountant. But it is not only labour which is highly specialised. Capital equipment is usually designed for a specific task. A modern blast furnace is a very effective means of producing iron, but it cannot be used for any other purposes; a petrol tanker cannot carry coal, and a combine harvester cannot dig ditches. Much of our capital equipment, therefore, is also occupationally immobile.

These may be very obvious points but they have important economic implications. These are times of rapid economic change and economic progress depends very much on the community's ability to adapt quickly and smoothly to changes in consumer demand, in technology, in world trade, and so on. When economic resources are highly specialised (i.e. *specific* to a particular task), it may be extremely difficult to transfer such resources from one use to another. The mobility of the factors of production is clearly an important economic problem. Let us now examine some of the causes of economic change.

Wars

Modern wars completely disrupt the economic life of a country. They increase the pace of economic and social change and in particular they speed up the rate of technological progress. Some industries undergo great expansion (e.g. chemicals, electronics, engineering), while many industries are forced to change the nature of their outputs. Large numbers of workers change their jobs and learn new skills. The structure of world trade is distorted and the pattern of exports and imports which develops after a major war is sometimes very different from that which existed before the war. The British economy has been particularly affected by export markets lost during wars (e.g. in cotton and coal).[1] While the prosecution of the war itself calls for a high degree of mobility of labour and capital, so does the need to adjust to the very different economic situation which emerges after the war.

Population changes

Emigration, immigration and movements in birth and death rates bring about changes in both the size and age composition of the population. Such population changes call for changes in the allocation

---

[1] This was only one of many reasons for the decline of these industries.

of resources to different industries. A rapidly increasing population will have a large proportion of younger people and there will be increasing demands for schools, schoolteachers, and those commodities consumed mainly by the young. A declining population will have an increasing proportion of older people. There will be a decreasing demand for social capital such as houses and schools and increasing demands for those things which meet the needs of older people.

Technological changes

Man's ingenuity produces a constant stream of technological innovations, and these in turn call for new methods of production, new types of capital equipment and changes in the skills required of the labour force. A good example is provided by recent developments in the ports where the container revolution based on the use of new types of capital equipment demanded a new range of skills from the dockers.

Political changes

The economy of a country is affected by political changes both at home and abroad. Changes in the structure of taxation and in the volume and distribution of government spending are important instruments of government policy which affect all sectors of the economy. Where industries are nationalised, the government, by varying the development programmes of these industries, can directly influence the allocation of resources. External political changes are also important, especially where a country is very dependent upon export markets.

Changes in taste and fashion

Changes in taste and fashion can influence the demands for most consumer goods to some extent, but they are particularly important to producers of such things as clothing, furniture, footwear, and domestic appliances. Advertising, of course, is a powerful agent in stimulating changes in demand of this type. Changes in income too play an important part. Rising incomes tend to bring about different patterns of consumption. A typical example would be the movement from public to private transport in recent years.

Occupational and geographical mobility

Changes in the character of the national output can only take place if the factors of production are mobile. There are two aspects of mobility: occupational and geographical.

Occupational mobility concerns the movement of a factor of production from one occupation to another. Most of the examples considered so far have referred to occupational mobility.

Geographical mobility describes the movement of a factor from one location to another. This is an important matter when new industries establish themselves in locations different from those in which the older industries were established.

Land

Land, quite obviously, is not mobile in the geographical sense, but a great deal of land has a high degree of occupational mobility. In the UK, for example, a large proportion of the land has many alternative uses. It might be used for farmland, for roads, railways, airports, parks, residential housing, industrial development, and so on. Some of the land, for example, the mountainous areas, has an extremely limited degree of occupational mobility, being useful perhaps for sheep grazing, or as a centre for tourism.

Capital

Capital is mobile in both senses, although some types of capital are extremely immobile. Such things as railway networks, blast furnaces, and shipyards are virtually immobile in the geographical sense. It may be physically possible to dismantle them and move them to different sites, but the cost of doing so will almost certainly outweigh any advantages of the new location.

Neither is such equipment mobile in the occupational sense; it can only be used for a specific purpose. Many buildings, however, can be effectively adapted to other uses. Many of the former cotton mills in Lancashire are now housing a variety of industrial activities. Some capital equipment is mobile both geographically and occupationally. Electric motors, machine tools, hand tools, and lorries, for example, can be used effectively in a wide variety of industries and are capable of movement from one location to another without great cost.

Labour

Theoretically we should expect labour to be the most mobile of the factors of production both occupationally and geographically. Economic history does indeed provide abundant evidence of great movements of labour from one industry to another and from one region to another. During the nineteenth century and the early years of this century, millions of people left Europe to settle in North America and in the British Dominions. In the second half of the nineteenth century there was the great westward movement in the United States, when large numbers of people left the eastern states to settle the interior and the western seaboard. The last quarter of the eighteenth century saw the beginnings of the great migration of the British people from the country to the town, a movement which is still taking place. More recent times have seen a large-scale movement of labour from the Mediterranean lands to the industrial nations in north-west Europe.

In spite of all this evidence of labour's mobility, we must bear in mind that most of these movements took place over fairly long periods of time, and in most cases there were severe political, economic, and social pressures stimulating the movements. There is plenty of evidence that labour is not very mobile geographically. Regions no more than 100 miles apart often record unemployment rates which are widely dissimilar. In the 1930s some areas of the UK experienced rates as high as 60 per cent while others had rates well below 10 per cent. If labour had been geographically mobile such divergencies would surely have been greatly reduced.

Occupationally, too, labour is relatively immobile. The evidence here lies in the large differentials in salaries and wages as between different occupations. A high degree of occupational mobility would certainly lead to a much narrower range of differentials.

Barriers to the mobility of labour

Geographical

1 Monetary cost. Moving a family together with all its possessions can be an expensive operation. In addition to removal costs it might well entail the numerous expenses involved in buying and selling a house. This latter aspect of mobility can be a deterrent to movements into areas where house prices are well above the national average (e.g. the London area).

2 Housing shortages. A housing shortage has been a feature of most economies since the war and this is undoubtedly the major barrier to geographical mobility. It is a particularly difficult problem in the case of rented accommodation; there is very little chance of a worker obtaining a rented house in a new area when virtually all local authorities have waiting lists for such houses.

3 Social ties. Many people are very reluctant to 'tear up their roots'. They do not wish to leave behind their friends and relatives and face the prospect of establishing new social relationships in a strange town. This is probably not such an important barrier for many professional groups where promotion often depends upon a movement to another town.

4 Education. Many families will tend to be immobile at certain stages of their children's education. They would regard it as inadvisable to move at some critical period in their child's schooling. This could also be a barrier if different parts of the country are operating different systems of education.

Occupational

1 Natural ability. People differ in natural ability and some occupations require a high level of intelligence, or particular natural aptitudes which are only possessed by a certain proportion of the population. For this reason surgeons, physicists, mathematicians, designers, and entertainers form a relatively small proportion of the population.

2 Training. The prevailing system of apprenticeship in many trades is geared to the training of people between the ages of 16 and 21 years. This tends to make it difficult for an older man to learn a new trade, especially when fully skilled status is only granted to those who have served the recognised period of apprenticeship.

Many professions demand a very long period of education and training (e.g. doctors, architects). In spite of the government aid in the form of training grants, such extended periods still require considerable financial sacrifice by the student and his family. The length of the training period itself may prove a deterrent to some people.

3 Capital. A certain amount of capital is required in order to enter some occupations. In order to establish oneself as an entrepreneur in the retail trade or some other form of one-person business (e.g. jobbing builder, or hairdresser), capital is needed to purchase the necessary stock and equipment. The purchase of a practice or partnership may be necessary if one wishes to become established as a solicitor, accountant, or estate agent. These requirements will constitute a financial barrier to many prospective entrants.

4 Class. It is held by many people that the existing class structure is responsible for some restrictions on the occupational mobility of labour. A particular type of social background with an education at one of the more famous public schools provide, it is believed, definite advantages in certain fields of employment.

Policies to assist mobility

The barriers to geographical mobility are quite formidable, and while the UK government does provide financial assistance towards the cost of removal for unemployed workers, it has tended to deal with the problem of regional unemployment by 'moving work to the workers' (see pp. 134–40). Many employers anxious to attract workers from other areas offer assistance with removal costs and sometimes provide accommodation.

One problem may be lack of knowledge; employers may not be fully-informed of the potential labour supply and workers may be ignorant of certain job opportunities. The UK government has recently embarked upon a major programme to extend and improve its information services in this area. The older and rather forbidding Employment Exchanges are being replaced by modern and attractive Job Centres which, it is hoped, will encourage both employers and job-seekers to use the facilities provided by the state. There are, of course, a number of privately operated employment agencies, and employers also make great use of the local press as a means of recruiting labour.

A most important feature of official policy on the occupational mobility of labour is the provision of Retraining Centres (currently known as Skill Centres) where workers can learn new skills.

The UK has about 60 such centres and is in the process of opening more of them. It is important, of course that adequate financial assistance is available to those people attending retraining centres since many of them will be older workers with family responsibilities. Since these are the people who are bearing the main burdens of economic change, it seems reasonable that the state should provide the necessary means to facilitate the redeployment of labour.

Other aids to mobility take the form of redundancy payments and Job Search and employment transfer schemes. The purpose of these schemes is to remove or reduce the financial hardship which a change of job often entails. The need for mobility shows itself when economic changes make people redundant and organised labour will usually resist such redundancies. Such resistance is perfectly understandable – no one likes to be told that his or her skill is no longer required. The provision of adequate financial assistance during the period when a worker is seeking a new job, or undergoing retraining is one way of helping to reduce the resistance to the redeployment of labour.

Industry itself plays an important part. Most of the larger firms offer training to new entrants. Increased mechanisation and the greater use of automatic and semi-automatic machinery has tended to reduce the problem of immobility. There are now far more jobs of a semi-skilled nature which call for no more than a few weeks training.

Labour turnover

While a measure of mobility in the labour force is essential, too much mobility is inefficient and costly. It appears that a great deal of the mobility which does take place is not of the type which leads to a more efficient distribution of the labour force. Studies of particular industrial regions have revealed that very large movements of workers into and out of certain industries are taking place while the totals employed in those industries remain relatively unchanged. Labour turnover, as this movement is called, often represents an aimless wandering from job to job – a restless movement of workers seeking a change rather than advancement to a better paid or more suitable situation. It is due in some part to the lack of job satisfaction referred to earlier although inadequate selection procedures may also be a cause.

A high degree of labour turnover is costly because each time an operative leaves his job and a replacement is required the employer incurs costs in the form of (a) a fall in output, (b) the costs of training a new worker, and (c) the loss of a skilled operative's output while he trains the new entrant.

The entrepreneur

The most mobile of the factors of production is probably the entrepreneur. While labour tends to be trained for some special task appropriate to some particular industry, the basic functions of the entrepreneur are common to all industries. Whatever the type of economic activity there will be a need to raise capital, to organise the factors of production, and to take the fundamental decisions on where, what, and how to produce. The creation of an efficient unit of production is a task of human relations the basic features of which are common to all industries. It requires qualities of initiative, leadership, organisation, and control. The relatively few people of first-class ability who possess such qualities are able to operate effectively in almost any industry.

5 Combining the Factors of Production

Varying the proportions

It is the task of management in providing a supply of goods and services to organise land, labour, and capital so that any given output can be produced at the lowest possible cost. In Chapter 6 we shall be concerned mainly with the relationship between output and monetary costs. In order to understand the economics of production, however, we have to start by examining the purely physical aspects; that is, the relationship between the units of capital, land, and labour employed and the resultant physical units of output.

In making a product, a firm does not have to combine the inputs in fixed proportions. Many farm crops can be grown by using relatively little labour and relatively large amounts of capital (machinery, fertilisers, etc.) or by combining relatively large amounts of labour with very little capital. In most cases a firm has some opportunity to vary the 'input mix'.

The effects of varying the proportions between the factors of production is a subject of great importance because nearly all short-run changes in production involve some changes in these proportions. When a firm wishes to increase (or decrease) its output, it cannot, in the short run, change its fixed factors of production, but it can produce more (or less) by changing the amounts of the variable factors (labour, materials, etc.). When farmers wish to increase their output they are usually obliged to do so by using more labour, more seed, more fertiliser (i.e. variable factors) on some fixed supply of land (the fixed factor).

Manufacturers are in a similar position. In the short run they cannot extend their factories or instal more machinery but they can adjust their output by varying the quantities of labour, raw materials, fuel, and power.

Diminishing returns

Many years ago economists pondered over the implications of varying the proportions in which the factors were combined and came up with a principle which has become famous as the Law of Diminishing Returns. They applied this law to agriculture (and we shall use agriculture in our illustration), but it holds true for all kinds of production. The operation of the law is best explained by means of a simple arithmetical example.

Let us assume that some particular crop is to be grown on a fixed area of land, say 20 acres. We shall also assume that the amount of capital to be used is also fixed in supply. Labour will be the variable factor. Table 2 sets out some hypothetical results obtained by varying the amount of labour employed.

Table 2 Non-proportional returns

(1) Number of people	(2) Total product (tons)	(3) Average product (tons)	(4) Marginal product (tons)
1	8	8	8
2	24	12	16
3	54	18	30
4	82	20·5	28
5	95	19	13
6	100	16·7	5
7	100	14·3	0
8	96	12	−4

Table 2 illustrates some important relationships, but before we examine them we must state the assumptions on which the table is based.

1 Labour is the only variable factor.
2 All units of the variable factor are equally efficient.
3 There are no changes in the techniques of production.

On the basis of these assumptions we can conclude that any changes in productivity arising from variations in the number of people employed are due entirely to the changes in the proportions in which labour is combined with the other factors.

Table 2 illustrates the Law of Diminishing Returns (or the Law of Variable Proportions) which states that, *'As we add successive units of one factor to fixed amounts of other factors the increments in total output will at first rise and then decline.'*

The details in Table 2 can be used to illustrate this law. Columns 1 and 2 are self-explanatory – they show the total products at different levels of employment. *Average product* (or output per worker) is shown in Column 3 and is obtained quite simply by using the formula

$$\frac{\text{Total product}}{\text{Number of workers}} = \text{Average product}$$

Marginal product, shown in Column 4, describes the changes in total output brought about by varying employment by one person. The addition of a third person adds 30 tons to total output, while the employment of a fourth person increases total output by 28 tons.

Returns to the variable factor

Since labour is the only variable factor, changes in output are related directly to changes in employment so that we speak of changes in the productivity of labour or changes in *the returns to labour*. As the number of people increases from 1 to 6, total output continues to increase, but this is not true of the average product (AP) and the marginal product (MP). As more people are employed, both the AP and the MP begin to rise, reach a maximum and start to fall. These movements are clearly seen in Figure 5. As the number of people increases from 1 to 3 the *marginal product* of labour is increasing. Up to this point the fixed factors are being underutilised – the people are 'too thin on the ground'. When the number of people employed exceeds 3 the marginal product of labour begins to fall – an indication that the proportions between the fixed and variable factors are becoming less favourable. Marginal product begins to fall before average product and we get the maximum average product of labour when 4 people are employed. If we now wished to increase output *and* main-

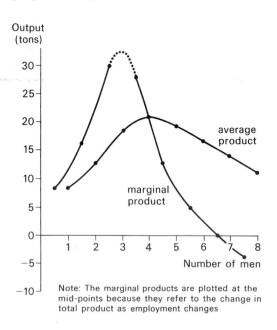

Note: The marginal products are plotted at the mid-points because they refer to the change in total product as employment changes

Fig. 5 Average and marginal productivity

tain the same productivity of labour it is obvious that an increase in the fixed factors must accompany the increase in the variable factors. This would be a change of *scale* and is the subject of the next section.

It is this feature of *increasing production* and *falling productivity* which is highlighted by the Law of Diminishing Returns. In Table 2 we see that diminishing marginal returns set in after the employment of the third person and diminishing average returns after the employment of the fourth person. Note that the marginal productivity of the seven person is zero – his employment does not change total output. This may not be so unrealistic as it first appears. In some underdeveloped lands where peasant families are confined to their individual plots, it is quite conceivable that the marginal productivity of very large families is zero.

Figure 6 makes use of the total product curve and provides another view of the relationships between employment and output where some of the factors are fixed in supply.

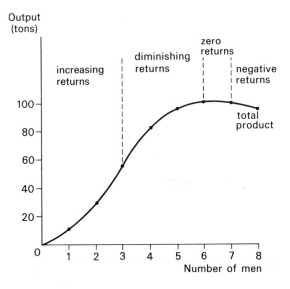

Fig. 6

We can summarise the possible effects of increasing the quantity of variable factors as follows:

1 Increasing returns – total product increases at an increasing rate (MP is increasing).
2 Constant returns (not illustrated) – total product is increasing at a constant rate (MP is constant).
3 Diminishing returns – total product is increasing at a decreasing rate (MP is falling).

4 Zero returns – total product is constant (MP is zero).
5 Negative returns – total product is falling (MP is negative).

It is important to note that although the illustrations used above have concentrated on labour as the variable factor, the law of variable proportions (or diminishing returns) is equally applicable to land and capital and, no doubt, to entrepreneurship. The marginal and average productivity of capital will, at some point, start to decline as more and more capital is applied to a fixed supply of land and labour. The same will apply to the productivity of land as more and more land is combined with a fixed amount of labour and capital.

Although the figures we have used in our example are hypothetical, a good many actual experiments have verified the pattern shown here. Experiments in which increased amounts of feed were given to a fixed number of dairy cows, and others where increased amounts of fertiliser were applied to a given area of land have clearly demonstrated the applicability of non-proportional returns. Increments in the yields at first increased more than proportionally but eventually there came a point where the law of diminishing returns asserted itself.

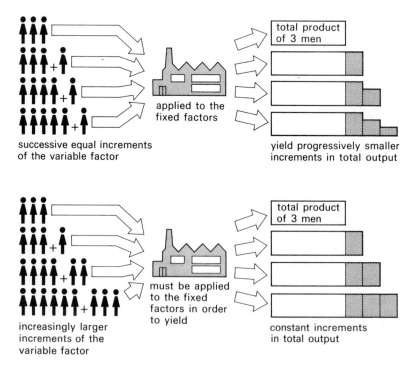

Fig. 7 Two views of the law of diminishing returns

The law of diminishing returns only applies when 'other things remain equal'. The efficiency of the other factors and the techniques of production are assumed to be constant. Now we know that these other things do not remain constant and improvements in technical knowledge have tended to offset the effects of the law of diminishing returns. Improved methods of production increase the productivity of the factors of production and move the AP and MP curves upwards. But this does not mean that the law no longer applies. It is still true that in the short period (when other things can change very little) increments in the variable factors will at some point yield increments in output which are less than proportionate. In some less developed regions where there is little or no technical change and population is increasing we can, unfortunately, see the law of diminishing returns operating only too clearly.

The least-cost combination

The preceding explanation of the law of diminishing returns should not be taken as an indication that the ratio of labour to land and capital which gives the maximum output per worker is the ratio which the firm should adopt. All we have done is to show the tendency of output per unit of the variable factor when the proportions between the factors are varied. The most profitable way of combining the factors of production depends upon their prices as well as their productivity.

In this section we have been concerned with physical inputs and physical outputs. In other words, we have been discussing technical efficiency. Our measurement has been the *physical productivity* of labour. But entrepreneurs are concerned with economic efficiency and for this purpose they will measure output and input in monetary terms. Their inputs they measure as costs and their output is measured in terms of revenue. They are interested in making profits and their aim will be to maximise the difference between costs and revenue. They will not be very interested in maximising the productivity of labour if labour is very cheap relative to the other factors.

We have already noted that there will be several different ways of combining the factors of production to produce any given output. Let us suppose that a firm wishes to produce 100 units per week of some particular commodity. This output we will assume can be produced with any of the following combinations.

	Land	Labour	Capital
Method 1	20	10	4
Method 2	20	7	7
Method 3	15	9	9

The question now arises, 'Which is the *best* method?'. Given our assumption that entrepreneurs will always try to maximise their profits, it follows that the firm will adopt that method which minimises costs. Let us assume that the prices of the factors of production are as follows:

Land is £20 per unit; Labour is £10 per unit; and Capital is £15 per unit. Now,

Method 1 will cost £560
Method 2 will cost £575
Method 3 will cost £525

The entrepreneur will choose Method 3.

The reader should now check the effects of varying factor prices. It will be observed that any significant changes in the *relative* prices of the factors of production will lead to a substitution of the relatively cheaper for the relatively dearer factor.

Returns to scale

The law of diminishing returns deals with what are essentially short-run situations. It is assumed that some of the resources used in production are fixed in supply. In the long-run, however, it is possible for a firm to vary the amounts of all the factors of production employed; more land can be acquired, more buildings erected and more machinery installed. What we are saying is that, in the long run, it is possible for a firm to change the *scale* of its activities. Strictly speaking a change of scale takes place when the quantities of all the factors are changed by the same percentage so that the proportions in which they are combined are not changed.

Table 3 Returns to scale

Units of labour	Units of land (*acres*)	Total output (*tonnes*)	Increase in size of firm	Increase in total output
4	20	100		
			100%	150%
8	40	250		
			50%	68%
12	60	420		
			$33\frac{1}{3}$%	$33\frac{1}{3}$%
16	80	560		
			25%	20%
20	100	672		
			20%	16%
24	120	780		

It is a feature of production that when the scale of production is changed, output changes are not usually proportionate. When a firm doubles its size, output will tend to change by more than 100% or less than 100%. The relationships between changes in scale and changes in output are described as *returns to scale*. In Table 3 some hypothetical figures are used in order to illustrate this important concept.

Table 3 shows the increases in total output as the scale of production increases. The firm increases its size but the proportion between the factors remains unchanged (i.e. 1 unit of labour per 5 acres of land). Using columns 4 and 5 we can compare the proportionate changes in total output with the proportionate changes in the size of the firm. As the firm increases its size from 4 people and 20 acres of land to 12 people and 60 acres of land, it experiences *increasing returns to scale* (output increases more than proportionately). A change of scale from 12 people and 60 acres to 16 people and 80 acres yields *constant returns to scale* (size and output change by the same percentage). Any further growth in the size of the firm yields *decreasing returns to scale* because output increases less than proportionately.

Those features of increasing size which account for increasing returns to scale are generally described as *economies of scale* and they are explained in Chapter 7. The causes of falling efficiency as the size of the firm increases are described as *diseconomies of scale*. These are also explained in Chapter 7, but, at this stage, we can note one possible cause of such diseconomies. While the inputs of land, labour, and capital may be increased proportionately, this may not be possible with regard to management ability. The entrepreneurial skills required to manage large enterprises are, it seems, limited in supply so that it is often difficult to match the increase in the supply of the other factors with a corresponding increase in the supply of management ability.

Part Three: The Organisation and Scale of Production

6 Costs of Production

Opportunity cost

Costs as we all know are usually measured in monetary terms and include such items as wages, rent, rates, interest, and the amounts paid for raw materials, fuel, power, transport, and so on. These are the costs measured and recorded by the accountant and they are an important part of the subject matter of economics. Before proceeding to analyse these costs, however, it is necessary to remind ourselves that economists also look at costs from a different viewpoint. They see the 'true' or 'real' costs of committing resources to a particular use as the output they might have produced had they been put to another use. This is the idea of opportunity cost explained on p. 4.

In order to obtain something of economic value we have to make a sacrifice since no economic goods are free. Since we all have limited incomes, the true or real cost of any article we buy is the next most desired alternative which is foregone. Opportunity cost is what we have 'to give up' in order to obtain something.

What is true of the individual is true of society as a whole. In devoting resources to the production of, say, roads, we have to forego the houses which might have been built with the same resources. In wartime, the opportunity cost of the tanks, guns, and military aircraft is the 'lost' output of motor cars, washing machines, railway equipment, and so on.

This way of looking at cost is important because 'money' or 'paid out' costs may not provide a true measure of the sacrifices incurred in producing a commodity. If the production of a good leads to pollution of the atmosphere or water supplies, the opportunity costs of production would include the clean air or clean water foregone by society as well as the costs of the factors employed in production. The idea of opportunity cost has an important bearing on the economist's view of profits. The difference between the traditional 'bookkeeping' costs and total revenue may not provide an accurate indication of the true profits. An obvious example is the case in which a businessman uses his own savings in order to establish an enterprise. Part of the true cost of running his firm is the interest foregone on his money capital. In using his savings for the purchase of stock and equipment he incurs a 'cost' in the form of the interest he might otherwise have received on his savings.

Output and costs

In dealing with the relationships between output and costs there are two situations to consider.

1 Short-run changes which cover periods when it is only possible to adjust the amount of the variable factors being used.
2 Long-run changes which apply to periods of time which are sufficiently long for all the factors to be varied.

We shall be mainly concerned with the short-run changes and our analysis of increasing and decreasing returns should give us a clue as to the behaviour of costs in the short period.

Increasing returns means that the ratio Output/Variable Input is increasing and this should mean that average cost is falling.

Similarly, diminishing returns means that the ratio Output/Variable Input is declining and we should expect average cost to be rising.

This may be clearer if we refer back to Table 2 (or Fig. 5) and see how many extra people are required in order to raise output by some given quantity, say, 18 tons. When 2 people are employed only $\frac{3}{5}$ extra people (1 person working part-time) will be needed to produce an extra 18 tons. When 4 people are employed, however, an additional 18 tons of output would require the employment of 2 more people. The cost per unit of output will be increasing under conditions of diminishing returns; it is falling when increasing returns are being experienced. These statements are based on the assumption that the prices of the factors do not change as more or less of them are employed. Changes in costs, then, arise directly from changes in productivity.

Classification of costs

Just as some inputs are fixed and others variable, so some costs are fixed and others variable.

Fixed costs

These are costs which do not vary as output varies. They are obviously the costs associated with the fixed factors of production, and include such items as rent, rates, insurance, interest on loans, and depreciation.

A major element in fixed costs, especially in capital-intensive industries, is the item known as *depreciation*. It may seem rather illogical to classify depreciation charges as a fixed cost for many people will think that the rate of depreciation of a capital asset is directly related to the extent to which it is used (i.e. to output). In fact the life of capital assets tends to be measured in economic rather than technical terms. Machinery depreciates even when not in use and, even more important, it becomes obsolete. It is normal practice, therefore, to fix an annual depreciation charge which will write off the cost of equipment over some *estimated* working lifetime. There are many ways of doing this, but the simplest is to make an annual charge equal to a fixed proportion of the total value. If a machine costs £20 000 and has an expected life of 5 years, then £4 000 per annum will be added to costs and placed in a depreciation fund to cover the expenses of renewal.

Fixed costs (sometimes described as *overhead* or *indirect* costs) are not influenced by changes in output. Whether a firm is working at full capacity or half capacity the items of costs mentioned above will be unaffected. Thus, when a super-tanker is lying empty in port, or a Jumbo-jet is standing in the hangar, or your new car is locked away in the garage, costs are still being incurred.

Variable costs

These are the costs which are related directly to output. The most obvious items of variable costs are the wages of labour, the costs of raw materials, and fuel and power. Variable costs are often described as *direct* or *prime* costs.

Total costs

Total costs represent the sum of fixed and variable costs. When output is zero, total costs will be equal to fixed costs since variable costs will be zero. When production commences, total costs will begin to rise as variable costs increase. Total costs will continue to rise as production increases, because there must be some increase in variable costs as output expands. What is important, however, is the *rate* at which total costs increase; if they are rising at a slower rate than output, average costs must be falling.

Average cost

Average cost (or cost per unit) is equal to Total Costs/Output. When output is small, average cost will be high because fixed costs will be spread over a small number of units of output. As output increases, average cost will tend to fall as each unit is 'carrying' a smaller element of fixed cost. Average cost will also fall because, for a time, there will be increasing returns to the variable factors as more of them are employed and more specialised methods adopted. There will come a point, however, when diminishing returns are encountered and average cost begins to rise. If we drop our assumption of homogeneous factors and fixed factor prices there are other reasons why average cost may increase at higher outputs. Management problems will tend to increase; less efficient stand-by equipment may be pressed into use; less efficient labour may have to be recruited; it may be necessary to work overtime at higher wage rates and increasing demand may cause the prices of materials to rise.

Economic theory, therefore, assumes that, for the individual firm with a fixed capacity, average cost will at first decline, but as output increases there will come a point where it will rise. In other words, the average cost curve will be U-shaped (see Fig. 8). When the firm is producing at its minimum average cost we say that it has reached its *optimum* output.

Marginal cost

The economist is interested in marginal quantities because most economic decisions involve changes in some existing situation. Marginal cost tells us what happens to total costs when we vary output by some small amount. More precisely, marginal cost is the extent to which total costs change when output is changed by one unit.

Marginal cost = Total cost of n units $-$ Total cost of $(n-1)$ units

Since marginal cost is a measurement of *changes in* total cost it is obviously influenced by variable costs but not by fixed costs. On the basis of our assumption that a firm expanding its output with a fixed capacity will, to begin with, experience increasing returns to its variable factors and, later, diminishing returns, it follows that the marginal cost curve will be U-shaped. We have already demonstrated that, under increasing returns, the cost of producing an extra unit will be falling and, under diminishing returns it will be rising.

Short-run cost schedules and cost curves

Table 4 is designed to illustrate the relationships between total, average, and marginal costs.

The derivation of the details in the different columns is quite straightforward. Column 4 showing total costs at different levels of output is obtained by adding together the figures in columns 2 and 3. Average cost in column 5 is the result of dividing the figures in column 4 by those in column 1. Marginal cost in column 6 is obtained from column 4 by the simple process of obtaining the *increments* in total costs for each unit increase in output.

(handwritten marginalia:) ✳ ÷ ✳ = ✳✳
↑ + ↑ = ↑↑
b − d = ∞

Table 4 Costs of production (£)

Units of output	Fixed costs	Variable costs	Total costs	Average costs	Marginal costs
0	18	0	18	Infinity	—
1	18	15·2	33·2	33·2	15·2
2	18	28·4	46·40	23·2	13·2
3	18	40·0	58·0	19·3	11·6
4	18	50·4	68·4	17·1	10·4
5	18	60·0	78·0	15·6	9·6
6	18	70·0	88·0	14·7	10·0
7	18	81·2	99·2	14·2	11·2
8	18	94·8	112·8	14·1	13·6
9	18	112·4	130·4	14·5	17·6
10	18	134·4	152·4	15·2	22·0

Notice that, as output increases, both the marginal and average costs begin to fall, reach a minimum, and then begin to rise. The relationship between average and marginal costs is an important one and it is clearly brought out in Fig. 8, which is a graphical representation of the details in Table 4.

The marginal costs have been plotted on the mid-points of the ordinates for reasons explained in Fig. 5. Both the AC and MC curves are U-shaped and the main point to note is that when MC is below

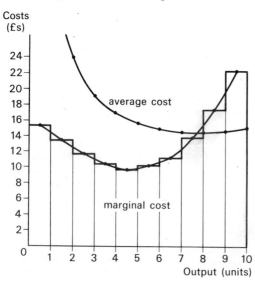

Fig. 8 *(handwritten:)* When marginal cost is below average cost, average cost is falling; When marginal cost is above average cost, average cost is rising.

AC, AC is falling; when MC is above AC, AC is rising. Marginal cost is equal to average cost when average cost is at its minimum value. These relationships can be proved mathematically, but they can also be easily understood on a common sense basis.

Consider a cricketer's batting average. If, in his next innings, his score (i.e. his marginal score) is less than his existing average, then his average must fall. If, in his next innings, he scores more than his existing average, his average score must increase. Very simply, then, if the marginal quantity < the average quantity, the average must be falling; if the marginal quantity > the average quantity, average must be rising.

Figure 9 presents another view of the cost relationships. It shows how the different kinds of costs can be derived from the total cost curve.

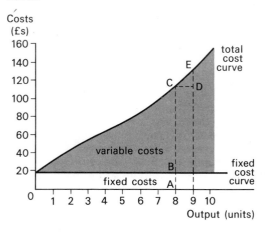

Fig. 9

When output is OA (i.e. 8 units), total costs = AC, and this is made up of fixed costs = AB and variable costs = BC. At this output, average cost = AC/OA, and marginal cost = ED.

The economies of large outputs

The use of mass production techniques to produce very large outputs of standardised goods provides a striking example of the relationships between output and average costs of production. This is especially true of those industries which are very capital-intensive and hence incur heavy fixed costs. The figures below are hypothetical, but they serve to demonstrate some very important features of the real world.

Let us take as an example the production of a typical mass-produced motor car. We assume the fixed costs are £400 million. This represents

65

expenditures on research and development, the purchase of a large number of new machines, the retooling of existing machinery and the costs of market research and preliminary advertising. We assume that variable costs are constant at £3 000 per car.

1 Assume the model is not very successful and only 50 000 of these cars are sold.

Total fixed costs	£400 000 000
Total variable costs	£150 000 000 (50,000 × 3,000)
Total costs	£550 000 000 ÷ 50,000 = 11,000
Average cost	£11 000

2 Assume the model is a great success and 2 000 000 of them are sold.

Total fixed costs	£400 000 000
Total variable costs	£6 000 000 000
Total costs	£6 400 000 000
Average cost	£3 200

This very simple example demonstrates that questions such as 'What does it cost to produce a car such as this?' are not very sensible questions. In order to make such a question meaningful some particular output must be specified.

7 The Scale of Production

We have already indicated that when an increase in the scale of production yields a more than proportionate increase in output, the enterprise is said to be experiencing *economies of scale*. These economies might be defined as those aspects of increasing size which lead to falling average costs. Economies of scale are conveniently classified as internal and external economies.

Internal economies of scale are those which arise from the growth of the firm independently of what is happening to other firms. They are not due to any increase in monopoly power or to any technological innovation; they arise quite simply from an increase in the scale of production *in the firm itself.*

External economies of scale are those advantages in the form of lower average costs which a firm gains from the growth of *the industry.* These economies accrue to all firms in the industry independently of changes in the scales of individual outputs.

Economies of scale are worthy of our attention because they are associated with important economic policies, and they help to explain important features of economic structure.

Internal economies of scale

Technical economies

Increased specialisation

The larger the establishment the greater the opportunities for the specialisation of men and machines. In the larger firm the process can be broken down into many more separate operations, workers can be employed on more specialised tasks, and the continuous use of highly specialised equipment becomes possible.

Indivisibility

Some types of capital equipment can only be employed efficiently in units of a minimum size, and this minimum may well be too large for the small firm. There is a lower limit to the size of a blast furnace, a rolling mill, a car assembly line, and a power press. This lower limit may be a technical limit; a smaller version of the equipment is impracticable. More generally the lower limit is an economic one; smaller versions of the equipment could be made but their usefulness would not justify their cost. Such indivisibility of plant means that firms with small outputs cannot take advantage of some highly specialised equipment. In a small firm this type of capital equipment would be standing idle for a large part of the time, the heavy fixed costs would be spread over small outputs, and average cost would be disproportionately high.

A research department must be of a certain size in order to work effectively. To the small firm this minimum effective size may represent a level of expenditure too large to justify any possible returns. To the large firm, however, the expenditure may be *relatively* small because the cost is spread over a large output.

Highly qualified specialists may also be regarded as 'indivisible' factors of production in the sense that the employment of such people on jobs other than those for which they have been specially trained represents an underutilisation of valuable economic resources. In the large firm they could be fully utilised, but it is doubtful if the smaller firm could find enough specialised work to keep them fully occupied. Small firms, however, can overcome this problem to some extent by 'buying out' such expertise as they require from specialised agencies of accountants, surveyors, lawyers, management consultants, and so on.

Increased dimensions

If one doubles the length, breadth, and height of a cube, the surface area is four times as great, and the volume eight times as great as the original. This simple arithmetical principle accounts for the remarkable increase in the dimensions of much capital equipment in recent years.

A modern oil tanker of 240 000 tons is only twice the size of a 30 000 ton tanker in terms of length, width, and height, and only four times as large in terms of surface area. It will require very few, if any, more people to operate her and she will certainly not require eight times the power to propel her through the water. In recent years the supertankers have been bringing oil to Europe from the Persian Gulf by way of the Cape of Good Hope, at a lower cost per ton than the smaller tankers managed on the very much shorter route through Suez.

Likewise the economies of the Jumbo-jet compared with the previous and much smaller generation of jets are most impressive. Economies of increased dimensions account for the tendency in industries which make use of tanks, vats, furnaces, and transport equipment to operate larger and larger units. In the domestic scene we can see the principle at work in trends towards larger packs and larger tubes of many packaged foods, toothpastes, and other household articles.

The principle of multiples

Most industries make use of a variety of machines, each machine carrying out a different operation. Each of these different machines is likely to have a different capacity. The machine which moulds the blocks of chocolate will operate at a much slower speed than the machine which wraps the blocks in silver paper.

Assume that a particular process requires a team of four machines, A, B, C, and D, the productive capacities of which are 50, 60, 20, and 30 units per hour. If the team comprises only one machine of each type, the maximum output per hour will be 20 units and machines A, B, and D will be working below capacity. This would be the kind of problem facing the small firm producing a small output. For small outputs it is not possible to obtain a balanced team of machines such that each machine is being fully utilised.

The lowest common multiple of 50, 60, 20, and 30 is 300. This is the smallest output per hour which will enable a sequence of machines of this type to work at full capacity. Such a balanced team of machines would be:

Machine A	Machine B	Machine C	Machine D
6	5	15	10

This assembly of machines would provide an output of 300 units per hour and all machines would be working at full capacity. If output is to be increased it will only be possible to maintain 100 per cent utilisation if production is increased by multiples of 300 units (i.e. 600, 900, 1 200, etc.). The reader can test this statement by trying to work out the most economic way of producing intermediate outputs of say 450 or 700 units.

The Economist 19.4.1980

'Modern mass-production methods were invented by the motor industry. The economy-of-scale rules for the conventional technology are the same the world over. For each model a manufacturer makes he must produce at least 800 to 1 100 cars a day, more than 250 000 annually of each of his so-called 'volume' cars. Otherwise the manufacturer's plant is under-utilised and his investment never recouped.

Making engines to put into the models is even tougher. The complicated transfer machine tools are very pricey. A manufacturer must make at least 2 500 of each of his engine types a day. And if they are modern lightweight aluminium ones (needing especially expensive pressure-die-casting tools) the break-even point is about 3 500 units a day. Sensible car firms tend to make only four body shapes, with perhaps two, or at most three basic engines.'

Marketing economies

A large firm is able to buy its material requirements in large quantities. Bulk buying enables the large enterprise to obtain preferential terms. It will be able to obtain goods at lower prices and be able to dictate its requirements with regard to quality and delivery much more effectively than the smaller firm. By placing large orders for particular lines bulk buyers enable suppliers to take advantage of 'long runs' – a much more economical proposition than trying to meet a large number of small orders from small firms each requiring a different colour, or quality, or design.

The large firm will be able to employ specialist buyers, whereas in the small firm, buying will be a function of an employee who will have several other responsibilities. Expert buyers have the knowledge and skill which enables them to buy 'the right materials, at the right time, at the right price'. Expert buying can be a great economy; unwise buying can be very costly.

The selling costs of the larger firm will be much greater than those of the small firm, but the selling costs *per unit* will generally be much lower. The selling costs of a large business might be £100 000 per annum while those of a small firm might be as low as £5 000 per annum. But if the large firm is selling 1 000 000 units while the small firm sells 20 000 per annum, the selling cost per unit in the large firm (i.e. 10p) is very much less than that of the small firm (25p). In selling, as in buying, the larger firm can afford to employ experts whose specialised skills can give it great economic advantages.

Packaging costs per unit will be lower. A package containing 100 articles is much easier to pack than 10 separate packages each containing 10 articles. The clerical and administrative costs of dealing with an order for 1 000 articles involves no more work than that involved in an order for 100, and, as we have just seen, transport costs do not increase proportionately with volume. Although many large firms spend huge sums on advertising, their advertising costs per unit sold may well be less than those of the small firm.

Financial economies

The large firm has several financial advantages. The fact that it is large and well known makes it a more credit-worthy borrower. Its greater selling potential and larger assets provide the lenders with greater security and make it possible for them to provide loans at lower rates of interest than would be charged to the smaller firm.

The larger firm has access to far more sources of finance. In addition to borrowing from the banks, it may approach a wide variety of other financial institutions as well as taking advantage of the highly developed market in the issuing of new shares and debentures (see pp.

108–110). Most of the larger financial institutions and the new issue market are not structured to meet the needs of the smaller firm.

The terms on which funds can be borrowed are more favourable to the large-scale borrower because the lending of money in large amounts, like the bulk supply of materials, yields economies of scale.

Risk-bearing economies

Large firms are usually better equipped than small firms to cope with the risks of trading. They can benefit from the law of averages or the law of large numbers. It is often possible to predict what will happen *on the average* when we have no idea what will happen in any individual case (insurance is based on this principle). The large firm, for example, can operate with smaller stocks *in proportion to sales* than the smaller firm. This is because variations in orders from individual customers and unexpected changes in customers' demands will tend to offset each other when total sales are very large. Total demand will be more stable and more predictable than will be the case with small firms where variations in individual orders will tend to have a relatively large impact on the total business.

This economy may be seen fairly clearly in the operation of a national grid to which many generating stations are connected. If each electricity-generating station supplied only its own locality, every station would have to maintain enough capacity to meet any possible exceptional demands. With a national grid, however, many of these exceptional variations in demand will be 'balanced' by occurring at different times or in different places so that the total capacity required to meet the national demand will be much less than would be the case with many separate generating stations each supplying its own area.

Many large firms are able to reduce the risks of trading by means of a policy of *diversification*. They manufacture either a variety of models of a particular product, or, more likely nowadays, a variety of products. All their eggs are not in one basket. A fall in the demand for any one of its products may not mean serious trouble for the firm; it may well be cancelled out by a rise in the demand for one or more of the other products. A small firm, on the other hand, is likely to be specialising in one product, any fall in the demand for which may have serious consequences. The larger firm is also likely to have a diversified market structure. In the national market, demand fluctuations between regions may offset one another; a fall in the demand in the home market might be balanced by a rise in the demand overseas. A small firm with a restricted market is much more vulnerable to changes in market conditions.

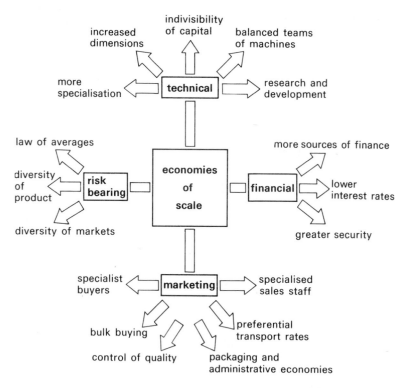

Fig. 10

Diseconomies of scale

Increasing size brings many advantages, but it can also bring disadvantages. While the present trend in industry is towards the growth of larger firms recent studies have shown that, in several cases, increases in the scale of production have not yielded the expected benefits in the form of greater industrial and commercial efficiency.

For each particular industry there will be some optimum size of firm in which average cost reaches a minimum. This optimum size will vary over time as technical progress changes the techniques of production. As firms grow beyond this optimum size, efficiency declines and average costs begin to increase.

There seems to be no good reason why such diseconomies of scale should arise from purely technical causes. Increased specialisation, increased dimensions, the principle of multiples, indivisibilities and so on should continue to offer potential reductions in average cost as the scale of production increases. Economists have usually attributed the major cause of diseconomies to management difficulties.

Management problems

There is no doubt that as the size of the firm increases, management problems become more complex. It becomes increasingly difficult to carry out the management functions of coordination, control, communication and the maintenance of morale in the labour force.

Coordination. Large organisations must be subdivided into many specialised departments (production planning, sales, purchasing, personnel, accounts etc.). As these departments multiply and grow in size, the task of coordinating their activities becomes more and more difficult.

Control. Essentially, management consists of two basic activities; the taking of decisions and seeing that these decisions are carried out. This latter function is that of control. The large firm usually has an impressive hierarchy of authority (managing director, director, head of division, head of department, foreman, and so on), but, in practice, the problem of seeing that 'everyone is doing what they are supposed to be doing, and doing it well', is a very difficult task.

Communication. The transfer of information in industry and commerce is a two-way process. It is not simply a matter of passing orders down the line; subordinates must be able to feed back their difficulties and problems. There must not only be a vertical line of communication, information must also move laterally, because one section of the firm must know what the other sections are doing. Keeping everyone informed of what is required of him or her, and on what is happening elsewhere in the firm is a very severe test of management's abilities.

Morale. Probably the most difficult problem for organisations with large numbers of employees is the maintenance of morale. The attitude of workers to management is of critical importance to the efficient operation of the enterprise, and the cultivation of a spirit of willing cooperation appears to become more and more difficult as the firm becomes larger. It is not easy to make the individual worker in a labour force of thousands feel that he or she is an important part of the firm and people low down the pyramid of control often lack an identification of interest with the firm and regard it with apathy and sometimes with hostility.

Prices of inputs

A further possible reason why growth in the size of the firm may lead to rising average costs may be increases in the prices of the factors of production. As the scale of production increases, the firm will increase its demands for materials, labour, energy, transport and so on. It may, however, be difficult to obtain increased supplies of some of these factors, for example, skilled labour, or minerals from mines which are already working at full capacity. In such cases a firm attempting to increase the scale of its production may find itself bidding up the prices of some of its inputs.

Although the difficulties mentioned above may give rise to inefficiencies as the size of the firm increases, the practical experience of firms in such industries as motor cars, chemicals, oil, and the manufacture of television tubes appears to contradict the idea that increasing size leads to diseconomies. It may be that the optimum size of the firm in such industries is very large indeed because the technical economies are so great that they more than offset any managerial and administrative diseconomies. We must also bear in mind a point made later in the chapter, namely, that economies of scale are only one of the motives for increasing the size of the firm.

Cost curves in the short-run and the long-run

The cost curves illustrated in Figure 8 (page 64) are short-run curves. They describe the behaviour of costs in a firm with a fixed amount of land and capital. In the long-run, however, there are no fixed factors; a firm can increase or reduce the amounts of all the factors it uses. It may expand by acquiring new plant and equipment or it may reduce its scale of operations by not replacing plant and equipment as they wear out, or it may dispose of such assets by selling them.

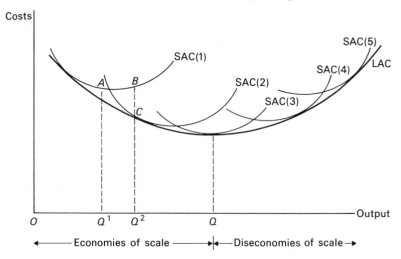

Fig. 11

Figure 11 helps to explain the changing cost structure of a firm as it changes its scale of production. If we assume that it begins operations as a small business, its original short-run average cost curve is represented by SAC(1). If this firm is successful and increases its size, a new short-run cost curve becomes effective for each particular scale of production. These short-run average cost curves are represented by SAC(2), SAC(3), SAC(4) and SAC(5). Each of these curves represents a different stock of capital and other fixed factors.

Assuming that a firm will always choose the size of plant and equipment which minimises the cost of producing any given output, we can see why it will tend to increase its scale of production as the demand for its product increases. Assume that initially it is operating on cost curve SAC(1) producing an output of OQ^1 at an average cost of AQ^1. Now in order to meet an increased demand, its output increases to OQ^2. With its existing size of plant this change in output would raise average cost to BQ^2. But by increasing the size of the firm and moving to cost curve SAC(2), an output of OQ^2 can be produced at an average cost of CQ^2. This same reasoning can be applied to explain movements to cost curves SAC(3), SAC(4) and SAC(5). Instead of moving up an existing cost curve, lower costs of production can be obtained by moving on to a cost curve of a plant with greater capacity.

The long-run average cost curve, therefore consists of a series of points on the different short-run cost curves. These points represent the lowest costs attainable for the production of any given output. If we assume that there are many such short-run curves, the long-run average cost curve will assume a shape similar to LAC in Figure 11. The LAC curve is described as an 'envelope curve' to the series of SAC curves.

In Figure 11 it is assumed that as the firm expands its capacity, it will experience economies of scale until it achieves output OQ on SAC(3). This is the optimum size of the firm since any further increase in the scale of production leads to rising average cost (i.e. diseconomies of scale). In fact empirical evidence seems to indicate that, in many manufacturing industries, the LAC falls as the scale of production increases and then levels out; constant returns seem to apply over very large ranges of output.

External economies of scale

External economies are the advantages which accrue to a firm from the growth in the size of *the industry* and they are especially significant when that industry is heavily localised. In this particular case they are often referred to as *economies of concentration*.

The cost advantages which a firm may obtain from the fact that a number of firms carrying out similar activities are situated in close proximity to one another are particularly relevant to policies on industrial location. We shall see later that these external economies of scale pose difficult problems for governments when they try to re-locate industries in new areas.

Labour

The concentration of similar firms in any one area leads to the creation of a local labour force skilled in the various techniques used in the industry. Local colleges develop special courses of training geared to the particular needs of the industry. The technical colleges in the Leicester area have important Hosiery and Footwear schools, while those in Bradford and Manchester have important Textile schools.

Ancillary services

In areas where there is a high degree of industrial concentration, sub-sidiary industries catering for the special needs of the major industry establish themselves. Thus we find the major manufacturer of footwear machinery located in the City of Leicester. Here too we find firms specialising in the marketing of leather, the wholesaling of footwear, and the processing of waste products from the local industries.

Disintegration

Where an industry is heavily localised there is a tendency for individual firms to specialise in a single process or in the manufacture of a single component. The classic example is to be found in Lancashire, where the production of cotton cloth is broken down into many processes each carried out by a specialist firm (spinning, weaving, dyeing, finishing, etc.). A glance through the Trades' Telephone Directory for centres such as Bradford, Coventry, Stoke-on-Trent, or Leicester will provide a very good picture of the extent to which industries in these areas have 'disintegrated' into many specialist activities. This develop-ment produces among the firms the same sort of advantages which result from the economies of scale in the single large firm. It means, for example, that each individual firm may obtain its components and other requirements at relatively low cost because they are being mass produced *for the industry*.

Cooperation

Regional specialisation encourages cooperation among the firms. A good example is provided by the research centres established as joint ventures by the firms in heavily localised industries. The pottery firms in Stoke-on-Trent, the footwear firms in the East Midlands, and the cotton firms in Lancashire have all set up research centres for their particular industries. The opportunities for formal and informal contacts between members of the firms are much greater where the firms themselves are all in one locality. The formation of trade societies, the publication of a trade journal and other such cooperative ventures are more easily stimulated in localised industry.

Commercial facilities

External economies also arise from the fact that the service industries in the area develop a special knowledge of the needs of the industry and this often leads to the provision of specialised facilities. Banking and insurance firms become acquainted with the particular requirements of the industry and find it worthwhile to provide special facilities. Transport firms may find it economical to develop special equipment (e.g. containers and vehicles) to deal with *the industry's* requirements. Again, each firm is a beneficiary, not because the firm itself is large, but because the industry as a whole provides a large demand for these services.

This tendency to conglomerate is an important reason for the survival of the small firm. A collection of relatively small independent firms can specialise on quite a large scale so that *collectively* they can achieve many of the economies of scale outlined earlier.

External diseconomies

A firm may also experience external diseconomies of scale as the industry to which it belongs becomes larger. A shortage of labour with the appropriate skills may develop so that firms in this industry may find themselves bidding up wages as they try to attract more labour (or hold on to their existing supplies). Increasing demands for raw materials may also bid up prices and cause costs to rise. If the industry is heavily localised, land for expansion will become increasingly scarce and hence more expensive both to purchase and to rent. Transport costs may also rise because of increased congestion.

The growth of the firm

Motives and methods

The motives which lead to growth in the size of the business unit are many and complex, but there are at least three which can be clearly distinguished.

1 The desire to achieve economies of scale.
2 The monopoly motive, or the desire to obtain a greater share of the market and hence greater market power.
3 The wish to achieve greater security by extending the range of products and markets.

There are two methods by which such growth may be achieved. The first of these is by *internal growth* where the firm increases its size by making more of its existing product or by extending the range of its products. It grows within the framework of its existing management and control structure. Although the Dunlop Company has since acquired other firms, it grew to a very large size on the basis of its original product (tyres) and by extending its range of products in the same field (rubber technology).

The second and much more common method nowadays is by *amalgamation, merger*, or *takeover*. A firm may amalgamate with one or more existing firms to form an entirely new enterprise, or a firm may take over another firm, the firm taken over losing its identity completely. Sometimes the amalgamation is carried out by forming an entirely new company for the sole purpose of acquiring the assets of a number of separate companies. Such a company is known as a *holding company*. The companies acquired in this way may retain their original identities but their trading policies are directed by the holding company. The Imperial Tobacco Company is a holding company controlling several major tobacco companies (Players, Wills, etc.). Sears (Holdings) Ltd. controls footwear, engineering, and shipbuilding companies as well as chains of retail stores.

Growth by merger or amalgamation is usually referred to as integration which, in turn, may be vertical, horizontal, or conglomerate, although this is by no means a watertight classification.

Vertical integration

When a merger takes place between firms engaged in different stages of the productive process we speak of vertical integration. It is 'vertical' in the sense that the combination is a movement up or down the productive process which runs from extraction to distribution. Thus, a large manufacturer of tea may take over tea plantations, a manufacturer of tyres may acquire rubber plantations, or a motor-car manufacturer may amalgamate with a body-building firm.

Backward integration

When the movement is towards the source of supplies we speak of vertical integration backwards. The examples quoted above are all of this type. It is often carried out so that a firm may exercise a much greater control over the quantity and quality of its supplies and be in a position of greater security with regard to their delivery. It may also have the aim of restricting the availability of such supplies to a competitor. An additional motive might be the absorption of the intermediate profit margins.

Forward integration

Where the movement is towards the market outlets the process is described as vertical integration forwards. The major breweries have now taken over the majority of public houses, and the large oil companies now control most of the petrol stations.

Important motives for this type of combination are the desire to secure an adequate number of market outlets and the wish to raise the standard of those outlets. Since manufacturers carry the main burden of advertising costs it is only natural that they should be concerned that their products reach the public in a form and in an environment which lives up to the image created by their advertising. Firms may be forced to take over some market outlets when a major competitor has already made a move in this direction – they must react or face the prospect of being squeezed out of the market.

Quite apart from providing greater security and control of supplies or markets, vertical integration may give rise to economies in production. This is most noticeable when a series of production processes are brought together in one large plant. In iron and steel making, for example, the hot pig iron from blast furnaces can be converted into steel with minimum loss of heat and by-product gases from the coke ovens can be used to heat furnaces in the finishing department. Some industries have remained integrated from an early stage in their development because it was the only way in which balanced growth at the different stages of production process could have been achieved. The companies which found crude oil were obliged to build the necessary oil refineries and to develop the means of transporting oil from oilfields to distant markets.

Vertical integration is sometimes adopted as a means of accelerating the development of new discoveries. The production and adoption of a new fibre or new plastic may be speeded up if the producer of the new material takes over facilities for fabricating it into marketable products.

Problems

There are some possible disadvantages. A manufacturer moving backwards to acquire the source of his raw materials may find himself with a rapidly depreciating asset if technology develops a superior substitute material. A rubber plantation may quickly lose its value if synthetic rubber proves a superior product in the manufacture of tyres. During a world recession raw material prices fall very sharply. The independent manufacturer will obtain very low-priced supplies – the burden of losses being borne by the supplier. The integrated firm, however, cannot avoid the losses due to the slump in raw material prices.

The optimum size of plants at different stages of production may be very different. The integration of firms with very different capacities will create the problem of finding enough 'outside work' to keep the plant with the larger capacity fully operational.

Horizontal integration

When firms engaged in producing the same kind of good or service are brought under unified control the procedure is described as horizontal integration. If several brewery companies or motor manufacturers amalgamate it would be a union of firms all engaged in *the same stage of production* and hence, in this sense, horizontal. Some of our largest companies have emerged as a result of a long process of horizontal integration. British Leyland, GEC, EMI, Associated Biscuits, and Metal Box are good examples.

Market domination is undoubtedly one of the motives leading to horizontal integration. When a number of firms producing the same or similar products form a single combine there is clearly a reduction in competition and the unified group will be able to exert more market power by virtue of the fact that a much greater proportion of the total market supply is now under its control.

Firms may be led to integrate horizontally by a desire to carry out some rationalisation of the industry's capacity, particularly when demand is falling. If there are, say, three firms making similar commodities and each firm is only working at two-thirds capacity, a merger will enable the new organisation to close down the least efficient plant and work the two remaining at full capacity.

Horizontal integration also enables the joint capacity of the amalgamated firms to be operated with a greater degree of specialisation. Suppose there are three independent firms each making a vacuum cleaner, a washing machine, and an electric heater. A merger, in this case, would enable the group to concentrate the production of each product in one factory with the obvious gains from larger scale production.

In many cases the horizontal combination is carried out with a view to obtaining economies of scale. The larger unit, as indicated above, will be able to achieve greater specialisation; it will also be in a position to take advantage of many of the other economies described earlier. By increasing the range of products (or models) horizontal integration provides greater security in the form of risk-bearing economies. Ford's wide range of vehicles provides it with a more stable pattern of demand than would be the case if it were highly dependent upon the demand for one type of vehicle.

Problems

The major criticism of the horizontal linking of firms is based upon the obvious tendency towards monopoly as the number of firms in an industry is reduced. This is one of the reasons why recent legislation in the UK has set up machinery for 'vetting' proposed mergers.

There is also the possibility of management diseconomies as the size of the firm increases. Integration may present particularly difficult management problems where a number of firms with different markets or using different technologies are brought together, or where firms are geographically dispersed. Problems also arise where it becomes necessary to weld together into one management team managers from firms having different histories, traditions, and outlooks.

Conglomerates

Conglomerates have been defined as those mergers or amalgamations which are neither substantially vertical nor substantially horizontal. They are generally understood to be those combinations of firms which produce goods or services which are not directly related to one another. For example, a firm producing cigarettes may take over a firm producing potato crisps, or a firm producing fertilisers may merge with a manufacturer of paint.

The major aim of the conglomerate is clearly to obtain a diversification of output so as to reduce the risks of trading. Conglomerate mergers may also arise where a firm believes that there is little scope for any further growth in the markets for its existing products. It may then satisfy a desire for further growth by taking over, or merging with, a firm in a different industry.

Although the output of a large conglomerate may appear to comprise a range of very different products, the diversification of output is rarely completely random. We often find that the products are linked by the use of common raw materials, a common technology, or common markets. Many of the products of the Dunlop enterprise (e.g. tennis balls, floor coverings, footwear, tyres, and upholstery materials) are linked by a common technology and a common raw material (rubber). Many of the products of the Schweppes-Cadbury merger are linked by virtue of the fact that they have a large number of common market outlets. This was also a factor in the proposed (but not fulfilled) merger between Imperial Tobacco and Smith's Crisps.

Vertical integration

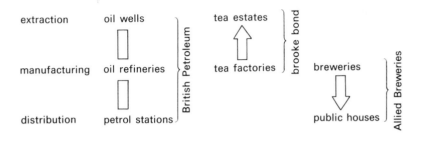

Horizontal integration

extraction — granite + gravel + sand quarries (Amalgamated Roadstone Ltd)

manufacturing — cars + vans + lorries + buses (British Leyland Ltd)

distribution — clothing + footwear + furniture shops
(Great Universal Stores Ltd)

Conglomerates

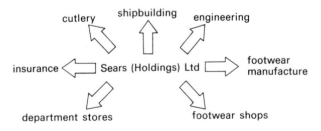

Fig. 12

Nevertheless there are several conglomerates where the only common links seem to be those of managerial and financial services. The justification for such mergers appears to lie in the promised injection of better management techniques and a more efficient use of the available resources. A conglomerate which consists of an amalgam of several sub-optimum firms operating in many different industries may not achieve any worthwhile economies of scale.

The survival of small firms

The preceding discussion would seem to indicate that there are substantial net advantages to be obtained from increasing the size of the business unit. There is, indeed, evidence to show that the number of large firms is increasing and that these are getting larger. Nevertheless the fact remains that about one half of the manufacturing output of the Western world issues from factories employing less than 500 workers and in the next section we note that about 80 per cent of UK factories employ between 1 and 50 workers.

There are hundreds of thousands of successful small firms in the UK (and in other developed countries) operating in all kinds of industries. In view of the many advantages of large-scale operation already discussed it is pertinent to ask why these small firms continue to survive and why industry and commerce is not dominated by a few giants.

Market limitations on mass production

The ability to profit from large-scale production is limited by the extent of the market. Where the market is small it is not possible to obtain significant economies of scale, most of which are dependent upon the existence of a large market for a standardised product. The size of the market may be restricted by a number of factors.

A demand for variety

Some industries are faced with the problem that consumers demand a wide variety of styles, patterns, and designs. The market for any one style or model may be very small indeed. Obvious examples are provided by the clothing, millinery, furniture, footwear, and jewellery trades. Firms in industries catering for such variety are confronted with the problem of 'short runs' and 'one off' types of production – they cannot set up their capital and labour for specialised production. Such firms are invariably quite small.

Geographical limitations

If the commodity has great bulk in relation to value, transport costs will be high relative to production costs. In such cases the market for the product is likely to be local rather than national. Bread, bricks, and coal may be cited as examples of commodities where markets have been confined to fairly small regions, although improvements in transport have tended to weaken this particular restriction on the size of the firm. Transport costs, however, still provide the village or suburban shop with some protection against the city-centre super store.

Personal services

Industries which provide services rather than commodities are usually characterised by a large number of small firms. Where the element of personal attention required by the purchaser is an important part of the service, then it is not possible to introduce standardisation and mass production methods. Thus, we find small firms in professions such as law, accountancy, architecture, and medicine where personal attention to individual problems is required. For similar reasons most firms specialising in repair work are relatively small. Hairdressing, the beauty parlour, and bespoke tailoring provide other examples of the demand for personal attention seriously limiting the size of the firm.

It is this same demand for personal service which accounts for the very large number of small firms in the retail trade although, in recent years, there have been major changes in the structure of this sector of the economy. New techniques in packaging, in food preparation, in the use of computers for stock control, and in shopping habits (e.g. the use of the motor car), have enabled the larger store to achieve great economies of scale. The supermarket and the discount store have successfully demonstrated that the public, for many of their requirements, prefer the lower priced, standardised article presented on a 'serve yourself' basis.

Luxury items

The market may be limited by price. Expensive sports cars, large limousines, luxury yachts, high quality jewellery and fur coats are examples of goods produced by small firms for very restricted prestige markets.

Disintegration

We have already referred to the tendency for mass production industries to disintegrate into a large number of specialist firms each supplying some standardised part to a large assembly plant. This has been a structural change which has operated very much to the benefit of the small firm. It is possible for the industry's total requirements of some particular component to be supplied by one relatively small firm.

Joint ventures

Cooperation between smaller firms may lead to the setting up of jointly-owned enterprises which enable them to enjoy many of the economies of scale obtained by larger firms. The smaller grocery shops have been successful in establishing links with wholesale groups (e.g. Mace, VG and Spar) for the marketing of standardised and branded goods on a large scale. Farmers have, for a long time, operated similar schemes (farmers' cooperatives) in order to obtain the benefits of bulk buying in feedstuffs, seeds, fertilisers, and so on. The collective ownership of large units of capital (e.g. combine harvesters) makes such resources available to small farmers on an economic basis. Small manufacturing firms in some industries (e.g. footwear and pottery) operate jointly-owned research establishments.

Part of the explanation for the prevalence of small firms lies in the fact that there seems to be no shortage of would-be entrepreneurs – there is always a large number of people eager to start their own business. Small firms are born in large numbers ever day. Some will survive and grow, others will die, but the ranks will be quickly filled by new entrants.

Many firms remain small because of the reluctance of the proprietor to accept the increased risks associated with growth – he or she may prefer a reasonable income and a 'quiet life'. Some firms remain small because they encounter difficulties in raising, on reasonable terms, the necessary finance for further expansion. Management problems may be a barrier to growth. Competent management is fairly easily obtained for a small-scale operation, but the ability to manage larger enterprises is probably a rather scarce commodity. The small firm is a more flexible unit than the larger firm; it is able to adjust quite quickly to changes in demand especially in those industries where fashions and tastes are subject to frequent changes.

8 British Industry – Size and Structure

Problems of definition

An industry

It is not easy to define an industry because economic activities can be grouped in a variety of ways. They may be classified according to the nature of the markets they serve, and this is how most people would define an industry, i.e. a group of firms making the same or very similar products. But economic units may also be grouped according to the process carried out, or on the basis of the kinds of factors of production they use, or the kind of technology they use.

The most common definition of an industry is that used in official statistics which groups firms into industries according to the physical and technical properties of their principal products. This classification is often self-evident as in the cases of footwear, furniture, or pottery where the nature of the product clearly defines the industry. Sometimes it is not so easy – is the extraction of chemicals from petroleum a part of the oil industry or the chemical industry?

It is often necessary to use the nature of the process as the distinguishing feature. It would be misleading, for example, to define the hosiery industry as comprising those firms which make stockings and socks since this industry produces a very wide range of garments. It is, in fact, defined as the collection of firms in which knitting is the principal activity.

Statistics of industrial production must be used with some caution because there are so many multi-product firms and the whole of such a firm's output might, under certain circumstances, be classified under the industry of its major product.

An enterprise

An enterprise is defined as the unit of ownership and control. In the great majority of cases it corresponds to what most people understand by *the firm*, but where there is a parent company with several subsidiary firms the whole group is classified as an enterprise. When we use the term 'firm' in this section it will have the same meaning as 'enterprise'.

An establishment

Units of production are officially referred to as establishments, but they are more commonly described as plants, factories, farms, shops, etc. A firm, of course, may own several establishments.

Size

Further problems of definition concern the methods used to measure the size of an industry, a firm, or a factory. Again there is no 'right' method. Size may be assessed on the basis of the capital employed, the value of output, or on the number of employees. The use of different methods will often produce different answers to questions about size. An industry which is being increasingly mechanised may be employing less labour but increasing its output. This is true of agriculture.

The number of employees is probably the most frequently used criterion, but it must be used with care. The chemical industry, for example, employs about 6 per cent of the manufacturing labour force, but it uses about 12 per cent of the total fixed capital in manufacturing industry.

The size of establishments (i.e. factories or plants)

In the UK, information becomes available from regular Censuses of Production on the size of firms and factories in manufacturing industry.

Table 5 Manufacturing establishments by size of employment in the UK in 1979

Numbers employed	Establish-ments	% of total	Employment (000s)	% of total	Net output[1] (£ million)	% of total
1–10	59 783	55·7	278·4	4·0 ⎫		
11–19	17 105	15·9	245·4	3·5 ⎬ 11 835·4	17·8
20–49	13 197	12·3	414·2	6·0		
50–99	6 683	6·2	472·2	6·8 ⎭		
100–199	4 682	4·4	654·7	9·5	5 829·5	8·9
200–499	3 602	3·4	1 117·4	16·1	10 717·1	16·1
500–999	1 318	1·2	911·2	13·2	9 018·2	13·6
1000–1499	460	0·4	556·2	8·0	5 468·8	8·2
1500+	563	0·5	2 276·0	32·9	23 482·4	35·4
	107 393	100·0	6 925·7	100·0	66 351·4	100·0

[1] Net output is calculated by deducting from gross output the cost of purchases and the cost of industrial services received.

Source: Business Monitor PA 1002

Table 5 shows that the great majority of plants are small. More than 90 per cent of them employ less than 100 workers, but these establishments employ only 20 per cent of the total labour force in manufacturing. On the other hand large units employing more than 1 000 workers represent only 1 per cent of the number of plants but they account for about 41 per cent of total employment in manufacturing.

The numerical predominance of small plants might, at first sight, indicate that economies of scale are either not important or are not being exploited. But the greater part of the total output is being produced by larger firms and it is likely that these firms are exploiting most of the potential of economies of scale. There have been several investigations into the extent of plant-level scale economies in different industries. These studies have attempted to estimate 'the minimum efficient plant size' (MEPS) for different industries. The MEPS may be defined as the point on the long run cost curve at which average costs cease to fall. The MEPS is relatively large for such products as sugar, ethylene, cigarettes, detergents, TV tubes, motor cars, and domestic electrical appliances. These studies seem to indicate that the size structure of plants in British industry is such that, for the most part, they are able to take advantage of such scale economies as are available. Nevertheless it is unlikely in industries subject to rapid technical progress that many existing plants will be of optimum size.

Over the longer period there has been a steady trend towards larger establishments. In 1935, plants with more than 1 500 workers accounted for about 15 per cent of total employment in private-sector manufacturing; in 1979 these larger plants accounted for about 33 per cent of employment in manufacturing.

Table 5 refers to manufacturing as a whole, but the size pattern revealed is fairly typical of that in individual industries. It is, perhaps, rather surprising to find that, for the majority of industries, there is no typical size of plant.

The size of firms (enterprises)

In the UK, some 2·5 million workers are employed by only 100 large industrial enterprises. These same firms control more than 3 500 different establishments and account for about 40 per cent of the total net output of manufacturing industry. The largest 100 companies in the UK are estimated to account for about 50 per cent of the capital employed by all industrial and commercial companies. In the average industry, the five largest firms account for approximately two-thirds of the industry's output.

These figures indicate quite clearly that the large industrial enterprises, whether large in the absolute or relative sense, are established features of the UK economy. Large industrial enterprises have been with us for a long time and in recent years they have been growing steadily in importance.

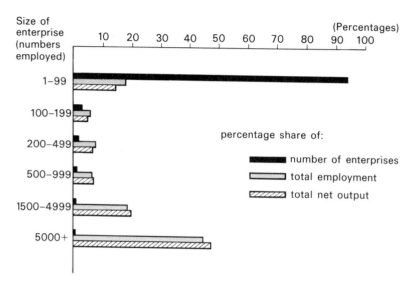

Source: Business Monitor PA1002

Fig. 13 UK manufacturing industry; size of firm (1979)

Figure 13 shows a size distribution of enterprises which is very similar to that for establishments. Most firms are very small, but in spite of their overwhelming numerical supremacy, these small firms account for a relatively small proportion of total employment and total output. One might expect Table 5 and Figure 13 to tell similar stories because the great majority of enterprises are single plant firms; the average number of plants per enterprise is only about 1·2. Figure 13 brings out the importance of the larger firms in manufacturing, but very large firms are also to be found in mining and quarrying, oil extraction and distribution, construction and retailing.

The large industrial enterprise has certain characteristics which tend to distinguish it from small and medium-size firms.

a The separation of ownership and control (explained on page 100).

b It is usually a multi-plant organisation operating plants in different parts of the country.

c In many cases it is a multinational corporation with production and distribution organisations in many different countries. Kodak, Ford, General Motors, Phillips, and Unilever are well-known multinational companies.

d It usually produces a range of different products. Dunlops, for example, in addition to the manufacture of tyres, produce an extremely wide variety of products including car and aircraft wheels, floor coverings, footwear, sports goods, upholstery materials, adhesives, and fire protection equipment.

Concentration – meaning and measurement

Recent trends towards larger and larger business units have led to an active debate on the possible dangers of the control of economic activity in certain industries passing into fewer and fewer hands. Some of these dangers are discussed later in the chapter on Monopoly, but it should be clear that when a firm becomes so large that it controls a preponderant share of the market, it may be tempted to use its market power to obtain excessive profits.

Economists have attempted to ascertain to what extent markets are becoming increasingly dominated by fewer and bigger firms. They have, therefore, devised a means of measuring the degree of *concentration* in an industry, that is, the extent to which an industry is dominated in terms of sales, employment or capital employed by the largest firms in the industry. The most commonly used concentration ratios measure the dominance of the 3, 5, or 7 largest firms. For example, if we are using employment as the measuring rod and the number employed by the 3 largest firms in the industry is 1 million, while the total employment in the industry is 4 million, the *three-firm employment concentration ratio* is 25 per cent.

Most recent studies of UK industry have tended to use the market share criterion and the most generally used measure is the *five-firm sales concentration ratio*. This gives the percentage share of the total sales of any product (or group of products) accounted for by the 5 largest firms. Table 6 gives some details of the five-firm concentration ratios for a number of industries selected to provide examples of relatively high and low concentration.

Concentration ratios are important indicators of market situations, but they can be misleading. The relative sizes of the top five firms may make a considerable difference to the degree of competition. A 75 per cent ratio may mean that the top five firms each supply 15 per cent of the total market or it may mean that one firm supplies 55 per cent and the other four each supply 5 per cent.

One must also take account of the number of firms in the industry and their average size. The five largest firms for example might account for 60 per cent of the market; the remaining 40 per cent may be shared by 50 firms or by only 5 firms. Concentration ratios unless supported by other data, do not clearly reveal the extent to which the largest firms exercise economic power. Another fact to be borne in mind is that some of these ratios only apply to domestic output. A high concentration ratio would not imply excessive market power if there is strong competition from imported goods.

Table 6 Total sales of the five largest enterprises as a percentage of total sales of the commodity in the UK in 1977

Industry	Concentration Ratio
Wooden furniture and upholstery	16·7
Trailers and caravans	34·1
Footwear	36·2
Cutlery	48·4
Pottery	48·7
Stone and slate quarrying	54·8
Domestic electrical appliances	62·0
Motor vehicle manufacture	70·1
Soap and detergents	82·7
Primary and secondary batteries	88·7
Fertilisers	91·2
Synthetic rubber	100·0
Tobacco	100·0
Cement	100·0
Sugar	100·0
Margarine	100·0

Source: Business Monitor PO 1006

The details in Table 6 refer to *market concentration*, that is the degree to which the markets for particular groups of products are dominated by a few large firms. For some purposes, however, *aggregate concentration* is of interest. This measures the percentage of manufacturing or total output accounted for by the larger firms. This aggregate measure is important when considering the extent to which the control of industry generally is concentrated. Aggregate concentration in the UK is usually measured by the share of total output accounted for by the 100 largest firms; this has increased substantially during the present century. In 1909 the 100 largest firms in UK manufacturing produced 16 per cent of the total output; in 1978 this share had risen to 45 per cent. Large firms tend to dominate the food, vehicles, chemicals, engineering, paper, textiles, bricks, and oil industries. In timber, clothing, leather, furniture, and footwear the degree of concentration is relatively low.

Concentration – causes and consequences

It is noteworthy that little of the increase in concentration in manufacturing has been due to increases in the size of the plant. The main explanation of increasing concentration lies in the increase in the average number of plants owned by the larger firms. This indicates that technical economies of scale justify only a relatively small part of the growth in concentration. Much of the increase in the extent of concentration has been brought about by mergers and the main motives for this activity appear to have been,

a the achievement of financial, marketing and administrative economies,

b the desire to achieve a diversified output,

c the elimination of excess capacity and the rationalisation of production,

d the acquisition of larger resources to finance research and development in capital-intensive industries where the costs of such development are relatively large (e.g. motor cars, aircraft, chemicals).

Increased concentration can yield benefits in the form of economies of scale, improved efficiency and a faster rate of technical progress. But it can also yield disadvantages in the form of reduced competition; this aspect of market concentration is discussed in the chapter on Monopoly.

In recent years governments in the UK have paid increasing attention to the role of small businesses in the economy and, to some extent, this has been due to the increasing attention being paid to the disadvantages of the growing concentration in industry. In particular measures have been taken (i) to make it easier for small firms to acquire finance either to start up in business or to expand, (ii) to reduce the overall weight of taxation on small businesses, and (iii) to reduce the administrative burdens on small firms. The small firm is seen to have certain advantages in the fields of,

a *Job creation.* Small firms tend to be labour-intensive and net job-creators. In America between 1969 and 1976 more than 80 per cent of new jobs were provided by small businesses.

b *Technical innovation.* A study of American industry showed that small firms produce more innovations per dollar spent on research than large firms.

c *Efficiency.* Small firms tend to have better labour relations than large firms and lose fewer days in strikes.

d *Competition.* The more independent firms there are in an industry, the greater the competition.

Against these points, however, have to be set the massive technical economies of scale attainable by modern capital-intensive industries.

9 Types of Business Organisation

We have discussed some of the factors which affect the size of the firm as a unit of production. In this and subsequent chapters we examine the ways in which firms are organised, controlled, and financed. The different types of business organisation to be found in the UK and most other countries in the non-communist world may be classified under five headings: the sole proprietor, the partnership, the joint stock company, the cooperative society, and the public corporation.

The sole proprietor

This is the simplest and oldest form of business enterprise and is often referred to as the one-person business. A single person provides the capital, takes the decisions, and assumes the risks. He or she is solely responsible for the success or failure of the business and has, therefore, the sole rights to such profits as may be made, or, alternatively, bears the sole responsibility for such losses as may accrue. The one-person business is still far more numerous than any other type of business organisation, but in terms of total employment, value of capital employed, or value of total output, it is relatively unimportant compared with the joint stock company.

The strength of this type of firm lies in the direct personal interest of the proprietor in the efficiency of his enterprise. Ownership and control are vested in one person who enjoys all the fruits of success and hence has a great incentive to run the firm efficiently. Since the proprietor is the sole decision-taker and has no need to consult colleagues when changes of policy are required we should expect this type of organisation to be extremely flexible and capable of quick and easy adjustment to changes in market conditions.

The great disadvantage of the sole proprietor form of enterprise lies in the fact that the owner is personally liable for the debts incurred by his firm and this liability is unlimited. All his personal possessions are at risk and may be seized to meet creditors' demands in the event of the business becoming insolvent. Another disadvantage of this type of firm is the strict limitation on its ability to acquire capital for expansion. Finance is restricted to the amounts which the entrepreneur is able to provide from his own resources and whatever sums he can borrow on his own security.

We find the one-person business prevalent in farming, retailing, building, repair and maintenance work, and personal services such as hairdressing.

The partnership

Partnerships are voluntary combinations of from 2 to 20 persons[1] formed for the purpose of carrying on business with a view to profit. This type of organisation represents a logical development from the one-person business since the obvious method by which such a firm may acquire further capital is to form a partnership. The motive, however, may not be financial and partnerships are often formed in order to bring new ability and enterprise into the business.

The partners usually share in the task of running the business, but a partner need not play an active role. A person who joins a partnership, supplying capital and sharing in the profits, but taking no part in the management is known as a dormant or sleeping partner. Partnerships are a common form of business organisation in such professions as law, accountancy, surveying, and medicine.

The advantages of this type of firm are similar to those of the one-person business. It is a flexible organisation which allows a greater degree of specialisation than the one-person business. Partners usually specialise in one or more aspects of the business; one may be responsible for buying, one for selling, one for production, and so on. Since it has greater access to capital, it can achieve greater size than the sole proprietor.

The great disadvantage, like that of the one-person business, is the fact that the liability of the partners is unlimited and they are all fully liable for the acts of the other partners. There are, however, some limited partnerships which have to be registered with the Registrar of Companies. In such firms some partners (e.g. dormant partners) may have their liability limited to some specified sum, but at least one of the partners must have unlimited liability.

The survival of a partnership depends upon the continued harmonious relationship between a number of people in situations which often give much cause for disagreement. Thus, where trading risks are very great, the partnership is not a very stable type of organisation.

The joint stock company

The most important form of business organisation in the UK is the joint stock company. Basically, it consists of an association of people

---

[1] Unlimited membership is allowed in the case of certain professional partnerships (e.g. solicitors, accountants).

who contribute towards a joint stock of capital for the purpose of carrying on business with a view to profit. A company may be defined as a legal person created to engage in business, capable of owning productive assets, of entering into contracts, and of employing labour in the same way as an individual.

Public and private companies

There are two kinds of joint stock company, the private company and the public company. At the present time there are some 600 000 joint stock companies in the UK of which about 15 000 are public companies. The public companies are much larger units and account for about two-thirds of all the capital employed by companies.

In general, private companies are small firms, often consisting of the members of one family. Both public and private companies must have at least 2 members. A public company must have a minimum allotted share capital of £50 000 of which at least one-quarter has been paid up (see page 98). A private company must include the word 'limited' in its name while a public company must have the words 'public limited company' at the end of its name although this can be abbreviated to *plc*.

The basic distinction between a private and a public company is that a public company can offer its shares and debentures for sale to the general public. In the case of a private company it would be a criminal offence to ask the public to subscribe to its shares. All companies must file annually, with the Registrar of Companies, details of their turnover, profits, assets, liabilities and other relevant financial information about their structures and activities.

Company formation

The state, through a succession of Companies Acts (the most recent being the 1980 Companies Act) has introduced many regulations governing the formation and organisation of joint stock companies. The main aim of this legislation is to ensure that shareholders (and others who deal with the company) are fully informed about the affairs of the company and are protected from fraudulent activities by promoters of companies. To this end companies are obliged to make public a great deal of information about their structure, ownership, and financial situation.

The persons forming a company (the promoters) are required to submit several documents to the Registrar of Companies; two of the most important are the Memorandum of Association and the Articles of Association.

1 The Memorandum of Association

This document must contain the name of the company, the address of the registered office, the amount of the authorised capital (the maximum the company is allowed to raise), and details of the objects for which the company is being formed. Since it is illegal for a company to carry out activities not specified in its objects, it is normal for these to be set out in the widest terms. A public company must clearly state in its memorandum that it is a public company.

2 The Articles of Association

This document sets out the proposed internal constitution of the company, that is, the rules and regulations governing the way it will be run. It will contain details of the manner in which its shares will be issued and transferred; the company's borrowing powers; the rights of the different classes of shareholders; the frequency and types of company meetings; the way in which the company will elect its officers, the powers of directors and so on.

When the various statutory documents have been submitted to the Registrar and have been duly accepted by him, he will issue a Certificate of Incorporation which bestows upon the company a separate legal identity. A public company, however, cannot commence business until it has declared that it has met the legal requirements regarding the size of its allotted share capital and the proportion of that capital which must be paid up.

All the various documents relating to a company's formation, together with any subsequent changes, and its annual statements of accounts are available for public inspection at the office of the Registrar of Companies.

Important features of the joint stock company

1 The first characteristic is the principle of *limited liability*. The company itself is fully liable for its debts in the same way as any other person, but the liability of the shareholders is limited to the amount they have agreed to subscribe to the capital of the company. When they have fully paid for their shares they cannot be called upon to meet any debts the company may incur. The introduction of the principle of limited liability was essential if people were to be persuaded to provide capital on the scale needed by modern industry. In the absence of limited liability the contribution of funds to business enterprise becomes an extremely risky undertaking – a very modest 'investment' would put all one's personal resources at risk.

2 A second feature of the joint stock principle is the prospect of *continuity* which it offers. Sole proprietorships and partnerships cannot continue in existence independently of the persons who own them. The death or bankruptcy of a sole proprietor or partner, or a mere unwillingness to continue, will bring an unincorporated business to an end. Modern industrial processes require resources to be committed for long periods of time and unless there is a real prospect of the continuing existence of the organisation such long-term investment will not be undertaken. A joint stock company offers just such a prospect, for its existence is independent of the lives and fortunes of its shareholders. If a shareholder dies his shares become the property of his heirs; if he does not like the way the company is being run he can sell his shares – the company is in no way affected.

3 Another very important feature of the joint-stock company is the *transferability of shares*. In order to perform its function a company must have permanent use of its capital, but very few, if any, investors are prepared to lend money on a permanent basis. Life is uncertain and no one is prepared to put himself in a position where, in a possible emergency, he could not convert his wealth into cash. This dilemma is solved by making shares transferable. The company has the use of the capital subscribed by the original share-holders who, if they wish, may sell their shares at any time on the open market. The market value of shares changes from day to day so that although a shareholder may convert his holdings into cash, he cannot be certain of the amount he will receive for them.

4 The joint stock principle enables those who cannot, or do not want to take an active part in management to contribute towards economic activity by providing capital. There are people that have technical and commercial expertise but do not possess the necessary resources to make effective use of their skills. The joint stock principle makes it possible for the resources owned by one group to be utilised by another group. This has raised interesting problems (discussed later) regarding the *divorce between ownership and management* which is a feature of modern capitalism.

The capital structure of companies

The *authorised* (or nominal) capital of a company is set out in the Memorandum of Association. The nominal[1] value of the shares actually issued is the *issued* capital of the company. Shares need not

---

[1] The nominal value of a share is its face value; the value printed on the share. It is usually referred to as the par value.

be fully paid for when they are issued. For example, a company may issue £1 shares by asking for 20p on application and 40p on allotment (i.e. when they are made available to the applicant). It may decide not to call up the remaining 40p per share for some considerable time.[1] These uncalled amounts can serve as a kind of reserve fund. Thus the amount of capital actually contributed by shareholders is known as the *paid-up* capital.

The authorised capital of a company may be divided into many different types of shares. We can only mention the more common types.

1 Preference shares

Preference shares, as their name implies, carry a prior right to a share in the profits of the company. The holders of these shares must receive payment of their dividends before the holders of other types of share (but they rank after debenture holders). Normally the rate of return on preference shares is a fixed percentage of their nominal values. A holder of a £100, 5 per cent, Preference Share is entitled to a return of £5 per annum from the profits of the company. If the company makes no profit then the holder will receive no dividend, but there is a class of Cumulative Preference Shares, and holders of these will receive payments of any arrears of dividend when the company has a profitable year.

Even when the company has an exceptionally profitable year, the preference shareholders will receive no more than the fixed rate of interest, unless they hold another class of preference share, the Participating Preference Share. This type of share entitles the holder to a fixed rate of return on his capital plus an additional share in the profits after the ordinary shareholders have received some minimum rate of return.

Preference shareholders usually have little say in the management of the enterprise since their income is less dependent upon the amount of profits than that of other shares. Their voting rights will be set out in the Articles of Association and normally they qualify for a vote at the annual meeting only if their dividends have not been paid.

2 Ordinary shares

The dividend on ordinary shares is not fixed and depends entirely on the profitability of the company and the policy of the directors with

[1] If the company became insolvent at this stage, shareholders could be called upon to pay the 40p share outstanding, but no more.

regard to the amount of profit to be retained in the company. The dividend may be very high or it may be zero. The ordinary shareholder is entitled to the residue of profits after all other claims have been met. Ordinary shares, therefore, are the riskiest type of investment and dividends on them may fluctuate from year to year. Since they bear the major risks, ordinary shareholders have the greatest say in the management and control of the enterprise, and most ordinary shares carry voting rights. The ordinary share capital of a company is usually referred to as the *equity* of the company.

3 Debentures

A debenture is not a share in the strict sense of the word. The investor who purchases debentures is making a special kind of loan and becomes a creditor of the company rather than an owner. A debenture is a kind of IOU. The rate of interest on debentures is fixed and debenture holders rank before all classes of shares for payments out of profits. The holders of these securities are normally given special rights which add to the security of their loans. The company may give a pledge that certain of its assets will be attached to the debentures so that, in the event of default by the company, the debenture holders may seize and sell these assets to secure repayment of their loans.

4 Profits, dividends and yields

The following simple example illustrates the manner in which profits are distributed and the variable nature of the return on ordinary shares (see note on *gearing* on p. 117).

The XYZ Company Limited

Loan capital	20 000 £1 6% Debentures	£20 000
Share capital	80 000 £1 Preference Shares (5%)	£80 000
	100 000 £1 Ordinary Shares	£100 000
		£200 000

Year 1

Profits available for distribution	£7 700
This will be distributed as follows:	
Debentures 6% of £20 000	£1 200
Preference Shares 5% of £80 000	£4 000
Ordinary Shares, dividend $2\frac{1}{2}$%	£2 500
	£7 700

Year 2

Profits available for distribution	£15 200

This will be distributed as follows:

Debentures 6% of £20 000	£1 200
Preference Shares 5% of £80 000	£4 000
Ordinary Shares, dividend 10%	£10 000
	£15 200

Yields. There is a difference between the dividend on a share and the yield on a share. This difference arises because shares have two valuations – the nominal or *par* value and the *market* value. The market value varies from day to day according to the supply of and demand for the shares. If it is higher than the par value, the shares are said to be at a *premium*; if it is lower, the shares are at a *discount*.

The rate of dividend is always expressed as a percentage of the nominal value of the share. The yield on a share is the amount of the dividend expressed as a percentage of the market value.

Example:

The XYZ Co. Ltd. declares a dividend of 10 per cent on its £1 Ordinary Shares (i.e. 10p per share).

The current market price of these shares is 175p.

$$\text{The Yield} = \frac{10p}{175p} \times \frac{100}{1} = 5 \cdot 7\%$$

Ownership and control

The owners of a joint stock company are clearly the shareholders who provide the money for the business, but the growth in the size of many public companies has meant that the shareholders are far too numerous and dispersed to be able to exercise the functions of management. Management is in the hands of directors who are elected by the shareholders. Shareholder control, therefore, often amounts to no more than the ability to vote against the recommendations of the directors at the annual general meeting and ultimately if necessary, to replace the directors.

But shareholders in the large companies are very numerous and may be widely dispersed throughout the country (many shares may be held overseas). Generally speaking only a very small percentage bother to attend the general meetings. Shareholders usually lack the knowledge and expertise to exercise effective control over the directors, and unless things are going badly wrong the directors will be fairly certain to have their policies endorsed. We must also recognise the fact that not all those who supply the capital have voting rights. Preference shareholders, at best, have very restricted voting rights and debenture holders are creditors not owners. It is the ordinary shareholders who enjoy voting powers, although, in recent years, it has become a practice (with increasing opposition from many institutions) to issue non-voting ordinary shares.

Where the owners are not completely in control of the policy of the company a divergence of interests may arise. Economic theory has tended to assume that the maximisation of profits is the principal aim of private enterprise. Where, however, the executive directors (those who actually run the business) have only very limited shareholdings (and this is often the case) they may pursue objectives other than profit maximisation. As long as some satisfactory rate of return for the ordinary shareholders is achieved, directors may attempt to maximise sales rather than aim for even higher rates of return on capital employed. The status and salaries of executives may be more closely related to the size of the firm than the rate of return on the capital employed.

One feature of capitalism which has an important bearing on the question of ownership has been the growth in *institutional investment.* The major providers of funds for the larger companies are institutions such as insurance companies, pension funds, investment trusts, unit trusts, and other types of trust funds. Such institutions often control a significant proportion of the voting shares in the large companies and they could, if they wished, exercise a real influence on the policy decisions of these companies. Normally, however, providing the company is reasonably profitable, the institutions prefer not to interfere in its management. Institutional investment means that share ownership is more widely dispersed than would appear from the lists of shareholders. The shares held by insurance companies and pension funds, for example, are purchased, indirectly, by the many thousands of contributors to such funds. In the case of Unilever Limited, one of the largest companies in the UK, some 70 per cent of the ordinary shares are held by institutions of various kinds, and 30 per cent by individuals (see Fig. 16).

Take-over bids and pyramiding

The capital structure of joint stock companies makes it relatively easy for one company to be taken over by another. It also makes it possible for very large amounts of capital to be controlled by a group which owns quite modest amounts of ordinary share capital.

If company A makes an offer to acquire the assets of company B, it does not have to find large sums of money for this purpose. It may simply offer shares in company A in exchange for the shares in company B. Alternatively it may decide to make the offer more attractive to shareholders in B by offering, say, one share in A plus some small amount of cash for each share in company B. In any event the amount of money required for such a transaction need be no more than a relatively small proportion of the market value of the shares in company B.

The fact that the capital of one company can be used to purchase the capital of another company makes possible the process known as 'pyramiding' whereby the ownership of quite small amounts of ordinary share capital can be used to control vast resources.

Let us take a simple example where we assume that voting rights are restricted to ordinary shares.

Company A

Capital:	Ordinary shares	£100 000
	Preference shares	£50 000
	Debentures	£50 000
		£200 000

The ownership of slightly more than £50 000 of the ordinary share capital ensures control of this company. Now suppose the whole of the capital of Company A is used to purchase one half of the ordinary share capital of Company B.

Company B

Capital:	Ordinary shares	£400 000
	Preference shares	£200 000
	Debentures	£200 000
		£800 000

Now this £800 000 might be used to purchase one half of the ordinary share capital of Company C.

Company C

Capital:	Ordinary shares	£1 600 000
	Preference shares	£800 000
	Debentures	£800 000
		£3 200 000

We have now reached the stage where a holding of rather more than £50 000 in ordinary shares has secured control of a sub-subsidiary with a capital of £3 200 000.

Our very simple and hypothetical example has served to illustrate the possibilities of minority control, and although in theory there is no limit to the process we have started here there are certain practical and legal limits. A company such as A in the example above which exists merely to hold shares in another company is known as *a holding company*. Such companies are usually formed for the purposes of bringing about the types of integration described in Chapter 4.

Cooperatives

There are basically two forms of cooperative enterprises, one which operates on the basis of worker control and one on the basis of consumer control. The second type has been much more successful in the UK than the first type.

Producer cooperatives

The idea of workers establishing their own production units, raising the capital by their own efforts, electing the management from their own ranks, sharing the profits according to some agreed formula, and sharing power on the basis of one member, one vote, is quite an old one. In the UK at the turn of the century there were some 200 such worker-controlled enterprises strongly supported by the cooperative retail societies which purchased much of their output. Since that time a serious decline reduced the number of this type of cooperative to about 30 in the late 1960s. Most of the survivors were in printing, clothing, and footwear.

In more recent years there has been a strong revival and many new cooperatives have been formed (see Table 7). Some of these newer worker-cooperatives differ in several respects from earlier experiments. They have sometimes been launched with government money and have been established as a result of workers' refusal (shown by 'sit-ins') to accept management's view that the firm is not a viable enterprise and should be closed down. Several of these cooperatives have been registered under the Companies Acts instead of the Industrial and Provident Societies Acts, as were the older cooperatives. In 1978 the government established a special agency to help worker-cooperatives with technical advice and expertise.

This type of business organisation has proved very successful in Danish agriculture and is being widely adopted in the agricultural sectors of developing countries. France has about 500 producer-cooperatives employing some 30 000 people, about half of them in the building trades. In Spain there are some 1 300 such cooperatives employing about 50 000 people. The Cooperative Development Agency reported that, in 1982, there were some 515 worker-cooperatives in the UK (see Table 7).

Consumer cooperatives

In the UK this form of cooperative enterprise has become widely estab-

Table 7 Worker cooperatives in the UK 1982

Activity	Number of Cooperatives
Advisory, consultative, educational, and office services	33
Building, house repair and decoration, cleaning, waste recycling, architecture, gardening services	69
Crafts, arts, carpentry, furniture-making, joinery	40
Engineering, electronics, chemicals, general manufacturing	41
Footwear, clothing, textiles	32
Printing and publishing	75
Provision and hire of transport, bicycle and motor vehicle repairs	13
Record, film and music making, theatre (including actors' agencies), leisure	46
Retail, distributive, catering and food processing	151
Umbrella cooperatives, workspaces	15
	515

Source: Cooperative Development Agency

lished and accounts for a substantial share of the retail trade. Beginning in 1844 when some poor weavers in Rochdale opened their own small retail shop, the movement has developed until it now has some 10·5 million members, about 200 local and regional societies and some 950 shops. The movement is based on consumer ownership and control – the members of the society who have the voting and dividend rights are the customers. The minimum shareholding is usually £1 and the maximum £1 000, but voting rights are strictly on the basis of one member one vote. The members of a society elect a management committee (usually part-timers) who are responsible for the general policy of the society, but the day-to-day operation is in the hands of full-time salaried management staff appointed by the committee.

Profits are shared out in the form of dividends related, not to the value of shares held, but to the value of the member's purchases. Nowadays the usual principle is that of 'instant dividend' where customers (members or not) receive dividend stamps, but members are usually entitled to special bonuses.

The number of cooperative societies has been falling quite rapidly due to a series of mergers designed to achieve greater economies of scale. Some of the retail societies are very large and about 80 per cent of the trade is accounted for by 57 societies. The largest of these is the Cooperative Retail Services Ltd which operates nationally and was formed to take over ailing societies. The Coops have about 7 per cent of the national retail trade and about 16 per cent of the grocery trade. They also supply about one third of the country's milk.

The needs of the retail societies are largely met by the Cooperative Wholesale Society which is now Britain's tenth largest business. It is collectively owned by the retail societies. The CWS is a large-scale importer and manufacturer and also operates a very large banking and insurance business. It is also Britain's largest farmer. The CWS manufacturing and other industrial operations are not run on the basis of worker ownership and control – they are controlled by the retail societies.

After losing ground to the multiples, the Coops, in recent years, have adopted a much more competitive approach with large-scale national advertising, the development of hypermarkets, the replacement of a multiplicity of brand names with the single Coop label, and the appointment of high quality management staff. The merger movement in bringing about larger and more efficient units has undoubtedly been successful, but the movement appears to be finding it difficult to reconcile the objective of efficient larger-scale operation with the traditional image of a local retail democracy. Cooperative societies started as working class movements and the loyalty of the working class was a very important feature of their early success. To the lower paid, the Coop dividend was a useful form of saving and this too played its part in establishing a loyal clientele. These things may not be so important nowadays as the cooperative societies seek to widen their markets, but the movement still retains important social and political objectives. It seeks the extension of worker and consumer control both through its own activities and in supporting political movements which advocate these principles.

The public corporation

In recent years whenever the state has decided to transfer the ownership of an industry from the private sector to the public sector, the public corporation has been the type of business organisation adopted for the purpose of running the industry. Some of these public corporations have been in existence for many years. The Port of London Authority was set up in 1909 to run the London docks, and the British Broadcasting Corporation was established in 1927. Most of the larger public corporations, however, date from the period of the Labour government, 1945–51, when several important industries were nationalised. We shall discuss the question of nationalisation later (Ch. 37); here we are only concerned with the type of business organisation which has been adopted to control and organise nationalised industries.

The public corporation is a separate legal identity like the company, but there are no private shareholders. The government owns the capital and appoints the members of the controlling Board who have functions very similar to directors except that they are answerable to the government and not to shareholders. In general, the policy to be pursued by a public corporation is determined by the government and a Minister of the Crown is usually given the responsibility for seeing that the corporation is acting within the broad policy requirements laid down by Parliament.

In its day-to-day management, however, the controlling board is given wide freedom of action. When commercial enterprises were brought under public ownership it was felt that the direct control by Parliament, as is the case with government departments such as health, education, pensions and so on, was not appropriate for enterprises where uncertainty and risk-taking called for quick decisions of a strictly commercial nature. The public corporation, therefore, is an attempt to obtain a satisfactory compromise between public responsibility and commercial efficiency. Parliament does not interfere in the day-to-day management of the public corporation.

The main purpose of the public corporation is to provide an efficient public service at a reasonable price. It does not aim to maximise its profits, but it is charged with the duty of paying its way. Any profits made by a public corporation must be used for capital investment, the lowering of prices, the raising of wages, or transferred to the Exchequer. Such losses as have been made by public corporations have been financed by government loans.

In contrasting the joint stock company and the public corporation the following features should be noted.

1 *Control.* The joint stock company is controlled by a board of directors elected by the shareholders, whereas the public corporation is controlled by a board appointed by the state.

2 *Ownership.* A joint stock company is owned by the shareholders, but there are no shareholders in the public corporation which is owned by the state.

3 *Size.* Some of the public corporations are much larger than the largest domestic joint stock company.

4 Finance. A joint stock company raises its capital by the issue of shares to the general public, but, at the present time, the public corporations obtain most of their capital requirements direct from the Exchequer.

5 Motives. While the joint stock company exists primarily for the purpose of making profits, the aim of the public corporation is to act in the public interest and to cover its costs. (See also the section on public ownership, Chapter 37.)

10   The Finance of Industry

In this chapter we discuss the ways in which firms raise the money required to finance their operations. The sources of funds for industry may be *external* or *internal*, that is, firms may borrow from different types of lender, or they may generate funds for investment purposes by allocating some of their profits for use within the firm. We shall deal first of all with external sources of finance.

It is also useful to distinguish between funds required for working or circulating capital, and funds required for longer term investment in fixed assets. Some institutions tend to specialise in the provision of short-term loans for working capital while others provide funds on a long-term basis.

The commercial banks [1]

By tradition British banks are providers of relatively short-term loans. A typical bank loan is often described as a 'self-liquidating' loan, because it finances the purchase of raw materials which are transformed into saleable products in a matter of weeks or months. In other words, the means of repaying the loan is generated in a fairly short period of time. Apart from the provision of this type of working capital, banks also provide 'bridging' finance. Although over the long period a firm's income may exceed its expenditures this is not likely to be always the case over relatively short periods of time; income and outgoings do not balance week by week. Temporary deficits will arise during periods when expenditures exceed receipts and these are usually covered by 'bridging' loans from the banks.

In more recent years the lending policies of the commercial banks have been changing. They now provide some loans of longer duration (up to 5 or 7 years in certain cases). Short-term loans, of course, can be renewed and continued for relatively long periods. The banks also, indirectly, through their ownership of finance companies and their participation in specialist finance institutions (discussed later), play a part in the market for longer term loans.

The new issue market

For the larger firms a major source of external funds is the new issue

[1] See p. 302.

market. Large sums of money may be raised by selling shares and debentures to the general public. It is very unlikely that an entirely new company would use the new issue market – it will be an unknown quantity to the people dealing in this market. New share issues are made by existing public companies seeking additional funds or when a private company decides to 'go public'.

The new issue market is only available to the public company and is only attractive when fairly large sums of money are required because many of the costs of making a new issue do not increase proportionately with the size of the issue. There are several ways of marketing new shares.

The public issue

In this case the company offering its shares for sale makes a direct approach to the general public. A public issue is usually handled on behalf of the company by an *Issuing House* which is an institution specialising in this type of work.

It may be one of the old-established merchant banks, a finance house, or a firm of issuing brokers. When the issuing house has decided on the class of shares to be offered, the issue price of the shares, and the rights they will carry, it will prepare the prospectus. This prospectus must be advertised in at least two national newspapers and must contain information on the company's financial position, trading prospects, and recent results, and other relevant financial information in considerable detail. A copy must be filed with the Registrar of Companies. The advertisement will contain an invitation to the public to apply for the shares and a closing date for applications will be announced. The next procedure is the allotment of the shares. If the issue has been oversubscribed the issuing house must allot to each applicant some proportion of the shares for which he has applied. If the issue is undersubscribed the issuing house will be left with unsold shares. This possibility is normally avoided by having the share issue underwritten. Underwriting is carried out by specialist firms and is, in effect, a kind of insurance against the failure of the issue. The underwriter, for a commission, will guarantee to take up any unsold shares.

The public issue, as mentioned earlier, is fairly costly, for it involves fees to the issuing house, underwriters' commissions, legal fees, stamp duties, advertising costs, and accounting charges.

Offers for sale

This is an alternative method of issuing shares in which the whole share issue is sold outright to the issuing house which then offers the shares to the public. In this case the issuing house is acting as a principal and not as an agent. Again the method is fairly costly because, like the public issue, it requires the preparation of a prospectus and national advertising.

Placings

The shares need not be offered directly to the general public. The issuing house or broker may attempt to place the shares. This means contacting institutions such as insurance companies or pensions funds, or perhaps Stock Exchange firms, and getting them to accept large blocks of the shares on offer. If they are placed on the Stock Exchange there are rules to ensure that any one firm does not acquire a monopoly position – the shares must be placed with more than one source of supply.

A rights issue

One method a raising finance which is commonly used and is probably the cheapest method of all is the rights issue. The company writes to its existing shareholders offering them the chance of buying new shares in proportion to their existing shareholdings. As shareholders they have 'rights' to a certain number of new shares. These rights are valuable since the new shares are offered at less than their current market price.

Issues by tender

The difficulties of estimating the true market value of a new issue when trying to fix the issue price has led to some movement towards issuing shares by tender. Here the subscribers are asked to nominate the prices they are prepared to pay and the shares are sold to the highest bidders. This method does have the advantage of bringing in market forces at the earliest possible stage.

Retained profits

By far the most important sources of company finance are internal. Something like 60 per cent of the capital funds of the larger quoted[1] companies derives from retained profits. Even in the case of the smaller companies most of the capital requirements are generated within the

[1] Companies whose shares are dealt in on the Stock Exchange.

company. If retained profits are subjected to a lower rate of taxation than distributed profits, companies may be encouraged to retain more of their profits. Such a system operated in the UK until 1973.

The annual accounts of the General Electric Company for 1980 contain the following information.

The Value Added [1] for the year amounted to £1 572 million. This was disposed of as follows:

		%
1 To employees		
Wages, Salaries, Pension Contributions etc.	£1 034m	65·8
2 To government		
Taxation	£156m	9·9
3 To providers of capital		
Interest on loans	£41m	2·6
Dividends on shares	£45m	2·9
4 Retained in business		
Depreciation	£82m	5·2
Retained profit	£214m	13·6
	£1 572m	100·0

Institutional sources of finance

There are a number of financial institutions which play an important part in the capital market. The role of these institutions is to collect savings from members of the public and channel them to industry and the government. By this means the individually very small but regular savings of millions of people can be aggregated into very large sums of money for investment purposes. Many of these institutions prefer to place funds where there is a high degree of security, and income is known and certain. Much of their investment, therefore, will be in debentures, preference shares, and government securities. Nevertheless they are large-scale buyers of ordinary shares.

Insurance companies

Insurance companies provide protection from certain risks in return for regular payments which are known as premiums. The annual total of premiums paid to insurance companies in this country is a very large sum indeed, part of which becomes available for investment in industry. They are easily the largest of the institutional investors.

---

[1] Value added = Turnover less goods and services purchased from outside (see also page 229).

Pension funds

Public and private pension schemes have grown very rapidly in recent years and funds from this source are an increasing element in the provision of capital for the government and industry. Much of the investment by these bodies goes into government securities, but an increasing proportion has been finding its way into the various stocks and shares of private industry.

Building societies

This is a rather specialised source of finance for industry since it provides funds almost exclusively for investment in buildings. Most of the funds of British building societies are used to finance the purchase of houses. Indeed, the demand for houses in the UK is extremely dependent upon the availability of mortgage funds provided by the building societies.

Investment trusts

Investment trusts are limited companies, registered in the usual way, but their assets do not consist of land, buildings, and machines as is the case with most companies. They exist solely for the purposes of holding shares in other companies. The managers of investment trusts are full-time experts in the field of investment. In purchasing a share in an investment trust, the investor is, indirectly, investing in a very large number of different companies. The income of an investment trust consists of the dividends it receives on its holdings in other trading companies, and this, in turn, is paid out as a dividend on its own shares.

Unit trusts

The unit trust is an organisation very similar in function to the investment trust. It aims to attract the small saver who is invited to buy 'units' in the trust. The funds accumulated in this way are invested by experienced managers in the shares of many different companies. Investors in unit trusts are entitled to a share of the returns on the invested funds. Whereas shares in an investment trust may be sold on the Stock Exchange (or privately) the holdings in a unit trust may only be resold to the trust itself. The managers of a unit trust will always repurchase units, but the market value of such units varies from day to day according to the value of the underlying investments.

Savings banks

The institutions most familiar to the small saver are the facilities
provided by the Trustee Savings Banks and the National Savings
Bank. The savings of any one individual in these institutions is limited
in amount, but there are many millions of accounts, so that the total
savings is very large. The funds collected by these savings banks are
invested in the securities issued by the government and other public
authorities.

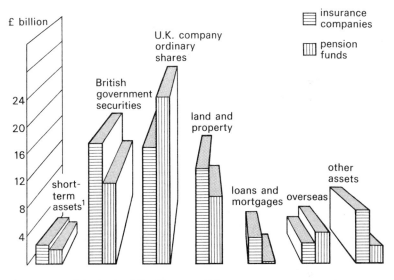

¹ Cash, Local Authority bills, Treasury bills, etc.

Source: *Financial Statistics*

Fig. 14 Insurance companies and pension funds: investments end 1980

Specialist finance agencies

In addition to the sources of funds already mentioned a number of
specialist institutions exist to satisfy particular needs. Several of them
are financed by clearing banks, merchants banks, insurance companies, and pension funds.

The Industrial and Commercial Finance Corporation (*ICFC*) is an important source of finance for the small to medium-sized firm. It
provides both equity and loan capital in amounts ranging from £5 000
to £2 million.

The Finance Corporation for Industry (*FCI*) supplies long-term fixed interest capital for medium and larger sized firms which cannot find the necessary finance elsewhere.

The ICFC and the FCI are subsidiaries of Finance for Industry Ltd (FFI).

Technical Development Capital (*TDC*) is a subsidiary of the ICFC and provides finance for high risk ventures. Its aim is to help people who are starting new businesses or expanding existing ones to develop technical innovations.

The British Technology Group (*BTG*) was formed in 1981 to absorb the functions of the former National Research Development Corporation (NRDC) which aims to provide financial support for industrial companies developing high technology or processes where there is a considerable degree of risk, and of the National Enterprise Board (NEB) which was set up to provide funds to assist in the restructuring of industry (see also page 132).

The above list is a very restricted selection of the specialist financial institutions; there are many others.

Table 8 Other financial institutions[1]

	Number of institutions	Holdings at end of 1980 £ billion
Building societies	276	54·3
Trustee savings banks[2]	17	6·3
Finance houses	500	....[3]
Insurance companies	850	65·2
Pension funds	800	54·7
Unit trusts	510	4·1
Investment trusts	200	7·3
Property unit trusts	23	1·1
Special finance agencies	5	1·3

[1] i.e. not part of officially defined banking sector
[2] from end 1981 part of banking sector
[3] not available

Source: Financial Statistics, Explanatory Handbook

Hire purchase

Hire purchase in industry and commerce works in much the same way as in the retail trade. After making an initial down-payment, and paying regular fixed amounts over an agreed period (covering interest and the balance of the capital cost), a business acquires ownership of the goods. When a firm buys goods on hire purchase it is, in effect, obtaining a loan from the finance company which supplies the funds to support the hire purchase scheme.

Leasing

Instead of using a medium-term loan to buy new assets, a firm may lease them. Under a leasing arrangement, the leasing company will purchase the plant, equipment or vehicles to the firm's requirements and then lease them to the firm for an agreed period at an agreed rental. The leasing company sometimes provides servicing and maintenance. The assets being leased remain the property of the leasing company.

Trade credit

Trade credit is an important source of finance for the smaller firm. When a company supplies goods on credit terms which allow the purchaser 3 or 6 months in which to make payment, it is, in effect, providing the buyer with a short-term loan. Trade credit, like leasing and hire purchase is an important source of working capital.

Loan capital and risk capital

Capital for industrial and commercial enterprises may be classified as either *loan capital* or *risk capital*. Loan capital consists of those funds advanced (by creditors) at fixed rates of interest which may or may not be secured by some kind of mortgage on the assets of the company (see debentures, page 99). The interest payments on loan capital are regarded as part of the fixed costs of the business and, hence, may be deducted from profits before any assessment is made for tax purposes. Risk capital is that part of the capital stock which is raised by the sale of shares. The interest and dividends payable on these shares do not rank as costs of production for taxation purposes and they must be paid out of profits after taxation demands have been met. On the other hand, the interest charges on loan capital must be paid each year whereas dividends and interest on risk capital need not be paid in those years when the company has not prospered. Companies which operate in industries where the market for the product is subject to continuous fluctuation would not take the risk of having a high proportion of loan capital. Loan capital is more appropriate to firms operating in stable markets and which have a large part of their assets

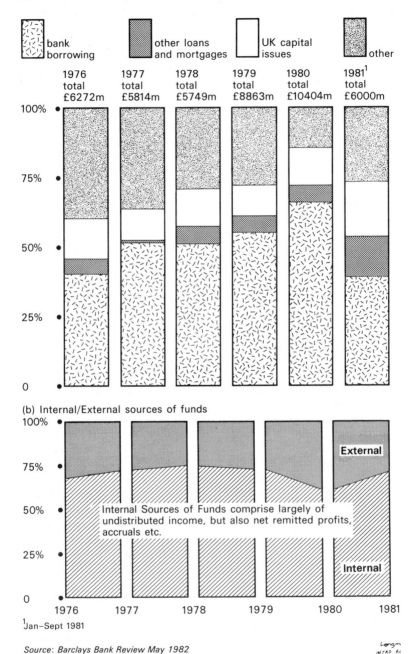

(a) External borrowing

bank borrowing · other loans and mortgages · UK capital issues · other

| 1976 total £6272m | 1977 total £5814m | 1978 total £5749m | 1979 total £8863m | 1980 total £10404m | 1981[1] total £6000m |

(b) Internal/External sources of funds

External

Internal Sources of Funds comprise largely of undistributed income, but also net remitted profits, accruals etc.

Internal

1976 1977 1978 1979 1980 1981

[1]Jan–Sept 1981

Source: Barclays Bank Review May 1982

Longm
INTRO Ec

Fig. 15 Industrial and commercial companies (UK) sources of funds

in the form of land and buildings which are good subjects for mortgages (e.g. brewery companies). Another feature of loan capital is that borrowing money in this form does not affect the pattern of ownership of the business. An issue of ordinary shares, of course, will cause the ownership of the business to be more widely dispersed.

The ratio of loan capital to risk capital is of some significance since it has considerable influence on the variability of the returns from investment. The ratio of a company's ordinary share capital to that part of the capital which carries a fixed rate of interest (preference shares and debentures) is known as *the gearing* of the capital structure. The greater the proportion of ordinary to other capital, the lower the gearing of the capital structure. Thus, if profits are rising, the dividends on the ordinary shares will rise very much faster in those companies with high gearing than in those with low gearing. The opposite will apply when profits are falling. The examples on pp. 99–100 may be used to illustrate this point. If the profits are unchanged but the proportions between the ordinary shares and the fixed interest securities are varied it will be found that the dividends on ordinary shares are much more variable when the gearing is greater.

Public money and private industry

One feature of the increasing extent of government economic activity in capitalist economies is the fact that governments have become increasingly large providers of capital to private industry. State aid to industry takes several forms and has a variety of objectives.

A large part of it, in the form of grants, loans and the direct provision of factories, is directed towards the task of changing the location of industry. This is an important component of the government's regional policy and is described in Chapter 12.

There are also nationwide schemes to encourage industrial investment. These take the form of tax allowances and, where the project is considered to be a valuable contribution to improved industrial efficiency, grants are also available. In recent years the state has also supplied funds to 'rescue' certain large companies which have found themselves in financial difficulties (e.g. British Leyland, Alfred Herbert and International Computers (ICL)). It is hoped that the financial resources provided by the government will allow these companies to rationalise and modernise both their means of production and their range of products. Besides the work done at government research establishments, the government also gives financial support to the development of marketable products by individual companies (up to 50 per cent of the cost). Most of these schemes are sponsored by the Department of Industry but public money may be directed to private industry through such institutions as the British Technology Group.

The steady increase in the level of unemployment during the late

117

1970s and early 1980s led to the introduction of several schemes to boost employment. These schemes provide subsidies, grants and other assistance to employers as well as employees (see page 459).

Funds from the EEC. The European Community is playing an increasingly active role in helping to finance industrial investment in member states. Loans and grants are provided by a variety of organisations, the European Regional Development Fund, The European Investment Bank, The European Social Fund, The European Agricultural Fund, and the European Coal and Steel Community. Some details on these sources of finance are given in Chapter 29. In the first seven years of its membership the UK received £4·5 billion in financial aid (grants and loans) from various EEC sources.

The problems of small firms

The Bolton Committee on Small Firms (Cmnd 4811) 1971 defined a small firm in manufacturing industry as one which had no more than 200 workers.[1] About 80 per cent of such firms are registered companies with limited liability and of these over 90 per cent are 'closely controlled', i.e. under the control of five or fewer persons. The vast majority are controlled, if not owned, by one or two people, very often from the same family.

Whereas large and medium-sized firms have a wide variety of sources of external finance available to them, internally generated funds and bank overdrafts tend to be the principal sources of finance for small firms. For some time there has been a widely held view that smaller firms are at a disadvantage compared with larger firms when seeking finance from external sources. These disadvantages have been identified as,

a some facilities are only available to the larger firm (e.g. the new issue market and some financial institutions do not deal with small loans),

b small firms have to pay more for their money than large firms; this is due to the greater element of risk and the fact that administrative costs of small loans are proportionately greater than those for large loans,

c the unwillingness of some family-owned firms to share control of the business.

Nevertheless, special sources of loan and/or equity finance for small firms do exist. Some have already been mentioned (e.g. ICFC, TDC, and BTG). There are several others including the Council for

---

[1] 'Small' was measured in different ways in different industries, e.g. Construction (25 employees or less), Road Transport (5 vehicles or less).

Small Industries in Rural Areas and the Small Business Capital Fund.

In 1981 the government announced several new measures designed to help small firms. *A Business Start-Up Scheme* is designed to encourage 'outsiders' to put money into new independent companies by offering the investor very attractive tax reliefs.

A Loan Guarantee Scheme allows the government to offer financial guarantees to lending institutions making loans to small businesses. The government also allocated additional funds to the Department of Industry's Small Firms' Service which provides advisory services on financial and other matters.

The Stock Exchange

The Stock Exchange is a market in existing securities (shares, debentures, and securities issued by public authorities). There are about 4 500 members of the Stock Exchange grouped into a number of firms the majority of which are partnerships. There are some limited liability companies, but even in these firms the directors personally must assume unlimited liability. The governing body of the Stock Exchange is the Council, which is elected by the members. The main trading floor and central administration is in London, but there are trading floors in Glasgow, Liverpool, Manchester, Birmingham, Dublin and Belfast.

Brokers and jobbers

The main function of the Stock Exchange is to provide a market for existing shares and securities. It aims to create a free market where people wishing to dispose of shares can always find a buyer and people who wish to buy shares can always find a seller. These facilities are provided by a group of traders known as Jobbers who stand ready to buy or sell securities. Jobbers trade on their own account (they are principals) and they obtain an income in the form of profits from the differences between their buying prices and their selling prices.

Competition between Jobbers tends to produce uniform equilibrium prices. These prices, however, vary from hour to hour according to changes in supply and demand. Jobbers cannot stand against the prevailing opinion of the value of a share. They have to move their prices in order to attract buyers if they are becoming overstocked with a particular share or to attract sellers if they are unable to meet the demand for a particular share. Jobbers do not deal with the general public; they only deal with Brokers.

These Brokers are the other type of trader in the Stock Exchange. They act as agents for buyers and sellers and for these services they receive a commission. Dealings on the Stock Exchange, then, are between Jobbers and Brokers. They are carried out in such a way that when a Jobber is approached by a Broker he does not know whether he is being called upon to buy or sell. The Broker will approach a Jobber and merely ask 'What are ICI?'. The Jobber will then quote two prices, say 180p and 177p. This means that he is prepared to sell these shares at 180p or buy them at 177p. The Broker will now obtain quotations from other Jobbers and finally deal with the one which offers the most favourable quotation.

The securities

Although the shares in public companies are freely transferable, only shares in *quoted public companies*[1] may be traded on the Stock Exchange. A quoted company is one which has satisfied the Stock Exchange Council's requirements with regard to its financial structure, control, and disclosure of financial information. Some 10 000 different shares and bonds are dealt with on the London Stock Exchange. These comprise;
a Gilt-Edged. These are securities issued by the government and they carry a fixed rate of interest. The gilt-edged market is the largest single market in the Stock Exchange.
b Local Authority and other Public Loans. These are similar to gilt-edged except that they are issued by Local Authorities, Public Boards, and Overseas Governments
c Debentures and Loan Stock
d Preference and Ordinary Shares

The investors

Broadly speaking there are two classes of 'Investors', those who buy shares because they are seeking income in the form of dividends and those who buy shares because they hope to make a capital gain from the resale of the shares. This latter group are known as *speculators* and they are usually described as *bulls* and *bears*. Speculators who buy in the expectation that share prices are about to rise are known as bulls. The bear sells shares that he does not possess because he expects prices to fall before the account is settled. If he anticipates correctly he will be able to buy the shares at a lower price than that at which he contracts to supply them.

Nowadays the terms 'bullish' and 'bearish' are more generally

[1] Often referred to as *listed* companies because their shares are listed on the Stock Exchange.

applied to describe markets where share prices are tending to rise or fall.

The private fortunes of wealthy individuals can no longer meet the huge demands for capital and more and more securities are bought by persons investing relatively small amounts of money either directly or indirectly. The number of direct investors in the UK is estimated to be about 2½ million. Millions more, of course, buy shares indirectly by virtue of their contributions to insurance companies, pension funds, unit trusts, and the like.

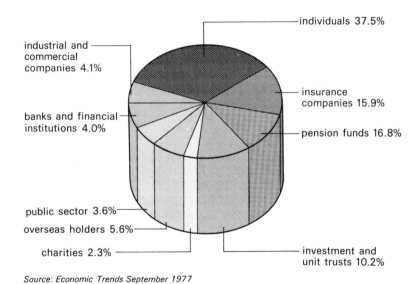

Source: *Economic Trends September 1977*

Fig. 16 Who owns ordinary shares (Dec. 1975) [1]

Share prices

Since the Stock Exchange is a relatively free market, share prices are subject to fluctuations as market conditions change. The Stock Exchange publishes its own Daily List showing the prices at which transactions have taken place. Prices are determined by supply and demand and the willingness to buy and sell is subject to many influences. The following is a brief list of some of these influences.

1 The recent profit record of the company and especially the recent rates of dividend paid to shareholders.

---

[1] Most recent data available in May 1982.

2 The growth prospects of the industry in which the company operates.

3 Government economic policy is a most important factor. Changes in taxation, in government spending, in monetary policy, and, particularly in recent years, in the operation of an incomes and prices policy, are some of the most powerful determinants of expectations on the Stock Exchange.

4 Rumours, and announcements, of mergers and take-over bids. Since take-over bids usually offer generous terms to the shareholders of the company being approached, the shares in that company tend to rise in price.

5 Industrial relations. The effectiveness and growing use of the strike weapon has meant that the state of mangement-labour relations has a very important bearing on the movements of share prices.

6 Foreign political developments are another important influence, especially where an economy is heavily dependent on world trade.

7 Changes in the rate of interest on government securities will often affect share prices. A rise in the market rate of interest might cause some 'switching' from shares to government securities.

8 The news of such things as a major oil strike tends to have a dramatic effect on the shares of the companies concerned. This happened in 1965 when natural gas was discovered in the North Sea.

9 The views of experts are an increasingly important influence. Articles by well-known financial writers can persuade people to buy or sell certain classes of share.

The role of the stock exchange in the economy

1 It provides a high degree of liquidity for what would otherwise be very illiquid assets. Shares are permanent loans to companies and many other securities represent long-term loans (i.e. they are not due to be repaid for many years). People will be prepared to purchase such shares and bonds much more readily when an institution such as the Stock Exchange provides a market where they can, if they wish, sell their securities. Thus, the raising of capital by private industry and governments is greatly facilitated.

2 It provides a daily 'barometer' of industrial and commercial efficiency to the extent that movements in share prices reflect commercial success. Stock Exchange price movements, therefore, tend to direct funds to those industries where share prices are rising. The assumption is, of course, that rising share prices indicate that the relevant companies are using capital more profitably than other companies. We must bear in mind, however, that irrational speculative pressures can also move share prices.

3 Stock Exchange prices provide a means of valuing wealth held in the form of securities. This is important for the assessment of taxes on capital and wealth. The market prices of shares are also used for the assessment of compensation payments when firms are nationalised.

4 The Stock Exchange is primarily a market for existing securities, although some new shares are privately placed with Stock Exchange firms.

11 The Location of Industry

Natural advantages

One of the fundamental decisions to be taken by entrepreneurs concerns the geographical location of their enterprises. They have not only to decide 'How to produce' and 'What to produce' but 'Where to produce'. We must now consider the various influences which bear upon this decision. The great importance of this particular aspect of economic activity is evidenced by the fact that the distribution of industry has now become a major feature of government economic policy.

From the entrepreneur's viewpoint the major determinant of location will be the private costs [1] associated with different locations. There are usually several locations where it would be possible for the firm to operate and the entrepreneur will tend to choose that which minimises the costs of production. Even so the firm, in deciding where to produce, will generally be faced with a rather difficult problem for its needs as a producer might conflict with its needs as a seller. One location might provide an excellent site in relation to the source of raw materials but another might be much more favourable in relation to the firm's markets. The final decision will rest upon some calculation of the maximum net advantages of alternative sites.

Transport costs

Raw materials and power

In the early days of industrialisation the great localising factors were the proximities to raw materials and power. The first factories were dependent upon water power and were sited on the banks of fast-flowing streams. Arkwright built his mill on the banks of such a stream at Cromford. The introduction of steam power moved industrial activity to the coalfields. Coal became the prime source of energy and since, in these early years, transport facilities were primitive and costly, any locations other than coalfield sites were hopelessly uneconomic. All the basic industries in Britain – cotton, wool, iron, and steel – became established on or near coalfields.

Iron and coal were found in close proximity in many areas, as were clay and coal. Hence, the iron and steel industry, the pottery industry, and brick-making all came to be established on coalfields. Industries highly dependent upon imported raw materials tended to be located

[1] See p. 22.

on coastal sites, especially where coal was also available (e.g. South Wales, North West England, and North East England.)

The sources of raw materials and power no longer exert such a strong geographical pull on industry. The electricity grid and the gas and oil pipe lines have made the newer sources of power available in all parts of the country. In addition great improvements in transport have cheapened the movement of raw materials and finished products. Nevertheless the location of raw materials where they happen to be particularly bulky still has some influence on industrial location. Where the industrial process is *bulk reducing* there is a strong incentive to carry out the processing at the source of the basic material. The iron and steel industry built plants on the Lincolnshire and Northamptonshire ore deposits. This was because British ore has a very low iron content and technical progress, in this industry, has led to great economies in the fuels used for heating purposes. The sugar beet processing plants are located on or near the beet fields, since the yield of sugar is very low in relation to the weight and volume of the beet. Chemical plants are located on the salt beds of Cheshire and South Lancashire for similar reasons.

Markets

When the process is *bulk increasing* the pull of the market will be very strong since transport costs will be much less for locations near to the market. Thus, we find much of the furniture industry and the manufacture of domestic appliances such as refrigerators and washing machines located near to the great centres of population in the South East and the Midlands.

Brewers and bakers produce commodities which are of low value in relation to their bulk so that these activities tend to be carried out fairly close to their markets. Proximity to the market may also be an important consideration where the product is durable and requires an efficient after-sales service.

The significance of these arguments depends upon the ratio of transport costs to total costs. Generally speaking this ratio has tended to decline in the UK. The industrial structure has been changing and a much greater proportion of total output is now made up of lighter, easily transportable products, while the role of the heavy industries where transport costs are relatively high has been declining. Added to this we have the facts that the UK is a small country and there have been major improvements in transport. For many industries it seems that transport costs may no longer be an important determinant of location.

Labour

The availability of labour is an essential requirement for economic activity, and when an industry is dependent upon particular labour skills, local supplies of such skills will exert a great influence upon the location decision. More important though is the general availability of labour since, for many modern industries, the bulk of the labour force can be quickly trained. Where there is a high national level of employment but significant variations as between regions, those areas with surplus labour will tend to attract firms which are unable to expand in areas where there are labour shortages.

Since we are concerned with the relative costs of operating in different locations any regional variations in labour costs will also influence location decisions. In a small country like the UK where there are strong trade unions, one would not expect to find any very great differences in regional wage rates, but, in areas of labour shortage, firms may be obliged to pay well above the agreed minimum wage rates.

Physical features and accessibility

For some industries the physical features of the site are of prime importance in deciding location. Industries producing steel, rayon, paper, and chemicals require very large quantities of water and tend to be found near rivers. The atomic power stations are all located on estuaries because of the vast quantities of water required for cooling purposes. Certain industries have serious problems of waste disposal, especially the chemical-based industries, and, again, they are usually located on river-bank sites. The problem of dust control has made it necessary to site cement works in fairly remote situations.

The accessibility of the site is an important factor. Before the development of efficient road transport, proximity to the railway network was an essential requirement for any large-scale enterprise. This is no longer the case since the overwhelming proportion of passenger and freight traffic now uses the road network and proximity to the new motorways has become an important localising factor.

The economic factors which have a bearing on location decisions do not provide a comprehensive explanation for the siting of a great deal of British industry. A general survey of the causes which have influenced location in the past gives the impression that their operation was frequently unknown or imperfectly understood by the original producers. In fact, many decisions on location seem to be haphazard or based purely on personal considerations. An important factor has been the local ties of the entrepreneur. He has tended to set up business where he is known and has useful local contacts and where he is more likely to raise finance from associates and local banks. Lord Nuffield established a motor car industry in his native Oxford; the Rowntree factory in York, and Pilkington's glassworks at St Helens are other examples of large industrial developments in the home towns of their founders. Nevertheless we cannot dismiss the economic factors. The success of such enterprises indicates that the locations must have had some favourable features. There is also the point that transport and labour costs have become relatively less important as far as many industries are concerned, or they do not vary significantly as between different regions, so that entrepreneurs are able to give more weight to personal preferences.

Acquired advantages

Once an industry has become localised the economic advantages of the situation in relation to other areas tend to increase. It is these acquired advantages of existing centres of industry which tend to exert the greatest influence on location decisions. These economies of concentration, as they are sometimes called, gradually develop and persist long after the initial localising factors have disappeared from the scene. The availability of local clays and coal was a major factor in the establishment of a pottery industry in Stoke-on-Trent, but this industry has for a long time been completely dependent on clay transported from Cornwall and the industrial heating is now supplied by gas and electricity. The industry, however, remains very heavily concentrated in the same area, because of the very important external economies of scale available to pottery firms. We discussed these external economies at some length in Chapter 7

The government and location of industry

In the UK, and most other countries, governments have come to play a major part in determining the geographical distribution of industry. The reasons for this development and the nature of the policies used by the political authorities are dealt with in Chapter 12 under the heading Regional Policies.

12 Government and Industry

In Chapter 2 we saw that the typical economic system in the non-communist world is the mixed economy, so called because it contains elements of both private and public enterprise together with some measure of government control over the activities of the private sector. The UK provides a good example of a mixed economy although the industrialised nations of Western Europe and North America are also typical.

In these countries the governments have accepted responsibilities in relation to the maintenance of full employment, the movements of prices, the balance of payments situation, and the rate of economic growth. It is these responsibilities which oblige governments to play an important part in determining the pattern and direction of economic activity.

In the UK, as far as industry is concerned, state intervention is quite extensive and has many strands. It is extremely difficult to classify all the elements of government policy towards industry, and all we can do at this level is to provide some very broad groupings.

Government and the behaviour of firms

Some of the government's measures may be seen as attempts to make the market mechanism work more efficiently by providing a framework of regulations aimed at encouraging a more competitive market structure and at preventing dishonesty in commercial dealings. Others are designed to protect groups which have relatively weak bargaining positions.

A series of Companies Acts regulate the formation, structure, and organisation of joint stock companies. They also require companies to make public certain information about their finances and operations so that people dealing with them should not be misled. The laws relating to Monopolies and Restrictive Practices (see Chap. 16) are designed to secure a more equitable balance of market forces so that individual firms or groups of firms cannot (or do not) exercise undue market power.

In the UK, firms are subject to many statutory controls which are intended to protect the interest of groups of people which might, in a free market, be vulnerable to 'unfair' exploitation. Thus, we have legislation regulating the working conditions in factories, shops and offices, and there are statutory Wages Councils which determine wages in occupations where union organisation has been particularly weak.

The Fair Trading Act (see p. 224) has the objective of providing protection for the consumer in his dealings with suppliers of goods and services. There are laws which give the purchaser the chance to have second thoughts about any hire purchase agreement he may have signed. The Trade Descriptions Act 1968 imposes strict controls on the claims a firm may make in advertising its product. Other regulations control the ingredients of processed food and patent medicines. There are many other examples of this type of regulation, and in more recent years we have seen a great extension of government intervention in the form of far-reaching price controls.

What we are now witnessing in many capitalist countries is a fundamental change in the traditional attitudes towards private enterprise. The generally accepted view, and, indeed, the underlying assumption of much of economic theory, has been that the main function of the firm is to earn maximum profits for its shareholders. Increasing political pressure is now obliging governments to ensure that the firm exercises much wider responsibilities. While the rights of shareholders to profits is generally upheld, the rights of employees, customers, and the general public must be given far more weight in the management decisions taken within the firm. Governments have increasingly intervened in determining the workers' share of the income of the enterprise and there is a growing demand for the state to enlarge the workers' participation in the management of companies. We have already noted the increasing attention being given to consumers' rights, and the rights of the community at large are receiving more and more attention, particularly in respect of the effects which a company's activities have upon the environment.

Government and industrial efficiency

Widespread dissatisfaction with the rate of economic growth has meant that governments have paid increasing attention to the performance of British industry. As far as the private sector is concerned, policies to improve industrial efficiency are mainly confined to financial inducements and exhortation. The emphasis has been on investment (the installation of new capital equipment) and research. Attempts to stimulate investment in private industry have taken the form of investment grants (the government contributes directly to the cost) and various tax concessions on investment expenditures. In addition, firms have been encouraged to build up reserve funds to finance investment by means of a tax system which treats retained profits more favourably than distributed profits.

Economic growth demands large expenditures on research and development, but this involves great risks, especially in the development stage. The development of the industrial process may cost ten or twenty times as much as the original research. The government has accepted the fact that much desirable research and development would not be undertaken without state subsidies. Two institutions mentioned earlier on page 114, the NRDC and TDC were both established to assist, with public funds, the development of new products and processes. The government also operates its own research institutions, and makes substantial grants towards approved research in the private sector (especially in aircraft, computers, electronics, and metallurgy).

The government takes an interest in industrial performance in many other ways. It has played a leading role in the development of management education and took the initiative in setting up the British Institute of Management. It provides a wide range of services to assist exporters most notably with the Export Credits Guarantee Department which, by providing a kind of insurance against the possibility of default by overseas buyers, reduces the risks attached to trading overseas. Another example of the state's efforts to improve industrial efficiency was the 1964 Industrial Training Act which empowers the Department of Employment to set up training boards (financed partly by levies on the firms) to provide training in particular industries.

Many authorities hold the view that the relatively slow growth of productivity in British industry is at least partly due to constant changes in government economic policy which, by creating uncertainty, make firms very cautious about embarking on expensive long-run modernisation programmes. In the 1960s the government attempted to deal with this problem by setting up some machinery to assist with long-term planning. It established the National Economic Development Council with members drawn from the trade unions, the employers, and the government. Its task is to propose measures which would remove obstacles to economic growth and improve Britain's economic performance. Its proposals aim to provide some basis for the government's economic policies, and the setting out of its findings, it is hoped, will encourage industry to frame appropriate development plans. The NEDC *indicates* desirable policies; it has no executive powers.

The earlier reports of the NEDC had relatively little effect because economic crises in the middle and later 1960s meant that long-term objectives had to be sacrificed in order to solve serious short-term problems. The NEDC remains in being and is mainly concerned with the organisation and coordination of the work of a number of Economic Development Committees which have been established to study the problems of particular industries. These EDCs aim to improve the performance of industry by looking at the needs of an entire industry in relation to the economy as a whole. They have no compulsory powers but they try to stimulate change and cooperation within the industry by producing convincing arguments supported by adequate evidence. They have looked into such matters as manpower problems, investment requirements, standardisation, export performance, and import trends. This information is circulated to firms by newsletters and in the form of detailed reports.

Government and industrial structure

Structural change may be considered necessary to improve the performances of exporting industries and/or import-saving industries; to arrest the decline of an industry; to speed up the movement of resources into a new technology (e.g. micro electronics) or to change the geographical distribution of industry.

Industries in decline have received government financial support to help them with the tasks of modernisation and rationalisation (to achieve smaller but more efficient industries). Cotton, steel, shipbuilding, and the aircraft industries have all received substantial government assistance on condition that certain structural changes were carried out.

In the 1970s, the government found itself helping several large firms in very serious difficulties. Rolls Royce, British Leyland, Ferranti, and Alfred Herbert were all 'rescued' by injections of public money. As a preponderant buyer of the output of several major industries, the government can use its position to put pressure on an industry to carry out the structural changes it thinks necessary.

The Industry Act of 1972 gave the government authority to provide financial assistance in the form of grants or loans for major projects which will produce a substantial improvement in industrial efficiency. This assistance, however, is only available for investment which would not go ahead without it. The government also attempts to encourage investment by making tax concessions. A firm can set off the costs of new capital equipment against its tax liability at whatever rate suits it best. It can, if it wishes, greatly reduce its initial outlay by setting the whole of its depreciation allowance against its tax liability in the year in which the new plant is purchased (i.e. 100 per cent initial allowance).

In addition to the use of financial inducements the government might influence the structure of industry by more direct means. It might, for example, acquire shareholdings in companies and, by placing government representatives on the boards of management, have a direct influence on the companies' policies. An interesting experiment in this field was the setting up, by the government, of the Industrial Reorganisation Corporation in 1966. The main purpose of the IRC was to use public money in order to encourage programmes of rationalisation through mergers and regroupings where such changes would lead to greater standardisation, substantial economies of scale and greater competitiveness in export markets. Its investment in any one project was intended to be relatively short-term. Once a scheme was successfully launched, the IRC would sell its holdings and reinvest the money elsewhere. The IRC played a leading role in some spectacular mergers (e.g. Leyland–BMC and GEC–AEI–English Electric) before being wound up in 1971.

An organisation with very similar functions to those of the IRC, the *National Enterprise Board* (NEB), was set up in 1975 with the following objectives:

a to hold government-owned shareholdings in joint stock companies.
b to promote industrial efficiency by restructuring companies where necessary.
c to extend public ownership.
d to extend worker participation in industry.

In 1980 the government severely restricted the role of the NEB. Its holdings in the more profitable companies were sold back to private enterprise and its functions were limited to those of (*a*) acting as a holding company for government shareholdings and (*b*) acting as a provider of capital for new high-risk ventures.[1]

Probably the most important aspects of government policy in respect of industrial structure are the measures it uses to influence the geographical distribution of industry; this is the subject of the next section.

Government and the location of industry (Regional policies)

Reasons for state intervention

We have discussed the purely economic factors which influence the location of industry, but at the present time these factors are rarely the sole, or even the main, determinant of industrial location. In most countries governments have a very large say in the geographical location of any medium- or large-scale new enterprise.

There are two main reasons why the government has taken powers to control the distribution of industry. The first of these, and the one which originally prompted government action, was the serious regional imbalance in the levels of economic activity. In the UK great discrepancies in local unemployment rates developed between the wars and these have persisted in the post-war period, although the absolute rates of unemployment have been much lower[2]. The second reason is the fact that a firm's location often involves important social costs which have to be borne by the community rather than the firm. Thus

---

[1] These functions were transferred to the British Technology Group in 1981 (see page 114).
[2] i.e. until the late 1970s.

a firm might choose a location which from its own point of view has great advantages, but which might increase congestion and lead to public expenditures on roads, houses, schools, etc., while similar social capital is being underutilised elsewhere. In such a case it is likely that the firm will be bidding up wages in a prosperous area while other areas have relatively high unemployment rates.

The nature of the problem

In the UK the problem of regional unemployment arises from the localisation of the major industries which provided the basis for industrial development in the nineteenth century. Since the First World War several of these basic industries have experienced a serious decline in their home and overseas markets. Thus coal, cotton, and shipbuilding declined because overseas buyers developed their own industries, or major new competitors appeared in foreign markets (e.g. Japan), or because technological progress produced new and superior substitutes (e.g. oil for coal), or new techniques which led to a massive replacement of labour by capital (e.g. mining and agriculture). These industries happen to be heavily concentrated in areas such as Lancashire, South Wales, Clydeside, North East, and North West England.

We live in a world of change so that at any moment of time there will always be some industries in decline, but others will be growing. A declining industry, therefore, would present no serious economic problems if labour and capital were extremely mobile; resources could move from declining to expanding industries. Unfortunately the newer industries which have developed during the twentieth century (e.g. motor vehicles, electrical appliances, radio and television, and food processing) have tended to prefer locations away from the traditional industrial centres. The attraction for these mainly consumer goods industries have been the large markets in the Midlands, London, and the South East. Given the serious barriers to the mobility of labour discussed earlier (pp. 48–49) the result has been a difficult and persistent regional imbalance in the labour market.

Regional policies

Faced with the problems outlined above governments have placed regional policies high on their list of priorities. Regional policy is a twentieth-century development designed to deal with *three basic problems*.

1 An excessive concentration of people in particular towns and cities.
2 Areas dominated by older declining industries.
3 Regions depressed due to a dependence on low-income extractive industries such as agriculture, forestry, and fishing.

In the UK the major problem is the second one, but the problems of London and the South East Lancashire and Midland conurbations provide examples of the first type, while the Scottish Highlands and the South West peninsula provide examples of the third type.

The main effects of an uneven regional distribution of unemployment are

a The unemployment in the less prosperous areas represents a serious waste of economic resources and national income is lower than it might otherwise be.

b The drift of population to the more prosperous areas leads to housing shortages and general overcrowding in these areas and there will be added social costs incurred in trying to overcome the problems of the overcrowded areas. In other regions community life might be damaged by the loss of population and the distortion of the age composition (since younger persons are the ones most likely to move). In addition there may be social costs in the form of underutilised social capital.

c When the total demand for goods and services is running at a high level, there is excess demand for labour (and other factors) in the prosperous areas giving rise to upward pressures on incomes and other prices. Inflationary pressures are generated while manpower resources are underutilised elsewhere.

Regional policy measures fall into three main groups.

1 Development of the infrastructure of the depressed areas by improving roads, railways, and airports, increasing the availability of fuel and power, and providing the necessary social capital and amenities.

2 Schemes to improve the occupational and geographical mobility of labour so that workers can move more readily to the new jobs provided by firms moving into areas with surplus labour.

3 Measures to stimulate industrial expansion and diversification in selected areas together with restrictions on expansion in more prosperous or overcrowded regions.

Regional policy in the UK

The extent of the regional problem is revealed in Table 9, which shows the variations in unemployment rates in the official planning regions of the UK. The government began to tackle the problem in a small way in the 1930s, but the measures had little or no effect mainly because the *national* rate of unemployment was high throughout the inter-war period. During the Second World War the problem disappeared, but the return to peace-time conditions saw the reappearance of the regional imbalance in unemployment rates and the problem has persisted with varying degrees of severity.

A series of Distribution of Industry, and Local Employment Acts has brought into being a wide range of policy instruments for dealing with the regional problems. The more important aspects of government policy are designed to 'take work to the workers' rather than 'taking workers to the work'. The reasons for this concentration on moving firms to areas with surplus labour are based upon the geographical immobilities of labour and the problems associated with large movements of population which have already been discussed.

Table 9 UK regional unemployment rates (excluding school leavers) (annual averages)

	1978	1979	1980	1981	1982[1]
North	8·2	8·0	9·9	14·1	15·4
Yorks and Humberside	5·5	5·3	7·0	11·3	12·6
East Midlands	4·7	4·4	5·9	9·5	10·6
East Anglia	4·7	4·3	5·3	8·6	9·8
South East	4·0	3·5	4·4	7·6	8·9
South West	6·1	5·4	6·2	9·3	10·3
West Midlands	5·1	5·1	7·1	12·8	14·5
North West	6·9	6·6	8·5	13·0	14·6
Wales	7·6	7·3	9·4	13·8	15·2
Scotland	7·6	7·4	9·1	12·7	14·0
Northern Ireland	10·5	10·3	12·5	17·0	18·8
United Kingdom	5·7	5·4	6·8	10·6	12·0

[1] May

Source: Department of Employment Gazette

Assisted areas

Certain regions of the UK have been designated as qualifying for special government aid. Although the level of unemployment is the chief determinant of an area's status as an assisted area, other factors such as population decline or a particularly slow rate of growth may also be taken into account. There are three types of assisted areas.

1 Development areas

These are mainly the older industrial regions where major industries have been in decline for many years. Development areas cover large areas of Scotland, Wales, and the Northern region, Merseyside, Cornwall, parts of Devon, Corby, and the whole of Northern Ireland.

1 August 1982 (subject to review)

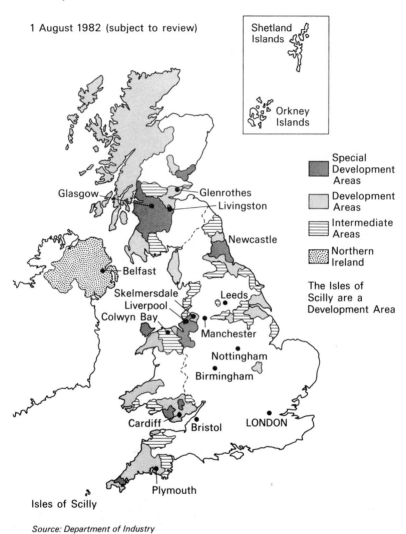

Source: Department of Industry

Fig. 17 Assisted areas

2 Special development areas

These are locations within the development areas where there are particularly severe problems of unemployment. They are situated in the Scottish, Welsh, and Northern regions and in parts of Cornwall.

3 Intermediate areas

These areas lie on the fringes of development areas and suffer from problems similar in kind but not in severity.

Until 1979 the assisted areas covered some 40 per cent of the employed population of Britain, but in that year changes in policy were announced which greatly reduced the areas qualifying for special treatment. Figure 17 shows the new boundaries which will mean that about 25 per cent of the employed population will be living and working in the assisted areas.

Policy measures

These consist of a variety of financial inducements designed to encourage firms to move to the assisted areas together with a form of deterrent to expansion elsewhere. It is sometimes described as 'a carrot and stick policy'.

Inducements

a The Department of Industry has the power to erect factories in the assisted areas and to make them available on very favourable terms (sometimes rent-free for limited periods).

b Government grants are available to help firms meet the costs of training labour in the development and special development areas.

c The most important form of financial aid takes the form of Regional Development Grants (RDGs) which in 1981 were available as follows,

In the Special Development Areas	22 per cent of the cost of new buildings and machinery
In the Development Areas	15 per cent of the cost of buildings and machinery
In the Intermediate Areas	RDGs were not available

d Regional Selective Assistance (RSA), usually in the form of grants, is available for projects which safeguard jobs, but this assistance is only provided where such projects would not otherwise go ahead. RSA is available in addition to RDGs.

e Firms in assisted areas tend to receive preference in the placing of government contracts.

Finance to help in the creation and safeguarding of jobs in the assisted areas is also provided by the European Investment Bank and the European Coal and Steel Community.

Direct controls

In the UK, it is not possible to obtain planning permission for the erection of a new industrial building occupying an area greater than 50 000 square feet unless the Department of Industry grants an Industrial Development Certificate (IDC). The fact that IDCs are not required in the assisted areas and may be refused in the more prosperous areas may persuade firms wishing to expand to locate the new plant in one of the areas qualifying for special treatment. In fact, very few IDCs were refused during the period of heavy unemployment in the late 1970s and early 1980s.

Mobility

An important part of regional policy consists of government measures to assist the mobility of labour so that workers can move more easily to the new jobs created by the other measures. In addition to the training grants paid to firms creating jobs in development areas, the government has established (and is establishing more) government training centres (GTCs) where redundant workers can learn new skills. Training grants are payable to workers who attend these courses. This programme of retraining together with the Redundancy Payments Scheme should, it is hoped, greatly increase the occupational mobility of labour. There are also schemes offering financial assistance to workers seeking to move to work in other areas. Travelling expenses, lodging allowances, and assistance with removal expenses may be provided by the Department of Employment.

Another aspect of regional policy in the UK has been the creation of the New Towns. About 20 new towns have been built and some other towns have been greatly enlarged under the same policy. The principal objective has been to reduce the congestion in the large conurbations (several of the towns have been created to take 'overspill' population from London and Birmingham), but others have been established in development areas in attempts to generate growth points.

Enterprise zones

In 1980 the government announced plans for dealing with the serious problems of decline and decay in the centres of several large industrial cities. Demolition of slums and older industrial and commercial properties had not been followed up by redevelopment and the centres of many large cities were becoming less and less attractive to new enterprises. The government decided to create 'enterprise zones' in a number of cities with a view to attracting firms to set up in inner-city areas. Firms located within an enterprise zone do not have to pay rates for up to 10 years; planning controls are less rigid so that factories can be built more quickly, and such firms can obtain very favourable tax treatment of their capital expenditures. By 1982 some 11 enterprise zones had been established.

Effectiveness of regional policy

It is difficult to assess the extent to which regional policy has been successful. In spite of the very substantial financial incentives the discrepancies in regional unemployment rates still remain. It is possible of course that without government intervention the divergencies would have been much greater. The policies have been criticised on several grounds.

1 A policy of diversification of industry in all the regions may result in the loss of external economies of scale. The motor car industry, which has built plants in several of the development areas, appeared to be rather reluctant to do so because it meant that these plants would lose the benefits of economies of concentration available in the established centres of the industry.

2 The policy of taking work to the workers may have been pushed too far. Firms which have been refused an IDC to expand their plants in prosperous areas may have cancelled their plans for expansion rather than accept the alternative of operating a branch factory at considerable distance from the parent plant. It has sometimes been found that even in areas of general labour surplus particular skills are just as scarce as they are in more prosperous areas.

3 Labour availability is only one criterion for industrial location and areas with surplus labour might well be high-cost areas in other respects. If so, pressures to locate firms in these areas might reduce their competitiveness – especially in export markets.

4 Some areas, it is held, are 'economically exhausted' so that no amount of financial assistance will persuade firms to move into these areas on a scale large enough to rehabilitate them.

As against these criticisms it must be said that many of them are largely based on the assumption that firms, left to themselves, will always choose the least-cost locations. It is difficult to prove this, and all sorts of personal factors seem to play a part in the location decision. Many modern industries appear to be 'footloose' in the sense that they could operate equally well in a wide range of different locations. In other words the costs of production of firms in these industries are not critically affected by location. Other studies indicate that relocation of industry does raise costs initially, but the cost differences tend to disappear after an interval of about 5 years.

A broader approach to regional planning to ensure balanced growth in all regions has led to the establishment of regional planning organisations. The whole country has been divided into ten regions. Each region has its own Regional Council consisting of representatives from industry, local government, and the universities together with a Regional Planning Board consisting of civil servants from the ministries concerned. These groups carry out regional studies, identify problems, and formulate regional plans.

There is a further discussion of state intervention in Chapter 37.

Part Four: Population

13 The Population Basis

World population

The population of the world is estimated to be 4·5 billion and it is growing at about 1·6 per cent per annum. The world's population has not grown at a steady rate. It took more than a million years for the world to achieve its first billion (1 000 million) people; the second billion was added in about 120 years, the third billion in about 32 years and the fourth billion was achieved in only 15 years. Figure 18 illustrates these startling developments.

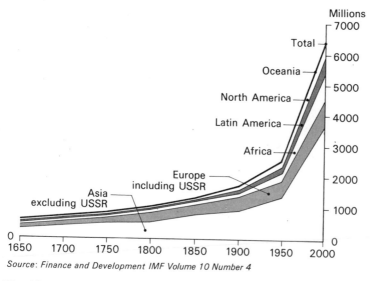

Source: Finance and Development IMF Volume 10 Number 4

Fig. 18 World population growth 1650–2000 (millions)

The first period of rapid population growth started in Europe about the time of the Industrial Revolution. Technical progress made possible the increases in productivity, the higher living standards, the improvements in sanitation and transport and the developments in medicine which brought about a fall in the death rate.

It was this fall in the death rate combined with continuing high birth rates which led to the high growth rates. On average, the time lag between the first substantial fall in death rates and the later fall in birth rates was about 70 years. In this transitional period very high growth rates were recorded and the population of Europe trebled in the period 1750–1914.

The first round of the demographic 'explosion' is over and the developed countries in Europe and North America have reached a kind of population equilibrium with low birth rates and low death rates; populations are virtually stable or increasing very slowly. The experience of the developed nations has led to the formulation of a theory that societies tend to move through three distinct demographic stages.

a High birth rates and high death rates with near stationary populations.

b High birth rates and falling death rates when populations will be growing, often quite rapidly.

c Low birth rates and low death rates with near stationary populations.

It took the developed world as a whole about 150 years to pass through this demographic transition.

The developing countries in Asia, Latin America, and Africa are now in the second stage of transition and are experiencing population growth of unprecedented magnitude. As a group their populations are growing at about 2·2 per cent per annum, a rate of growth which, if maintained, would cause their populations to double in about 33 years. One explanation of the present great upsurge in population is the application of medical science developed over the past century. In Europe medical knowledge advanced relatively slowly and the growth of population, by present standards, was at a modest rate. In the developing world the accumulated knowledge of a century or more is immediately available and death rates have fallen much faster than they did in Europe. For example, Sri Lanka in the years between 1945 and 1953 had as great a decline in the death rate as had occurred in Sweden in the entire century between 1771 and 1871.

A basic problem in the developing countries is the fact that they are still agricultural societies. In Europe, the growth of population accompanied the Industrial Revolution and the growth of production more than kept pace with population growth. In the developing countries, rapid population growth has tended to precede economic development. There are, however, strong indications that in many parts of the developing world birth rates are beginning to fall and that *the rate of* population growth has passed its peak.

Malthus

The current trends in world population have revived interest in the population theories of the Rev. Thomas Malthus, whose *Essay on Population* (1798) led to the first really serious discussions of the problem. Malthus wrote at a time when the British population was increasing rapidly and his observations seemed to confirm his views that increasing numbers could only increase the misery of the masses. He declared that population has a persistent tendency to outstrip the means of subsistence. Any rise in the living standards of the mass of the people would only lead to earlier marriages, more births, and more babies surviving. The increased numbers would simply lower living standards back to the bare subsistence level. His purpose was to demonstrate 'That the increase in population is necessarily limited by the means of subsistence. That population does invariably increase when the means of subsistence increase and that the superior power of population is repressed, and the actual population kept equal to the means of subsistence by misery and vice.'

The checks on population which Malthus summarised as misery and vice were famines, plagues, wars, and infanticide. He was, of course, concerned with the British problem and believed that agricultural output could not possibly increase at the rate at which population tends to grow. In this he was undoubtedly influenced by the Law of Diminishing Returns because he saw the supply of land as relatively fixed. He was proved wrong in the case of Britain for the population quadrupled during the the nineteenth century. He did not foresee the great improvements in transport and technology which enabled the British people to be fed from the vast lands of the new continents. Nor did he foresee that rising living standards bring falling birth rates as they did in most western nations after 1870.

Nevertheless the germs of truth in his doctrines are still important for an understanding of the population problems in much of Asia and Africa where the balanace between the numbers of people and the means of subsistence is often precarious. Where inexpensive science greatly reduces the death rate without increasing productivity Malthus still has some relevance.

Changes in population

Changes in population come about in two ways, (i) by movements in birth and death rates, and (ii) by migration. The crude birth rate is usually expressed as the number of births per annum per thousand of the population and the crude death rate is the number of deaths per thousand of the population per annum. The natural growth rate will be the difference between these two rates.

Natural Growth Rate = Birth Rate − Death Rate

Thus if a country has a birth rate of 40 per 1 000 and a death rate of 20 per 1 000, its population has a natural growth rate of 2 per cent per annum. The actual rate of population growth is calculated by adjusting the natural growth rate by the extent of net immigration or emigration.

Migration has been an important factor in the population development of several countries. Between 1846 and 1930 over 50 million Europeans sought new lives overseas, the bulk of them going to North America. The decline in the population of Ireland after 1840 was partly due to large scale emigration (mainly to the USA). In the UK one third of the increase of 52 000 in the total population between 1961 and 1962 was due to immigration, but, as Figure 19 indicates, there has been a small net outflow from the UK in most recent years.

The factors which affect the natural growth rate are well summarised in the following quotation from the *World Development Report 1981* published by World Bank.

'The reasons why world population is, as a minimum, going to double can be briefly stated. Mortality is declining; current fertility is high; the marriage age in developing countries is still low; populations are young, and the number of women in, or about to enter, the child-bearing age groups is growing rapidly.'

Figure 19 illustrates the movements in some of the main determinants of the size of the UK population.

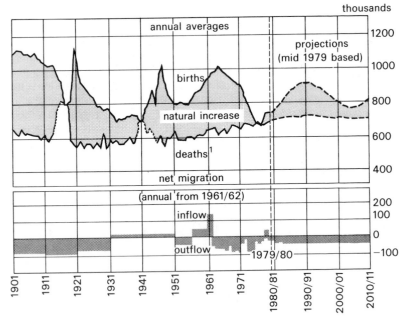

[1] The dots on this line cover the periods 1914 – 18 and 1939 – 45 which include deaths of non-civilians and merchant seamen who died outside the country.

Source: Social Trends

Fig. 19 UK population changes and projections

Age distribution

The age distribution (or age composition) of the population refers to
the numbers of people in the different age groups. The most popular
way of presenting this information is in the form of a bar graph as
shown in Figure 20 where the length of each bar indicates the number
of people in that particular age group.

A country with a high birth rate and high death rate will have a
large proportion of young people in its population. The expectancy of

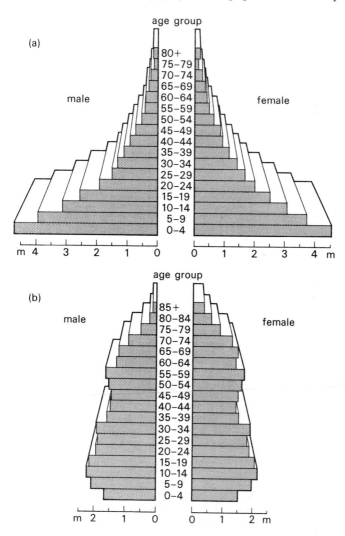

Fig. 20

145

life will be relatively low because the death rate will be high in all the age groups and only a small percentage of those born in such a country will reach the older age groups. This situation is typical of most developing countries and is illustrated by the population 'pyramid' in Figure 20 (a). In countries with this type of age distribution, between 40 per cent and 45 per cent of the population will be below the age of 15 years and only about 4 per cent will be older than 60 years.

Figure 20 (b) illustrates an age distribution which is typical of most developed countries. It indicates a near stationary population with a low birth rate and a low death rate. Expectancy of life is high and most people survive into the older age groups. The percentage of young people in such a society is typically between 20 per cent and 25 per cent; about 15 per cent of the population will be over 60 years of age.

The economist is interested in the age distribution of a population because it reveals the proportions between the numbers in the working age groups and the numbers in the non-working age groups. This *dependency ratio*, as it is called, is measured in the following manner.

Dependency Ratio =
$$\frac{\text{Numbers below school leaving age} + \text{Numbers over retirement ages}}{\text{Numbers between school leaving age and retirement ages}}$$

The dependency ratio will be relatively high in the developing countries. In the Federal Republic of Germany and the Soviet Union, for example, there are two people of working age for every one that is too young or too old to work. In Mexico and Nigeria there is only one.

The economics of population

An optimum population

Countries are often described as underpopulated or overpopulated. From the economist's viewpoint these terms do not refer to the population densities (i.e. the number of persons per square mile), but to the relationship between the numbers of people and the supplies of land, capital, and technical knowledge available to them. That size of population which, with the existing stock of land, capital, and knowledge, would give rise to the maximum output per head is described as *the optimum population*. Thus, the terms underpopulated and overpopulated refer to sizes of population less than or greater than the optimum. A country with more than adequate supplies of fertile land and capital may be underpopulated with 300 persons per square mile, whereas a poor country may be overpopulated with no more than 20 persons per square mile.

The optimum population is not a static concept since the state of technology and the stock of capital are subject to constant change. An increase in the national stock of capital, improvements in the techniques of production, and in the fertility of the land will all tend to increase the size of the optimum population. But measures other than output per head may be taken into account when assessing the optimum population. A nation might relate the preferred size of population to the problem of pollution, or the destruction of valuable amenities, or the rate at which non-replaceable resources are being used up.

An increasing population

Whether an increase in the size of a population brings economic advantages or disadvantages depends very much on the size of the existing population in relation to the other economic resources available to it; in other words, whether it is above or below the optimum size. When population is growing due to an excess of births over deaths there will be an increase in the numbers in the dependent age groups.

A high dependency ratio is adverse to economic development because the resources needed to care for children and to educate them might have been devoted to industrial investment and training which in turn would yield increases in output per head. This is a serious problem for areas such as Africa and Asia where, even if fertility falls rapidly, the number of children in the 6 to 11 age group will increase by 92 per cent (Africa) and 62 per cent (Asia) by the year 2000.

A growing population increases the demands for social capital and the resources needed to meet this *increased* demand might have been used to raise the living standards of the existing population. Some idea of the nature of this problem might be gained from the fact that in some less developed countries where population is growing rapidly, about 65 per cent of total investment is devoted to *maintaining* existing living standards whereas in the advanced countries this proportion is about 25 per cent.

When a country is heavily dependent on world trade for a major part of its requirements of food and basic materials a rapidly rising population might give rise to serious balance of payments problems. Quite apart from the need to import more food, creating work for the increasing numbers will require larger imports of raw materials and other capital goods. To pay for these additional imports the country will have to achieve a substantial increase in its exports.

We must not assume, however, that a slowing down in the growth of population will remove the causes of poverty. Some of the poorer countries would no doubt benefit from a less rapid growth of population since they could then devote more resources to *improving* their facilities rather than to *extending* them. In other regions, however, population growth may not be undesirable. An expanding population will create increased demands for goods and services and growing markets tend to stimulate investment and create employment. A growing population will be able to take more advantage of specialised production and economies of scale. We have seen that many of the more efficient modern production techniques can only be utilised economically in large-scale production. Comprehensive road and rail networks, power supplies, and other public utilities can only be operated at relatively low cost when there is a relatively large population to ensure full utilisation.

A country with a growing population, and hence a young age structure, will probably be more amenable to change and better able to carry it out. The labour force will be more mobile. With increasing numbers entering the working population, expanding industries will have little trouble in recruiting labour. A more rapid rate of technical progress is possible when the population is expanding, because new industries, new factories, and new techniques of production can come into operation alongside the older ones. With a static or declining population these changes might have to wait for the redundancy of the older equipment.

The population of the UK

A full census of the UK population is taken every 10 years. The first official census was carried out in 1801.

Table 10 UK population (millions)

1801	10·5
1841	20·3
1881	31·2
1921	44·2
1961	52·9
1971	55·7
1981	55·9
1991	57·2 (estimate)
2001	58·4 (estimate)

Sources: Census Report 1981 and *Population Trends*

During the nineteenth century Britain's population grew fairly rapidly at a rate of nearly $1\frac{1}{2}$ per cent per annum, but during the first half of the twentieth century there was a marked fall in the rate of growth to about $\frac{1}{2}$ per cent per annum. The density of population in the UK is one of the highest in the world. In mid-1968 it was about 587 persons per square mile. In England and Wales there were about 833 persons per square mile.

Birth rates and death rates

For most of the nineteenth century the birth rate was about 35 per 1 000 and the death rate just over 20 per 1 000. Both birth and death rates fell during the last 30 years of the century. The high birth and death rates produced a population of low average age, but the rapid fall in the death rate after 1880 more than offset the fall in the birth rate and population continued to increase. By the 1930s the birth rate had fallen to less than one half the rate experienced during the nineteenth century. The population continued to increase slowly but the average age increased considerably. The fall in the birth rate ceased in 1933. It rose during the Second World War and reached a post-war peak in 1947. It then declined slightly, rose again in 1964, but in the early 1970s had again started to fall. Towards the end of the 1970s there was an upward trend in fertility. The birth rate for the UK rose from 11·8 per thousand in 1977 to 13·5 per thousand in 1980. The death rate has remained relatively unchanged at about 12 per thousand in recent years.

Sex distribution

The ratio of male births to female births varies little from 106:100. Although there are more male births than female births, the number of females in the total population exceeds that of males. In 1980 there were approximately 105 females to every 100 males. This situation arises because stillbirth rates and mortality rates at almost all ages are higher for males. But the pattern is changing. Until fairly recently women outnumbered men in every age group from adolescence onwards, but the reduction in infant mortality and in the number of stillbirths has significantly changed the sex ratio in most of the age groups. Males now exceed females in every age group up to 50 years. On the other hand the lengthening expectancy of life has been rather more marked for women than for men so that there are now some 177 women over 70 years of age to every 100 men.

Age distribution

In 1981 some 17·5 per cent of the population was over the normal retirement ages of 65 for men and 60 for women. Table 11 shows that the percentage of people over retirement age has more than doubled since 1921. There has also been a substantial increase in the dependency ratio. In 1931 there were 55 people under 16 or over retirement age for every 100 in the working age groups whereas in 1981 there were 66 people in the dependent age groups for every 100 people in the working age groups. Over this same period there has also been a steady increase in the average age of the population.

In the last two decades of the present century, however, the dependency ratio will tend to move more favourably for the following reasons.

a There has been a fairly substantial fall in the *number* of births since the mid-1960s so that the percentage of young dependents will be falling.

b The number reaching retirement age will also be falling because of the relatively low birth rates in the 1920s.

c There will be little change in the death rate.

Table 11 Age structure of UK population (percentages of total population)

	Under 16 (school age and under)	16–64/59 (working ages)	65/60 and over (retirement ages)
1921	29·7	62·1	8·2
1931	25·9	64·3	9·8
1941	22·2	66·0	11·8
1951	23·7	62·7	13·6
1961	24·7	60·8	14·5
1971	25·5	58·2	16·3
1981	22·3	60·2	17·5
1991	21·8	60·7	17·5
2001	23·5	60·2	16·3

Source: Social Trends

Regional distribution

The South East and Midlands occupy 28 per cent of the land area of the UK, but contain about 50 per cent of its population. The most densely populated area, however, is the North West with a density of 3·4 persons per acre. This heavy density is due to the large conurbations centred on Manchester and Merseyside. The next most densely populated region is the South East with 1·9 persons per acre followed by the East and West Ridings of Yorkshire with 1·67 persons per acre. The most sparsely populated regions are Scotland, Wales, and Northern Ireland.

There is considerable internal migration in the UK, a major part of which, until very recent years, has taken the form of a movement from the North to the South East and Midlands. In the last decade the picture has changed slightly due to the large movement from the Inner London area, and the South East now records a very small net outward movement – although its very dense population gives it a very high natural growth element. The 1981 census showed that over the previous decade there had been a steady drift from the cities with fairly large scale movements out of the large conurbations of London, Glasgow, Liverpool, Manchester, and Birmingham.

The size of the UK working population

The working population comprises all those who are in work, those serving in H.M. Forces and those who are on the unemployment register. In 1981 the working population of the UK was 26 million out of a total population of 56 million. Of those in the working age groups, about 90 per cent of the men, 60 per cent of the married women and about 70 per cent of the non-married women were economically active (i.e. in work or registered as seeking work).

Between 1961 and 1979, the working population increased by about 2 million, due mainly to the large increase in the number of married women wishing to work outside the home. The activity rate for married women increased from 29 per cent in 1961 to more than 50 per cent in 1980. Over the same period there was a fall in the activity rate for males due mainly to more people taking early retirement. Increasing numbers entering full-time further education reduced the activity rates in the younger age groups.

In spite of a fairly substantial increase in the numbers of working age, the recent recession led to a fall in the size of the labour force. It is estimated that between 1977 and 1981 the population of working age grew by over 700 000, but the total labour force fell by 150 000. This was due to increasing numbers taking early retirement and a fall in the activity rates of married women.

Occupational distribution

Figure 21 shows recent trends in the occupational distribution of the labour force by sector and by industry.

The three important changes in employment in the UK over the past twenty years have been:

a the large increase in employment in the public sector, both in absolute terms and as a proportion of total employment.

b the continuing expansion of employment in services matched by a fall in employment in mining, agriculture, and manufacturing industries.

c the growing importance of the role of married women in employment.

The UK has a relatively large public sector and the central government, local authorities and the public corporations together account for nearly 30 per cent of total employment. The numbers employed in

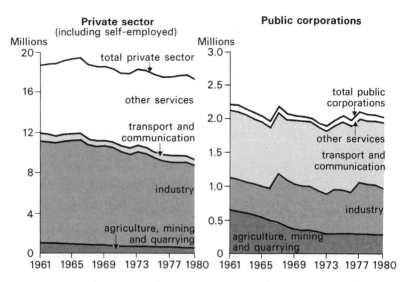

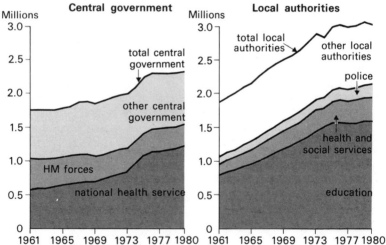

Source: Social Trends 1982

Fig. 21 People in employment: by sector and industry in the UK

the national health service, local authority educational services and local authority health and social services doubled between 1961 and 1979. About 45 per cent of the employees in the public sector are women and of these more than 40 per cent are working part-time.

Figure 21 shows the significant shift in employment away from production industries towards services, especially the services provided by the public sector (education, health and public administration). The long-term decline in employment in primary industries (mining and agriculture) continues although there has been increased employment in the extraction of oil and fears about the future supplies of oil make the prospects for the coal industry seem much brighter.

There has been a steady fall in the numbers employed in manufacturing industry which now employs less than 30 per cent of the labour force. Employment in manufacturing fell very sharply during the recent recession. Between 1979 and 1981 the number of people employed in manufacturing industry fell by 14 per cent (about 1 million), but, in the service industries, the fall was only $2\frac{1}{2}$ per cent.

In the service industries the growth areas in the 1960s and 1970s were the professional and scientific services (particularly education and health) and the insurance, banking and financial services. In some services, however, employment remained fairly stable (e.g. the distributive trades) or declined (e.g. transport and communications). In the UK, services account for about 60 per cent of total employment.

Official forecasts of future manpower requirements indicate that recent trends will continue with an increasing proportion of the labour force being employed in a wide variety of service-type occupations and a continuing fall in employment in industry. 'Blue collar' jobs requiring limited skills will continue to disappear as will many of the traditional craft jobs. There will be an increasing demand for technicians and technologists.

14 How Prices are Determined

Price and value

In this chapter we discuss the basic determinants of price. *Price* is not the same thing as *value*. Things are 'valuable' because people think they are, and for no other reason. The 'value' which an individual places on a commodity cannot be measured; its value will be different for different people. This kind of subjective value is not the concern of the economist who is interested only in 'value in exchange'. The economic worth or value of a good can only be measured in some kind of market transaction which reveals the value of the good in terms of what is offered in exchange for it. If 5lb of potatoes will exchange for 1lb of sugar, then the 'price' of 1lb of sugar is 5lb of potatoes. Nowadays practically all exchanges represent an exchange of goods and services for money, and prices in terms of money are the market values of the things we buy.

Markets

Prices arise in exchange transactions and this implies some kind of market. This need not, necessarily, be a fixed location – a building, or a market place. We are all familiar with the open and covered markets in the centres of our towns, but in the modern world the word 'market' has a much wider meaning. Any effective arrangement for bringing buyers and sellers into contact with one another is defined as a market. The small ad. columns of the local newspaper provide a very efficient market for second-hand cars. Face to face contact between buyers and sellers is not a requirement for a market to be able to operate efficiently. In the foreign exchange market, buyers and sellers are separated by thousands of miles, but the knowledge of what is happening in the market is just as complete, and the ease of dealing is just as effective as if the participants were in the same room.

For some commodities, notably fresh fruit and vegetables, the traditional market is still the normal arrangement, but for most goods the market is a national one. Most consumer goods, in developed countries, are bought and sold on a countrywide basis. For other commodities the market is worldwide. This is particularly true of the more important primary products such as rubber, tin, copper, and oil, and of the basic foodstuffs such as meat, wheat, sugar, tea, and coffee. Most of the products of advanced technology also have world markets; for example, computers, aeroplanes, ships, and motor cars.

The price of any economic good, under market conditions such as we find in the capitalist world, is determined by the forces of supply and demand. There is some kind of market arrangement where buyers and sellers are in contact with one another, and the forces of supply acting through the sellers and the forces of demand acting through the buyers, determine the market price.

Demand

The first thing to understand is that demand is not the same thing as desire, or need, or want. We are looking for the forces which determine price, and the strength of the desire for something will not, in itself, have any influence on the price. Only when desire is supported by the ability and willingness to pay the price does it become an effective demand and have an influence in the market. Demand, in economics, means effective demand, and may be defined as *'the quantity of the commodity which will be demanded at any given price over some given period of time'*.

Consider the following statements;

1 The demand for commodity X is 1 000 units.

2 The demand for commodity X, at a price of 6p per unit, is 1 000 units.

3 The demand for commodity X, at a price of 6p per unit, is 1 000 units per week.

Note that only the third statement is meaningful. The first statement is incomplete because the quantity demanded will be different at different prices. The second statement tells us the quantity demanded at a given price, but it does not tell us how long it will take to sell 1 000 units. Any definition of demand must say something about the quantity, the price, and the time period.

For the great majority of goods and services, experience shows that the quantity demanded will increase as the price falls. This particular characteristic of demand may be illustrated by a table described as a *demand schedule*, or, as is more usual, by *a demand curve*, which is a graphical representation of the data in the demand schedule. Figure 22 provides an example of the manner in which information about demand is usually presented.

Demand and utility

Why should demand curves slope downwards from left to right? Why should the quantity demanded increase as the price falls? One ex-

planation of this aspect of consumer behaviour is based upon the
notion of *diminishing marginal utility*. Utility is defined as the satisfaction which is derived from the consumption of some good or service.
A person buys a commodity because it yields him utility or satisfaction. As he buys more of any good the total utility he derives increases,
but the increase in total utility is not proportionate to the increase in
his consumption.

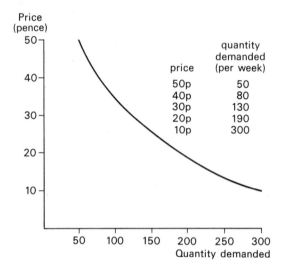

price	quantity demanded (per week)
50p	50
40p	80
30p	130
20p	190
10p	300

Fig. 22

The additional utility derived from the last unit purchased is defined
as the *marginal utility* of the commodity and it is generally accepted
that marginal utility diminishes as consumption increases. After a
strenuous session of work, the first cup of tea provides us with great
satisfaction; the marginal utility of the first cup is very high. A second
cup of tea might also be very welcome, but it will not yield as much
utility as the first, while a third cup will provide an even lower level of
satisfaction. If we continue to consume cups of tea we should eventually reach a stage where it became positively distasteful and marginal
utility would become negative.

Utility cannot be measured, because it is a *subjective* evaluation and
will vary from person to person. Tobacco for the smoker has a high
degree of utility, to the non-smoker its utility is zero. The utility of a
good will vary for the same person according to his particular situation. In the middle of a desert, a drink of cold water will possess
great utility, but the same person on a cold wet day in London would
derive very little, if any, utility from the commodity.

Nevertheless, the law of diminishing marginal utility is a valid
generalisation of human behaviour; the more of a commodity we con-

sume, the less the utility to be derived from the consumption of one more unit. This relationship between consumption and satisfaction might be used to indicate the sacrifices which a consumer will be prepared to make in order to obtain further units of a given commodity. Imagine such a consumer being placed in a position where he faces a sole supplier who is prepared to extort the maximum price for his goods. The picture of consumer behaviour revealed by such an experiment might be something like this:

If he possesses 0 units of the good, he will pay 25p for the 1st unit
If he possesses 1 unit of the good, he will pay 19p for a 2nd unit
If he possesses 2 units of the good, he will pay 10p for a 3rd unit
If he possesses 3 units of the good, he will pay 5p for the 4th unit

This information can be rearranged to show us how this consumer would behave in a free market when faced by different market prices.

When the market price is 25p he will buy 1 unit
When the market price is 20p he will buy 1 unit
When the market price is 15p he will buy 2 units
When the market price is 10p he will buy 3 units
When the market price is 5p he will buy 4 units

This is nothing more than the consumer's individual demand schedule for this commodity, for it shows us how much he will buy at different prices. It could be represented by a demand curve which would slope downwards from left to right. The total demand curve for the product would be the summation of all these individual demand curves.

We have not *measured* utility, but assumed that the sacrifices people are prepared to make in order to obtain something gives us an indication of the utility they derive from that thing. Price measures sacrifice in the sense that it indicates what other things might have been obtained with the money. Since marginal utility diminishes, consumers will only be tempted to buy more of a good if its price is lowered.

Income and substitution effects

The shape of the typical demand curve may also be explained in terms of the income and substitution effects of price changes. Other things being equal, when the price of a good changes, the real income of the consumer changes. The purchasing power of his money income will be greater when the price of the good falls, it will be less when the price rises. When the price of a good falls, therefore, we would expect consumers to buy more because they can afford to buy more (the income effect). Existing buyers will probably increase their purchases and new buyers, who did not purchase at the higher price, will tend to enter the market.

A fall in the price of a commodity also makes it *relatively* cheaper when compared with competing goods. There will probably be some 'switching' of purchases away from the now relatively dearer substitutes towards the commodity which has fallen in price. This is the substitution effect.

The opposite effects will apply when the price of a good rises.

The demand curve

The demand curve tells us what quantities would be demanded at any given price, *if other things do not change.*[1] These other things are discussed later in the chapter, but it is most important to realise, right at the beginning, that the demand curve tells us what happens to quantity demanded *when price changes* and there is *no change* in any of the other factors influencing demand (e.g. incomes, taste, fashion, and so on).

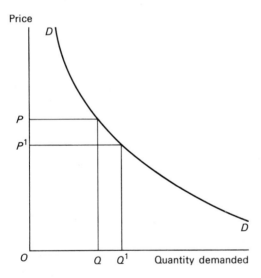

Fig. 23

Figure 23 shows a typical demand curve and we can see that at a price of OP the quantity demanded would be OQ. If price fell to OP^1 quantity demanded would increase to OQ^1. Alternatively we can use the demand curve to tell us the price at which any quantity would be taken off the market. If suppliers wished to dispose of quantity OQ^1, they could not charge any price higher than OP^1.

---

[1] This is sometimes referred to as the *ceteris paribus* assumption.

The area of the rectangles under the demand curve represent the Total Revenues forthcoming at different prices, since they are equal to Price × Quantity.

The movement illustrated in Fig. 23 is referred to as a *change in quantity demanded*. When price falls from OP to OP^1, the quantity demanded increases from OQ to OQ^1. It is very misleading to speak of this as a *change in demand* since this term is usually applied to movements of the whole demand curve. Movements along a demand curve are sometimes referred to as extensions and contractions of demand. It is most important to distinguish between movements along a demand curve (changes in quantity demanded) and movements of the demand curve (changes in demand).

Exceptional demand curves

All the demand curves illustrated in this book slope downwards from left to right and hence obey the general law that more will be demanded at lower prices than at higher prices. There are, however, some unusual demand curves which do not obey this 'law' and which represent conditions where 'more will be demanded at a higher price'.

A much quoted illustration of such a perverse demand curve is the behaviour of buyers in markets where expectations of future price changes play an important role. In the Stock Exchange, for example, falling share prices often lead to a fall in the quantity demanded because potential buyers expect the trend to continue. They anticipate being able to buy at even lower prices in the near future. Rising share prices will often stimulate an increase in quantity demanded when buyers expect prices to continue rising. This particular pattern of behaviour might possibly be explained in terms of a series of shifts in the demand curve rather than in terms of an exceptional demand curve.

Examples of exceptional demand curves are sometimes provided by goods which have a 'snob' appeal. Some people buy expensive things because they are expensive; the ownership of such goods puts them in a rather exclusive class. Where goods are bought for ostentatious reasons a fall in price might cause them to lose some of their appeal and the quantities demanded might fall. They will not be so effective as a means of displaying wealth.

Probably the most important exception to our general law of demand is provided by the demands for the staple foodstuffs such as potatoes, bread, rice, and corn in countries where living standards are very low. In these countries expenditure on basic foodstuffs comprises the greater part of the income of most families. In circumstances like these, an increase in the price of the stable food could well lead to *an increase* in the quantity demanded. If consumers' income and the

159

prices of other goods remain unchanged, people will be obliged to buy at least the same quantity of potatoes, or rice, as before and they would have less to spend on other things. The amount of money remaining for the purchase of those 'extras' to the staple diet may now buy such negligibly small amounts of them that consumers may well decide that they would get much better value by using the remaining income to buy more of the staple foods. A fall in the prices of basic foodstuffs, under the conditions outlined, would tend to have the opposite effects.

Changes in demand

A change in demand means that one or more of the factors which determine demand (other than the price of the product) have changed. It means that the whole demand curve will move.

An increase in demand means that more is now demanded at each and every price.

A fall in demand means that less is now demanded at each and every price.

These changes are illustrated in Fig. 24, which may be used to illustrate either an increase or a decrease in demand. An increase in demand would mean that the curve D^1D^1 has replaced curve DD. We can see that the result of the movement is that an increased quantity is now demanded at any given price. At the price OP the quantity demanded has increased from OQ to OQ^1; at the price OP^1 the quantity demanded has increased from OQ^2 to OQ^3.

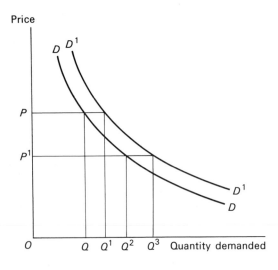

Fig. 24

A fall in demand would mean that the demand curve had moved from D^1D^1 to DD and less would be demanded at any given price.

In the modern world there are many possible causes of changes in demand. The following are some of the more important of these causes.

Changes in disposable real income

For most commodities the really important determinant of demand is the level of incomes. If incomes are rising, the demand for most goods and services will tend to increase. A striking example of this tendency has been the remarkable increase in the demand for motor cars which has accompanied the general rise in incomes since the war.

Rising incomes, however, may cause the demands for some goods to fall. These items are described as *inferior goods* and comprise such things as the cheaper basic foodstuffs and cheaper clothing. An example is provided by the demand for bread which has been declining in Western Europe for several years.

In considering the relationship between changes in income and changes in demand we must note that it is disposable real income which is the relevant variable. *Disposable income*, as the name implies, refers to the amount of income which the individual has available for spending. It differs from the amount of income he is paid for services rendered by the amount of taxation he pays and/or the various state benefits he might receive in the form of family allowances and other social security benefits. Changes in demand, therefore, will be brought about by changes in government policy on taxation and on social expenditures.

Finally we should note that purchasing power is related to *real income* rather than to money income. If money incomes rise by 5 per cent, but over the same time period prices rise by 10 per cent, real income will have fallen, and this means that people's ability to buy things has fallen.

Changes in the prices of other goods

Many of the goods and services we buy have close *substitutes*, and, in making our purchases, we are influenced by the relative prices of competing goods. The demand for a commodity will be influenced by changes in the prices of substitutes. If the price of butter fell, the demand for margarine would probably fall. An increase in the fares on public transport might increase the demand for private transport. Thus a change in the price of a substitute will move the demand curves for competing goods.

The demands for some goods will be affected by changes in the prices of *complementary goods*. Goods are complementary when they are jointly demanded – the use of one requiring the use of the other. The demand for tapes is linked to the demand for tape recorders; the demand for petrol is associated directly with the demand for motor cars. Thus a sharp increase in the price of motor cars might cause the demand for petrol to fall.

Changes in taste and fashion

The demands for some goods and services are very susceptible to changes in taste and fashion. Particularly affected are the clothing trades, but industries producing furniture, processed foods, and beverages are also subject to movements in taste and fashion. Until fairly recent times there was a large industry making hats, but as these have now gone out of fashion there has been a sharp decline in the number and size of firms catering for this trade. The changing public taste in entertainment has led to the closing down of thousands of cinemas in recent years.

Advertising

In advanced capitalist societies, advertising is a powerful instrument affecting demand in many markets. Its aim, quite clearly, is to move the demand curve to the right. In highly competitive markets, a successful advertising campaign will move the product's demand curve to the right and at the same time move the demand curves for competing goods to the left.

The availability of hire purchase finance

In developed countries the demands for many durable consumer goods depend very much on the provision of hire purchase facilities. Any changes in the terms on which this type of finance can be obtained will have a marked effect on the demands for such things as motor cars, electrical appliances, furniture, and other types of household equipment. A similar situation applies in the housing market since the overwhelming majority of houses are purchased with borrowed funds and a shortage of funds in the building societies can lead to a drastic fall in the demand for houses.

Changes in population

The influence of this factor is of a longer term nature unless the change comes about by large-scale migration. Changes in the total population and changes in the age distribution will affect both the total demand for goods and services and the composition of that demand.

Supply

The demand curve shows the relationship between prices and the quantities demanded. The supply schedule and supply curve show the relationships between market prices and the quantities which suppliers are prepared to offer for sale. Supply is not the same thing as 'existing stock' or 'amount available'. We are only concerned here with the amounts actually brought to market and these amounts depend to a large extent on the ruling market price. If a farmer ploughs in his cabbages because he thinks the market price is too low – the cabbages were a part of the existing stock but they never became part of the current supply.

The basic law of supply says *'More will be supplied at a higher price than at a lower price'*.

Supply curves, therefore, will slope upwards from left to right as in Fig. 25 which is derived from the accompanying supply schedule.

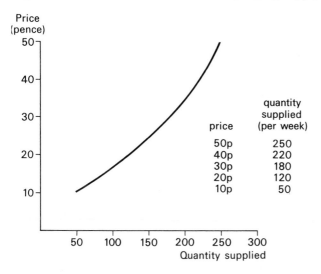

price	quantity supplied (per week)
50p	250
40p	220
30p	180
20p	120
10p	50

Fig. 25

Later in this chapter we shall examine the basis of the supply curve in more detail, but, for the moment, we shall content ourselves with an explanation of the supply curve which is based largely on common sense and our own limited experience of commercial life. An increase in price usually means that production will become more profitable and we would expect existing producers to expand their outputs in response to rising prices. In addition, in the longer run, an increase in price (and hence profits) would tend to encourage new firms to enter the industry. For these reasons it would seem plausible to accept the view that the supply curve will slope upwards from left to right.

As was the case with the demand curve, the supply curve is drawn on the assumption that when the price of the product changes no 'other things' change. Movements along the supply curve are referred to as *changes in the quantity supplied*. The term *change in supply* means that the whole supply curve has moved.

Changes in supply

An increase in supply means that more is supplied at each and every price. A decrease in supply means that less is supplied at each and every price.

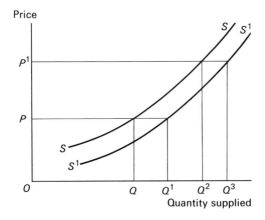

Fig. 26

These movements are illustrated in Fig. 26.

An increase in supply would be represented by a movement of the supply curve from SS to S^1S^1 leading to an increase in the quantity supplied at any given price. For example, at the price OP suppliers are now prepared to offer quantity OQ^1 whereas under the original supply conditions, at this price, they were only prepared to supply quantity OQ. Similarly at price OP^1 the quantity supplied has increased from OQ^2 to OQ^3.

The diagram may be used to illustrate a fall in supply. In this case we assume that the supply curve has moved from S^1S^1 to SS. The effect will be to reduce the quantities supplied at all prices.

A movement of the supply curve indicates some basic change in the conditions governing supply. The most obvious cause of such a movement would be a change in the costs of production. If producers are prepared to supply greater quantities at given prices, shown by a movement of the supply curve from SS to S^1S^1, they have probably experienced some reductions in their labour costs, material costs, or capital costs (or they have decided to accept lower profit levels). Similarly a movement of the supply curve from S^1S^1 to SS means that suppliers now require a higher price before they supply any given quantity, indicating that they have experienced an increase in their costs of production. Some possible causes of changes in the conditions of supply are set out below.

Weather

The output of agricultural products is seriously affected by variations in weather conditions. Output in this industry is subject to variations from year to year which are independent of the acreage planted, and hence independent to a large extent of the costs incurred in preparation and planting. An unfavourable season which results in a poor harvest may be seen as an increase in the average cost of production since a given outlay on fertilisers, ploughing, seeds, and planting yields a smaller return than it would have done in a good season. A bad harvest means that the supply curve moves to the left; a bumper harvest is represented by a movement of the supply curve to the right.

Technical progress

Technical progress is a term which covers improvements in the performances of machines and labour, in the quality of raw materials, in organisation and management, in factory layouts, in communications, in techniques of production, and so on. It is the main source of improvements in productivity and these increases in output-per-person-hour will move the supply curve to the right, because, if other things remain unchanged, average costs of production will fall.

Changes in the prices of the factors of production

An important determinant of changes in the conditions governing supply, especially in recent years, is changes in the prices of the factors of production. Movements in wages, the prices of raw materials, fuel and power, rates of interest, rents, and other factor prices will clearly affect the costs of production. It must be pointed out, however, that movements in factor prices may be offset by changes in the productivity of the factors so that factor cost may not change very much, if at all. For example, if wage rates rise by 10 per cent, but labour productivity also increases by 10 per cent, then labour costs per unit have not changed. In fact, in recent years factor prices have risen quite sharply, far more than movements in productivity, so that the supply curves for most products have been moving to the left. If factor prices fall, of course, the supply curve moves to the right.

Changes in the prices of other commodities

Changes in the prices of other goods may affect the supply of a commodity whose price does not change. If, because of increases in demand, the prices of other goods increase, the production of these goods will become more profitable, and resources would tend to move towards the industries making these higher-priced commodities. The production of goods, with prices unchanged, would now be less attractive to suppliers.

Taxation and subsidies

The imposition of indirect taxes will bring about changes in supply. As explained on p. 185, a tax on a commodity may be regarded as an increase in the costs of supplying that commodity and the supply curve will move to the left. Subsidies will have exactly the opposite effect. They lower the costs of bringing the goods to the market and increase the supply.

Market price

We have very briefly surveyed the two market forces which determine price. For each economic good there is a supply schedule and a demand schedule. If the two are brought together we find that the quantity demanded and the quantity supplied will be equal at one and only one market price. This is *the equilibrium price*. The equilibrium price may be determined from the supply and demand schedules, or, as is more usually the case, from the point at which the demand and supply curves intersect. In Fig. 27, for example, the equilibrium price is 30p, for only at this price is the quantity brought to the market by willing sellers equal to the amount taken off the market by willing buyers.

At prices higher than the market price (e.g. 40p) the quantity supplied will be greater than the quantity demanded and the excess supply would oblige sellers to lower their prices in order to dispose of their output. This situation is sometimes described as a buyers' market.

At prices lower than the market price (e.g. 20p) the quantity

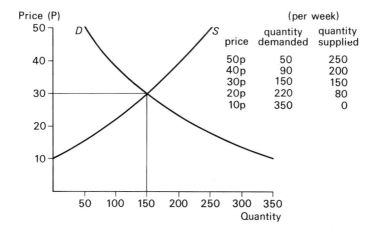

Fig. 27

demanded will exceed the quantity supplied, giving rise to a shortage. Competition between buyers will force up the price giving rise to a condition known as a sellers' market.

The equilibrium or market price is 30p, because at any other price there are market forces at work which tend to change the price.

Changes in market prices

Market prices are determined by the interaction of demand and supply and in competitive markets changes in market prices must be due to changes in demand or supply, or both. Price does not move independently of the demand and supply situations.

The effects of shifts in demand

The effects of changes in demand may be stated in terms of economic 'laws'.

1 *Other things being equal, an increase in demand will raise the price and increase the quantity supplied.*

2 *Other things being equal, a decrease in demand will lower the price and reduce the quantity supplied.*

These statements are generalisations based upon observations of human behaviour, and since they indicate what happens in the great majority of cases they are decribed as laws. Fig. 28 shows the effects of a change in demand.

We can use Fig. 28 to explain the effects of an increase in demand by assuming that *DD* is the original demand curve so that the equili-

167

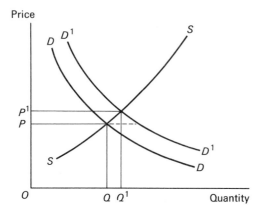

Fig. 28

brium price is OP and the quantity OQ is demanded and supplied. Assume that demand now increases from DD to D^1D^1. The immediate effect is to cause a shortage (shown by dotted line) at the ruling price OP. This shortage will cause the price to be bid upwards and quantity supplied will increase until a new equilibrium price is established at OP^1. The quantity demanded and supplied is now OQ^1. Figure 28 can be used to explain the effects of a fall in demand if we assume that the original demand curve is D^1D^1 and the ruling market price is OP^1. If demand falls from D^1D^1 to DD there will be a surplus at price OP^1 (equal to the horizontal distance between the demand curves). Suppliers will be obliged to lower prices in order to clear their stocks. This fall in price will tend to reduce the quantity supplied and increase the quantity demanded until a new and lower equilibrium price is established at OP.

The effects of shifts in supply

The effects of changes in supply may also be summarised in the form of two economic 'laws'.

1 *Other things being equal, an increase in supply will lower the price and increase the quantity demanded.*

2 *Other things being equal, a decrease in supply will raise the price and reduce the quantity demanded.*

Figure 29 demonstrates the effects of a change in supply.

If we wish to use Fig. 29 to show the effects of an increase in supply, we assume that SS is the original supply curve so that OP is the equilibrium price and quantity OQ is demanded and supplied. An increase in supply moves the supply curve from SS to S^1S^1. The immediate effect is a surplus (shown by dotted line) at the ruling price OP. This surplus will force the price downwards, quantity demanded

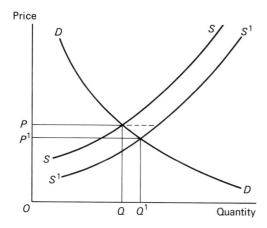

Fig. 29

will increase and eventually a new equilibrium price OP^1 will be established. The quantity demanded and supplied will be OQ^1.

Figure 29 can be used to demonstrate the effects of a fall in supply by assuming that S^1S^1 is the original supply curve and OP^1 is the original market price. When supply falls from S^1S^1 to SS there will be excess demand at price OP^1 (equal to the horizontal distance between the supply curves). This excess demand will cause the price to rise; quantity demanded will fall and quantity supplied will increase until a new equilibrium price is established at OP.

A common confusion

Students beginning the study of economics often find this part of the subject matter rather puzzling. One of the most common difficulties arises when they are asked to analyse causes and effects of price changes. Having learned the first law of supply and demand (i.e. 'more is demanded at lower prices'), many students then automatically associate an increase in price with a fall in the quantity demanded and vice versa.

But this is not necessarily the case. One cannot draw any conclusions about the *effects* of a price change unless one knows the *cause* of the price change. For example, Fig. 28 can be used to illustrate the case where an *increase in price* is associated with an *increase in the quantity sold* (the cause of the change is an increase in demand). On the other hand, Fig. 29 may be used to show how an *increase in price* is associated with a *decrease in the quantity sold* (the cause of the change is a fall in supply). By reversing the movements just described one can see that a fall in price may be associated with an increase or a decrease in quantity demanded – it all depends upon what caused the price change.

These problems are not difficult to overcome if one remembers that changes in price are due to *either* changes in demand *or* changes in supply and, at the same time, one keeps clearly in mind the possible causes of such changes.

Elasticity of demand and supply

We have noted that changes in demand and supply will lead to changes in market prices and in the quantities demanded and supplied. We know the direction of such changes, but it is also important to know the extent of such changes. Will a fall in supply have a large or small effect on price? Will it lead to a large or small reduction in the quantity demanded? Similarly we wish to know the extent to which changes in demand affect prices and quantities supplied. Economists have two important concepts which relate changes in price to changes in quantities demanded and supplied. They are the elasticities of demand and supply.

Elasticity of demand

Elasticity of demand refers to the responsiveness of quantity demanded to a change in price. Where quantity demanded is very responsive to price changes – a small change in price leading to a relatively large change in quantity demanded – we say that demand is elastic. Where quantity demanded is relatively unresponsive to price changes we say that demand is inelastic. To be more precise, *elasticity of demand is the relationship between the proportionate change in price and the proportionate change in quantity demanded.*

The main point to note is that the concept of elasticity is concerned with proportionate changes in price and quantity and not absolute changes. Elasticity of demand can be given a numerical value by using the following formula:

$$\text{Elasticity of Demand} = \frac{\text{Percentage change in quantity demanded}}{\text{Percentage change in price}}$$

Where this ratio is greater than 1, demand is elastic
Where this ratio is less than 1, demand is inelastic
Where the ratio is equal to 1, demand has unit elasticity

A few examples may make this clearer. If a 10 per cent increase in price leads to a 5 per cent fall in quantity demanded, demand is inelastic. If a 10 per cent increase in price reduces quantity demanded by 15 per cent, demand is elastic. Where a 5 per cent change in price causes quantity demanded to change by 5 per cent, elasticity of demand is unity.

170

These simple examples indicate that we may check whether demand is elastic or inelastic by examining the change in total revenue when price changes. Taking another look at the examples above, we can see that in the first one, total revenue will increase; in the second case, total revenue will fall, and in the third example total revenue will be constant.

Using the formula given above it is possible to derive the following relationships.

If demand is elastic (proportionate change in Q > proportionate change in P).

1 An increase in price will reduce total revenue.

2 A fall in price will increase total revenue.

If demand is inelastic (proportionate change in Q < proportionate change in P).

1 An increase in price will increase total revenue.

2 A fall in price will reduce total revenue.

If elasticity of demand in unity (proportionate change in Q = proportionate change in P)

a change in price will leave total revenue unchanged [1]

Fig. 30 demonstrates the effects of changes in supply when (a) demand is inelastic and (b) when demand is elastic in the price ranges illustrated.

Fig. 30a   **Fig. 30b**

In Fig. 30a, demand is inelastic in the price range illustrated since total revenue at the higher price is clearly greater than it is at the lower price.

---

[1] See mathematical note at the end of this chapter.

In Fig. 30b, demand is elastic in the price range illustrated since total revenue is greater at the lower price.

Elasticity of demand and the gradient of the demand curve

Elasticity of demand is *not* measured by the slope or gradient of the demand curve. Normally, on any demand curve, elasticity will be different at different prices (the exceptions are explained below). In order to avoid any confusion between elasticity and the gradient of the demand curve we can demonstrate that a downward sloping *straight line* demand curve does *not* have constant elasticity.

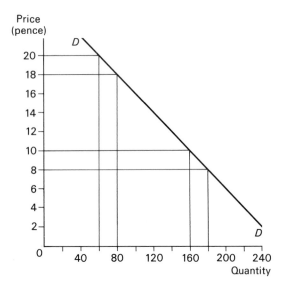

Fig. 31

Let us examine the elasticities of demand in the price ranges illustrated in Fig. 31. In each case there has been a price change of 2p and, since the demand curve is a straight line, the resulting quantity changes are also equal (i.e. 20 units), but the elasticities of demand are certainly not equal.

1 When price changes from 20p to 18p,

Elasticity of demand $= \dfrac{\text{Percentage change in quantity demanded}}{\text{Percentage change in price}}$

$$= \frac{33\frac{1}{3}}{10} = 3.33$$

2 When price changes from 10p to 8p,

$$\text{Elasticity of demand} = \frac{\text{Percentage change in quantity demanded}}{\text{Percentage change in price}}$$

$$= \frac{12\frac{1}{2}}{20} = 0 \cdot 625$$

This example brings out very clearly the fact that elasticity of demand is a relationship between proportionate and not absolute changes in price and quantity demanded.

The three exceptional cases where elasticity of demand is the same at all prices are illustrated in Fig. 32 (a–c).

Elasticity of demand is clearly an important factor which must be

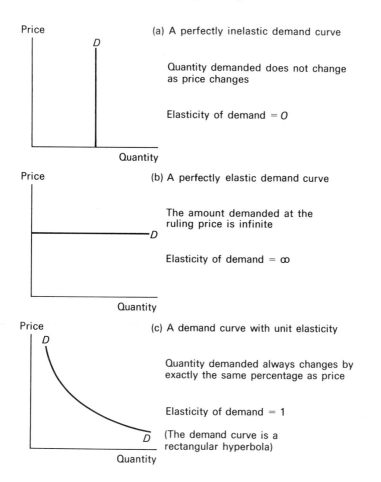

Fig. 32

Introductory Economics

taken into account when we are considering the effects of a change in supply. Figure 30 demonstrates how similar changes in supply will have very different effects on price and quantity demanded when elasticities of demand in the relevant price ranges are different.

The determinants of elasticity of demand

1 The major influence on elasticity of demand is the availability of close substitutes. When a close substitute is available in the relevant price range, demand will be elastic. If the supplier of such a commodity were to raise the price, many buyers would turn to the close substitute. If the supplier were to lower his price he would attract many customers away from the substitute. For example, the demands for a particular brand of cigarettes or paint will be elastic, because there are several other brands which are close substitutes. The total demands for cigarettes and paint, however, will be inelastic because there are no close substitutes for these commodities.

2 The proportion of a consumer's income which is spent on the commodity is also a determinant of the degree of elasticity of demand. Where this proportion is very small, demand will tend to be inelastic. Matches account for a very small part of our total expenditure and a relatively large percentage increase (or fall) in their price would have little effect on the quantity bought.

3 It is sometimes held that the demands for necessities will be inelastic and the demands for luxuries will be elastic. The demands for necessities such as housing, clothing, and basic foodstuffs are certainly inelastic, but is this not another aspect of the availability of substitutes? The demand for luxuries, it is argued will be elastic because we can manage without them and, if their prices rise, many people will certainly do so. But the demands for motor cars, petrol, tobacco, and alcoholic drinks have proved to be extremely inelastic. These are hardly 'necessities' in the strict sense of the word. The use of the words 'necessity' and 'luxury' causes many problems in economics. The goods and services which are classified as luxuries or necessities depend upon the current standard of living. In an economy where real incomes are steadily rising, the luxuries of one generation tend to be regarded as necessities by the next.

4 Some commodities are habit forming and the demands for such goods will obviously tend to be inelastic.

Elasticity of supply

An understanding of the market mechanism will obviously require us to know something about the manner in which the quantity supplied responds to changes in price. For this purpose the concept of elasticity

174

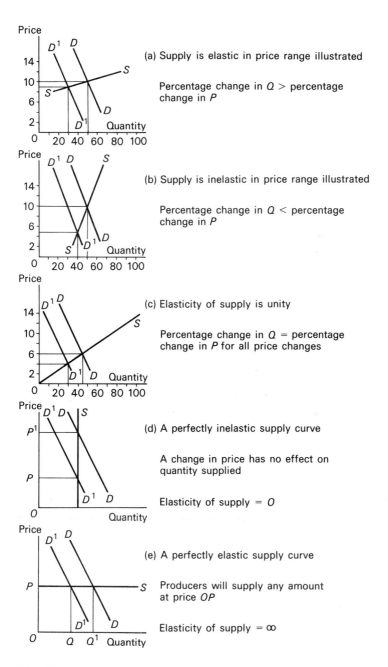

(a) Supply is elastic in price range illustrated

Percentage change in Q > percentage change in P

(b) Supply is inelastic in price range illustrated

Percentage change in Q < percentage change in P

(c) Elasticity of supply is unity

Percentage change in Q = percentage change in P for all price changes

(d) A perfectly inelastic supply curve

A change in price has no effect on quantity supplied

Elasticity of supply = 0

(e) A perfectly elastic supply curve

Producers will supply any amount at price OP

Elasticity of supply = ∞

Fig. 33

is used in very much the same manner as described above. *Elasticity of supply is a relationship between the proportionate changes in price and the associated proportionate changes in quantity supplied.* The formula used to measure elasticity of supply is similar to that used for the elasticity of demand.

$$\text{Elasticity of Supply} = \frac{\text{Percentage change in quantity supplied}}{\text{Percentage change in price}}$$

Where this ratio is greater than 1, supply is elastic
Where this ratio is less than 1, supply is inelastic
Where this ratio is equal to 1, supply has unit elasticity

Figure 33 (a) illustrates a situation where supply is elastic since the proportionate change in quantity supplied is greater than the proportionate change in price. Figure 33 (b) is an illustration of a situation where supply is inelastic. In Figure 33 (c) elasticity of supply is unity at all points on the supply curve. *Any* straight line passing through the origin will have this property. The proportionate changes in quantity supplied will be equal to the proportionate changes in price at any point on the line.

Figure 33 (d) and (e) demonstrate the extreme cases where supply is perfectly inelastic and perfectly elastic.

Elasticity of supply is an important concept, because we cannot determine the likely effects of a change in demand unless we have some knowledge of the elasticity of supply. Figure 33 (a) and (b) illustrate the very different effects of similar changes in demand when the supply conditions have different elasticities.

The determinants of elasticity of supply

The extent to which supply is elastic depends upon the flexibility or mobility of the factors of production. If production can be expanded very easily and quickly in response to an increase in demand, supply will be elastic; if not, supply will be inelastic. Similarly, when demand falls, supply will be elastic if it can be cut back very quickly to match the lower demand. To make this more realistic we should discuss some possible supply conditions in the real world.

1 Where an industry is operating below capacity and there are unemployed resources, supply will be elastic. The industry will be able to expand production fairly easily by engaging more variable factors and bringing into use its idle fixed factors.

2 Where suppliers are holding large stocks, supply will be elastic. In this case an increase in demand can be met by running down stocks, and while these last, supply will be elastic. Once the stocks are depleted, however, it may be difficult to increase output and supply will then be inelastic.

3 In a situation of full employment, the supply of most goods and services will be inelastic. Supply may be increased by improved productivity, but in the short run no significant increases in output will be possible. Supply in the home market may still be elastic if it is possible to obtain supplies from abroad, but this may lead to balance of payments difficulties.

4 In the case of agricultural products, supply in the short run must be fairly inelastic because the quantity supplied in any one year is governed by the acreage planted in the sowing season. Some commodities such as natural rubber, coffee, and cocoa will be inelastic in supply over fairly long periods of time since it takes several years for newly planted trees to reach maturity. Thus, in the short run, an increase in demand will lead to a sharp increase in price. The supplies of products such as beef and milk will also be inelastic because it takes a considerable time to increase the sizes of the herds of beef and dairy cattle.

5 In some industries the expansion of capacity takes a long time. Once such industries are operating at full capacity, therefore, supply will be inelastic (as far as expansion is concerned) for several years. This is true of mining industries because the sinking of new mines and the extension of existing ones is a lengthy procedure. Thus, the supply of most minerals tends to be inelastic.

An increase in the demands for primary products (such as those mentioned above) cannot call forth an immediate increase in supply. Inevitably the short-run effect is an increase in price. The extraordinary increases in the world prices of basic commodities which took place in the early 1970s can be largely explained in terms of a rise in world demand for commodities which have inelastic supply conditions.

Income elasticity of demand

Our discussion of elasticity has concentrated on what is more accurately described as *price elasticity* since we have been examining the relationships between price changes and quantity changes. We noted earlier, however, that one of the most important determinants of demand is the level of income and the concept of elasticity is also used to define the relationships between changes in income and changes in demand. This relationship is known as the *income elasticity* of demand. It is measured by the following formula:

$$\text{Income elasticity of demand} = \frac{\text{Percentage change in quantity demanded}}{\text{Percentage change in income}}$$

For most goods, of course, income and quantity demanded will move in the same direction – an increase in income will lead to an increase in quantity demanded and vice versa – so that the income elasticity of demand will be positive. For example, if a 5 per cent increase in income leads to a 10 per cent increase in the demand for motor cars, we have

$$\text{Income elasticity of demand} = \frac{10\%}{5\%} = +2$$

In the case of inferior goods, as explained on p. 161, increases in income will lead to decreases in the quantities demanded so that income elasticity of demand will be negative. Here income and quantity demanded move in opposite directions.

When quantity demanded does not change as income changes, income elasticity of demand is zero.

For any particular commodity, income elasticity of demand depends very much on the current standard of living. In Western Europe, relatively expensive household goods, motor cars, and holidays abroad have a positive income elasticity of demand, while the demands for some staple foodstuffs (e.g. bread), poor-quality clothing, and public transport have negative income elasticities of demand. In developing countries, however, commodities such as clothing and footwear, which in Europe probably have zero income elasticities, will have large positive income elasticities of demand.

Cross elasticity of demand

The relationship between changes in the price of one commodity and the resulting changes in the quantity demanded of another commodity is described as the cross elasticity of demand. This concept is useful as a means of assessing the extent to which goods are close substitutes or closely related complementary goods. This form of elasticity is measured as follows,

$$\text{Cross elasticity of demand} = \frac{\text{Percentage change in quantity demanded of Good A}}{\text{Percentage change in price of Good B}}$$

In the case of substitute goods, cross elasticity of demand will be positive; an increase in the price of B will lead to an increase in the quantity demanded of A (and vice versa).

In the case of complementary goods, the cross elasticity of demand will be negative; and increase in the price of B will lead to a fall in the quantity demanded of A (and vice versa).

If the two goods are very close substitutes, cross elasticity of demand will have a high positive value. Thus, if an increase of 10 per cent in the price of one brand of petrol leads to a rise of 40 per cent in the sales of another brand, the cross elasticity of demand is +4. Similarly, when two goods are closely related complements, the cross elasticity of demand will have a high negative value.

Demand and supply – the time factor

The effects of changes in demand and supply on price and quantity vary according to the time period being considered. The short-run effects can be very different from the long run effects. Generally speaking while changes in demand can take place in the very short period, especially in markets subject to changes in fashion or where advertising is very effective, changes in supply, because of technical problems and the immobilities of the factors of production, take much longer. It is usual to distinguish three time periods in supply and demand analysis.

The momentary period

This is defined as the period of time during which supply is restricted to the quantities actually available in the market. Supply is fixed (i.e. perfectly inelastic) in the momentary period, and the supply curve will be a straight line parallel to the price axis. Normally, this period will be a very short one. In the case of perishable goods such as fish, fruit, and vegetables, the supply for the day, in local markets, is limited to the quantities delivered in the morning.

The short period

The short period is the interval which must elapse before more can be supplied with the existing capacity. More fish can be supplied by trawlermen fishing longer hours or further afield. More fruit can be supplied by speeding up the harvesting, or by using up existing stocks more quickly. More shoes can be produced by taking on more labour or by working overtime. The short period in some industries (e.g. manufacturing) may be only a matter of a few days, but in others (e.g. housebuilding) it may be many months. The short period, then, is the period of time which allows for changes to take place in the quantities of the variable factors employed. Changes in supply in this period are shown as movements along the normal supply curve. The supply curves used in most of our supply and demand analysis are short period supply curves.

The long period

This is the time interval which is long enough for fundamental changes to take place in the scale of the industry. In other words, in the long period, the quantities of both fixed and variable factors of production may be changed. Existing firms may expand (or contract) their capacity; they may extend their factories, instal more machines, adopt new methods and so on. New firms may enter (or existing firms leave) the industry. The fishing industry may expand by bringing new boats into use; the supply of fruit may be increased by planting more trees; and the output of the steel industry may be increased by building new plants.

The long period may be a matter of months in the case of some manufacturing industries, or several years in the case of mining, steel production, electricity generating, or fruit growing. The long-period changes in supply represent changes in the basic conditions of supply (the capacity of the industry has changed) and these changes involve a series of shifts in the short-period supply curves. Each short-term supply curve describes the supply situation *for a given capacity*.

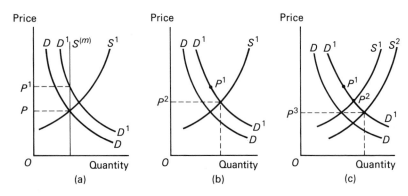

Fig. 34

The relationships described above are illustrated in Fig. 34, which shows the effects of an increase in demand, in the momentary period, the short period, and the long period. $S^{(m)}$ is the momentary period supply curve and S^1 the original short-period supply curve.

In Fig. 34 (a) we see the situation following an increase in demand in the momentary period. Supply is perfectly inelastic and price rises from OP to OP^1, that is, by the full extent of the change in demand.

Fig. 34 (b) shows the situation after sufficient time has elapsed for the industry to react to the increase in demand. The higher price has stimulated an increase in output and this is represented by a movement along the existing short-period supply curve. Quantity supplied has increased and price has fallen from OP^1 to OP^2. This higher (short period) price, if sustained, will lead to changes in the productive capacity of the industry. Existing firms will be encouraged to expand and new firms will enter the industry.

In Fig. 34 (c) we see the effects of this increase in the scale of production. The new supply situation is represented by an entirely new short term supply curve S^2. The increase in supply has caused the price to fall from OP^2 to OP^3 and the quantity demanded has increased. The price OP^3 may be higher or lower than the original price OP depending upon the extent to which the expansion of the industry has yielded economies of scale.

Demand and supply – some relationships and applications

Joint demand

Some goods are jointly demanded; they are *complementary* in the sense that the use of one implies the use of the other. The demand for petrol is associated with the demand for motor cars; the demand for tennis balls is linked to the demand for tennis racquets. Where goods are complementary a change in the price of one of them will cause a change in the demand for the other. For example, technological progress might lead to a drastic reduction in the costs of producing tape recorders and make them available at much lower prices. Such a development would almost certainly increase the demand for tapes (the complementary good). Figure 35 provides a diagrammatic explanation of the movements just described.

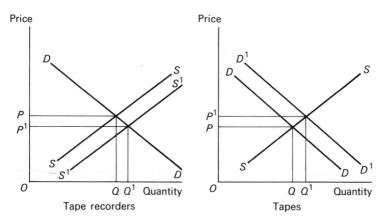

Fig. 35

Competitive demand

Goods which are close substitutes for one another are said to be in competitive demand. Other things being equal, the demand for a commodity will tend to vary directly as the price of its substitute. If the

181

price of butter falls we should expect the demand for margarine to fall. Figure 36 explains this relationship between goods in competitive demand. In Fig. 36 (a) we note that a fall in the supply of beef has raised the price and reduced the quantity demanded. This has caused an increase in the demand for pork, an increase in its price, and an increase in the quantity supplied, as shown in Figure 36 (b).

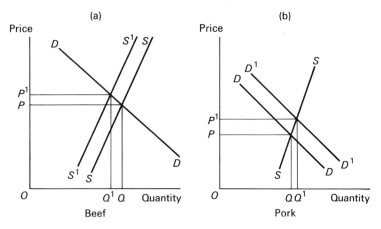

Fig. 36

Composite demand

A good is said to be in composite demand when it is demanded for several different uses. The demands for such goods are the aggregates of the demands of the various users. Wool will be demanded by the textile industry, carpet manufacturers, blanket manufacturers, the hosiery industry, and many others. An increase in the demand for wool by any one industry will raise the price and affect the prices of all the other commodities made from wool. Copper, nylon, and rubber provide good examples of basic commodities widely used in many different industries. Thus, we might have a situation where a large increase in the demand for central heating (copper pipes) might increase prices in the electrical components industries (printed circuits and cables).

Joint supply

An interesting relationship, and one which gives rise to a number of difficult economic problems, is that of joint supply, where the production of one good automatically leads to an output of another. Lead and zinc are found in the same ore so that the extraction of one leads to the extraction of the other. We cannot produce beef unless we produce hides and the production of mutton leads to a supply of wool. An oil refinery produces many different fuels from crude oil and, in the short period, an increased output of any one product, say petrol, will automatically increase the output of the others (benzine, fuel oil, etc.).

One very important, but not so obvious, example of this relationship is to be found in the transport industry. Haulage contractors, bus companies, and the railways cannot, normally, supply an outward journey without supplying an inward journey. This gives rise to the very costly problems of 'empty running'.

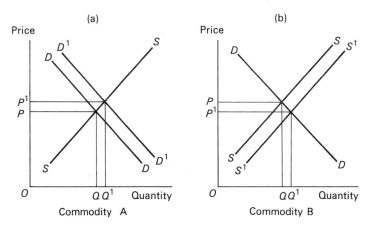

Fig. 37

Where commodities are in joint supply an increase in the demand for one of them will cause a fall in the price of the other. This is demonstrated in Fig. 37. We have two commodities, A and B, which are jointly supplied. In Fig. 37 (a) the demand for A increases, causing the price to rise from OP to OP^1 and the quantity supplied to increase from OQ to OQ^1. But this increase in the quantity supplied of A means an increase in the supply of B. The effect of this is shown in Fig. 37 (b).

Price fixing

In times of emergency such as wartime, or when there is a serious economic crisis in peacetime, governments often resort to the use of price controls on the real necessities of life. Where serious market shortages would cause the free market price to rise to levels which might put these 'essentials' beyond the means of many people, governments will be under great pressure to use measures which limit the extent to which prices can rise.

Supply and demand diagrams make clear the consequences of price

Price

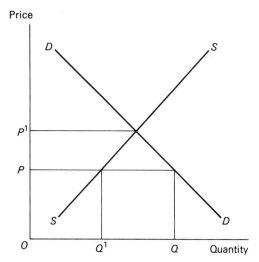

Fig. 38

fixing. In Fig. 38 the free market price is OP^1, but this is considered to be politically unacceptable and the government fixes a statutory maximum price of OP. At the controlled price OP the quantity demanded is OQ, but the quantity supplied is only OQ^1. The market shortage is clearly QQ^1. If no further action is taken, the situation will be very unsatisfactory. Firstcomers will satisfy all their demands, leaving nothing for the less fortunate latecomers. Queues will form outside shops as soon as information is received that supplies have arrived. Some shopkeepers will probably favour their regular customers and friends by keeping some of their supplies 'under the counter'. The excess demand will tempt some people to resell the goods at higher prices (i.e. a black market will develop). Another feature of this situation, especially in the markets for durable goods, will be the use of waiting lists (although this is really another form of queueing).

Since price controls are usually imposed on the basic necessities of life, they are normally accompanied by some form of official rationing where everyone is given a legal entitlement to some quantity of the rationed goods. For example, in Fig. 38, the quantity demanded at the controlled price is about twice as great as the quantity supplied, so that a rationing system would allow people to have about one-half the quantity they would be prepared to buy at this price.

Indirect taxes

Taxes placed on goods and services are known as indirect taxes as opposed to direct taxes which are placed on income and wealth. When a tax such as a purchase tax, a value-added tax, or an excise duty is levied on a commodity it has the same economic effects as an increase in the costs of production. The costs of bringing the good to market are now increased by the amount of the tax. In terms of supply and demand analysis, therefore, the imposition of a tax may be seen as a fall in supply. This will be clear from the data in Table 12.

Table 12 The effects of imposing a tax of 2p per unit

Market price	Quantity supplied (before tax)	Quantity supplied (after tax)	Quantity demanded
(p)			
10	1 100	900	100
9	1 000	800	200
8	900	700	300
7	800	600	400
6	700	500	500
5	600	400	600
4	500	300	700
3	400	—	800
2	300	—	900

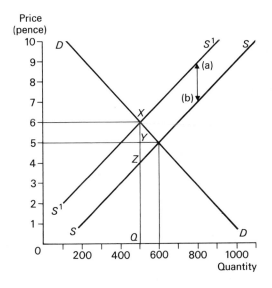

Fig. 39

185

The second column of Table 12 shows the quantities supplied at different prices before the tax is imposed, and the first two columns of the table are represented by the supply curve SS in Fig. 39.

The third column in Table 12 shows the quantities supplied at different prices after the tax has been imposed. It is derived fairly easily from columns one and two. In the new situation, a *market price* of 10p represents a *supply price* of 8p. Producers do not receive the full market price; 2p per unit is now taken by the government. It is, however, the supply price which determines how much suppliers are prepared to offer to the market. Thus when the market price is 10p, the market supply will now be 900 units. Similarly a market price of 9p will only give rise to a market supply of 800 units and so on.

What has happened in fact is that supply has fallen; less is now supplied at each and every market price. Columns one and three make up the new supply schedule which is represented by the supply curve S^1S^1 in Fig. 39.

All the data in Table 12 is contained in Fig. 39. The supply curve has shifted upwards by the amount of the tax (i.e. ab = 2p). At the original equilibrium price (5p), 600 units were demanded and supplied. The imposition of the tax reduces supply, price rises to 6p, and the quantity demanded falls to 500 units.

Note that the price has not risen by the full amount of the tax. The burden of the tax has been shared by producers and consumers. The amount of the tax per unit is equal to XZ. Of this, XY is borne by the consumers in the form of higher prices. YZ, however, is the part of the tax borne by suppliers since they now receive ZQ per unit whereas before the tax they were receiving YQ per unit.

In terms of the hypothetical figures used in the example,

Original equilibrium price   = 5p
New equilibrium price   = 6p (consumers pay 1p per unit more)
New supply price   = 4p (suppliers receive 1p per unit less)
Total revenue   = 3 000p (i.e. 500 × 6p)
Tax yield   = 1 000p (i.e. 500 × 2p)
Suppliers receive   = 2 000p (i.e. 500 × 4p)

The incidence of the tax burden. In the example above the burden of taxation was shared equally between buyers and sellers, but this is a particular case. The incidence of an indirect tax depends upon the particular supply and demand conditions in the market. Whether the tax is borne largely by producers or whether they can pass the greater part of it on to consumers in the form of a higher price depends largely on the elasticities of demand and supply. Figure 40 shows the effect of a tax under differing demand conditions.

In Fig. 40 (a) the demand is elastic and suppliers experience a fall in supply price greater than the increase in market price experienced by the buyers ($YZ > XY$).

In Fig. 40 (b) demand is perfectly elastic; if suppliers raise the price demand falls to zero. In this case suppliers must bear the whole burden of the tax and the supply price falls by the amount *YZ*. Market price does not change but there is a substantial fall in quantity demanded.

In Fig. 40 (c) demand is perfectly inelastic so that suppliers can

(a)

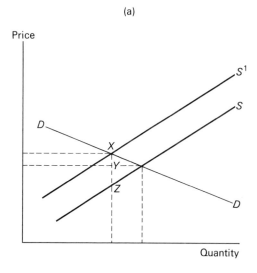

(b)

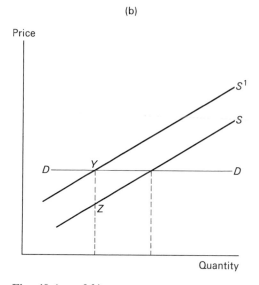

Fig. 40 (a and b)

(c)

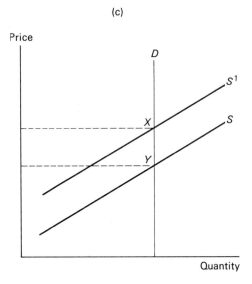

Fig. 40 (c)

pass on the full amount of the tax in the form of a price increase. The consumers bear the whole burden of the tax.

But the elasticity of supply is also relevant. It would be an instructive exercise if the reader now used supply and demand diagrams to show that the more inelastic the supply curve, the greater is the proportion of the tax borne by the producers. In general, if elasticity of demand is greater than elasticity of supply, the producers bear the greater share of the tax burden; if elasticity of demand is less than the elasticity of supply, the consumers bear the greater share.

This analysis, obviously, has great relevance in respect of budgetary policy. If the Chancellor wishes to raise large sums of money from indirect taxation he must concentrate heavily on those commodities for which demand is inelastic (although this is not the only consideration).

Subsidies

Subsidies may be regarded as negative taxes. They normally take the form of payments by governments to producers and are particularly important in the case of agricultural products (wheat, milk, meat, etc.). The effect of a subsidy is to reduce the costs of supplying a commodity. In terms of our supply and demand analysis this means that the supply curve moves downwards by the amount of the subsidy – more is now supplied at any given *market price*. Price will fall and the quantity demanded will increase. This is demonstrated in Fig. 41. Initially the equilibrium price was OP and quantity OQ was demanded and supplied. A subsidy to producers has moved the supply curve from SS to S^1S^1, price has fallen to OP^1 and quantity demanded has increased to OQ^1.

The amount of the subsidy is XZ. Consumers have benefited by a price fall equal to YZ. They now consume more at a lower price. Producers have benefited from an increase in the *supply price* from YQ^1 to XQ^1. They now supply more and receive a higher supply price.

If the demand is elastic, the granting of a subsidy would lead to a relatively small reduction in price, but a relatively large increase in consumption. If demand were inelastic, the movement of the supply curve would lead to a relatively large fall in price and a relatively small increase in the quantity demanded.

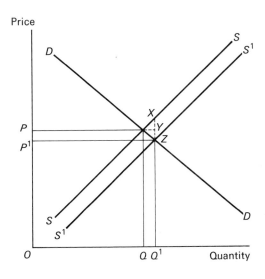

Fig. 41

Guaranteed prices

It is fairly common for governments committed to policies of assisting their agricultural industries to offer farmers guaranteed prices for some of their products. The aim of the government is to provide some stability in farm prices and farm incomes. Fig. 42 helps us to analyse this particular market situation. The true market price is OP but the guaranteed price is OG. At the guaranteed price farmers supply quantity OQ^1, but consumers are only prepared to buy quantity OQ. The government buying agency will be obliged to purchase and store quantity QQ^1. If, in the future, an increase in demand or a fall in supply raises the market price above *OG*, the official stocks can be released in order to maintain an equilibrium at the guaranteed price *OG*. If this guaranteed price approximates to the long-run market price, then the additions to stocks and releases of stocks over the longer period will be roughly in balance.

Another alternative is for the government to buy up the entire output at the guaranteed price and then resell to the public at whatever price it will fetch in a free market. In Fig. 42 this price would be *OR* and the government would be obliged to absorb a loss equal to *OG–OR* on each unit sold.

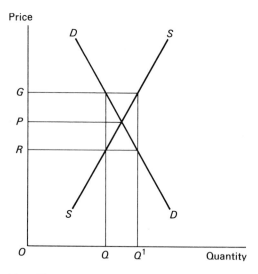

Fig. 42

Mathematical note

Elasticity is a concept which involves the ratio of infinitesimally small changes in price to the resulting changes in quantity. The demand curve is drawn on the assumption that price can be varied by infinitely small amounts. When we come to measure elasticity, problems arise because real world changes in price are *relatively* large.

When we are expressing changes in price and quantity as *proportionate* changes it is usual to take the actual change in *P* or *Q* and express it as a proportion of either the original or final value of *P* or *Q*.

For example, if price changes from 10p to 8p we can express this as either a 20 per cent change or a 25 per cent change. Which is the correct measurement? For most purposes in economics it does not matter which measurement we take, but we should recognise that both calculations will give us a very crude average of an infinitely large number of very small price changes over the range 10p to 8p. The same reasoning can be applied to the quantity changes.

It would, in fact, be more accurate to express the actual changes in P and Q as percentage (or proportionate) changes from the mid-values of the old and new values of P and Q.

For example,

Price	Quantity	Total revenue
40p	140	5 600p
35p	160	5 600p

The fact that total revenue is constant indicates that elasticity of demand over this price range is unity. If, however, we use the conventional calculation of proportionate changes we get,

$$\frac{\text{Proportionate change in } Q}{\text{Proportionate change in } P} = \frac{\dfrac{20}{140}}{\dfrac{5}{40}} = 1 \cdot 14$$

Now using the alternative method,

$$\frac{\text{Proportionate change in } Q}{\text{Proportionate change in } P} = \frac{\dfrac{20}{150}}{\dfrac{5}{37\frac{1}{2}}} = 1 \cdot 0$$

15 Competition in Theory and Practice

We are still concerned mainly with the free enterprise or capitalist system where price movements are a major factor in determining the actions of producers and consumers. It is now time to turn to a study of the various market conditions under which these prices are determined. The capitalist system is said to be based upon the principle of competition and we must, therefore, examine the nature and extent of competition in the markets for goods and services.

In order to assess the degrees of competition in different markets it is necessary to have some kind of 'measuring rod', or 'standard of comparison'. We begin, therefore, by looking at the conditions necessary for a state of perfect competition [1] – an extreme situation in which competition reaches its highest possible degree.

Perfect competition

The economist's model of perfect competition is highly theoretical, but it does provide a useful tool of economic analysis and helps us to make some sense of real world conditions. The real world is much too complicated to understand all at once; it is necessary to examine one feature at a time. Economists are able to use their model of a perfect market as a means of assessing the degree of competition in real world markets. They set out the conditions necessary for a perfect market and then contrast these with the situations found in the markets for goods and services. The degree of competition in these real markets is based upon the extent to which they approximate to the model of perfect competition. It is necessary to point out that the competition referred to here is *price competition*. Firms are assumed to be engaged in a rivalry for sales which takes the form of underselling competitors.

In a market operating under the conditions of perfect competition, there will be one, and only one, market price, and this price will be beyond the influence of any one buyer or any one seller. These conditions can only be satisfied in a market which contains certain characteristics. They are:

1 All units of the commodity are homogeneous (i.e. one unit is exactly like another). If this condition exists, buyers will have no preference for the goods of any particular seller.

---

[1] This should not be taken to mean that it is in some way the most desirable situation.

2 There must be many buyers and many sellers so that the behaviour of any one buyer, or any one seller, has no influence on the market price. Each individual buyer comprises such a small part of total demand and each seller is responsible for such a small part of total supply that any change in their plans will have no influence on the market price.

3 Buyers are assumed to have perfect knowledge of market conditions; they know what prices are being asked for the commodity in every part of the market. Equally sellers are fully aware of the activities of buyers and other sellers.

4 There must be no barriers to the movement of buyers from one seller to another. Since all units of the commodity are identical, buyers will always approach the seller quoting the lowest price.

5 Finally, it is assumed that there are no restrictions on the entry of firms into the market or on their exit from it.

We can now see why, in a perfect market, there will be one and only one market price which is beyond the control of any one buyer or any one seller. Firms cannot charge different prices because they are selling identical products, each of them is responsible for a tiny part of the total supply, and buyers are fully aware of what is happening in the market.

The individual firm under perfect competition

Under conditions of perfect competition the firm is powerless to exert any influence on price. It sees the market price as 'given', that is, established by forces beyond its control. For example, in most countries, the individual farmer has no influence on the prices at which he sells his wheat, or beef, or milk, or vegetables. Any changes in the amounts of these things which he brings to market will have negligible effects on their prices. The firm, under perfect competition, is a 'price-taker'.

The demand curve for the output of the single firm, therefore, must be a horizontal line at the ruling price; in other words, a perfectly elastic demand curve. No matter how many units the firms sells it cannot change the price. It can sell its entire output at the ruling market price. If it tries to sell at higher prices its demand will drop to zero, and there is obviously no incentive to sell at lower prices. Again, we must guard against a common misunderstanding. The demand curve for the product of *the firm* will be perfectly elastic, but the *market demand curve* for the output of *the industry* will be of the normal shape (i.e. sloping downwards from left to right). Market price will be determined by the total demand and supply curves. Figure 43 should make this clear.

Figure 43 (*a*) shows the determination of the market price (*OP*) by the forces of market demand and supply. D^1D^1 is the demand curve facing the industry and *SS* is the total supply provided by all the firms

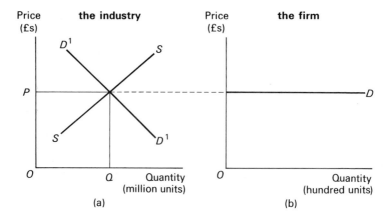

Fig. 43

in that industry. In Fig. 43 (*b*) we have the situation facing the individual firm. Market price (*OP*) is externally determined and the firm sees the demand for its product as being perfectly elastic. In the two diagrams, the scales on the price axes will be the same, but the scales on the quantity axes will be very different, because the firm supplies a negligibly small part of the total output of the product.

Average and marginal revenues

When a firm faces a perfectly elastic demand curve, how does it determine its output? In theory it could sell an infinite amount at the existing market price, because no matter what quantity it sells, it has no influence on the price. The answer to the question is to be found in the shape of the firm's average and marginal cost curves. As explained earlier these curves are assumed to be U-shaped and, if increasing output eventually leads to rising unit costs, there must come a point where the cost of producing a unit of output will exceed its price. It should be apparent that a firm will continue to expand its output as long as the revenue it receives from additional output exceeds the cost of producing that additional output. This leads us to consider how a firm's revenue changes as its output changes. There are three ways of looking at a firm's revenues.

a Total revenue (TR) is quite simply the money value of the total amount sold.

b Average revenue (AR) is another name for price because it is equal to revenue per unit sold.

i.e. $AR = \dfrac{\text{Total revenue}}{\text{Number of units sold}}$

In economic theory, the demand curve or price line is often referred to as the average revenue curve.

c Marginal revenue (MR) is the additional revenue obtained when sales are increased by one unit, or, more precisely, it is the change in total revenue when the quantity sold is varied by one unit. For example,

The marginal revenue of the 10th unit	=	Total revenue from sale of 10 units	*minus*	Total revenue from sale of 9 units

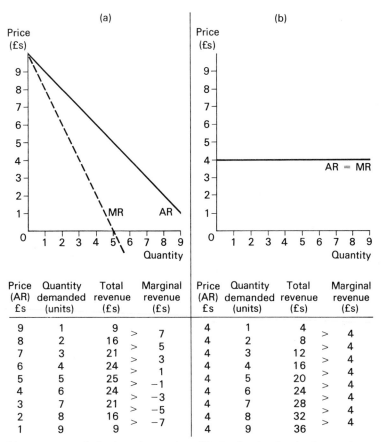

Price (AR) £s	Quantity demanded (units)	Total revenue (£s)	Marginal revenue (£s)
9	1	9	
8	2	16	7
7	3	21	5
6	4	24	3
5	5	25	1
4	6	24	−1
3	7	21	−3
2	8	16	−5
1	9	9	−7

Price (AR) £s	Quantity demanded (units)	Total revenue (£s)	Marginal revenue (£s)
4	1	4	
4	2	8	4
4	3	12	4
4	4	16	4
4	5	20	4
4	6	24	4
4	7	28	4
4	8	32	4
4	9	36	4

(a) Downward sloping demand curve

(b) Perfectly elastic demand curve

Fig. 44

The purpose of Figure 44 is to demonstrate the relationships between AR and MR under different market conditions.

1 A downward-sloping demand curve

In Figure 44 (*a*) the demand curve slopes downwards from left to right indicating that sales can only be increased by cutting prices. In these circumstances the sale of one more unit of output does not increase TR by an amount equal to the price at which that unit is sold. An examination of the table under Figure 44 (*a*) should make this clear. For example, in order to increase sales from 3 units to 4 units, price must be reduced from £7 to £6. The extra unit will be sold for £6, but TR will only increase by £3. The net gain in revenue (MR) of £3 is equal to the additional £6 from the sale of the 4th unit minus the revenue foregone (£3) resulting from the £1 reduction in the price of the first 3 units. If the demand curve slopes downward, therefore, MR will always be less than AR (i.e. price).

2 A perfectly elastic demand curve

In Figure 44 (*b*) we have a perfectly elastic demand curve of the type faced by the firm operating under perfect competition. In this case MR must always be equal to AR. As the quantity sold increases, the price remains unchanged so that each additional unit sold increases total revenue by an amount equal to its price.

The output of the firm under perfect competition

a In the short-run

We assume that the firm is in business to make profits and that it will aim to maximise profits. As long as the price (AR) it receives for each unit exceeds the average cost of production, the firm will be making profits. Thus, in Figure 45 when price = OP, the firm will be making profits in the range of output OQ to OQ^3, because at all outputs in this range, AR is greater than AC.

We have to determine which output between OQ and OQ^3 yields the maximum profit. It should be apparent that output OQ^1 will yield the maximum profit *per unit*, but firms seek to maximise total profit not profit per unit. We notice that,

a As output increases from OQ to OQ^2, the firm's total profit will be increasing because for each additional unit produced, the increase in total revenue (i.e. MR) is greater than the increase in total cost (i.e. MC). Remember that in this particular case, MR = AR.

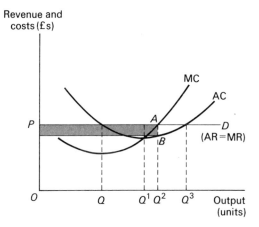

Fig. 45

b As output is expanded beyond OQ^2, total profit will be decreasing, because, for each additional unit produced, the increase in total revenue (i.e. MR) is less than the increase in total cost (i.e. MC).

Therefore since total profit is increasing up to OQ^2 and falling beyond OQ^2, profits must be maximised when output is at OQ^2, that is, when Marginal Revenue = Marginal Cost. It is important that the explanation above is fully understood, because the relationship which has been derived, i.e. *profits are maximised when output is at the point where MR = MC*, applies to all firms whether they are operating in perfect competition or are monopolies.

In the case of the perfectly competitive firm illustrated in Fig. 45, demand is perfectly elastic so that AR = MR. Thus, in this particular case, we can say that maximum profits will be earned where AR = MR = MC.

Normal and abnormal profit

The economist takes the view that some level of profit, described as *normal profit*, should be regarded as a cost of production. Normal profit is the minimum level of profit which will persuade an entrepreneur to stay in business. It will vary from industry to industry depending upon the degree of risk involved. Since production will not continue unless this minimum level of profit is forthcoming, normal profit may be legitimately regarded as a cost of production. Normal profits, therefore, are included in the calculations which produce the AC curve. Therefore, when price exceeds average cost, the firm is said to be earning *abnormal profits*. Excess or abnormal profits are illustrated by the shaded area in Fig. 45. When output is at OQ^2, the cost per unit is equal to BQ^2, but the price is equal to AQ^2. Abnormal profit per unit, therefore, is AB. Total abnormal profit is equal to the area $AB \times OQ^2$ (i.e. the shaded area).

(b) In the long-run

Although the *firm* in Fig. 45 is in equilibrium, the *industry* is not in equilibrium. There will be forces at work tending to change the size of the industry. One of the assumptions of perfect competition is freedom of entry. The situation depicted in Fig. 45 will not persist in the long run, because the abnormal profits being earned by the existing firms will attract other firms into this industry. As new firms come in, total supply will increase, market price will fall, and the process will continue until the abnormal profits have been 'competed away'. What happens is that the supply curve in Fig. 43 (a) will move to the right and bring down the market price. The long-run equilibrium of the firm is shown in Fig. 46. The market price has fallen to OP^1 and the most profitable output is now OQ^1, where AR = MR = MC. Note that price, or average revenue, is now equal to average cost so that the firm is making only normal profits. There is no incentive for firms to enter or leave the industry so that both the firm and the industry are in equilibrium. The long-run equilibrium of the firm, therefore, is to be found where,

$$AR = MR = MC = AC$$

In theory, the system of perfect competition produces a long-run equilibrium where all firms earn only normal profits *and* produce at minimum cost.

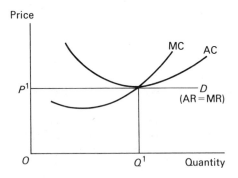

Fig. 46

The above analysis is based on the assumptions that (i) factors of production are perfectly mobile, (ii) there is perfect knowledge, and (iii) there are no barriers to entry. All the firms, therefore, are assumed to have identical cost curves and, in the long run, they will all be in the position shown in Fig. 46.

This is not a very realistic assumption. Even if all units of land, labour, and capital were equally efficient and available to all firms on identical terms, it is most unlikely that all entrepreneurs will have the same outlook, the same ability, and the same energy. If equally efficient entrepreneurs are not freely available to all firms, we must allow that the cost curves of individual firms will not be the same. There will be high-cost and low-cost firms. Equilibrium in the industry will now obtain when the least efficient or *marginal firm* is just making normal profits. Some firms, therefore, even in the long term, will be making abnormal profits.

Perfect competition is not to be found in the real world, although it is possible to point to some markets where there is some rough approximation to this 'ideal'. There are hundreds of thousands of wheat producers all over the world and no one of them is large enough to influence the world price of wheat. The world markets for a number of agricultural products contain many of the features of a perfect market. There are many producers and many buyers; modern methods of communication make knowledge of market conditions almost perfect, and the standardised grading of commodities means that the products in any one grade are regarded as homogeneous. Another, often quoted, example of a market which bears some resemblance to a perfect market is the Stock Exchange, the market in stocks and shares.

A note on the supply curve

The foregoing explanation of how a firm under perfect competition determines its output may be used to explain the shape of the individual firm's supply curve and the general shape of the total supply curve for the industry. It has been shown that firms attempt to set their outputs at the point where MR = MC. For the firm in perfect competition, MR is always equal to AR (i.e. price) so that the individual firm will try to adjust its output so as to equate price and marginal cost.

In the conditions shown in Figure 47, when the market price is OP the firm will produce output OQ. If the market price falls to OP^1, the firm, in trying to maximise profit, will reduce output to OQ^1. The MC curve, therefore, is acting as the firm's supply curve, because it is determining the quantity supplied at any given price. If the market price falls to OP^2, the firm will adjust its output to OQ^2 (where price equals marginal cost). At this point, however, Price = MC = AC so that the firm will be making no more than normal profits.

If market price falls below OP^2, the firm will be making losses because, at all outputs, price will be less than average cost. Thus when

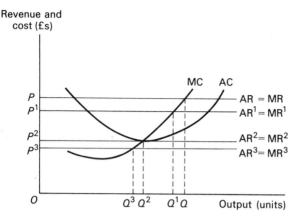

Fig. 47

price is OP^3 the firm will be making losses, but at this price, OQ^3 still represents the 'most profitable' output in the sense that it represents the output at which losses are minimised. In the short-run, the firm may still produce even when price is less than average total cost. As long as price exceeds average variable cost, the firm will be receiving some revenue which can be used to pay part of the fixed costs whereas if the firm were to shut down temporarily, it would still have to meet the whole of its fixed costs.

What this analysis demonstrates is the fact that the supply curve of the individual firm, in the long run, is that part of the MC curve which lies above the AC curve. It slopes upwards from left to right because increasing output gives rise to increasing marginal cost. The total or market supply curve for a commodity is obtained by adding together the supply curves of all the firms producing that commodity. This total supply curve is described as the industry supply curve. We must bear in mind, however, that the supply curve for an industry is affected by the movement of firms into and out of the industry. If market price rises, not only will existing firms produce more, there will also be new firms moving into the industry. Similarly, falling prices will cause existing firms to reduce output and some of the higher cost firms will be driven out of the industry.

Monopoly

Monopoly power

Monopoly in the market place indicates the existence of a *sole supplier*. It may take the form of a unified business organisation, or it may be an association of separately controlled firms which combine, or act together, for the purpose of marketing their products (e.g. they may charge common prices). This latter example indicates that monopoly power is concerned with *supply* – it does not necessarily mean that there is one producer. The main point is that buyers are facing a single seller.

A monopolist has the power to determine *either*,

a The price at which he will sell his product.
b The quantity he wishes to sell.

He cannot determine both price and quantity, because he cannot control demand. If he decides on the price at which he is prepared to sell, the demand curve will determine the quantity he can dispose of at the chosen price. If he wishes to market a given quantity per month, then the demand curve will determine the price at which this quantity may be disposed of. The monopolist's power to influence price depends upon two factors.
(i)   The availability of close substitutes.
(ii) The power to restrict the entry of new firms.
These two features are closely related because (ii) has some influence on (i).

If there are a number of substitutes available,[1] the prices of which compare favourably with the price of the monopolist's product, his market power will be very limited.

Monopoly power has been defined as the ability to earn *long-run* abnormal profits. We know from our analysis of perfect competition that this will only be possible if there are some effective barriers to the entry of new firms. The more effective the restrictions on the emergence of new firms, the greater will be the power of the monopolist to exploit the consumer by charging prices well above his average cost.

Monopoly output

Since the monopolist is a sole supplier of a commodity, the demand curve for his product is the total or market demand curve. The AR and MR curves for the monopolist, therefore will be similar to those illustrated in Figure 44 (a). If we combine these AR and MR curves with the conventional cost curves, as in Figure 48 we can determine the most profitable output. It has already been demonstrated that this output occurs where MR = MC.

Figure 48 is an important diagram and may be interpreted as follows.
1 Maximum profits are attained when output is at *OQ* where MR = MC. The reasoning should now be familiar. At lower outputs each

---

[1] See p. 211 for reference to branded goods.

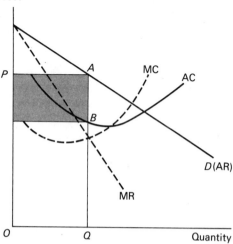

Fig. 48

unit produced adds more to revenue than to costs. When output is greater than OQ each additional unit adds more to costs than to revenue.

2 The price at which output OQ can be sold is determined by the demand curve. Thus, output OQ will be marketed at price OP.

3 At the output level OQ, average cost equals QB and abnormal profit per unit is AB.

4 Total abnormal profit, therefore, is equal to $AB \times OQ$ and is represented by the shaded area.

We can now summarise some of the distinctions between a monopolist and a firm operating under perfect competition.

a The monopolist does not have to take price as given; he can vary the price of his product by varying output. The perfectly competitive firm is a price-taker.

b The demand curve for the monopolist's product is less than perfectly elastic. The firm under perfect competition faces a perfectly elastic demand curve.

c The monopolist has the power to restrict the entry of new firms. Under perfect competition there are no barriers to entry.

d The monopolist can earn abnormal profits even in the long run. Under perfect competition, abnormal profits will be competed away in the long run.

Restrictions on entry

Monopoly power depends upon the effectiveness of the barriers which prevent potential competitors from entering that particular industry. These restrictions on entry can arise in a number of ways:

a Concentration of raw materials

The geographical distribution of natural resources is very uneven and the known or workable deposits of some materials are concentrated into very small regions (although new discoveries are continually changing the situation). At one time most of world's nickel was obtained from a certain area in the Rockies; a large proportion of the total world supply of gold and diamonds comes from South Africa; and, until the development of artificial fertilisers, Chile had a virtual monopoly of the world supply of nitrates. Peculiarities of soil and climatic conditions can also provide certain regions with monopoly powers. Until quite recently parts of the southern USA had a monopoly in the supply of soyabeans. This particular feature is most strikingly illustrated in the supply of wines where we have such products as Champagne, Burgundy, and Moselle clearly associated with the areas where they are produced.

b Technical barriers

In modern capitalist states there are a number of industries which are dominated by a few giant firms. Where the existing firms are already operating on a vast scale, making use of expensive indivisible units of capital, and enjoying extensive technical economies of scale, the barriers to the entry of new firms are quite formidable. There is very little prospect of a new entrant starting in a small way and growing larger by increasing his share of the market. The smaller producer could not compete with the existing firms because his average cost of production would be so much greater. Only by commencing operations on a scale comparable to that employed by existing firms would a new entrant be able to compete effectively. Even this would be very risky unless the market had a very large growth potential, because the large increase in supply would seriously depress market prices. Existing firms in such industries are in a protected position and this is an inducement to form a monopoly.

c Advertising and branding

Where a market is dominated by one, or very few, large firms each of which is marketing a number of heavily advertised brands, it is extremely difficult for a new firm to break into the market. The initial advertising costs of establishing a new brand in such a market is a formidable deterrent. For example, if there are 3 existing firms each selling 4 brands, a new producer faces the prospect of very costly advertising in order to establish his product. But, even if he succeeds in taking a proportionate share of this market, he will only have one-thirteenth of it – he is competing with 12 brands rather than 3 firms.

d Legal barriers

Probably the most formidable restrictions against the entry of new firms are legal barriers where the law of the land operates to prevent the emergence of competing firms. This particular form of restriction has a long history. The great overseas trading companies formed in the fifteenth and sixteenth centuries were granted monopoly rights in specified geographical areas. These rights were granted by the Crown in the form of Royal Charters. The Hudson's Bay Company and the East India Company are two of the more famous of these trading companies which were granted the sole right to trade in certain regions. Much later, public utility companies formed by Act of Parliament to provide water, gas, and electricity were granted local monopoly powers, but were subject to some degree of public regulation (they were privately owned).

More recently we have the examples of the nationalised industries where the controlling boards have been granted monopoly powers. The National Coal Board, for example, has complete monopoly powers over the production and wholesale supply of coal in the United Kingdom.

The granting of patent rights is a further important example of competition being limited by law. The firm holding the patent is protected from the threat of competition from new firms (or existing firms) making identical products, at least for the period of time which is the life of the patent, usually 16 years.

e Transport costs and tariffs

Although two or more firms may be making identical products and operating at similar costs, it is possible for such firms to enjoy local monopoly positions. Firm A will be able to sell more cheaply in its own locality than Firm B since Firm B's additional transport costs will increase its selling prices in Firm A's local market. Thus Firm A will be able to raise its prices, in the local market, above its production costs by an amount which does not exceed Firm B's transport costs. We know that shops in villages or suburbs are sometimes able to charge a little more than the larger stores in city centres because they have some degree of protection in the form of transport costs (e.g. bus fares).

Tariffs operate to protect a home market against competition from foreign producers. They have the same economic effect as transport costs, for they raise the price in the home market above the foreign producer's costs of production. Tariffs may encourage the formation of monopolies among domestic producers since, as a monopoly, they could raise market price by the extent of any differential between their own costs and the artificially high price of the foreign commodity.

f Restrictive practices

Although in most countries they are now subject to legal control and many of them have been made illegal, agreements between firms to restrict competition in an industry have been an important means of establishing monopoly situations. There are many ways in which the existing firms in an industry can combine to prevent the entry of new firms. For example, they might act collectively to withhold supplies from any wholesaler or retailer who stocks the goods of any new producer. These restrictive agreements are discussed in the next section.

Monopolistic practices

Although the word 'monopoly' conjures up a picture of a single large firm, this is by no means the general form taken by monopoly organisation. Much more pervasive in the structure of industry, prior to the UK legislation on monopolies, was the situation where groups of independently controlled firms actively collaborated in operating agreements to restrict competition within an industry. If an industry is made up of say 10 or 20 firms but they agree to restrict competition between themselves, say by means of a price agreement, then we have a monopoly situation. Effectively the buyers are facing a single seller. A report by the UK Monopolies Commission in 1955 indicated that such *restrictive trade practices* were a common feature of the business world. As already noted, many of these practices have now been abandoned or declared illegal, but it might be interesting to look at some those which were widely practised.[1]

Exclusive dealing and collective boycott

Producers agree to supply only recognised dealers, normally only one dealer in each area, on condition that the dealer does not stock the products of any producer outside the group (or trade association). Should the dealer break the agreement, all members of the group

---

[1] Some are still practised, with official approval.

agree to withhold supplies from the offender. This practice has proved a very effective restriction on competition for it means that any new firms would find it extremely difficult to secure market outlets for their products.

Price and output agreements

The firms in an industry (or the majority of them) may agree not to compete on price and, where the product is fairly standardised, they may agree to charge common prices. The agreed price is normally well above the average costs of the more efficient firms since, in order to persuade enough firms to join the scheme to make it operational, the price must be high enough to provide profits for the less efficient. In order to make the price effective, a price agreement is usually supported by a complementary agreement to limit output (e.g. firms agree to accept output quotas).

Cartels

In its most developed form a cartel comprises a selling syndicate, formed by a group of firms, through which the outputs of the member firms are marketed. The syndicate or selling agency pays the producers a fixed price for their outputs and markets the product as a single seller. Profits are distributed to member firms in proportion to outputs. Marketing boards such as the British Milk Marketing Board are, in fact, a type of cartel.

Collusive tendering

There are many goods which are not produced 'in anticipation of demand', but are made 'to order'. The buyers announce their requirements by publishing a specification and producers are invited to tender for the contract to supply. This is the normal procedure in the building industry, the civil engineering industry, shipbuilding, and heavy engineering. The preparation of a tender for the building of a bridge or the erection of large industrial plant can be an expensive operation and, since only one firm can succeed in getting the contract, the unsuccessful bidders incur heavy nonrecoverable expenses. In some industries producers have combined to eliminate competition by means of schemes which ensure that the available contracts are shared out between the cooperating firms. This may be done by the various firms agreeing not to submit lower tenders than the firm which is entitled to the next contract.

The pooling of patents

In some industries, especially the technically advanced industries, competition may be seriously restricted when the existing firms combine for the purpose of pooling the patents held by individual firms. Technical cooperation of this type means that the firms which are party to the agreement have access to a substantial amount of technical expertise and specialised equipment which is denied to any potential competitors.

Resale price maintenance

This is the practice whereby the manufacturer fixes the price of his product at each stage of distribution. Although the goods are being distributed by independent wholesalers and retailers they are obliged to charge prices which are laid down by the manufacturers. It means, of course, that the profit margins at these subsequent stages are being fixed by the manufacturers. Resale price maintenance can be enforced by manufacturers either collectively or individually by the threat of withholding supplies if the distributor breaks the price agreement. At one time in the UK manufacturers were given the right to enforce RPM through the courts. RPM is a practice which prevents price competition taking place at the retail stage. Shops cannot pass on any improvements in efficiency in the form of lower prices. It almost certainly maintains prices at higher levels than would be the case if RPM were not in force. Manufacturers anxious to maintain the maximum number of retail outlets tend to fix retail prices at levels which give satisfactory profits to the less efficient retailers. Legislation in 1964 effectively ended the practice of RPM in the UK. (See page 224.)

Discriminating monopoly

One of the criticisms of monopoly is based on the fact that a monopolist is often able to discriminate in his pricing policy. He can charge different prices in different markets for the same commodity. Three basic conditions are necessary for such a policy to be effective and profitable.

1 In order to charge different prices the seller must be able to control the supply otherwise competitors would undersell him in the dearer market. Only a monopolist has the power to determine the price (or prices) at which he sells his commodity.
2 The markets must be clearly separated so that those paying lower prices cannot resell to those paying higher prices.
3 The demand conditions in the separate markets must be different so

that total profits may be increased by charging different prices. It is really a matter of separating a group of consumers willing to pay higher prices from those that are only able or willing to pay lower prices.

We have plenty of evidence from our everyday experience to show that these conditions can be met. Markets may be separated by a time barrier. Most passenger transport undertakings charge cheaper rates for off-peak journeys. Electricity and telephone charges are varied according to the time at which they are consumed. These are examples of services which cannot be transferred from the cheaper to the dearer market.

Markets may be separated by transport costs and tariffs. Firms often sell their goods more cheaply in export markets than in the home market. The price differential, of course, cannot exceed the cost of transporting the good back to the home market plus any tariff on imports.

A third type of price discrimination is found where it is possible to separate buyers into clearly defined groups. Before the National Health Service was established doctors commonly charged lower fees to poorer patients than to their wealthier clients. Milk is sold more cheaply to industrial users than to householders. Electricity charges also vary according to the type of consumer.

Price discrimination means that some groups are charged higher prices than others and although this may be regarded as an 'unfair' practice it is possible for price discrimination to be beneficial. Where it leads to a great expansion of sales and output and a significant fall in average costs of production, even those in the higher priced market may be obtaining goods at lower prices than they would be charged in a single market. For example, a large export market (gained by selling at prices lower than the home price) may lead to economies of scale which benefit home consumers even though the home price is higher than the export price.

Monopoly and competition – some comparisons

Prices and outputs

Economic theory indicates that, under monopoly, output will be lower and price will be higher than would be the case under perfect competition. We have seen that firms in a perfect market produce where price equals marginal cost, and competition between these firms forces price downwards until it is equal to minimum average cost (see Figs. 45 and 46).

A monopolist, however, has the power to restrict market supply and he will adjust his output until marginal revenue equals marginal cost. At this output, as Fig. 48 shows, price is greater than marginal cost, and greater than average cost.

Under perfect competition,   PRICE = MC = AC
Under monopoly,   PRICE > MC and PRICE > AC

This is probably the major argument against monopoly. Critics point to the power to exploit consumers by charging prices well above average cost and they assume that the desire for profits will lead to the abuse of this market power. Allied to this argument is the charge that monopolists can indulge in price discrimination and oblige one group of consumers to subsidise another group. The argument here is not against the principle of subsidisation, but against the system which allows the monopolist to decide which group should benefit and which group lose.

Economies of scale

The argument that monopoly will lead to higher prices and lower outputs is based upon the assumption that, if a competitive industry were monopolised, the costs of production would be unaffected. This is not very realistic. If a number of small competing firms are combined into one large integrated enterprise then many of the economies described in Chapter 7 become attainable. These economies of scale, if achieved, would mean that the cost curves of the monopolist would be lower than those of a competitive industry.

In industries where there are many competing firms each producing its own particular design or model (e.g. parts and components in electrical and mechanical engineering), monopolisation would make possible a much greater degree of standardisation. This would be an important factor in making larger scale production possible.

It may be that in some industries the total market (e.g. for some small standardised part for motor cars) could be supplied by one firm of optimum size. In this case a single supplier would operate at much lower cost than several smaller competing firms.

The economies of scale argument in favour of monopoly is very strong in the case of the public utilities supplying water, gas, electricity, and telephone services. In all these industries fixed costs form a very high proportion of total costs and competition would mean a wasteful duplication of fixed capital. A number of competing firms would have fixed costs similar to those of a single supplier (e.g. competing electricity supply companies would all have to lay main services), but they would each have only a fraction of the total market over which to spread their fixed costs. Average cost would be much higher in a competitive industry than in a monopoly.

Economies of scale are attainable where the monopoly takes the form of a unified enterprise which takes advantage of the possibilities arising from rationalisation and standardisation. It does not follow that these gains will always be achieved by a monopoly organisation, neither does it necessarily follow that any economies so achieved will be passed on to consumers in the form of lower prices.

Efficiency and innovation

Those who believe in the virtues of competition argue that the absence of such competition will lead to less efficient production. The monopolist is not 'kept on his toes' by the pressures from competing producers. He does not have the same incentive to improve his product and his methods as does a firm in a competitive framework. On the other hand it is pointed out that, when there is a single supplier, much of the 'waste' of competitive advertising is eliminated. Competition may lead to an excessive variety of product which prevents the industry achieving economies from large-scale production.

The monopolist, of course, does have an incentive to improve his performance since any reduction in costs means larger profits. The fact that a monopolist is earning profits cannot, in itself, be taken as an indication that the firm is efficient since a monopolist can use his market power to raise prices in order to cover costs.

The lack of competition is often used to support the view that monopoly leads to a slowing down of the rate of technical progress. The monopolist, it is argued, has little incentive to innovate, that is, to develop new products and new techniques of production. If he does not innovate, his control of the market means that he can still make profits. The competitive firm, however, may fear that if it does not innovate it will lose its market to its competitors who *will* take advantage of new developments. Monopoly is also accused of retarding technical progress by restricting the entry of new firms. It is important that entrepreneurs with progressive ideas should be free to put them to the test in the open market. When an industry is monopolised, this source of new ideas may be lost to the community.

On the other hand there is much support for the view that monopoly organisation encourages technical progress. A unified monopoly is more likely to have the resources required for research and development than a small firm in a competitive market. In addition the monopolist has more incentive to innovate since his secure market ensures that he obtains all the gains from any successful new technique or product. He can, moreover, retain these gains over the long run. Under competition any innovation will soon be copied and the gains to the innovator will be short-lived (although the patent laws provide some protection).

Stability

One argument in favour of monopoly is that it provides greater stability of output and prices. In a competitive market producers respond to market signals (i.e. price changes) in the expected manner. If an increase in demand leads to higher prices, producers will react by revising their production plans upwards. But the aggregate effect of a very large number of individual decisions to raise output is likely to be excess supply in the next marketing period. This will lead to a sharp fall in prices and producers will revise their output plans downwards. Again, the total effect is likely to be an over-adjustment and a severe shortage in the next marketing period with a corresponding rise in prices. A highly competitive market, especially where there is a substantial time lag between the decision to produce and the availability of supplies, is likely to be characterised by fairly extensive price swings.

A monopolist, on the other hand, is likely to react to demand changes in a more effective manner. He supplies the total market and should be capable of estimating the true extent of market trends much more accurately than a small firm supplying a tiny part of the market. His adjustments of output, therefore, are likely to bring about an equilibrium situation fairly quickly. This particular argument provides the basis for many cartels (often government inspired) in the markets for agricultural products such as coffee, cocoa, and milk.

Monopolistic competition (Imperfect competition)

Perfect competition is not to be found in the real world and absolute or pure monopoly is also virtually impossible to achieve since it implies operating in the absence of competition (i.e. no substitutes). While it is not difficult for a firm to become a sole supplier (by the use of brand names and trade marks) it is extremely difficult to achieve a situation where there are no substitutes for the product. A more realistic definition of monopoly would be 'a sole supplier of a commodity for which there are no very good substitutes'. In fact the degree of monopoly in the real world tends to be judged on the basis of the share of the total market accounted for by any particular supplier. If a single enterprise accounted for, say, 50 per cent of the total market, it would be deemed to have a significant degree of monopoly power (i.e. the power to influence the prices of the products in this market).

Product differentiation

Modern capitalism is characterised by a large number of 'limited' monopolies. They are sole suppliers of branded goods, but other firms compete with them by selling similar goods with different brand names. This is the market situation described as *monopolistic* or *imperfect competition*. Thus the commodities produced by any one industry are not homogeneous; the goods are differentiated by *branding* and the use of trade marks. The individual firm has a monopoly position (e.g. only ICI can supply Dulux), but it faces keen competition from firms supplying very similar goods. It has, therefore, only a limited degree of monopoly power – how much depends upon the extent to which firms are free to enter the industry. Product differentiation is emphasised (some would say, created) by the practice of *competitive advertising* which is, perhaps, the most striking feature of monopolistic competition.

Advertising is employed to heighten in the consumer's mind the differences between Brand X and Brand Y. It is important to realise that we are concerned with the differentiation of goods in the economic sense and not in the technical sense. Two branded products may be almost identical in their technical features or chemical composition, but if advertising and other selling practices have created different images in the consumer's mind, then these products are different from our point of view because the consumer will be prepared to pay different prices for them.

Output and price

Although each producer is a monopolist, and the demand curve for his product will slope downwards, the availability of close substitutes will mean that the demand curve for his product will be fairly elastic. The market situation of the firm under monopolistic competition is shown in Fig. 49. The demand curve (AR) slopes downwards because brand loyalties exist. An increase in price would result in some loss of sales, but some customers would be retained. A cut in price would capture some customers from competitors, but others will remain loyal to the brands they have become accustomed to.

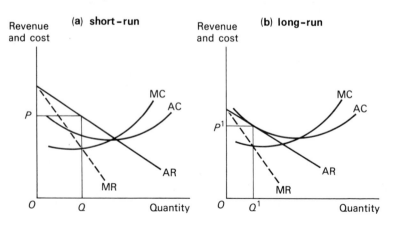

Fig. 49

In the short run (Fig. 49a), output is determined where MC = MR and abnormal profits are earned. This would be typical of a successful new product. In the long run, if there are no barriers to entry, new firms would be attracted by the abnormal profits and the increased competition would push the demand curve to the left until it was tangential to the AC curve (Fig. 49b). In this situation the firm is only making normal profits. At any output other than OQ^1 the firm would be making losses. The most profitable output (OQ^1), as always, is determined where MC = MR.

Oligopoly

In many industries, especially the science-based, and technologically advanced industries, we find a market situation known as oligopoly. As the name implies, this is where the market is dominated 'by the few'. In other words, a small number of very large firms account for practically the whole output of the industry. Good examples of oligopoly are to be found in the industries producing oil, detergents, tyres, motor cars, synthetic fibres, and cigarettes.

Where there are important technical economies of scale to be gained, the processes of merger and amalgamation have drastically reduced the number of firms in an industry and brought into being some very large business units. In several industries in the UK more than 90 per cent of the market is supplied by no more than three or four firms.

Competition among the few, especially where each one of the few is a giant firm supplying a significant share of the market, presents very difficult problems in economic analysis. Oligopoly does not really fit into the framework we have used for monopoly and perfect competition for the simple reason that we cannot use the assumption that 'other things remain equal'. Remember that the demand curves used in the preceding analysis are drawn on the assumption that if a firm changes its price other things will not change. We cannot make this assumption for oligopoly because each firm has such a powerful influence on the total market that any change in its marketing policies is almost certain to provoke some reaction from its rivals. But what that reaction will be is uncertain. If a firm cuts its price it may finish up with increased sales, or it may find itself selling less. It all depends on how its rivals react. If they counter-attack by making even larger price cuts, the firm which started the process may well lose some of its market. If its competitors react with relatively smaller price cuts, the firm may be able to increase its share of the market. The uncertainty about what happens when an oligopolist changes his price means that we cannot use the normal demand curve in analysing the determination of output. Economists do, however, use a diagram of a kinked demand curve in order to explain why price in oligopolistic markets tends to be much more stable than in competitive conditions.

A kinked demand curve

In Fig. 50 the price is *OP* and output is *OQ*. The demand curve is kinked at *G*. At prices higher than *OP*, demand is very elastic. The explanation is that the oligopolist fears that if he raises price his competitors will not follow him and he will lose a large part of his market. At prices lower than *OP*, demand is inelastic because the oligopolist believes that if he cuts his price his rivals will follow suit and he will gain relatively little in the way of additional sales.

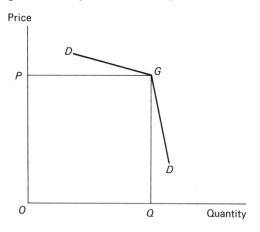

Fig. 50

Oligopolists, therefore, are not very keen to indulge in severe price competition. They know that any move on the part of one firm to reduce its price will provoke similar action from the other firms. The final result is likely to be that all the firms will finish up selling at lower prices while their market shares remain much the same as before the price war.

Non-price competition

This unpleasant prospect encourages oligopolists to favour some sort of tacit agreement on prices. They may decide to accept price leadership from the largest firm – moving their prices in line with that firm's prices, or arrange in some other way for their prices to stay in line (although in most countries restrictive price agreements are illegal). The level at which prices are fixed depends upon the effectiveness of the barriers to entry. Where these are not very restrictive, prices may be very little higher than the competitive price, but, if the existing firms are very large, the barriers are likely to be formidable and prices could be fixed much higher than the competitive price.

The reluctance to indulge in price competition has given rise to many types of non-price competition. We are all familiar with the free gift schemes, the use of trading stamps, and 'special offers'. Firms also compete on the bases of better or more attractive packaging, improved after-sales service, and more luxurious retail outlets. The most important form of non-price competition, of course, is advertising.

Do firms maximise profits?

In the real world of imperfect competition, firms have some degree of discretion in determining the prices of their products. In the previous discussions on this subject it has been assumed that firms will always adjust prices or outputs so as to maximise profits. There is much argument as to whether this is a realistic assumption about the behaviour of firms in modern industrialised societies. The validity of the assumption of profit maximisation has been questioned on several grounds.

1 It has been pointed out that many businesspeople are not aware of the concepts of marginal revenue and marginal cost and, of those who do have knowledge of these ideas, many would find it extremely difficult to obtain any precise measurements of MC and MR. It is sometimes said, therefore, that firms do not maximise profits because they lack the knowledge necessary for them to do so.

But even if the foregoing assertions are true, they do not destroy the profit-maximisation theory. If businesspeople try to increase profits by trial and error adjustments of their prices, they will be tending towards the output where $MR = MC$, even if they are unaware of these concepts.

2 If firms tried to maintain output at the point where $MR = MC$, it is likely that prices would be very unstable because firms would have to adjust price and output levels following every change in cost and demand conditions. Many firms are reluctant to carry out frequent changes in price because such changes impose administrative costs and they lead to a loss of goodwill on the part of their customers. Instead of making frequent changes in price so as to equate MR and MC and maximise profits in the short-run, firms may be more concerned with the longer-run effects of their pricing policies, that is, they will take into account the effects of today's prices on tomorrow's sales. It has been suggested that this type of behaviour does not conflict with the idea that firms try to maximise profits since they are attempting to maximise long-run rather than short-run profits.

3 Some studies of businesspeople's activities have led to the view that, rather than trying to maximise profits, some firms tend to opt for a 'quiet life'. They seem content with some acceptable level of profit which might be less than they could earn if they adopted more fiercely competitive policies. Managements may be reluctant to accept the increased risks and pressures which go with more aggressive and ambitious practices. While this option may be available to a firm with some degree of monopoly power, firms in very competitive markets, where no firm has any significant market power, must attempt to maximise profits in order to survive.

4 The fact that larger firms are not directly controlled by shareholders (the people most likely to be interested in profit-maximisation), but by professional managers provides another basis for criticising the theory of profit-maximisation. The status, prestige, and remuneration of managers is closely linked to the size of the firm and it is likely, therefore, that such people will be more interested in maximising sales rather than maximising profits. They cannot be indifferent to the profit and loss account of the firm, but, having achieved a level of profit which they believe will satisfy shareholders, managers are more inclined to make sales-maximisation their major objective.

5 Several investigations into business practices have revealed the fact that a large number of firms fix their prices on what is described as a *full-cost* basis. Estimates are prepared of the firm's average total cost. There is evidence that this may be constant over a wide range of output. To this average cost figure management adds some conventional profit margin (described as the 'mark-up') and this determines the price at which the product is marketed. Sales are determined by what the market will absorb at this price (i.e. by demand). Under this system the critical decision is the extent of the mark-up. It seems that the mark-up is periodically adjusted in the light of changes in demand conditions and the extent of competition from other firms. If this is so, full-cost pricing may be the industrialist's way of moving towards the price/output combination which yields maximum profits.

We must recognise the fact that there is no theory of the behaviour of the firm which commands general acceptance. Firms clearly can have several goals, for example, profits, stability, maximum sales, protecting their share of the market, management status, and so on. There is no theory which successfully embraces all these aspects of decision-making. The assumption of profit-maximisation is useful because it is simple to understand and enables us to construct a theory of business behaviour. It possibly describes the way in which firms behave at least as well as any other plausible assumption.

16 Monopoly and Public Policy

The bases of the policy

There appears to be a generally held opinion that monopoly is against the public interest. The case against monopoly is based mainly on the assumptions we have already outlined, namely, higher prices, abnormal profits (i.e. a redistribution of income from consumers to producers), price discrimination, and the lack of competition which leads to inefficiency and a slower rate of technical progress.

For centuries the common law in Britain has held that 'agreements in restraint of trade' are against the public interest, but the courts have tended to interpret this law very leniently. Legislation specifically designed to deal with monopoly and monopolistic practices was not introduced in the UK until 1948. In spite of a generally unfavourable public opinion, the legislation has not made monopolies illegal (as was the case in the USA). It has been recognised that there might be circumstances where monopoly organisation could be justified. For example, monopoly in the home market might be necessary in order to obtain important economies of scale which, in turn, would lead to lower-priced exports. Firms which operate agreements to restrict competition between themselves might, as a consequence, collaborate in cost-reducing research and development. An agreement to restrict competition might be necessary in order to ensure a domestic source of supply. For example, an efficient plant designed to produce some synthetic fibre might have to be very large and require an enormous outlay on capital equipment. A firm may hesitate to embark on such an investment unless it can be guaranteed the whole of the home market. If a competitor were allowed to operate in the market, it would probably mean two large plants each working well below capacity with much higher costs per unit, lower profitability, and reduced prospects in export markets.

It is possibilities such as these which have persuaded legislators in the UK to establish machinery for the examination of monopoly situations and to decide each case on its merits. Nevertheless there is a presumption that monopoly is against the public interest.

The public interest

The great problem with this approach to monopoly is that it requires some indicators of what is meant by 'the public interest'. The people who have to administer the policy have to come to some decision on whether the trading practices they find in the business world are operating in the public interest or against it. Unfortunately the legislation has not given any very clear guide lines. The 1948 Act (see p. 220) laid down that in judging whether a monopoly was operating contrary to the public interest the investigators should consider

> all matters which appear in the particular circumstances relevant ... and among other things ... the need to achieve the production, treatment and distribution by the most efficient and economical means of goods of such types and in such quantities as will best meet the requirements of home and overseas markets.

The 'other things' to be taken into account included,

> the organisation of industry and trade in such a way that their efficiency is progressively increased and new enterprise encouraged; the fullest use and best distribution of men, materials, and industrial capacity in the UK; the development of technical improvements, and the expansion of existing markets and the opening up of new markets.

These guide lines have been described by one former member of the Monopolies Commission as a string of platitudes, much too wide and general to be of any great assistance to those who had to reach some conclusion on a particular case. One problem of course is that some of these objectives might, in particular circumstances, be incompatible. For example, a measure which leads to greater efficiency may lead to greatly increased local unemployment. It is interesting to note that the 1948 Act did not specifically mention 'competition' among the public interest criteria. The 1973 Act (see p. 220) provides more guidance in the form of a new definition of the public interest. This includes such phrases as 'the desirability of maintaining and promoting effective competition', the need for 'promoting through competition the reduction of costs and the development of new techniques and new products, and ... facilitating the entry of new competitors into existing markets'. The emphasis is now much more on competition as a means of stimulating efficiency, but the 1973 Act clearly lays down that 'all matters which appear relevant' must be considered, and it makes particular mention of the need to maintain a balanced distribution of industry and employment in the UK. The aim of promoting competition, therefore, will not be the overriding consideration. An increase in monopoly power (e.g. by merger) which, it is believed, would improve employment prospects in, say, a development area would most probably be judged to be in the public interest.

Identifying monopoly

If the authorities are going to control monopoly, they have to define it in such a way that a monopoly situation can be clearly identified. The most widely used indicator of monopoly power is that of the market share. In the 1948 Act monopoly was defined as a situation in which at least one third of the supply of a commodity is accounted for by one firm or group of firms under unified control. The 1973 legislation has reduced the market share which is considered to be *prima facie* evidence of monopoly to *one quarter*.

The market share test is probably the most workable measurement for administrative purposes since it is fairly easily measured. It does not follow that, in itself, it is a good guide to monopoly power. A firm with one quarter of the total market may have great market power (where the rest of the market is shared by numerous small firms), or it may face very keen competition (where the rest of the market is supplied by four or five firms of almost equal size).

Another test of monopoly power is the level of profits. It is usually assumed that the existence of profit levels substantially above those being earned in similar industries (or in industry generally) is evidence of the exercise of monopoly power. But, again, this is not conclusive evidence. Such profits may be due to greater efficiency as compared with competitors, and the Monopolies Commission has shown that the existence of monopoly power may reveal itself in low profits due to the inefficiency of companies sheltered from competition.

Monopoly might also be identified by the nature and extent of the barriers to entry. The existence of such barriers would certainly be a factor in deciding whether monopoly conditions existed, but it might be very difficult to measure their effectiveness.

The machinery of control

The legal control of monopoly has been substantially extended and modified since the first legislation in 1948. The laws relating to monopoly have three major targets.

1 Monopolies. In law a monopoly exists when (*a*) one firm has at least 25 per cent of the market for the supply of a particular good or service (i.e. a scale monopoly), or (*b*) when a number of firms, which together have a 25 per cent market share, conduct their business so as to restrict competition (i.e. a complex monopoly).

2 Restrictive trade practices. These are agreements between independent firms in respect of price or other conditions of supply which are designed to restrict competition between the parties to the agreements.

3 Mergers. These as explained in Chapter 7 may be horizontal, vertical, or conglomerate.

The investigation and control of monopolies and monopolistic practices is carried out by three important institutions, The Office of the Director-General of Fair Trading, The Monopolies and Mergers Commission, and the Restrictive Practices Court.

1 The Director-General of Fair Trading (DGFT)

This very important office was created by the Fair Trading Act of 1973. The Director-General is obliged to maintain a continuous survey of and collect information on all types of trading practices in relation to the supply of goods and services. He is, in fact, a kind of official watch-dog in the market place. The Office of Fair Trading operates in three main areas.
i Competition policy: monopolies, restrictive trade practices, mergers.
ii Consumer credit.
iii Consumer affairs.
The responsibilities of the Director-General of Fair Trading are explained in the sections which follow.

2 The Monopolies and Mergers Commission (MMC)

This organisation formerly known as the Monopolies Commission was established by the 1948 Monopolies and Restrictive Practices Act. The functions of the MMC are to investigate monopolies and proposed mergers referred to them and to report on whether they consider the existing situation or the proposed changes to be in the public interest. They also make recommendations to the government on any actions they think are necessary to protect the public interest. The MMC consists of a full-time chairman, two part-time deputies and twenty-two other part-time commissioners drawn from such fields as administration, industry, commerce, trade unions and the academic world. There is also a professional full-time staff. The MMC does not have the power to initiate investigations; it can only take action when a case is referred to it by the DGFT or by the Secretary of State for Trade. It has no powers to enforce its recommendations; whether any action is taken on the findings of the MMC rests upon a decision by the Secretary of State.
The number of investigations is limited by the resources of the MMC. Its maximum capacity is about 15 investigations of monopolies and mergers at any one time. In practice the MMC is able, on average, to produce about 6 monopoly reports and 6 merger reports each year.

The duties of the MMC are to conduct enquiries into:
a monopolies in the supply of goods and services;
b merger proposals;
c local (or geographical) monopolies;
d the general effects of specific monopolistic practices (e.g. price discrimination);
e the efficiency, costs, and quality of services provided by public enterprises;
f anti-competitive practices pursued by any individual firm whether or not it is a monopoly.

Monopolies

As mentioned earlier the MMC can only carry out an investigation where a company has a 25 per cent market share or where two or more companies together having a 25 per cent market share are acting together so as to restrict competition. The DGFT has the duty to keep the UK market under continuous review and to ascertain the existence of monopoly situations. He decides the priority for references to the MMC. The Commission looks into the supply of particular goods and services and not into the activities of large companies as such. This means that a large multi-product firm may be the subject of more than one MMC investigation.

The way in which the MMC works has been criticised for being a much too lengthy process; there is an average interval of about two years between the initial reference and the publication of the MMC's report. The reports have been wide ranging and have provided detailed authoritative accounts of the structure and performance of the firms investigated. They have greatly extended public knowledge of the way in which the business world conducts its affairs.

There has also been criticism because some of the reports and recommendations of the MMC have not been followed by strong legal action by the government. The Secretary of State for Trade has the power to make orders giving legal effect to any recommendations of the MMC, but this power has rarely been used. Even so the reports of the MMC have led to substantial changes in business practices. Adverse comments have usually led to voluntary agreements by the firms concerned (in negotiations with the Secretary of State) to modify or abandon the offending practice. The fear of investigation and unwelcome publicity may also have had some beneficial effects on business behaviour.

Over the years the MMC have made a variety of recommendations for the control or modification of firms' policies. These have included proposals for price reductions; government supervision of prices, costs and profits; the lowering of tariffs on competing imports; substantial reductions in advertising and other selling costs, and the prohibition of any further take-overs of competitors.

Mergers

A proposed merger may be referred to the MMC for investigation where it would involve the transfer of gross assets of at least £15 million or where the merger would lead to a monopoly situation (i.e. the control of at least 25 per cent of the market). The Director-General of Fair Trading has the responsibility of keeping himself informed of all merger situations qualifying for possible reference to the MMC. He carries out preliminary investigations and then advises the Secretary of State on whether the proposed merger should be referred to the MMC; only the Secretary of State can refer a proposed merger to the MMC. In fact only a small percentage of mergers have been referred to the MMC and of these about 60 per cent were either found to be against the public interest or were abandoned. The restraining effects of merger control are certainly greater than the official statistics indicate because many merger proposals are dropped after informal consultations with the DGFT.

Decisions on merger references are taken on a case by case basis. In deciding whether a proposed merger is likely to operate against the public interest the MMC will take into account such matters as:

a the extent to which competition is likely to be reduced;

b the possible gains in efficiency from rationalisation, economies of scale and better management;

c the likely effects on employment;

d the possibilities of increased competitiveness in overseas markets;

e whether the merger is likely to stimulate innovation and technical progress;

f the possible effects on the regional distribution of industry;

g the effects on consumers and suppliers: for example a merger might create a large preponderant buyer which would be in a very strong bargaining position if its suppliers were numerous and small.

Until quite recently the official policy on mergers was based on the view that mergers are generally not against the public interest. Current attitudes appear to be more critical and the tendency is for more proposed mergers to be sent to the MMC for their consideration. This change of attitude is largely due to the fact that several recent studies of the effects of mergers have shown that a high proportion (at least 50 per cent) of them have proved unprofitable or much less successful than had been anticipated. One explanation for this may be the fact that the planned gains from mergers often depend upon substantial reorganisation of production facilities which may include the closure of some plants with inevitable redundancies. Such changes are likely to meet with strong resistance especially from organised labour and hence may take a long time to carry out. There is also concern that many mergers appear to have been motivated by a desire to increase market power (by reducing competition) rather than by a desire to increase efficiency.

Newspaper mergers are treated as a special case. The written permission of the Secretary of State is required for any merger where the buyer actually or potentially controls newspapers with a circulation of 500 000 copies or more.

The Restrictive Practices Court

The legal regulation of restrictive trade practices began with the Restrictive Trade Practices Act of 1956, the provisions of which have been extended and modified by several other Acts of Parliament. There is an obligation on the parties to certain types of restrictive agreement to place them on a public register which is maintained by the Director-General of Fair Trading. An agreement is registrable if the parties to it include two or more persons (whether individuals or companies) who are engaged in business in the UK in the manufacture or supply of goods or in the supply of services. Two or more parties to the agreement must accept restrictions (i.e. some limitation on their freedom to make their own decisions) on such matters as prices, conditions of sale, persons dealt with and areas or scale of production. Typical examples of the types of practice which are registrable are given on pages 205–207.

It is the job of the DGFT to select practices on the register for reference to the Restrictive Practices Court which then has the task of deciding whether or not the practices are operating in the public interest. The RP Court has the status of a High Court and its judgements become the law of the land. All registered agreements are presumed to be against the public interest and the onus is on the parties to the agreements to prove to the satisfaction of the court that they are not harmful to the public interest. By the end of 1980 some 3 500 agreements relating to goods had been placed on the register of which about 650 had been referred to the Restrictive Practices Court. Very few of these have been contested and only 11 agreements have been successfully defended as being in the public interest. There were about 500 service agreements on the register at the end of 1980 and four of these were being defended before the RP Court.

The great majority of restrictive agreements on the register have been voluntarily abandoned or have been modified so that they do not qualify as registrable agreements.

The firms or trade associations which choose to defend their agreements must select a form of defence from a restricted list set out in the Restrictive Practices Act. There are eight approved grounds for defence, generally referred to as the eight 'gateways' (see Appendix at end of chapter). The defendants must, in addition, show that any gain from the operation of the practice is not outweighed by any detrimental effects on persons not party to the agreement. For example, in the case of the Lancashire Yarn Spinners, the firms proved to the satisfaction of the court that the abandonment of the restrictive agreement (a minimum price scheme) would lead to increased unemployment in South Lancashire. They succeeded in getting through 'gateway' number 5, but they were unable to satisfy the court on the second requirement. The Restrictive Practices Court decided that the higher yarn prices which resulted from the operation of the restrictive practice did more harm to the public interest in the form of higher consumer prices (and possible harmful effects on exports) than the benefits obtained by one section of the community.

The number of cases considered by the court has not been very great, but by carefully selecting the agreements to be judged by the court it has been possible to make each reference a test case for a large number of similar agreements. If a particular case is lost then similar agreements are likely to be abandoned. The Restrictive Practices Court has tended to be severe in upholding the general principle that the restriction of competition is against the public interest and less than 1 per cent of the *registered* agreements have been found to be consistent with the public interest.

The effects of the court's earlier judgements have varied. In some cases the breaking of agreements led to keen price competition, but in other cases registrable agreements were replaced by open-price or *information agreements* where firms avoided keen price competition by keeping each other informed about their proposed price changes. Information agreements have now been made registrable. Certain agreements are exempt from registration and in addition the Secretary of State has powers to exempt from registration certain restrictive agreements where such exemption would help to promote important commercial or industrial projects (e.g. agreements for joint research and development).

One particular restrictive practice was the subject of its own legislation. The Resale Prices Act of 1964 prohibited resale price maintenance, but made provision for suppliers to claim exemption. The procedure for this is similar to that for restrictive agreements in general; RPM agreements must be registered and defended before the Restrictive Practices Court. There are five 'gateways' which might be used as justifications for RPM (see Appendix at end of chapter). The great majority of RPM agreements have been voluntarily abandoned and in only two cases, books and proprietary medicines, have RPM agreements been upheld.

Consumer protection

Although the legal control of monopolies and restrictive practices now has a fairly long history, the idea that government should provide organisations for a general oversight of consumers' interests is relatively new. The Fair Trading Act of 1973 made the Director-General of Fair Trading responsible for safeguarding the interests of consumers. He proposes new laws to end unfair trading practices, encourages trade associations to produce codes of practice for member firms to follow when dealing with consumers, and deals with manufacturers and traders who persistently indulge in unfair practices. In this matter he is assisted by a Consumer Protection Advisory Committee (CPAC) whose functions are to investigate undesirable trading practices referred to it by the DGFT and to consider his proposals for dealing with the practices. The types of unfair practice with which the CPAC is concerned are those which:

a mislead consumers about the nature, quality, or quantity of goods involved in a transaction;

b mislead consumers about their rights and obligations;

c subject consumers to undue pressures to buy;

d cause the terms or conditions of sale to be so adverse as to be inequitable.

If the CPAC is satisfied that the practice adversely affects consumers and agrees with the DGFT's proposals, the Secretary of State can make an order banning the practice.

The work of the CPAC and the Director-General has resulted in many codes of practice being adopted by various trade associations (e.g. the servicing of electrical appliances, mail order trading, laundry and dry cleaning services, package holidays and footwear retailing). The Office of Fair Trading has also investigated many other practices (e.g. advertising, door-to-door selling and one-day sales) and has obliged many individual companies to give undertakings to modify their business practices.

The DGFT also has important responsibilities as a result of the Consumer Credit Act of 1974. Under this Act all businesses involved in the granting of credit or the hiring of goods (including hire purchase) to individuals, sole traders or partnerships require a licence from the DGFT. An important aim of the legislation is that the consumer should be given sufficient information about the credit being offered and its true cost. A court may be asked to reopen a credit agreement which is deemed to be extortionate and a consumer is also given the right to complete payment of hire purchase or credit agreements early and obtain a rebate of the credit charges.

Appendix

The Restrictive Practices Acts

The eight gateways

The respondents must show that the agreement confers benefits in one or more of the following ways:

1 By protecting the public against injury in connection with the installation, use or consumption of goods.

2 By making available other specific and substantial benefits.

3 By counteracting restrictive measures taken by any one person who is not party to the agreement.

4 By permitting negotiation of fair terms for the purchase or sale of goods or services with buyers or sellers who represent a preponderant part of the trade.

5 By preventing the occurrence of serious and persistent unemployment in an area heavily dependent upon the particular trade.

6 In maintaining the volume or earnings of the export trade in the commodity or service where this is substantial in relation to the export trade of the UK as a whole, or in relation to the whole business of the particular trade.

7 In maintaining some other restriction which the Court holds to be justified on its own merits.

8 The restriction does not directly or indirectly restrict or discourage competition.

The Resale Prices Acts

The five gateways

Exemptions may be granted if, through the ending of price maintenance, the public suffered detriment by reason of:

1 Substantial reduction in the variety and quality of goods.

2 Substantial deterioration in after-sales service.

3 Substantial loss of retail outlets.

4 Goods being sold under conditions likely to cause danger to health and safety by misuse.

5 The possibility that prices might rise in the long term.

Natural Monopoly - Diamond Industry

Services Monopoly - British Telecom

Temporary Monopoly - Firm that corners market for short w

Social Monopoly - water, electricity, gass boards

legal Monopoly - (laws patent and trade marks)

Part Six: The National Income and Its Distribution

17 National Income

Up to this point most of the subject matter discussed has been concerned with the various aspects of production. The factors of production, the laws of production, the types of business organisation, the location of industry, and the prices of the goods and services are all important aspects of the problem of producing those things which satisfy material wants. We now turn to the problem of measuring the results of economic activity. The output of goods and services is a continuous process so that in trying to measure what is produced we are in fact dealing with a *flow* and not a stock. We have to measure a flow of output over time and the time period used for this purpose is invariably one year. Note that the total national product includes *services* as well as goods, because production is defined as any economic activity which satisfies a want and for which people are prepared to pay a price.

The problems of measurement

Money values

The first problem which arises is that of valuation. Total output consists of a vast range of different goods and services whose quantities cannot be added together in physical units. We cannot add kilograms of wheat, to metres of cloth, to tonnes of coal in physical terms. The only possible common unit of measurement is money. If all commodities have money prices, the products of the quantities and prices will give us total money values. Although the use of money as a measuring rod is the only feasible way of measuring total output, it does give rise to difficulties. For example, we must assume that *relative* prices are a reasonable reflection of the relative amounts of satisfaction provided by the different commodities. If commodity A is priced at £5 while the price of commodity B is £2·50, it means that one unit of A counts for twice as much output (i.e. renders twice as much satisfaction) as one unit of B. Another problem arises when the value of money itself changes. This makes it difficult to compare the value of output in one year with that of another year.

Public services

Difficulties are also encountered when goods and services do not have market prices. This is true of many public services such as defence, law and order, education and health services. They are certainly part of the national output since they satisfy wants and use up scarce resources. The solution adopted is to measure their values 'at cost'. The salaries of teachers and policemen are taken as a measure of the values of their outputs. The total money cost of providing public services is assumed to be a fair representation of the value of output.

Self-provided commodities

Similar problems are encountered with the goods and services which people provide for themselves. For example, farmers consume some of their own output, a great deal of repair and improvement work is carried out on a 'do it yourself' basis, and many people make their own clothes. In such cases there is no market measurement of the value of the output. Where similar goods and services are sold in the market it is possible to give self-provided goods and services an imputed valuation – an estimate of their values can be included in the national income figures. This method is used, for example, in the case of owner-occupied dwellings. The market rents of similar properties are used as guide lines for the imputed rents of premises occupied by their owners. Where there is no reliable market indicator, the assumed value must be an arbitrary estimate or it may be decided to omit the commodity from the calculations of the national output. This latter solution is adopted in the case of housewives' services.[1]

Double counting

Adding up the total outputs of all the enterprises in the economy will give us an aggregate many times greater than the true value of the national product. The problem here is one of 'double counting'. It arises because the outputs of some firms are the inputs of other firms. Suppose the annual output of the flour mills sells for £15 m. and the value of the output of the bakeries is £25 m. Added together they give a total output of £40 m., but the value of the flour has been counted twice. If we added together the value of the wheat output from the farms, the flour output from the mills, and the bread from the bakeries, we would be counting the value of the wheat three times!

There are two possible ways of dealing with this problem. National output can be measured by adding the values of the *final products*, or by totalling the *values added* at each stage of production. In the ex-

---

[1] Rough estimates put the value of housewives' services at about one-fifth of the national income.

ample used earlier the bakeries added £10 m. to the value of the flour they purchased from the mills – this is the true measure of their outputs. The total of the values added at each stage will be exactly the same as the total value of the final products. Table 13 should make this clear. We assume the whole process of producing bread begins with the farmer and ends with the retailer.[1]

Table 13 The values added at each stage of the production of bread (£ m)

	Value of output	Cost of intermediate goods	Value added
Farmers	10	0	10
Millers	15	10	5
Bakers	25	15	10
Retailers	30	25	5
	—		—
			30
			—

Intermediate goods and materials are the material inputs at the various stages of production – the goods each firm purchases from other producers. It can be seen that the value of the final product (which includes additions to stocks) is exactly the same as the total of the values added by the various production processes.

Factor cost

The value of the national output is measured at factor cost, that is, in terms of the payments made to the factors of production for services rendered in producing that output. Using market prices as measures of the value of output can be misleading when market prices do not accurately reflect the costs of production (including profits). Nowadays, most market prices contain some element of taxation and a few of them include an element of subsidy. Thus about two-thirds of the market value of tobacco purchased in the UK will consist of tax payments and only one-third represents payments to the makers and sellers of this tobacco. In order to arrive at the factor cost value, taxes on expenditure must be deducted and subsidies must be added to the market price valuations. It would be very misleading to use the figures for national income at market prices since it would mean that the value of national output could be increased by an increase in the rates of taxation.

---

[1] In fact the seed will be part of a previous year's output.

Gross national product and national income

In the UK, the main official measurement of total output is described as the *Gross National Product* (*GNP*). In 1981 its value was £211 792 m. The word 'National' requires some explanation because GNP is *not* the value of the total output produced within the UK. The total product of all the resources located within the UK is known as the *Gross Domestic Product* (*GDP*). The difference between GNP and GDP is largely a matter of ownership. Some of the UK output is produced by resources owned by foreigners and this leads to a flow of income (interest and profits) out of the country. On the other hand, British-owned assets abroad lead to a corresponding flow of income from overseas into the UK. The net difference between these flows is recorded as *net property income from abroad*. If this item is added to GDP we arrive at the GNP figure. Thus,

Gross Domestic Product + net property income from abroad =
Gross National Product

GNP, therefore, is the total output from resources owned by the residents of a country wherever these resources happen to be located. GDP is the total output from all the resources located in a country wherever their owners happen to live.

The word 'Gross' indicates that no deduction has been made for that part of total output which is needed to maintain the nation's stock of capital assets. The value of the output required to replace obsolete and worn-out capital is known as *depreciation*, or *capital consumption*. The total output of capital goods is described as Gross Investment and the net additions to the stock of capital is known as Net Investment. We have, therefore,

Gross Investment − Depreciation   = Net Investment

Gross National Product − Depreciation = Net National Product

Net National Product consists of all the goods and services becoming available for consumption together with the net additions to the nation's stock of capital. This is the total which is generally known as the *National Income*.

We should note, however, that it is extremely difficult to obtain an accurate estimate of the annual amount of depreciation and economists often use the figures for Gross National Product for purposes of analysis.

Measuring the national income

There are three possible approaches to this problem and they are based on three different views of the national income.

First of all the national income may be viewed as the total output from domestically owned resources during the course of one year (the *Output approach*).

Secondly, national income may be viewed in terms of the incomes earned by the factors of production engaged in producing the national output. Since the total product is valued at factor cost, it must be exactly the same as the total value of the incomes (wages, interest, rent and profits) which have been paid out to the factors of production. National income, then, may be measured by totalling these incomes (the *Income approach*).

Thirdly, national income may be looked at from the point of view of its disposal. The national output must either be bought for use or added to stocks. If we assume that net additions to stocks amount to 'expenditure' by the firm on its own output, we can measure national income by the amount of money spent on purchasing the national output (the *Expenditure approach*).

It should be apparent, therefore, that

National Output ≡ National Income ≡ National Expenditure

These totals are identically equal since they are merely different ways of looking at the same thing. We have defined the terms in such a way that they must be equal. There are, however, a number of possible pitfalls in measuring the national income by these different methods because the totals of income, output, and expenditure presented to us in real world statistics are, very often, not the factor cost valuations.

The output method

The most direct method of measuring the national output or income is to use the output figures of all the firms in the country. We have already noted the problem of double counting so we must either use the 'value added' method, or take the total value of all final products.

Exports are included because they are part of the national output, but imported materials and services must be excluded. If the value added method is used, imports will be automatically excluded since we only record the values added in this country. This will now give us the GDP and to this total must be added the net property income from abroad.[1] If the general level of prices has been changing during the course of the year, it is necessary to make an adjustment for the purely monetary changes in the value of stocks. A rise in prices increases the value of existing stocks even when there is no change in their volume. In order to obtain an estimate of the *real* changes in

---

[1] This item may of course be negative.

stocks it is necessary to make a deduction equal to the 'inflationary' increase in value. This deduction is described as *Stock Appreciation*[1] in the official tables (see Table 14).

The income method

The main point to note here is the fact that *all* personal incomes are not included in the national income. We must only take account of those which have been earned for services rendered and in respect of which there is some corresponding value of output. In any advanced society a sizeable proportion of total personal income is made up of *Transfer Payments*. These payments take the form of social security payments such as unemployment pay, old age pensions, child benefits, and the like. All these are transfer payments *not* because they are paid out of taxes, but because they are not payments for services rendered – there is no contribution to current real output by the recipients. The test of whether an income payment is a transfer payment or not is quite simple. We ask, 'Is this a payment for services rendered during the period in which the income was received?' If the answer is 'No', then it is a transfer payment.

The official statistics record incomes in the form in which they are received. Thus we find figures for wages, rent, interest and profits, and a separate category for the incomes of the self-employed (The reason for this is explained on pp. 287–8). It must be noted that factor incomes are recorded gross (i.e. before taxes are paid), because this is the measure of the factors' contributions to output.

We must also take account of the fact that all the income generated in production does not find its way into personal incomes. Some part of company profits may be added to reserves, and the profits of nationalised undertakings go to the government and not to persons. These *undistributed surpluses* must be added on to the totals of factor incomes received by persons.

We have already noted that some of the income derived from economic activity within the country will be paid to foreign owners of assets located here, while income from British-owned assets abroad will be moving in the opposite direction. The income account, therefore, must be adjusted by including the item 'net income from abroad'. Finally the stock appreciation adjustment must be made in order to eliminate the element of windfall gain in the profits received (see Table 14).

The expenditure method

In estimating the value of the national product by the expenditure

[1] This would be added when prices had been falling.

232

method we must only record *final expenditures*. All the expenditure on intermediate goods and services must be excluded. It is the usual practice to break down total expenditure into five large categories: Consumption, Government Spending, Investment, Imports, and Exports. This classification is extremely useful for purposes of analysis. There are several adjustments to be made to the total national expenditure in order to arrive at a figure for the national income at factor cost.

1 The available statistics provide us with national expenditure at *market prices*. These prices differ from the factor cost values by the amount of taxes and subsidies they contain.

Thus,

National Income at market prices − Indirect taxes + Subsidies = National Income at factor cost

2 We must be careful to include only that part of government expenditure which represents payments for goods and services – government spending on transfer payments must be excluded.

3 The expenditure method also necessitates some adjustments to take account of international transactions. Total domestic expenditure includes spending on foreign goods and services (imports) which does not generate factor income at home. On the other hand it does not include expenditures by foreigners on domestically produced goods and services (exports) which do generate income at home. Thus exports must be added and imports subtracted from total domestic spending.

4 The expenditure which actually takes place on capital goods (i.e. investment) must be supplemented by an estimated value of the additions to stocks, and work in progress. Incomes will have been earned in the production of these incomplete or unsold goods which have not yet reached the market. In order to arrive at the factor cost value of total output we include an imputed expenditure on these items. In other words we assume that the producer himself has 'purchased' the additions to stocks and the unfinished goods.

Using the information

The measurement of the national income by official sources was first carried out in 1941 and the information is now published annually in the publication *National Income and Expenditure*, more commonly known as the Blue Book.

Real income and money income

Using a monetary system of measurement gives rise to certain problems. Difficulties arise when we wish to compare the national income

Table 14 United Kingdom national income in 1981 (£ million)

Output[1]		Income		Expenditure	
Agriculture, forestry, fishing	4 867	Income from employment	147 197	Consumers' expenditure	151 042
Oil and natural gas	11 972	Income from self-employment	18 569	Public authorities' current expenditure on goods and services	55 151
Mining and quarrying	3 455	Gross trading profits of companies	27 101	Gross domestic fixed capital formation	39 377
Manufacturing	49 916	Gross trading surpluses of public corporations	7 551	Value of physical increase in stocks and work in progress	−4 160
Construction	13 545	Gross trading surpluses of other public enterprises	242		
Gas, electricity, water	6 670	Rent	15 282	Total domestic expenditure at market prices	241 410
Transport	10 935	Imputed charge for consumption of non-trading capital	2 318	Exports	67 854
Communications	5 858	Less Stock appreciation	−5 692	Less Imports	−60 866
Distributive trades	20 088	Residual error	−1 780	Net property income from abroad	1 004
Insurance, banking, finance	19 251			Less Taxes on expenditure	−43 471
Ownership of dwellings	13 869			Subsidies	5 861
Public administration and defence	15 988				
Professional and scientific services	28 467				
Other services	20 057				
Less Adjustment for financial services[2]	−12 370				
Residual error[3]	−1 780				
Gross domestic product at factor cost	210 788	Gross domestic product at factor cost	210 788		
Net property income from abroad	1 004	Net property income from abroad	1 004		
Gross national product	211 792	Gross national product	211 792	Gross national product	211 792
Less Capital consumption	−30 613	Less Capital consumption	−30 613	Less Capital consumption	−30 613
National income	181 179	National income	181 179	National income	181 179

[1] The contribution of each industry to the gross domestic product after providing for stock appreciation.
[2] To avoid some double counting of interest paid on loans and interest received by financial institutions.
[3] The estimates of GDP are built up largely from independent data on incomes and expenditure. The residual error is the difference between these estimates. It is placed in the income and output tables purely as a matter of convenience. It does not imply that expenditure estimates are superior in accuracy.
Source: *National Income and Expenditure* 1982 Edition HMSO.

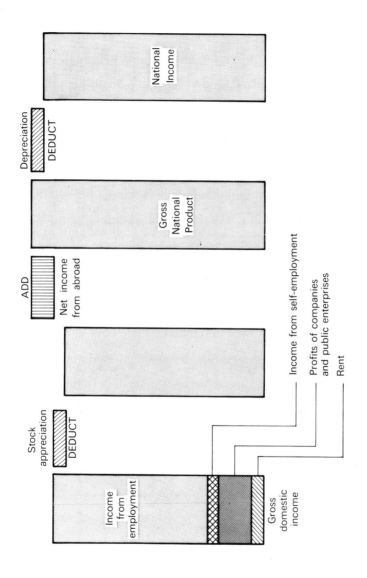

Fig. 51 National income – income method

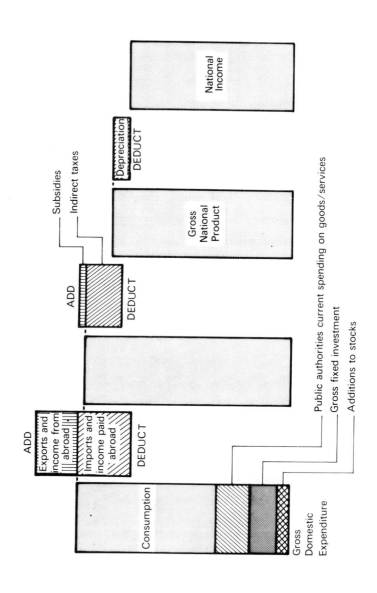

Fig. 52 National income – expenditure method

of one year with that of another because the value of money itself may change. When the general level of prices is changing, the value of money is changing and the standard of measurement becomes variable. National income statistics are often used to provide some indication of changes in the economic welfare of the citizens and for this purpose we need to know what has been happening to real income (i.e. the *volume* of output).

If the general price level has been changing during the period under consideration, the figures recorded for the different years will have to be adjusted to take account of the price changes. What is needed is a measure of what the national income would have been in the latter year, had prices remained constant. A simple example should make clear the manner in which the national income of one year may be compared *in real terms* with that of another year.

	Year 1	Year 2
National income (£ million)	10 000	12 000
Index of prices	100	105

National income of Year 2 expressed in terms of the prices ruling in Year 1

$$= \frac{12\,000}{1} \times \frac{100}{105}$$

$$= £11\,428 \cdot 5\text{m}.$$

The example shows that, although the national income in monetary terms had increased by 20 per cent, in real terms the increase was only about 14·3 per cent.

The standard of living

Since income represents a flow of real output, movements in the national income are often used to indicate changes in the standard of living. Great care must be exercised in using the figures for this purpose. We have already pointed to the problem of changing prices. Account must also be taken of changes in the population because it is *income per head* which is relevant when living standards are being discussed. A 5 per cent increase in total real income which is accompanied by an 8 per cent increase in the population probably means that the average standard of living has fallen.

It is also necessary to take note of the composition of total output. A large increase in total output which is due to an increased output of capital goods or defence equipment will not mean any immediate increase in economic welfare.

International comparisons

Statistics of national income per head are the most frequently used bases for comparing living standards in different countries. There are many reasons why such comparisons must be used with caution. The levels of accuracy in measurement may differ very widely. In countries where subsistence agriculture is the main activity there is a large element of guesswork in the final compilation. There are great discrepancies in the patterns of income distribution in different countries. Two countries may have the same income-per-head figures but the standards of living will be very different if in one the income is fairly evenly distributed, while in the other income distribution is very unequal. The composition of total output may be different. For example, one country may devote a much greater proportion of its resources to defence than another country and yet the two countries may have very similar figures for income per head.

Some differences arise from climate or geography. Inhabitants of cold countries have to spend a relatively large proportion of their incomes on keeping warm, while people living in sparsely populated countries will have to spend relatively more on communications and transport. It does not follow that living standards are lower where these expenditures are lower.

International comparisons require the conversion of values measured in one currency to values measured in another currency. The UK national income is measured in pounds sterling, that of the USA in dollars. To make these figures comparable, use is made of the official exchange rate. This rate of exchange, however, may not be a good indicator of the relative domestic purchasing powers of the two currencies. For example, if £1 = $2, it does not follow that $2 in the USA will purchase more or less the same volume of goods and services as £1 in the UK. The official exchange rate only takes account of the commodities entering into international trade and these may represent a very small selection of the commodities traded within each nation. The exchange rate may also be held at an artificially high level due to various measures of exchange control. The use of national income figures for the purpose of comparing international standards of living need to be supplemented by various social indicators such as the number of hospital beds and doctors per head of the population, numbers in further education, and the nature and quality of the different welfare services.

Environmental effects

Some of the 'costs' of economic growth are not accounted for in the calculations of the national income. Pollution, noise, congestion, and mental strain may be the by-products of a rapidly increasing national income. If a nation spends, say, £10 m. on increasing the output of some commodity and then has to spend £1 m. on mitigating the nuisances associated with this output, it would be rather misleading to say that 'output' had increased by £11 m. The quality of life is not accurately measured by purely economic indicators.

The Blue Book presents a variety of break-downs of the national income figures. These make it possible to analyse the behaviour of different sectors of the economy. Tables are available to show changes in consumption, investment, savings, public expenditures, the outputs of different branches of industry, and the distribution of income. This kind of data is an essential requirement for the formulation of economic policy.

The distribution of income

The next section of this book deals with the manner in which the national income is distributed. The economist, as such, is not concerned with the question of whether the national income is shared out on an equitable basis, but with the forces which determine the shares going to the different income groups. Incomes, as we have seen, may be subdivided into factor payments and transfer payments. At this stage we are interested in the first category since it is these payments which comprise the national income. The payments for the services of the factors of production may be classified as

a Those incomes which are rewards for personal services (i.e. wages and salaries).
b Those paid to owners of property for the services rendered by that property (i.e. rent and interest).
c A surplus accruing to the entrepreneur which is generally regarded as a reward for risk-bearing (i.e. profits).

In the chapters which follow we deal with the determination of these factor incomes. They are identified according to the nature of the services provided. Thus:

Wages are payments for the services of Labour.
Interest is a payment for the services of Capital.
Rent is a reward for the services of Land (although *economic* rent applies to other factors too).
Profits are a return to the risk-bearing function of the Entrepreneur.

Although these incomes are described as returns to the various factors, they all accrue to individuals – or they are retained within the enterprise as undistributed profits and surpluses. Figure 53 presents a picture of the distribution of the UK national income. Incomes may be regarded as prices. There are markets for land, labour, and capital just as there are for the things they produce. Like other prices, incomes are determined by demand and supply and, as is the case with other commodities, we shall find that some of these factor markets are highly competitive and some are monopolistic.

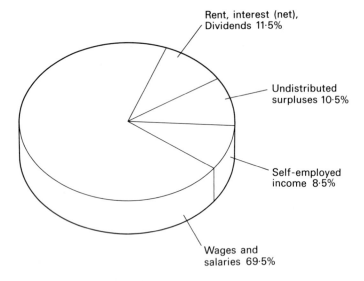

Source: National Income and Expenditure 1982 HMSO.

Fig. 53 Shares in the gross national product, United Kingdom, 1981

18 Wages

Wage differentials

A wage is a payment, normally made under contract, for the services of labour. We are all aware of the fact that there are very great differences in wage rates as between different occupations and the commonsense explanation for this would be that labour is not a homogeneous factor. There are very great differences in the skills and abilities of, and in the demands for, different types of worker giving rise to not one labour market, but many different markets each with its own supply and demand conditions. The variations in the conditions of supply and demand as between these markets will give rise to different prices, hence the existence of wage differentials.

This is all very true, but we have to explain why these wage differentials persist. Why is there no large-scale movement of workers from the lower-paid jobs to those more highly paid? Such a movement would tend to equalise wages, for the movements out of the lower-paid jobs would reduce the supply of this type of labour and raise its price, while the movements into the more highly paid jobs would increase the supply and tend to lower the price. Adam Smith asked the question, 'If labour were perfectly mobile would wages in all occupations then be equal?' In fact, they would not, because some jobs are more attractive than others. If wages were equal in all occupations, the dirty and disagreeable jobs would attract little labour, most people would seek the jobs with pleasant and congenial conditions. Smith pointed out that under such circumstances it would be the *net advantages* of occupations which would tend to equality. There would be differences in money wages and these differentials would measure, in money terms, the values which people placed on other aspects of their work such as the degree of security, the element of danger, and the satisfaction of the work. If we turn to the real world again, we find that dirty and disagreeable work is often less well paid than the more pleasant and attractive jobs. It is apparent that existing wage differences do not equalise the attractiveness of different occupations. To explain why one job pays £x per week while another pays £y per week, we must examine the supply and demand conditions to find out what makes them equate at different price levels in the different markets.

The demand for labour

There are four basic propositions regarding the demand for labour:
1 The demand for labour is a derived demand. Labour is required not

for itself, but for what it will produce. The demand for labour derives directly from the demand for the product of labour. The greater the demand for the product, the greater the demand for labour. No matter how skilful the worker, no matter how long his period of training, if what he produces is no longer in demand, his services will no longer be required.

2 The elasticity of demand for labour is directly related to the elasticity of demand for the product. If labour is producing a commodity which has a very inelastic demand, an increase in wages will have a relatively small effect on the demand for labour. Even if the whole of the increase in wages is passed on in the form of higher prices, the fall in the quantity demanded of the product will be relatively small, and there will be a correspondingly small reduction in the demand for labour. If, however, the demand for the product of labour is very elastic, a small increase in price will lead to a relatively large reduction in the quantity demanded. Under these circumstances an increase in wages which is passed on in the form of higher prices will cause a relatively large reduction in the demand for labour.

3 The elasticity of demand for a given type of labour varies according to the proportion of total costs accounted for by labour costs. Where wages account for only a small proportion of total costs, the demand for labour will tend to be inelastic. Some industries such as house-building, are labour-intensive and labour costs make up a large part of the total costs of the product. Other industries are capital-intensive (e.g. chemicals and oil refining) and in these industries the cost of labour accounts for a relatively small part of the cost of the product.

Let us assume that wages increase generally by 10 per cent while productivity remains unchanged. In a labour-intensive industry, labour costs might account for, say, 60 per cent of average total cost and the effect of the increase in wages will raise unit cost by 6 per cent. In a capital-intensive industry where labour costs are, say, 20 per cent of average total cost, the increase in wages will raise unit cost by only 2 per cent. If these increased costs are passed on in the form of higher prices, the effects on the demand for labour are likely to be much greater in the former example than in the latter.

4 The demand for labour will be more elastic the easier it is to substitute other factors for it. Other things being equal, an increase in wage rates will increase the cost of labour relative to the costs of the other factors. Where possible, therefore, entrepreneurs will tend to substitute other factors for the now relatively dearer labour. As wages increase, the substitution of labour-saving machinery becomes more and more attractive. In low-wage countries like India and China we find that methods of production are labour-intensive and it is countries with relatively high wage rates such as the USA which make the most use of labour-saving machinery. Where it is fairly easy to substitute capital for labour, the demand for labour will become more and more elastic as wage rates rise relative to other factor prices.

These four propositions are important features of the demand for labour, because they help us to explain some of the reasons for the differing demand conditions for labour in different industries and occupations. What we have to do next is to establish that the demand curve for labour is of the normal shape, that is, sloping downwards from left to right.

Marginal revenue productivity

Entrepreneurs will employ labour when there is a demand for the product of labour. Although they are interested in the physical productivity of labour, entrepreneurs are more concerned with the revenue yielded by labour's efforts. We assume that the objective of entrepreneurs is to maximise profits so that their main concern is the difference between the cost of employing labour and the revenue yielded by selling the product of labour. We define the amount added to the firm's revenue by employing one more worker as the *marginal revenue product* of labour. If the firm is operating *under conditions of perfect competition,* the price of the product does not change as the firm changes its output so that the MRP of labour is clearly equal to the marginal physical product of labour multiplied by the price of the product.

MRP of labour = MPP of labour × Price of product

Table 2 and Fig. 5 illustrate the changing values of the average and marginal physical products of labour when a fixed amount of capital and land is combined with varying amounts of labour. The law of diminishing returns tell us that the AP and MP of labour will, sooner or later, begin to decline. If these average and marginal products are multiplied by the price of the product (we are still assuming perfect competition), we obtain the average and marginal revenue products. All we have done, of course, is to change the basis on which we measure labour's productivity from physical units to monetary units. The vertical scale on the diagram is now measured in pounds sterling.

In Fig. 54 we see how the ARP and MRP of labour vary as the individual firm combines different numbers of workers with a fixed amount of land and capital. If we assume that the firm is one of a very large number of buyers of this type of labour and cannot influence the wage rate, the supply of labour (to the firm) will be perfectly elastic at the ruling wage rate. It can obtain as many workers as it wishes at the market wage. How many workers will it employ?

The equilibrium condition is already familiar to us since it has been encountered when dealing with the output of the firm. The profit-maximising firm will employ additional workers as long as those

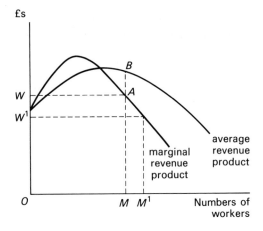

Fig. 54

workers are adding more to the firm's revenue than to the firm's costs. In other words, *labour will be employed up to the point where its marginal revenue product is equal to the wage rate.* Since the wage rate is constant, we can regard it as the marginal cost of labour, so that our equilibrium is nothing more than another application of the MC = MR profit-maximising condition.

The demand curve for labour

In Fig. 54 when the wage rate is OW the firm will employ OM workers. At this wage, as employment increases up to OM, each additional worker is adding more to the firm's revenue than to the firm's costs. Beyond OM the employment of extra workers adds more to costs than to revenue. If the wage rate falls to OW^1, employment will rise to OM^1. It now becomes worthwhile to employ MM^1 extra workers since the marginal revenue products of these workers are higher than the new lower wage rate. The MRP curve then tells us how much labour will be demanded at any given price (i.e. wage). Since this is the function of a demand curve, *the MRP curve is the firm's demand curve for labour.* But note that it is only that part of the MRP curve which lies below the ARP curve which is relevant. The ARP curve represents the average monetary return per worker employed. When OM workers are employed, the ARP is equal to MB so that the firm is earning a surplus per worker equal to AB. The section of the MRP curve which lies above the ARP curve is not part of the demand curve because a firm will not employ labour when the wage is higher than the ARP of labour; it would be making a loss on each worker employed.

We have established that the firm's demand curve for labour will be of the normal shape sloping downwards from left to right. Although we have assumed that the firm sells its output in a perfect market, the same conclusion applies to a firm operating in an imperfect market. In this case it will have to cut its price in order to increase its sales so that the marginal revenue yielded by an extra unit of output will be less than its price. Thus, where a firm faces a downward sloping demand curve, the value of the marginal product of labour will be equal to the marginal physical product multiplied by the marginal revenues obtained from the sale of the extra units of output.

MRP of labour = MPP of labour × Marginal Revenues yielded by sale of additional output

We have used Fig. 54 to show how changes in the wage rate will cause changes in the amount of labour demanded by the firm. What about movements of the ARP and MRP curves themselves? The revenue product of labour is determined by (i) *the physical productivity of labour* and (ii) *the price of the product* (changes in price cause changes in marginal revenue in both perfect and imperfect competition). A change in either or both of these variables will move the ARP and MRP curves. An increase in the productivity of labour and/or an increase in the price of the product will shift the curves upwards. This means that the demand curve for labour moves outward from the origin and more labour will now be demanded at any given wage rate. Similarly a fall in productivity or a fall in the price of the product will reduce the amount of labour demanded at any given wage.

The analysis of the firm's demand curve for labour is based on the assumption that other things remain equal. In other words we assume that a change in the wage rate does not affect the ARP and MRP curves. This assumption does not hold true when we are dealing with the industry as a whole, because a change in the wage rate will cause all the firms in the industry to change the amount of labour they employ. For example, if the wage rate falls, all the firms in the industry will take on more labour and increase their outputs. This increase in total supply will lower the price of the product and the ARP and MRP curves of all the individual firms will move inwards towards the origin. This means that we cannot obtain the industry's demand curve for labour by adding together the individual firms' demand curves. These complications are dealt with in more advanced texts, but they do not affect the conclusion that the industry's demand curve for labour will slope downwards from left to right as does the individual firm's demand curve. This must be so because (i) an increase in employment will reduce the marginal physical product of labour and (ii) as total output increases the price of the product will fall.

The main point we have established is that the profit-maximising firm will employ labour up to the point where the last unit of labour hired adds as much to the firm's revenue as it does to the firm's costs. This reasoning applies equally to the other factors of production. The firm will increase its stock of capital up to the point where its marginal revenue product is equal to its price. In Chapter 19 we use the marginal productivity theory to show that the quantity of capital demanded is a function of its price (the rate of interest) and its marginal revenue productivity. Exactly the same analysis can be applied to determine the demand for land.

The marginal productivity theory helps us to understand the determinants of the demand for labour (and other factors) – it does not tell us how the price of labour is determined because this depends upon demand and supply. We now look at the determinants of the supply of labour.

The supply of labour

In Chapter 3 the question of the total supply of labour was dealt with in some detail. It was pointed out that the supply of labour refers to the number of hours of work which is offered by the labour force. This, in turn, depends upon such factors as the size of the population, the age composition, the numbers in full-time education, the numbers of married women at work, the rates of pay, and so on. In this study of wages we are concerned not so much with the total supply of labour as with the forces which determine the supply of labour to a particular occupation.

The individual's supply of labour

In many occupations individual workers cannot freely choose the number of hours they are prepared to work. Most trades have some agreed and contractual working week. It is true that most self-employed persons such as taxi-drivers, shop-keepers, and small-scale builders can vary the number of hours they work, and many employed persons can exercise some choice on the amount of overtime they are prepared to work, but for the vast majority of the working population the length of the working week is settled by negotiation between trade unions and employers. But the choice between work and leisure is, indirectly, available to individual workers by virtue of the part they can play in deciding union policy.

The supply curve of labour for the individual worker will be of the normal shape for only part of its length. A higher price (i.e. wage rate) will call forth a greater supply up to a point. Beyond this point a higher price will probably lead to a reduced amount of labour being supplied. As income rises so does the demand for more leisure. As real income increases people can buy a much wider range of goods and services and they will demand more leisure in order to enjoy the consumption of these commodities. One has only to think of such activities as motoring, sailing, golf, and foreign travel to appreciate the increasing preference given to leisure as income rises. As the hourly wage rate rises, there will come a point at which the individual's supply curve of labour will bend backwards. This is illustrated in Fig. 55.

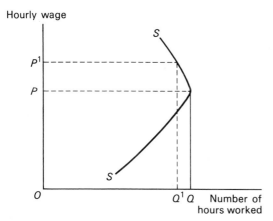

Fig. 55

As the hourly wage rate increases up to the level OP, the worker is tempted to work longer hours – the higher price calls forth a greater supply. As the wage rate rises above OP, the worker reduces the number of hours he is prepared to work. At the wage rate OP^1 he offers OQ^1 hours of work per week. This does not mean of course that he is reducing his weekly income. For example, he might be prepared to work a 44-hour week when the wage rate is £2·50 per hour, giving him a wage of £110. If the hourly wage rate increases to £3·50 he might offer 40 hours of work each week giving him a wage of £140 per week.

What we are saying is that, up to the rate OP, the substitution effect is more powerful than the income effect. Leisure is becoming more costly in terms of income forgone and the individual chooses more work and less leisure. At wage rates higher than OP, however, the income effect predominates. Alternatively, in terms of utility analysis, we can say that at wage rates higher than OP the marginal utility of leisure exceeds the marginal utility of income. This is true of the labour supplied by an individual; it will not be true of the supply of labour to an industry. The supply curve of labour to an industry will be of the normal shape because higher wages will attract *more workers* to that industry.

The supply of labour to a given occupation

Occupationally, labour is not perfectly mobile; there are many restrictions on the supply of labour to a particular occupation. Most of these barriers to entry are discussed on pp. 48–49. Where the restrictions on entry are severe, the supply of that particular skill will be very inelastic. For example, an increase in the demand for surgeons cannot be met by an increased supply for several years. The supply of unskilled or semi-skilled labour in any one industry will be fairly elastic because a relatively small increase in wages will attract workers from similar jobs in other industries.

Barriers to entry which make the supply of a particular kind of labour inelastic do not, in themselves, cause the wage rates to be relatively high. One occupation is not paid a higher rate than another because it requires a much longer period of training, or a higher level of education, or a greater degree of natural ability. The possession of skills and knowledge for which there is no demand is of no economic significance. Knowledge, skill, and training are important influences on the level of wages only in so far as they affect the *supply* situation. Wage differences can only be explained by an examination of the *supply and demand* conditions.

The wage rate in a particular occupation

We can now bring together the various strands of supply and demand analysis to explain wage differentials. The wage rate will be determined by the supply and demand conditions in the market for the particular grade of labour.

The demand for labour depends upon the physical productivity of labour and the price of the product. These two facts determine the marginal revenue productivity of labour and hence the shape of the demand curve. The elasticity of the demand for labour in any occupation depends upon:

a The elasticity of demand for the product.
b The possibility of substituting other factors for labour.
c Whether labour costs form a large or small proportion of total costs.

The supply of labour to an occupation depends upon:

a The standard of living and the extent to which workers value leisure relative to income.
b The mobility of labour, i.e. the extent to which restrictions on entry such as education, training, and skill requirements are applicable.
c The prevailing social attitudes towards the nature of the work, i.e. the rating which the work is given in terms of 'job satisfaction'.
d The extent to which trade unions and professional associations are able to control recruitment.

It is fairly obvious that these different influences on supply and demand will apply to very different degrees in the different labour markets and hence give rise to different wage rates. In each labour

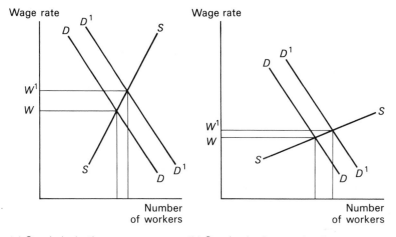

(a) Supply inelastic –
labour highly skilled–
long training period required

(b) Supply elastic – no barriers to entry–
labour unskilled –
little or no training required

Fig. 56 Effects of a change in demand for labour

market the wage rate will be determined by the interaction of the relevant demand and supply curves. Fig. 56 shows the effects of an increase (or decrease) in demand in two such markets. In one of the markets the supply of labour is elastic; in the other it is inelastic. There is not a separate market for each and every occupation, but rather separate markets for groups of occupations. Within these groups it is possible for labour to move from one occupation to another (e.g. a bus driver may become a lorry driver). Nevertheless for the highly skilled professions and those which require long periods of training each occupation does represent a separate labour market.

It should now be possible for the reader to discuss, analytically, questions on wage differentials. If asked to explain, for example, why solicitors earn more than their clerks, it is necessary to seek out those factors which give rise to different supply and demand conditions for these professions.

Quite apart from the differences in wage rates as between occupations we also find wage differences *within* an occupation. These arise for many reasons. In many occupations, particularly those of a clerical, administrative, or professional nature, there are scales of pay which allow for annual increments over a period of years, presumably because it is believed that labour's productivity varies directly with experience as well as education and training. The more senior workers, therefore, will be receiving higher wages than those who have recently joined the profession. There are various methods of remuneration which apply the payment-by-results principle (e.g. piece-work and bonus schemes) and in these cases wages will vary according to the individual worker's output. There may also be regional discrepancies in the wages paid to the same occupation. Workers with a particular skill may be in short supply in one area but not in another, but union negotiations, conducted on a national basis, tend to eliminate such regional differences in wage rates. Regional differences in the cost of living also play a part and the national scales for many occupations make provision for an additional allowance to be paid to those workers living in the London area.

Table 15 is included to provide some evidence of the variation in earnings as between very broad occupational groups. There will of course be wide variations within each group.

Table 15 UK earnings by occupation (selected groups) full time adult men in April 1981

Occupational Group	Average gross weekly earnings (£s)
Medical practitioners	297·1
Finance, insurance, tax specialists	244·7
Journalists	194·2
Engineers (mechanical)	192·4
Scientists and mathematicians	188·1
Architects and town planners	187·3
Accountants	174·4
Secondary teachers	172·2
Compositors	164·2
Plumbers	132·9
Postmen	119·7
Carpenters and joiners	119·0
Skilled motor vehicle mechanics	114·7
Machine tool operators	114·4
General clerks	112·5
Painters and decorators	108·7
Chefs and cooks	107·9
General labourers	102·8
Shop assistants	95·4
Caretakers	94·5
General farm workers	85·4

Source: Department of Employment. New Earnings Survey 1981 (Part A)

Trade unions and collective bargaining

The wages and salaries of the great majority of the working population are settled by some kind of collective bargaining procedure. The individual worker is in a weak bargaining position and the main purpose of a trade union is to remove this weakness by forcing the employer to negotiate with representatives of the whole, or the great majority of his labour force. The growth of trade unions has been accompanied by the growth of employers' associations and collective bargaining is the process whereby representatives of the employers in any one industry negotiate with representatives of the workers in that industry.

In the UK, trade union membership numbers about 11·5 million workers which is rather less than one half of the total working population. But there are large numbers of employees who belong to associations which carry out trade union-type functions but which are not strictly classified as such. A greater percentage of male workers than female workers belong to trade unions. Although large numbers of workers are not members of trade unions, it would be true to say that in the great majority of cases their pay and working conditions are settled by trade union negotiations. Such settlements are widely applied and are not normally confined to trade union members.

There are about 450 trade unions in the UK; the great majority of them are very small. The movement is dominated by a small number of very large unions. The 7 largest account for more than 50 per cent of total trade union membership (see Table 16). Trade unions are autonomous bodies, that is, they have complete freedom to act in their own interests. Most unions, however, are affiliated to the central body, the Trades Union Congress, which speaks for the movement as a whole and has an important role in bringing trade union points of view to bear on government decisions.

With so many different unions in the UK it is almost impossible to classify them into any clearly defined groupings. We can, however, distinguish four basic types of trade union.

Craft unions

The oldest unions, the craft unions, were formed originally to organise the workers according to their particular skills. Thus, engineers, printers, pattern makers, and boilermakers formed their own unions. These unions are spread horizontally across the industrial structure since the members of any one union will be found in many different industries. The spread of mechanisation and changing techniques of production have blurred the distinctions between many of the older crafts and have led to many 'demarcation' disputes as the craft unions argue about which particular trades should have the right to carry out new processes. The decline in the demand for some particular crafts has led many of these older unions to recruit semi-skilled and unskilled workers.

Table 16 The twenty largest trade unions 1982

Trade Union	Membership (thousands)
Transport workers (TGWU)	1 700
Engineers (AUEW)	1 020
Municipal workers (GMWU)	866
Local government (NALGO)	796
Public employees (NUPE)	704
Shopworkers (USDAW)	438
Managerial staff (ASTMS)	428
Electricians (EETPU)	395
Builders (UCATT)	275
Miners (NUM)	250
Printers (SOGAT)	237
Health workers (COHSE)	231
Teachers (NUT)	224
Civil servants (CPSA)	210
Postmen (UCW)	202
Engineers (TASS)	186
Railwaymen (NUR)	160
Bank staff (BIFU)	148
Printers (NGA)	136
Telecom Staff (POEU)	133

Source: Economist 11.9.82.

Industrial unions

These unions attempt to organise all the workers in a particular industry, regardless of the type of job done by the worker. This type of union is much more common in Europe and America than in Britain, where the National Union of Mineworkers and the National Union of Railwaymen provide examples. In the UK, where trade union organisation has a much longer history than in most other countries, it has proved very difficult to persuade workers with different skills (and those with no clearly recognised skill) to join forces in one union. The advantage of this form of union organisation, it is held, would be a great reduction of the demarcation-type of dispute within an industry.

General unions

These unions are usually prepared to accept anyone into membership, regardless of his place of work, the nature of his work, or his industrial qualifications. General unions have a very large unskilled membership and tend to overlap one another and also other types of union. The Transport and General Workers' Union and the National Union of General and Municipal Workers are two very large general unions in the UK.

'White-collar' unions

In the UK, in recent years, there has been a very marked increase in both the size and influence of the so-called 'white collar' unions (see Table 16). These unions recruit administrative and clerical staff (salaried employees) and other non-manual workers. They are very strong in teaching, banking, the civil service, local government, and among the technicians and other salaried employees of the nationalised industries and the larger industrial firms. Some of these are organised on an 'industry' basis, e.g. the banking and teacher unions, while others are organised across the industrial structure.

Trade unions and wages

Trade unions have two major functions:
1 To bargain on behalf of their members for better pay and working conditions.
2 To persuade the government to pass legislation in favour of the working class. Quite early in their history unions realised that many of their aims could only be achieved by political action. Trade unions played a leading part in the development of the Labour Party and they remain a major source of its funds.

It is the first function which is of most concern to us in this section.

Wages and collective bargaining

How great is the power of unions to influence wages? At one time it was thought that the unions' powers depended very much on the conditions in the labour market. In a situation of full or near-full employment when their membership would be high and their funds in a healthy state unions would be very strong. Employers, it was believed, would be much more vulnerable to union pressures when there was no excess supply of labour. Events in the early 1970s have cast serious doubts on this theory because unions have demonstrated their ability to push up wages even when unemployment is *relatively* high. This point is discussed more fully on p. 343.

Whether unions can exert a significant influence on *real wages* is a more difficult question to answer. Real wages depend upon the movements in money wages relative to the movements in prices. Increases in money wages unaccompanied by any increases in the output of goods and services are almost certain to lead to increased prices. Real wages then are determined very much by the movements in productivity.

To the extent that unions cooperate in schemes to increase efficiency they may play an important part in raising real wages although their very real fears of redundancy may lead them to resist the introduction of new techniques of production. They may also believe that, given the monopolistic structure of many industries, an increase in productivity may result in higher profits rather than higher wages. Even when there has been no increase in productivity it is still possible for trade unions to increase real wages if they can increase labour's share of the national income at the expense of profits, interest, and rent. This point is explained below. It is also possible for one union to increase the real wages of its own members at the expense of other income groups including other wage earners. Each union tends to direct its efforts at increasing the welfare of its own members; this, after all, is the main reason for its existence. The more powerful unions, if they make full use of their bargaining strength, could succeed in getting proportionately larger and/or more frequent wage increases than the weaker groups. If the share of income going to labour remains the same, this will mean a redistribution of income within the wage-earning groups from those with weaker bargaining powers to those with stronger positions.

In the 1970s there was an increasing tendency for bargaining on pay and working conditions to move away from industry-wide negotiations to company or plant-level bargaining. This development was accompanied by the increasingly important role being played by shop stewards in the worker-employer relationship and by a more widespread adoption of the closed shop principle.

A *shop steward* is not a full-time union official but one of the firm's employees who is granted time off during working hours to deal with trade union matters. In some larger companies and plants a shop steward may be employed full-time on industrial relations although his wage will be paid by the employer. As 'the person on the spot' he or she will have first-hand knowledge and experience of labour problems at the plant whereas the full-time union officials will have responsibilities for many factories and places of work in their areas. There has been a growing tendency, therefore, for management to deal directly with shop stewards (at plant level) on matters of pay and working practices.

A *closed shop* is an agreement that particular employees have to join particular unions in order to obtain and retain employment. In 1981 closed shop agreements covered about one-third of British factories.

The bases of wage claims

Trade union demands for higher wages are normally based on one or more of four grounds:
1 A rise in the cost of living has reduced the real income of their members.
2 Workers in comparable occupations have received a wage increase.
3 The increased profits in the industry justify a higher return to labour.
4 Productivity has increased.

1 The cost of living argument. If the rise in the cost of living is due to a rise in costs of production brought about by a previous wage increase then it seems difficult to justify the wage claim on purely economic grounds. If productivity has not increased and the share of income going to profits, rent, and interest does not change, an increase in wages can only lead to a further increase in prices. This is the familiar pattern of the wage-price spiral. If the cost of living has increased because of a rise in import prices, then, once again, if other things do not change, any wage increase must lead to a further rise in prices. If the rise in the general price level is due to an increase in monopoly profits, labour would seem to be quite justified in claiming a compensating wage increase, although the community as a whole would benefit from more competition, lower prices, and the elimination of the excess profits. The cost of living argument is one which attracts powerful social and political support and, in recent years, its acceptance has led to the widespread use of measures which link wages to the retail price index (a process generally described as 'indexation').

2 The differential argument. This argument rests on the widely held conviction that it is 'fair' that workers doing similar jobs should get similar rewards. One of the problems here is the meaning given to the term 'comparable occupation'. In many cases it is difficult to establish strict comparability; is there a job which is strictly comparable to, say, that of a policeman or an engine-driver? But the differential argument is also applied in a way which often leads to a situation where a wage settlement in one sector of the economy causes a chain reaction of wage claims in other sectors of the economy. If one occupation is granted a wage rise it means that the existing pattern of wage differentials has been upset. This will invariably provoke demands in other occupations for wage increases to restore the previous differentials. There is a strongly held conviction that wage differentials which have existed for a number of years are 'fair'. One often hears complaints from workers in different industries that they 'have lost out in recent wage settlements'.

The economic case against the differential argument is based on the necessity for a high degree of mobility in the labour force. If differentials are frozen, how do we get workers to move from declining or less 'essential' industries to the expanding industries? The only practical way in which such a movement may be brought about in a free society is by using wage differentials. If the growth industries offer higher rates of pay they will attract workers from other industries. But if these higher rates of pay lead immediately to compensating awards in other industries, the differentials remain unchanged, and there will be no monetary incentive for labour to move.

3 The profitability argument. The individual union in pursuing the interests of its own members feels completely justified in pressing for an increase in wages whenever the profits in the industry are increasing. In view of the imperfections in the product markets and the labour markets, it is difficult to say that the union claims are unjustified. Yet it appears from the point of view of the community as a whole that certain privileged groups (the shareholders and workers in these industries) are gaining at the expense of the general public. If the degree of competition were not restricted and the markets were more perfect, more labour and capital would move into these more profitable industries, more would be produced, prices would be lower, and excess profits would be eliminated.

4 The productivity argument. Improvements in labour productivity are widely accepted as justifiable reasons for increases in wages and most official incomes policies seem to accept this argument. There are, however, some serious problems involved. Most increases in productivity arise from improvements in the quality and performance of the capital equipment on which the labour is employed. Many would regard it as unfair that workers who happen to be employed in those industries where there is a rapid rate of technical progress should obtain all the benefits from the resulting increases in productivity. A large number of workers are employed in occupations where it is difficult or impossible to measure productivity, or where, due to circumstances beyond their control, it cannot be increased (e.g. increased traffic congestion *decreases* the productivity of the bus driver).

It can also be argued that gains from technical progress should accrue to the whole community in the form of lower prices. Where increases in productivity result from the workers' acceptance of new methods of production which impose greater strain, or responsibility, or call for retraining, claims for higher rewards are fully merited since the MRP of labour will have increased. A good example of this sort of change would be where labour agrees to drop some traditional restrictive practice.

Whatever the cause of increased productivity, where competition is ineffective, workers might reasonably argue that if they did not take the gains from the higher productivity in the form of higher wages, they would go to the owners of capital in the form of increased monopoly profits.

Trade unions and economic theory

It is often said that the determination of wages is a matter for unions and employers to settle by negotiation and the theory of supply and demand has little relevance in fixing wages. But market forces do have a part to play and they are, as it were, 'present at the bargaining table'. Employers and unions must take some account of the various supply and demand considerations discussed earlier. They will be aware of the extent to which labour can be substituted by capital and they will be conscious of the extent to which changes in labour costs affect total costs. They will also have some idea of the elasticity of demand for the product. Whether labour is in short supply or excess supply will also have some influence on the attitudes of the two sides. These matters will tend to set some limits to the range in which bargaining can take place. The power of the unions rests ultimately on their ability to call an effective strike and employers must consider the effects of such a strike on their costs and future sales. The unions' bargaining power also depends upon their ability to control the supply of labour to the industry. In cases where the union has established a *closed shop*, only union members may be employed and the union can effectively control the supply of labour. Trade unions can also influence recruitment in other ways such as by enforcing apprenticeship regulations and restricting employment to those who possess qualifications acceptable to the union. These latter restrictions are particularly important in such professions as law and medicine.

The trade unions' argument for closed shops and similar restrictive practices is that with open-shop bargaining (union membership is not compulsory) any agreement made between unions and employers applies to trade unionists and non-trade unionists alike. Those who are not members of the union get the benefits of trade union action without paying the dues, taking the responsibilities or sharing the risks associated with union membership.

When a trade union negotiates an agreed minimum wage and has the power to enforce that wage, the individual firm is faced with a similar situation to that shown in Fig. 54 and reproduced in Fig. 57. In Fig. 57 the free market wage is OW and at this wage the firm employs OM workers. A union is formed and negotiates a wage of OW^1 which it has the power to enforce on all firms in the industry. According to our theory the effect of the union action will be to cause the firm to reduce employment to OM^1. Indeed if this were a profit-maximising firm and other things remained equal this is exactly what would happen. But unions, as we have seen, have the power to control the supply of labour and might react to any reduction of employment by threatening strike action. The line AB shows the scope for bargaining between employer and union. AB represents the surplus earned on each worker employed when the wage rate is OW and the number of workers employed is OM. It might well be that when the wage is

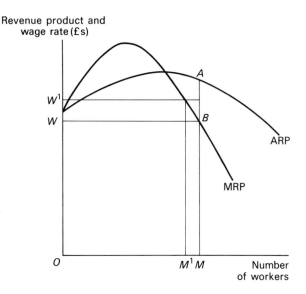

Fig. 57

raised to OW^1 and *employment remains at OM*, the firm is still making profits in excess of normal profits. In this case the union might be able to raise wages *and* resist any cut in the numbers employed.

We can present a similar picture for the industry as a whole. In Fig. 58, DD^1 and SS^1 represent the free market demand and supply curves for a particular type of labour. The free market wage will be OW and

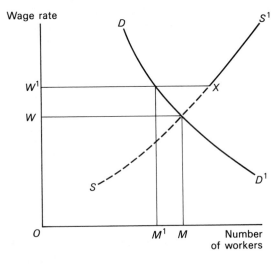

Fig. 58

OM workers will be employed. A trade union negotiates a minimum wage of OW^1. This means that the dotted part of the SS^1 curve now has no relevance because, although some workers will be willing to work for less than OW^1, they will not be allowed to do so. The supply of labour to this industry is now represented by the line $W^1 XS^1$ and the equilibrium position is where the demand curve crosses this line. At this point OM^1 workers will be employed. The result of the union action, according to this representation, has been to reduce employment by MM^1 workers. But this analysis assumes that other things remain equal and there is no change in the demand for labour. In fact, an increase in wages might well stimulate efforts to improve the productivity of labour and, if they are successful, the MRP curve will move upwards. The demand for labour will increase and there might well be no net reductions in the numbers employed. If this particular increase in wages is part of a general increase in wages there will be an increase in the demands for most goods and services. Firms will be able to raise prices and the ARP and MRP curves of labour will move upwards. Again, the increased demand for labour might well offset the increased wages so that numbers employed are not seriously affected. Unfortunately, as we shall see in Chapter 25, an increase in wages followed by an increase in prices is likely to provoke a chain reaction of events known as cost-push inflation.

Wages councils

The agreements made under collective bargaining procedures are not legally binding on the unions: they depend for their observance on the good faith of the parties to the agreement. In certain industries, however, where there is no effective machinery for collective bargaining, or where the voluntary arrangements are thought to be inadequate, there are statutory bodies known as Wages Councils. These councils are made up of equal numbers of employers' representatives and workers' representatives together with some independent members. Wages Councils submit proposals on wages and working conditions to the appropriate Minister who may then make an order giving legal force to the agreement. This method of wage-fixing is to be found in such industries as catering, distribution, road haulage, clothing and textiles. Wages and working conditions in agriculture are determined by a similar body known as the Agricultural Wages Board.

Trade unions and the law

Trade union power rests ultimately on the ability to withdraw the supply of labour, that is, the strike weapon. There is no doubt that the strike, or the threat of a strike has become increasingly effective as an instrument in collective bargaining. Modern industry based on extensive specialisation is increasingly vulnerable to disruption. A stoppage in any one part, no matter how small, of the linked processes of mass production can very quickly bring an entire industry to a halt. As industry becomes more capital-intensive, fixed costs are rising relative to labour costs so that stoppages of work are becoming increasingly costly; fixed costs remain high even when output drops to zero. A firm which has a large export market is particularly susceptible to strike action since, in highly competitive export markets, the ability to meet promised delivery dates is a vital factor.

The growth of unofficial strikes has become one of the most familiar features of the British system of industrial relations. Unofficial strikes are those which do not have full support of the trade union and they account for the great majority of all stoppages of work; most of them are of very short duration. Official statistics of the incidence of strikes, however, do not give a complete picture of the economic effects of industrial action since they do not record the effects of 'go slow' and 'work to rule' types of dislocation, neither do they indicate the numbers laid off as a result of strikes.

Successive governments in the UK have attempted to limit the powers of trade unions by getting them to cooperate on incomes policies and to accept legal limitations on their activities. British trade unions enjoy an immunity under the law from liability for damages (e.g. losses) caused by breaking contracts (e.g. strike action) which are carried out 'in furtherance of a trade dispute'. Britain's strike record and the recent growth of mass picketing have led to a widespread belief that trade unions tend to abuse the freedoms they enjoy under British law. In fact, in the UK, the number of days lost per annum through strike action (per 1 000 employees) is rather less than it is in several other industrialised countries.

Nevertheless growing concern about the state of industrial relations has persuaded successive governments to consider measures to bring industrial relations more closely within the framework of the law. In 1969 the Labour Government seriously considered bringing in an Industrial Relations Bill which would have given the government powers to intervene in industrial disputes. This proposal was abandoned in the face of united trade union opposition. The succeeding Conservative Government passed an Industrial Relations Act in 1971. It was a complex measure which aimed under certain circumstances to make collective agreements legally binding contracts. It established a Register of Trade Unions and only those unions whose rules met certain requirements were eligible for registration. Unions whose rules did not accord with certain basic principles could not be registered and hence could not be given legal status. They could not, therefore, obtain the legal privileges which went with that status. The Act proved largely inoperative because of union resistance and the next Labour government repealed the measure. The Conservative Government elected in 1979 made a fresh attempt to introduce the law into the field of industrial relations. The Employment Act of 1980 contained measures designed to make it more difficult to create new closed shop agreements (80 per cent of the work force must agree to the proposal); to provide some measure of protection for workers who object to the closed shop principle on grounds of conscience or religious belief; to encourage the use of secret ballots before strike action is taken; to limit lawful picketing to the employees' own place of work, and to place some restrictions on secondary action such as 'blacking' (e.g. refusing to accept or handle goods from firms where workers are on strike).

Equal pay

One of the most marked differentials in the national pay structure is that between the average earnings of men and the average earnings of women. In 1971, taking a wide range of occupations, it was found that within each broad occupational group women earned about 64 per cent as much as men on an hourly basis.[1] There are many reasons for this very substantial discrepancy.

Women tend to be over-represented in the low-paying occupations and within any one group they hold a disproportionate number of jobs at the lower end of the pay scale. The turnover and absenteeism rates for female workers tend to be higher than those for male employees. This, it is believed, gives employers less incentive to bear the cost of female training. Girls may also have less incentive to finance their own training (in terms of income forgone during training), because they believe they will spend a substantial period out of the labour force and hence will not receive proportionate benefits for the earlier sacrifices. If females do leave the labour force for several years, they will accumulate less experience and seniority than the male employees. For these reasons, among others, women are less likely to progress up the promotion ladders. Women workers, too, are less well organised in unions and tend to predominate in areas where trade union organisation has proved difficult (e.g. shops, hairdressing, small offices, etc.)

These reasons may explain why women hold fewer of the better paid jobs, but they do not provide good reasons for the fact that women are often paid less than men for the same work. Here we must accept the fact that habit and custom have tended to perpetuate differentials which are based on the idea that women's 'needs' are less than those of men. But this argument could equally well be used to

[1] It had risen to about 73 per cent in 1981.

support differentials between men – some men's 'needs' are far greater than those of other men. There is no doubt that prejudice plays a part in maintaining the sex differentials in pay. Demarcation between men's jobs and women's jobs persists long after technology has removed the skill element or the need for physical strength. There is certainly no evidence to support the view that men are 'better' workers than women.

An Equal Pay Act was passed in 1970 and came into force in December 1975. Its aim is to eliminate any discrimination between a man and a woman in regard to wages and other conditions of employment. It is difficult to foresee the effects of this legislation. For some considerable time the principle of equal pay has been supported by many trade unionists because they see it as a way of protecting men's jobs. As long as women are receiving less pay for the same work employers will use female labour as a means of lowering their costs of production. Cheap female labour is seen as a threat to male employment. The enforcement of equal pay could mean that these employers will show a preference for male workers.

There is something of a dilemma here. Sex differentials in pay almost certainly increase the demand for female labour and in doing so they increase the wages of women workers as a whole. It is of course unjust to the women workers who are doing the same work as men for less pay. Equal pay legislation might have the effect of reducing the demand for women workers and, if this is so, it will tend to depress the wages in exclusively women's jobs by increasing the numbers competing for them.

19 Interest

Interest has already been defined as the earnings of capital, or the price which has to be paid for the services of capital. In a monetary economy it may be regarded as the price which has to be paid for the funds which are required to purchase capital equipment. Loans are demanded, however, for purposes other than the purchase of capital and it would be more realistic to describe interest as a payment for the use of money. In order to create a supply of loans, people with the necessary financial resources have to be persuaded to lend. In normal circumstances, loans can only be obtained when lenders are offered some reward for the sacrifices, risks, and trouble involved. This reward is the rate of interest and it contains several elements.

a A payment for the sacrifice of current spending power. The lender forgoes the opportunity to spend and consume *now*.

b A payment for the risks involved. The future is always uncertain and circumstances are always changing. All lenders run the risk that the borrower may default.

c A payment to compensate, if only partially, for any fall in the value of money. In recent years most countries have experienced some degree of inflation and lenders have come to expect some payment to make up for the loss in the purchasing power of the money loaned.

The rate of interest is generally seen as a reward to lenders, but it is also the 'price' which has to be paid when a purchaser of an asset uses his own savings. In this case the rate of interest is the opportunity cost of using one's own resources; it is the interest forgone when one decides to buy rather than lend.

If the rate of interest is a price, then, in a free market, it must be determined by the forces of supply and demand. We shall deal with two well-known theories which attempt to explain the rate of interest in terms of supply and demand. The Classical Theory explains the rate of interest in terms of the demand for capital (i.e. investment) and the supply of savings. The Keynesian or Monetary Theory holds that the rate of interest is the price which equates the demand for money (i.e. the desire to hold wealth in the form of money) and the supply of money.

The classical theory

The classical economists regarded money as no more than a medium of exchange. In their view if people are prepared to pay interest for borrowed money it must be because they want money to buy real assets. Money is not demanded for its own sake, that is, to serve as a means of holding wealth. The demand for funds reflects the demand for capital goods.

Likewise the supply of funds available to borrowers must represent the willingness to forgo the goods which that money could buy. In other words the supply of loanable funds depends upon the ability and willingness to save.

The classical theory maintains that the rate of interest is the price which balances the community's saving with its capital investment.

The demand for capital

Capital is demanded because it is productive; it makes possible a much greater future output. Firms invest (i.e. create capital) because they expect to earn profits. They anticipate that the newly created capital will yield a series of returns during its lifetime which will exceed the costs incurred in its purchase and maintenance. The firm undertaking investment will estimate the net additional profits to be derived from the increased output and these expected net annual receipts can then be expressed in the form of a percentage annual return on the initial outlay. This percentage yield is the productivity of capital. We express the productivity of capital in this way because it is the only way in which we can compare the productivity of capital in different industries. If additional investment in the chemical industry is expected to yield a return of 20 per cent per annum while an addition to the stock of capital in the footwear industry is expected to earn 15 per cent per annum, capital will tend to flow to the chemical industry rather than to the footwear industry.

If we assume that the stock of capital is being increased relative to the stocks of the other factors of production, the returns to capital will be diminishing. Capital, like the other factors of production, is subject to the Law of Diminishing Marginal Productivity. The marginal product curve, then, will slope downwards from left to right. The analysis of the demand for capital follows exactly the same lines as that used to determine the demand for labour.

In Fig. 59 the *DD* line represents the marginal productivity of capital. It shows us the expected net profitability of additions to the firm's stock of capital. The price of capital is taken to be the current rate of interest on the funds available to purchase capital equipment, and we assume that the individual firm cannot influence this market rate of interest. In Fig. 59, therefore, the price of capital appears as a horizontal line. The entrepreneur will employ capital up to the point where the value of its marginal product is just equal to its price. In Fig. 59, when the rate of interest is *OR*, the firm will expand its capital stock to *OQ*. Any further additions to the capital stock would only reduce the firm's profits because the cost incurred in acquiring the capital (i.e. the interest charges) would exceed the expected annual returns from

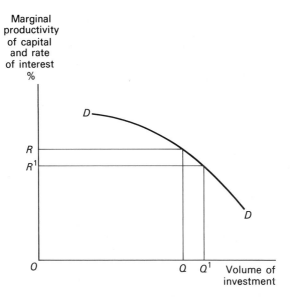

Fig. 59

the extra units of capital. If the rate of interest falls to OR^1, the demand for capital increases to OQ^1. Investment projects (QQ^1) which appeared unprofitable at the higher interest rate will now offer the prospect of profitable employment. Similarly an increase in the rate of interest will reduce the demand for investment goods. This analysis applies whether the firm is borrowing money or using its own savings. The rate of interest is the opportunity cost of investment in both cases. When the firm uses its own savings to purchase capital it sacrifices the interest it could have earned on those savings.

The marginal productivity curve tells us what quantity of capital will be demanded at any given price and it is, therefore, the demand curve for capital. The equilibrium condition for the firm is the familiar one. It will employ additional units of capital up to the point where the last unit employed adds as much to revenue as it does to costs. More formally we say that profitability is maximised when,

The MP of Capital = The Rate of Interest

The marginal productivity of capital, like that of labour, has two components, (i) the physical productivity of the capital, and (ii) the price of the goods produced with that capital. Changes in either of these components will shift the MP curve which is, of course, the demand curve for capital. The demand curve will move outwards when the efficiency of capital increases (due to technical progress) or when the price of the product increases. A fall in the price of the product will move the demand curve inwards towards the origin.

An important point to remember is that the calculations of the marginal productivity of capital are based on little more than guesswork. In trying to assess the profitability of an addition to the capital stock, the business person must estimate his revenues and costs for several years into the future (the expected life of the capital). It is the *expected profitability* of capital which is the basis of the investment decision. All manner of political, economic, and technical developments can influence entrepreneurs' views regarding the future prospects for their enterprises and for this reason we must expect private investment to be a fairly unstable element in the economy.

The supply of funds

According to the classical economists, the major determinant of the supply of funds for investment purposes is the current rate of saving. In return for a reward (i.e. interest) people will be prepared to forgo some current consumption in order to enjoy a higher level of consumption in the future. This reward is necessary because people have a *time preference*. They prefer present satisfactions to the promise of satisfactions in the future. The greater a person's time preference, the greater the inducement required to overcome it. If you are presented with the choice of having £100 now, or £110 in one year's time and you feel that £10 is just sufficient compensation for waiting, a rate of interest of at least 10 per cent is required to overcome your time preference. It would seem logical, therefore, to assume that a higher rate of interest will bring forth a greater supply of saving, since, as interest rates rise, people with a stronger time preference will be persuaded to start saving, and existing savers will increase their rate of saving. On this basis the classical economists assumed that the supply curve of savings was of the normal shape sloping upwards from left to right. The rate of interest then is determined by the interaction of the demand for loanable funds (derived from the demand for capital), and the supply of these funds (derived from current saving). This is shown in Fig. 60.

The classical theory – qualifications

The explanation of the rate of interest given above is very simple – unfortunately it is too simple and is subject to several qualifications.
1 The demand for loans is not derived solely from firms' demands for new capital. Householders also borrow. They borrow in order to purchase new houses and durable consumer goods and for these purposes make use of a variety of hire purchase arrangements and bank loans. People also demand loans in order to buy existing assets both financial (e.g. securities) and real (e.g. second-hand houses). The government is

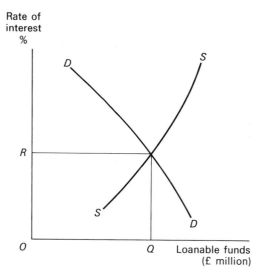

Fig. 60

also a large-scale borrower of loanable funds.

2 Although the demand for capital *is* affected by changes in the rate of interest, there are other influences at work and the relationship between the demand for capital and the rate of interest is not so straightforward as that outlined above. The level of economic activity is a powerful influence on business people's expectations. If they are confident that boom conditions will continue, an increase in interest rates may not deter them from carrying out an expansion of their investment, while very low interest rates may not persuade them to invest if they are convinced that a depression is just around the corner. Furthermore, a large proportion of total investment is carried out by public authorities (central and local governments and nationalised industries) and these projects will be strongly influenced by political and social considerations; changes in the rate of interest may have little effect on public investment.

3 The supply of loanable funds is not dependent solely on the level of current saving, and the current level of saving is not the same thing as the supply of loanable funds. Saving makes lending possible, but it does not follow that what is saved is automatically loaned. The rate of interest is a reward for *lending* rather than saving. People may abstain from consumption, but they may be reluctant to lend. In addition to the supply of funds from current saving, the banks are able to create additional supplies of money which may be made available as loans. A further supply of loanable funds becomes available when people decide to reduce the amount of wealth they are holding in the form of money – this means that lending may increase even when there is no increase in the current rate of saving.

4 It is extremely doubtful whether there is any simple direct relationship between the amount of saving and the rate of interest. The next section discusses the determinants of saving and provides evidence for the view that the rate of saving may be largely independent of changes in the rate of interest.

Savings

The level of savings

Table 17 provides background data to the subsequent discussion.

Table 17 Savings in the UK in 1981

	£ million	Per cent of total
Central government	−2 963	−6·1
Local authorities	2 515	5·2
Public corporations	5 419	11·2
Financial companies	3 369	7·0
Industrial and commercial companies	15 987	33·2
Personal sector	23 816	49·5
	48 143	100·0

Source: Financial Statistics

The community's level of saving is influenced by many factors.

Income

The most obvious requirement is the ability to save and this depends upon the level of income. No one can save until the level of income is sufficient to cover what are considered to be the necessities of life. As income rises beyond this level so does the ability to save. As we earn more, we spend more, but the *proportion* of income which is devoted to consumption spending tends to fall. A person earning £100 per week might spend £80 of it on consumer goods and services, whereas a person earning £150 per week might spend £100; a greater sum of money, but a smaller proportion of his income. What is true of the individual is also true, in this case, of society as a whole. The rate of saving in rich countries is much higher than that in poor countries.

Social attitudes

The prevailing social attitude towards thrift has a significant influence on the level of saving. Where thrift is regarded as a virtue, more will be saved. In Victorian times, hard work and careful saving were regarded as admirable personal characteristics, and they were important contributors to the rapid industrial progress during that period. Other communities place a higher value on leisure and consumption and in such societies the thrifty person might be despised as a mean person. Where this is the case, the level of savings would obviously be relatively low.

The financial framework

In the developed countries, all kinds of institutions for the safe deposit of savings are available. Savings banks, commercial banks, insurance companies, and building societies are all widely known, easily accessible, and have the confidence of the people. By prudent investment of the funds they obtain they are able to offer potential savers both security and income. This range of opportunities not only stimulates savings but ensures that most of the potential saving is made available to borrowers. In less developed countries there are few such institutions, they are not widely known or easily accessible, neither do they have the confidence of the majority of the people, who lack knowledge and experience of institutional forms of saving.

Savings and the rate of interest

As already mentioned, there is great uncertainty about the influence of the rate of interest on the level of savings. The reasons for this uncertainty should be fairly clear when we have looked at the nature of savings in our type of economy.

Much saving is habitual

Many people firmly believe that saving is a good moral habit, that is, people *ought* to save. Others like to have the feeling of security which comes with the possession of 'something in the bank'. Changes in the rate of interest are not likely to affect this type of saving.

A large part of total saving is contractual

This type of saving is carried out through insurance companies, pension funds, and building societies. The individual saver puts himself under a contractual agreement to pay a fixed annual sum (e.g. the insurance premium or superannuation contribution). Variations in the rate of interest will have little or no effect on existing contracts, although they might alter the nature of future contracts.

Many people save in order to achieve some definite objective

Many savers have a definite target such as the deposit for a new house, the purchase price of a motor cycle, or the cost of a holiday abroad. Saving in order to accumulate a fixed and known sum of money is not likely to be influenced greatly by changes in the rate of interest. In fact, an *increase* in the rate of interest might well *reduce* the level of such saving since, at the higher interest rate, the required sum will accumulate at a faster rate.

A large part of total saving is carried out by companies

Companies save in order to build up reserves which will act as a cushion against future business fluctuations and provide funds for future expansion. Company savings are not likely to vary with the rate of interest since the main purpose of such saving is not to achieve income in the form of interest.

A part of total saving is made up of government saving

When government revenue from taxation exceeds government expenditure we have a form of public saving. This will occur when the government feels that the purchasing power of the community is excessive in relation to the available supply of goods and services at current prices. Public saving of this type will not be varied to take account of any changes in the rate of interest.

The motives for, and nature of, saving provide sufficient evidence to support the view that the rate of interest and the rate of saving are not linked in any simple straightforward manner. Very high and very low rates of interest might well have some marked effects on the level of saving, but any 'normal' changes in the rate will probably have very little effect.

The liquidity preference, or monetary theory

Liquidity

Keynes emphasised the points made earlier that the demand for money was not related solely to the demand for new capital goods and the supply of funds was not dependent solely on the current level of saving. He pointed out that money was demanded not simply because it was a medium of exchange – it was also in demand as an *asset*. When he speaks of the 'demand for money', Keynes is referring to a demand for money *to hold*. In everyday speech the expression 'a demand for money' is usually taken to mean a demand for money to spend, but this is not a demand for money as such, but a demand for the things which money will buy. In monetary theory, 'the demand for money' must be interpreted literally; it refers to a desire to hold wealth in the form of money.

This preference for money over other kinds of assets is known as *liquidity preference*. Liquidity describes the readiness with which an asset can be converted into cash without any significant loss in value. Wealth held in the form of money provides us with the maximum freedom of action, because it is readily convertible into any other type of asset, and money, by definition, has a constant money value. If we exchange money for, say, a share in a company, the money value of our wealth is now uncertain, but we have an income-yielding asset. Money has the disadvantage that it does not earn an income. The great advantages of holding money are that it is the most liquid of all assets and its money value is certain. Note, however, that during inflation its exchange value falls.

Money, therefore, is one way in which an individual may choose to hold his or her wealth, but it is only one of many ways. Wealth may be held in the form of land, buildings, works of art, jewellery, bonds and shares, and so on. People hold wealth in all these forms and they adjust the proportions held in each form according to their means, desires, and the circumstances prevailing. We shall assume that decisions to change the amount of money they hold will cause people to hold more, or less, fixed-interest government securities (bonds).[1] A decision to hold less money will give rise to an increased demand for bonds, and a desire to hold more money will lead to a greater willingness to sell bonds.

The demand for money

There are three motives for holding money.

1 The transactions motive

Most of us receive our incomes at regular intervals (per week or per month) and spend it fairly evenly over the intervals between pay days. We receive regular payments in the form of a cash balance and then

---

[1] i.e. the next most liquid asset.

run it down over the intervals between one pay day and the next. We may not, of course, spend it all – some of it may be transferred to a savings account, but in most cases the greater part of it will be held as a cash balance to finance day-to-day expenditures. There is no alternative to this procedure because it is not feasible to transfer our incomes into income-earning assets and then to sell, each day, enough shares or securities to provide our cash requirements for that day. The pattern of daily life, therefore, means that, nationally, a large stock of money is demanded for transactions purposes.

The amount of money held as transactions balances depends upon the level of income, the movements in prices, and the frequency with which income payments are made. If our income rises, we tend to buy more and better goods and services and so we will hold larger transactions balances. If prices rise, we would hold larger cash balances because the things we buy now cost more. The frequency with which income is paid also has an important influence on the size of the average transaction balance. If a person receives a weekly wage of £120 and spends the whole of it evenly during the week, her average balance over the week will be £60. If she is now paid at the same rate but receives her remuneration monthly (i.e. £480 per month) and she maintains the same spending pattern, her average daily holding of money will be £240.

2 The precautionary motive

In addition to the cash balances needed to finance the regular day-to-day expenditures, most people hold additional money balances to deal with emergencies or to take advantage of some unexpected bargain. We may have to make an unplanned journey; unexpected visitors may involve us in unplanned spending on entertainment; something in a shop window catches our eye, or some domestic appliance requires urgent repair; such are the contingencies which encourage people to hold precautionary balances.

The transactions and precautionary motives are equally applicable to firms. A firm will hold a 'working balance' to meet payments during periods when the flow of income is less than the flow of expenditures. It will also need money balances to meet unexpected deviations in the pattern of trade (e.g. an unexpected rise in costs). The amount of money held for transactions and precautionary purposes is determined by factors which are not likely to change significantly in the short run.[1] The demand for these *active balances*, as they are called, will be fairly stable and will not be influenced by changes in the rate of interest.

[1] An increasing rate of inflation would have short-run effects.

3 The speculative motive

Any money which is held in excess of the requirements outlined above must be held for speculative purposes. People holding money in excess of the amounts needed for transactions and precautionary purposes must be convinced that, for the time being, it is more rewarding to hold money than financial, or real, income-earning assets. Why should people prefer to hold a sterile asset rather than one which brings them an income? In the case of government securities, for example, the income is guaranteed – there is no risk of default. But there is a risk of making a capital loss. People will prefer to hold money rather than securities when they believe that the prices of securities are about to fall.

Example: An undated government security, face value £100, bearing interest at $2\frac{1}{2}$ per cent per annum, stands at £30 in the open market. The purchase of 100 such securities will cost £3 000 and bring in an annual income of £250. This is a yield of $8\frac{1}{3}$ per cent.

Now suppose a prospective purchaser believes that over the coming year security prices will fall and decides to hold on to his money. In the event he is proved correct and at the end of the year the price of this particular security has dropped to £15. £3 000 will now purchase 200 such securities giving an annual return of £500 (i.e. $16\frac{2}{3}$ per cent).

By waiting for one year our investor has sacrificed £250 in the form of income foregone, but he will enjoy a net gain of £250 per annum as long as he holds these securities.

We can see, therefore, how an expectation of falling security prices will increase liquidity preference while expectations of rising security prices will reduce liquidity preference.

The prices of securities and the rate of interest

When the prices of fixed interest securities change, the rate of interest changes. The rate of interest is quite simply the current yield on undated government securities. This is often described as the 'basic' rate of interest because the government is able to borrow at lower rates than any other borrower. Government securities are described as 'gilt-edged' because there is no risk of default. A simple example should make the relationship between security prices and the rate of interest quite clear.

a An undated 5 per cent security, nominal value £100 (i.e. owner receives £5 per annum), stands at £80.

$$\text{Yield} = \frac{5}{80} \times \frac{100}{1} = 6\frac{1}{4} \text{ per cent} = \text{current rate of interest}$$

b The price of the security now falls to £60

Yield $= \dfrac{5}{60} \times \dfrac{100}{1} = 8\frac{1}{3}$ per cent $=$ current rate of interest

c The price of the security rises to £120

Yield $= \dfrac{5}{120} \times \dfrac{100}{1} = 4\frac{1}{6}$ per cent $=$ current rate of interest

Thus, the rate of interest varies inversely as the market prices of fixed interest securities.

Liquidity preference and the rate of interest

The reasons for holding money form the basis of the Liquidity Preference or Monetary Theory. For purposes of analysis the transactions and precautionary demands are usually added together and described as *active balances*. We have already noted that the demand for such balances will not be influenced by changes in the rate of interest and so it appears as the vertical straight line L^a in Fig. 61 (a). Before proceeding further it is necessary to emphasise the relationship between changes in the prices of fixed interest securities (or bonds) and changes in the rate of interest. A statement about one of these changes implies a statement about the other. Thus, if we read that interest rates are falling we know that the market price of securities must be rising (see examples above). If we read that the market prices of fixed interest securities are falling we know that interest rates are rising.

The speculative demand for money *is* influenced by changes in the rate of interest (i.e. in security prices), or, to be more accurate, by *expected changes* in the rate of interest. We saw this fairly clearly in the arithmetical example on p. 273. When security prices are expected to fall, speculators will be anxious to sell securities and hold money balances in order to avoid capital losses and also because they can increase their income by buying the securities at a later date when security prices are lower (as did the person in our earlier example). Now expectations of falling prices will be very strong when security prices are high – the next movement is likely to be downwards. Putting it another way, we are saying that *when interest rates are low, liquidity preference will be high*. There is the further point that the opportunity cost of holding cash balances will be low when interest rates are low (the amount of interest forgone is relatively small).

When security prices are low (i.e. interest rates are high), speculators will expect the next movement in prices to be upwards. They will want to buy securities now, before prices rise, either in anticipation of reselling at the expected higher price, or to secure the higher yield which the low-priced securities now offer (i.e. before rising prices reduce this yield). Speculators will, therefore, be anxious to exchange their money balances for securities. Thus, *when interest rates are high, liquidity preference will be relatively low.*

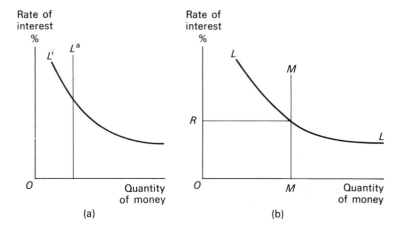

Fig. 61

This analysis indicates that when the quantity of money demanded is related to the rate of interest we shall obtain a demand curve of the normal shape. At high rates of interest very little money is demanded for speculative purposes; at low rates of interest, large amounts of money are demanded. The speculative demand for money is represented by the curve L^i in Fig. 61 (a). Note that the curve becomes horizontal at a positive rate of interest. This is because it is believed that some minimum reward (about 2 per cent?) is required to persuade people to forgo the advantages of holding money.

If the demand for active balances (L^a) is added to the demand for speculative balances (L^i) we obtain the total demand curve for money (LL) and this is shown in Fig. 61 (b). This curve is the liquidity preference schedule which tells us how the quantity of money demanded varies as the rate of interest varies. Speculative balances are often referred to as *idle balances.*

The rate of interest determined

The supply of money is determined by the monetary authorities (The Treasury and the Bank of England) and can be taken as fixed in the short run. It is identified as the vertical line (MM) in Fig. 61 (b). The rate of interest is now determined by the intersection of the demand curve for money (LL) and the supply curve (MM). It is equal to OR.

Let us now examine the effects of changes in the demand for money and the supply of money. For this purpose we make use of Fig. 62.

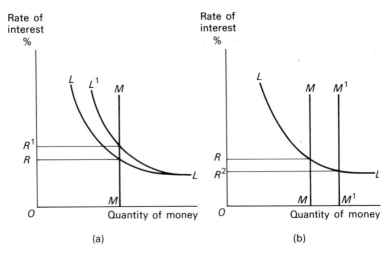

Fig. 62

An increase in liquidity preference (i.e. a stronger desire to hold money) brought about by an increase in income, or an increase in prices, or a widely held conviction that prices in general are about to fall, will raise the liquidity preference curve from LL to L^1L (See Fig. 62 (a)). This causes the rate of interest to rise from OR to OR^1. What happens is that the increased preference for money balances leads to an increased desire to sell securities and the increased supply of securities in the market depresses their prices. In other words, the rate of interest rises. A fall in liquidity preference, other things being equal, will lower the rate of interest as the demand for securities increases.

The effect of a change in the supply of money is illustrated in Fig. 62 (b). When the supply of money increases from MM to M^1M^1, the rate of interest falls from OR to OR^2. This comes about because an increase in the supply of money must leave some groups holding excess money balances (assuming no change in liquidity preference). They will be holding a greater proportion of their wealth in the form of money than they wish to hold at current rates of interest. In trying to adjust the distribution of their wealth among the different types of asset these people will try to buy more bonds. The increased demand for bonds increases their prices and the rate of interest falls. A fall in the supply of money will leave the community with less money that it wishes to hold at current interest rates. People will try to increase their money balances by selling securities and in doing so they will raise the rate of interest. Note that an increase in the supply of money when the LL curve is horizontal will have no effect on the rate of interest. This horizontal part of the LL curve is known as the 'liquidity trap' because any increase in the supply of money in this range will be held in *idle balances*.

The structure of interest rates

Throughout this chapter we have been discussing the rate of interest as though there were one and only one rate of interest. In fact, the slightest of contacts with the real world reveals not one but very many rates of interest. The National Savings Bank may offer us, say, 7 per cent on deposits, the building societies may tempt us with offers to pay 8 per cent on our savings, we are asked to pay, perhaps, 11 per cent for a mortgage and so on.

The rate of interest referred to in the foregoing analysis is the rate of interest on undated government securities which, as explained earlier, represents the lowest rate at which funds can be borrowed. Rates of interest paid by other borrowers will differ from this basic rate by margins which depend upon the factors discussed a little later in this section. The existence at any given moment of time of different rates of interest does not invalidate the preceding analysis of the forces which determine the rate of interest. There is a particular structure of interest rates and while one individual rate may change relative to another, the whole structure will be affected by changes in the demand for and supply of money. The general level of interest rates will tend to move with the basic rate of interest. The major reasons for so many different rates of interest existing at the same time are as follows.

1 The duration of the loan

The longer the period for which the money is borrowed, the greater the risk of default by the borrower. The future is uncertain and the longer the period of the loan, the greater is the uncertainty. Short-term loans, therefore, will normally carry lower rates of interest than long-term loans. The lender will accept a lower price because she feels more capable of estimating the course of events over the next few months than over the next few years, and, of course, she is postponing the ability to consume for a shorter period.

Note that a current account in a bank carries no interest because these funds are subject to immediate withdrawal, whereas a deposit account earns interest because the money is loaned for at least seven days.

2 The credit-worthiness of the borrower

Lending is a risky business and the degree of risk varies according to the evidence of the borrower's ability to repay. The risk of default by the government is negligible because it has the power to tax the whole of the nation's wealth in order to meet its liabilities. Borrowers with a credit standing almost as high as governments are the great industrial and commercial companies. Lenders will demand relatively low rates of interest from borrowers such as these. Individuals and firms with low credit ratings (probably because they are unknown quantities) will be charged much higher rates of interest. Much depends upon the nature of the security which the borrower can pledge against his loan. Borrowers who are able to offer claims on land and property as securities for loans will be able to borrow at relatively low rates.

3 The marketability of the IOU

Loans are made to governments when lenders purchase financial claims on the government in the form of Treasury Bills or longer term securities. Loans are made to companies by purchasing shares or debentures. These certificates (or IOUs) may or may not be easily marketable. Most government securities are marketable and may be bought and sold on the Stock Exchange (or in the Money Market). The same is true of the shares in most public companies. Where the ownership of the claim can be transferred very easily, the lender has a liquid asset. He can, if he wishes, 'change his mind' about lending his money and recover his cash. If he does decide to sell his security he cannot be sure of recovering the full amount of his loan, because the market prices of securities are always changing; he may get more than he loaned, he may get less. Where the acknowledgement of the loan is in the form of a marketable security, the loan will attract lower rates of interest, because the loan is a liquid asset.

The rate of interest is an important influence on economic activity. It will be referred to many times in subsequent chapters and it was necessary, therefore, to spend this time in trying to understand some of the rather difficult ideas concerning the determination of this particular price.

20 Rent

Everyone is familiar with the procedure of renting something. It is a procedure which has undergone rapid development in recent years and it is now possible to rent land, houses, factories, machines, offices, cars, television sets and almost any durable good. Rent, in everyday speech, simply means the periodical payment which is made for the use of some particular asset. It is a contractual payment fixed in terms of money and normally arranged on an annual basis. The type of payment ordinarily known as rent, the rent payable for the use of a car for example, contains an element of wages (labour is employed in providing the service), an element of interest (money has been invested in the business), and an element of profit.

Ricardo and rent

Economists have given a much more restricted meaning to the word Rent. It is used to describe all, or part, of the payment to a factor of production which is fixed in supply. When the theory of rent was first propounded, it was applied specifically to land. David Ricardo, one of the classical economists who formulated the theory, said that rent was a payment for 'the original and indestructible powers of the soil'. Although the concept of economic rent is applied to the earnings of all the factors of production, it is best to outline the theory in relation to land.

Economic rent

In the early nineteenth century Ricardo was very much involved in the disputes about the Corn Laws and the high cost of food, particularly the price of corn. Many people blamed the high prices on the landlords who, it was believed, were keeping the price of corn high by charging high rents for their land. Ricardo held that this explanation was completely wrong. He put forward the view that the rent of land did not determine the price of corn, but was, in fact, *determined by* the price of corn. The essence of Ricardo's theory is the fact that the supply of land, unlike the supply of capital and labour, cannot change in response to a change in demand. Land has no supply price. The amount available does not depend upon the market price; higher prices do not lead to larger quantities being supplied, and falling prices do not reduce the amount available. The *supply price* of a factor may be defined as the minimum reward necessary to retain a factor in its present employment. Any payment to a factor of production which is greater than its supply price is a kind of surplus and it is this surplus which is known as economic rent. Thus,

Present Earnings − Supply Price = Economic Rent

The supply of land is perfectly inelastic and if we assume that it has only one use, say the growing of corn, the whole of the landlord's income may be looked upon as economic rent. Since the supply of land is inelastic, any increase in the demand for food must lead to higher food prices and these higher food prices make it possible for landlords to charge higher rents, but they could *not* charge higher rents unless the land yielded higher revenues. If the demand for food falls, they cannot reduce the supply of land in order to hold up the level of rents. Ricardo believed that landlords were the class which stood to gain most from the rapid increase in population which was taking place during his lifetime. 'They would be able to reap where they never sowed.' In other words, the increasing demand for food would inevitably bid up the rents of land and landowners would receive increasing surpluses without making any kind of personal contribution to the increasing profitability of their land.

Economic rent more generally applied

The assumptions made in the preceding paragraph are not very realistic. Most land can be put to different uses, and the supply of land *for any one use* is not fixed. The supply of building land may be increased at the expense of agricultural land, and the supply of wheat land at the expense of grass land. The removal of the assumptions, however, does not invalidate the idea of economic rent as a surplus. It does mean that it is a concept which is not peculiar to land; it can be applied to the other factors of production. Whenever a factor is earning more than its supply price, it is receiving a part of its income in the form of economic rent. This situation arises when demand increases and the supply cannot fully respond to the increased demand. Factors of production already employed will experience an increase in income so that they must be earning more than their supply prices. There are particular circumstances where labour, capital, and the entrepreneur may all be receiving part of their remuneration in the form of economic rent.

Economic rent and transfer earnings

The *transfer earnings* of a factor of production is the minimum payment required to prevent that factor transferring to another employer or another occupation. It is determined by what that factor could earn in its next best paid employment. Transfer earnings may be regarded as the *opportunity cost* of keeping a factor of production in its present use, or, as we said earlier, it may be regarded as the factor's *supply price* in its present occupation. For example, if a person will work as a lorry driver for £100 per week, but not for £99 per week, and he is, in fact, receiving £125 per week as a lorry driver, his transfer earnings are £100 and he is receiving £25 per week in the form of economic rent.

Economic rent, therefore, may be defined as any payment made to a factor of production which is in excess of its transfer earnings.

Just how this concept may be applied to any factor of production may be seen in Fig. 63.

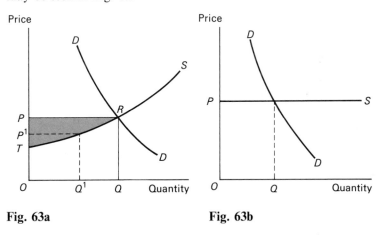

Fig. 63a   **Fig. 63b**

In Fig. 63 (a) we have the demand and supply curves for a factor of production. The equilibrium price is OP and OQ units of the factor are employed. Total earnings are equal to the area $OPRQ$, and all units of the factor receive the same reward, OP (it will be the wage rate if the factor is labour). But all units of this factor, except the last one taken into employment, were prepared to offer their services at prices less than OP. For example, OQ^1 units would be available to firms at a price of OP^1. Provided that the supply curve slopes upwards (i.e. it is less than perfectly elastic) an increase in demand will give rise to rent payments to those factors which were already employed at the original price. The shaded area PRT is the economic rent element in the total earnings. The area $OTRQ$ represents the total transfer earnings. Only the last unit of the factor to be employed earns no rent, because the price OP is the supply price of this particular unit.

In Fig. 63 (b) we have a situation where the supply of the factor is perfectly elastic, as it might be to the individual firm where there is perfect competition in the factor market. Thus, the firm can obtain any amount of the factor at the ruling price OP. At prices less than OP there will be no supplies available to the firm. The whole of the factor earnings represent transfer earnings, and, in this case, an increase in demand will not give rise to any economic rent. The price *OP* is the minimum payment which will prevent the factor leaving the firm.

Economic rent and labour

The amount of economic rent in the return to labour obviously depends upon the elasticity of supply and the level of demand. The greater the occupational mobility of labour, the smaller will be the element of economic rent. If labour is very mobile, quite small changes in the wage rate will cause large movements of labour, into the industry when wages rise, and out of the industry when wages fall.

Highly specialised labour is in very inelastic supply. This is true of specialists such as surgeons, highly qualified architects, physicists, and first class managers. The earnings of such persons probably contain a large amount of economic rent. Their relatively high rewards are due to the fact that they are in very scarce supply relative to the demands for their services. Their transfer earnings will be very much less than their current remuneration because their market values outside their own specialised professions are probably very low.

A most frequently quoted example of earnings which contain a large proportion of economic rent are those of 'star' entertainers, and particularly those of pop stars. Each one has, it seems, some unique characteristic and the supply of his or her particular talent is perfectly inelastic. The earnings of pop stars can reach amazing figures in a very short time period and there is no doubt that transfer earnings make up only a very small percentage of their incomes. In many cases the economic rent element in their earnings is, unfortunately, only too clearly revealed. The popularity of many individuals and groups is very short-lived and the weekly earnings collapse almost as quickly as they rose.

Economic rent and capital

Much of the nation's capital consists of very specialised equipment. It is designed for a particular purpose and cannot be transferred to another use. Once the equipment (e.g. a blast furnace) has been installed it could be said that any income greater than the variable costs is economic rent. No matter how low this net revenue falls, the equipment cannot be transferred to another use and any net return (i.e. greater than operating costs) is better than no return at all. It will only be beneficial to leave the equipment idle when the revenue falls below the running costs. This view is perfectly correct if we take the short-run view. Looking at the situation over the life of the existing equipment we can say that its transfer earnings are the current operating costs – if it does not cover these expenses it will leave the industry (i.e. go out of use). But if we take a longer-term view, there will come a time when the capital equipment will be worn out, and it will not be replaced if its earnings have not been sufficient to cover both variable costs and depreciation. If it does not earn this minimum return the supply of capital to this particular use will cease. Over the longer period, therefore, the transfer earnings of capital will be the variable costs plus the fixed costs.

Economic rent and land

In the case of land which has only one use (i.e. it is completely specific) the whole of its income is economic rent. The land cannot transfer to another use and it will remain in that use indefinitely even when its earnings are zero. Most land, however, has alternative uses and whenever this is the case a particular piece of land will be earning economic rent only to the extent that its income in its present use exceeds what it could earn in its next most remunerative use.

Suppose some land is being used for growing wheat and farmers are paying a rent of £90 per acre for it. Its next most profitable use would be for growing barley, but farmers are only prepared to pay £75 per acre for barley-land. Payments for the land in its present use, therefore, contain an element of economic rent equal to £15 per acre. Now *any* price greater than £75 per acre will lead to land being transferred from barley to wheat – why pay £90 per acre? The explanation lies in the strength of demand relative to supply. If wheat is a very profitable crop, farmers will bid against each other for suitable and available land and this could lead to prices rising well above the land's transfer earnings.

The land values which have attracted most attention in recent years have been those paid for urban land and especially for city-centre sites. The number of sites in the High Street is strictly limited – no matter what price is paid, there is no way of increasing the land available in this location for offices, shops, restaurants, cinemas, and so on. The high prices paid for such sites is explained by the inelasticity of supply and a rapidly increasing demand. Since these sites have many alternative uses the economic rent element in the price paid for any one use may be quite small, although the price itself may be very high. Fig. 64 illustrates the situation. D^1, D^2, and D^3 represent different demands for a particular urban site. D^1 may be the demand from companies building cinemas, D^2 the demand from supermarket developers, and D^3 the demand from developers of office blocks. The highest bids come from people wishing to build office blocks and the market price is OP^3. Of the total revenue only the shaded area represents economic rent.

Price

Fig. 64

Land tax

The fact that the total supply of land in a country is fixed and the view that the income derived from the ownership of land is a kind of 'unearned' surplus have led to much support for measures to tax economic rent. In most countries in the non-communist world increasing population and rising incomes have increased the demand for land and landowners have benefited from rising land prices, although they may have contributed little or nothing to the increase in the value of their land. The main attraction of a tax on economic rent is the fact that the whole of the tax would fall on the landlords. The best price (i.e. rent) they could get for their land will be determined by demand and supply. They cannot influence the demand for land, and since the total supply is fixed neither can they influence the supply. Thus a tax on land values cannot change the market price – it must fall on the landlords and must, therefore, reduce the revenue they receive as landowners. It should be remembered, however, that economic rent is not unique to landlords; it accrues to any factor which is fixed in supply and faces an increasing demand.

Much of the increased value of land arises from the efforts and expenditures of the community as a whole. Public expenditures on the infrastructure such as that on roads, water, gas and electricity services will dramatically increase the values of land which is adjacent to such services. There is a strong case to be made out for much (or all) of the increase in the value of the land accruing to the community rather than to the landowners. Many countries have introduced a Development Tax which is levied on any increase in the market value of land.

Quasi rent

We have noted that where the supply of a factor is less than perfectly elastic an increase in demand will lead to some units of that factor receiving economic rent. This rent may be of a temporary nature, however, because the higher price may lead to an increase in supply which will, in turn, lower the price. Increased earnings in an occupation may persuade more people to undertake the necessary training, increased freight rates may persuade shipowners to order more ships, and higher copper prices may encourage firms to sink more mines. That rent which is earned only during the period which must elapse before supply can be increased is termed *quasi rent*; true economic rent refers to the remuneration of factors which are fixed in supply.

21 Profit

Measuring the rate of profit

Once again we find ourselves using a word which has a number of different meanings. Profit is commonly understood to be the difference between receipts and costs. In the business world, however, the word is used in a variety of contexts.

The profit margin

This notion of profits refers to the difference between the cost price and the selling price per unit. This is the kind of relationship found in the examples in an arithmetic textbook.

e.g. Cost Price 50p   Selling Price 55p   Profit 5p

a Percentage Profit $= \dfrac{5}{50} \times \dfrac{100}{1} = 10\%$

A percentage return on turnover

In the previous example profit was expressed as a percentage of the cost price. It is a very common business practice to calculate profit as a percentage of total sales revenue.

e.g. Sales Revenue £1 000 000   Profits £150 000

b Rate of Profit $= \dfrac{£150\,000}{£1\,000\,000} \times \dfrac{100}{1} = 15\%$

This is a very useful view of profit to the trader, because the sales figure is the one which is most immediately available to him, and he can assess the movements in his profits on a day to day basis.

A rate of return on capital employed

In this case the profit is expressed as a percentage yield on the value of capital employed in the business. For example:

Sales receipts £1 000 000   Total costs £800 000   Capital £1 200 000
Profits £200 000

c Return on capital $= \dfrac{£200\,000}{£1\,200\,000} \times \dfrac{100}{1} = 16.66\%$

Economists are concerned with profit as an income and not as a percentage differential on individual transactions. The most relevant view of profit is that of a return on the capital employed, because, as we shall see later, it is this measurement which enables profit to serve as an important indicator to potential investors.

In any discussion of profit it is important to be aware of the particular view of profit which is being employed. A crude rate of profit, without any further analysis, can be very misleading. In the following example we have two firms, one making a very small profit on each unit sold, but having a large turnover, the other making a large profit on each unit, but having a small turnover. Each firm has the same amount of capital employed in the business. Profit margins are expressed as percentages of the selling prices.

Firm A

    Capital employed £1 000 000   Sales £5 000 000
    Profit margin 5%   Profit £250 000

a Return on capital employed $= \dfrac{£250\,000}{£1\,000\,000} \times \dfrac{100}{1} = 25\%$

Firm B

    Capital employed £1 000 000   Sales £500 000
    Profit margin 20%   Profit £100 000

b Return on capital employed $= \dfrac{£100\,000}{£1\,000\,000} \times \dfrac{100}{1} = 10\%$

Although Firm B is operating with a profit margin four times as great as Firm A, the return on its capital is very much less than that earned by Firm A. This example should help us to understand why firms which carry large stocks in order to provide a wide choice, such as jewellers and ladies' fashion shops, have much larger profit margins on the goods they sell than do supermarkets. In the case of the jewellers and fashion houses, the stock 'turns over' very slowly whereas in the supermarket the stock 'turns over' very quickly.

The nature of profit

It is very difficult to isolate the return described as profits from the other factor incomes, wages, interest, and rent. This is especially the case when the owners of capital are also the managers. The small proprietor who works in her own business may declare that she has made £5 000 'profit' during the year. The figure she refers to will invariably be her gross profits which she obtains by deducting her purchases from her sales revenue. Her true profit will be much less than £5 000 because this figure will contain elements of wages, interest, and rent. The entrepreneur who contributes her own labour to the business must deduct from the gross profits an amount equal to what she might earn as a salaried employee. She will almost certainly have invested her own savings in the business so that some part of the £5 000 represents interest on capital. If she owns the premises in which the business is conducted then a further deduction must be made from the gross profit figure. This will be equal to the rent she would have received had she let the premises to a tenant. The opportunity cost to the entrepreneur of using her own labour, capital, and premises in the business represents *implicit* wages, interest, and rent, and these items must be deducted from the gross profit figure in order to obtain the true, or pure profit.

A major problem is to distinguish between interest and profit because the terms are often used as though they were interchangeable. Both are payments made to the providers of capital. If the funds for investment are supplied by creditors of the company in the form of loans, the returns to capital are described as interest. When the money is provided by shareholders, who by purchasing shares become owners of the business, the returns to capital are described as profits. Strictly speaking, the opportunity cost principle described above should be applied to shareholders' profits. Shareholders have forgone the interest their funds might have earned if they had been used to buy virtually risk-free bonds. A deduction equal to this implicit interest should be made from their dividends in order to arrive at the true profit. In practice it is very difficult to isolate pure profit and the profit figures produced by the accountant will include elements of implicit wages, interest, and rent. Profit differs from the other forms of income in three ways.

1 Profit may be negative. Capitalism is a *profit and loss* system. A firm may make losses, but wages, interest, and rent are most unlikely to be negative items.

2 Profit fluctuates far more than other forms of income. Rent, interest, and wages are normally fixed at some agreed rates for some given period of time (e.g. a wage of £150 per week, or interest at 10 per cent per annum). Profit cannot be agreed in advance because future revenue and costs are uncertain.

3 Profit is a residual item. Profit is what remains of the receipts after all expenses have been met. Wages, interest and rent are usually fixed in advance of the performance of the services for which they are payments.

Risk-bearing and profits

We have spent some time trying to distinguish profits from other forms of factor income. It is also necessary to distinguish the particular function or service which justifies the making of profits in a capitalist system. We know that profits accrue to the factor we have identified as the entrepreneur whose role is to hire, combine, and organise land, labour, and capital in a manner which, he believes, will maximise his profits.

The entrepreneur's decisions are based on his expectations – he cannot know how things will turn out, and in a changing world he has to take risks. These risks arise from uncertainty. The entrepreneur must risk his capital in carrying out production *in anticipation of* a successful outcome – he cannot guarantee success, neither can he insure against the risks of failure. Profit is usually defined as a reward for bearing the burden of uncertainty, or as a return to the function of risk-bearing.

The risks incurred in running a business are of many kinds. Some of these, such as the risk of loss due to flood, fire, or burglary, or injuries to employees, are insurable, because the laws of probability can be applied to such events, and insurance companies can calculate the degree of risk involved. But no statistician can calculate the numerical probability that a firm, or group of firms, will make profits or losses in the future. Economic conditions are changing all the time and the success or failure of a particular enterprise in the past is no good guide as to the likely success or failure of a similar enterprise in the future. Profits then are the reward for taking non-insurable risks.

Some economists emphasise the role of profit as a necessary incentive for innovation. All enterprises in a capitalist economy involve a degree of risk, but the introduction of a new product, or a new method of producing an existing product, or the attempt to open up a new market, are examples of innovations which carry a much higher degree of risk. It is this type of activity – trying something new – which is so vitally necessary for economic growth. Successful innovation provides a great stimulus to new investment and may well lead to the growth of large new industries. Innovators may well be encouraged by the prospects of large profits which may, and often do, accrue to the first in the field.

Profit and rent

Normal profits have been defined as the minimum rate of return which is required to keep an entrepreneur in his existing line of business. This rate of profit might be regarded, therefore, as the entrepreneur's transfer earnings, and any profit in excess of normal profits must be a form of economic rent. Normal profits will vary from industry to industry according to the degree of risk involved. The minimum expected rate of profit required to persuade a firm to carry on prospecting for oil will obviously be much greater than that needed to keep a firm in the brewing industry. Excess or abnormal profits can only be maintained in the long run where there is a monopoly situation. Such abnormal profits are often described as monopoly rent.

The role of profit

We can now summarise the role of profit in a capitalist society.

a A reward for bearing the uncertainty associated with carrying on business.

b A stimulus to innovation. Profit is seen as the necessary inducement which encourages people to introduce new products and new techniques.

c A source of funds for investment. We saw in Chapter 10 that retained profits provide an important means of financing expansion and modernisation.

d An indicator for potential investors. Profit plays an important part in determining the allocation of resources. Industries earning high profits will attract more resources than those where profits are relatively lower.

Note on stock appreciation and profit

The increasing rate of inflation in recent years has led to a fierce debate on exactly what 'profits' should be subject to a profits tax. Inflation rates of 20 per cent per annum or more have led to large increases in the *money values* of the stocks held by businesses. Corporation tax is levied on gross profits and these include any increase in the value of stocks. The values of the stocks held therefore have an important influence on the level of gross profits and *stock appreciation* during inflation will swell the profit figures. Briefly

Gross Profits = Current Sales − Current Purchases + Stock
Appreciation

The problem is that stock appreciation is only a 'book' profit; it cannot be spent or distributed to shareholders unless the stocks are sold. But if the firm is continuing in business the stocks must be replaced and if prices remain at their present level or continue to rise the 'profit' on stocks held will be swallowed up in the replacement cost. Firms complained that they were being charged profits tax on a profit which they never received, and, in 1974, the Chancellor agreed that, in assessing profits for taxation purposes, some allowances should be made for this inflationary element in gross profits.

Part Seven: Money and Banking

22 Money

Money is one of man's greatest inventions and the fact that all but the least developed of human societies use money indicates that it is an essential tool of civilisation. In the absence of some form of money, exchange must take the form of *barter* which is the direct exchange of goods and services for goods and services. Barter will serve man's requirements quite adequately when he provides most of his needs directly and relies upon market exchanges for very few of the things he wants. As the extent of specialisation increases, the barter system proves very inefficient and frustrating. In the simplest society each family will provide by its own efforts most of its needs and perhaps some small surpluses. A farmer will exchange any small surplus of food, wool, or hides for the surpluses of other producers. But this system of exchange becomes very cumbersome as economic activities become more specialised. A specialist metal worker must seek out a large number of other specialists in order to obtain, by barter, the variety of goods he needs to satisfy his daily wants.

The great disadvantage of barter is the fact that it depends upon a 'double coincidence of wants'. A hunter who wants to exchange his skins for corn must find, not merely a person who wants skins, but someone who wants skins *and* has a surplus of corn for disposal. The alternative is to exchange his skins for some other article and then carry out a series of similar exchanges until he finally gets his corn. Time and energy which could be devoted to production is spent on a laborious system of exchange.

Quite early in his history man discovered a much more convenient arrangement. The use of some commodity as a medium of exchange makes exchange triangular and removes the major difficulty of the barter system. If a commodity is generally acceptable in exchange for goods and services, it is money. A producer now exchanges his goods for money and the money can then be exchanged for whatever goods and services he requires.

The essential characteristic of money is that it must be *generally acceptable*. Unless the medium of exchange is freely acceptable by everyone, no producer is going to take the risk of accepting it in exchange for his products. He must have confidence that the 'money' will, in turn, be accepted by the sellers of the things he wishes to buy.

The functions of money

Money has several functions and these will be outlined before we proceed to examine the development of the modern forms of money.

1 A medium of exchange

As we have already explained, the use of money as a medium of exchange makes possible a great extension of the principle of specialisation. In an advanced society the use of money allows us to exchange hours of labour for an amazing variety of goods and services. We can exchange, for example, two weeks' labour for a holiday abroad just as easily as we can exchange it for a piece of furniture or a year's rent on a television set. Such exchanges are taken for granted yet they would be inconceivable without the use of money.

2 A measure of value

The first step in the use of money was probably the adoption of some commodity as a unit of account or measure of value. Money, most likely, came into use within the barter system as a means whereby the values of different goods could be compared. The direct exchange of goods for goods would raise all sorts of problems regarding valuation. For example 'How many bushels of corn are equal in value to one sheep, if twenty sheep exchange for three cows and one cow exchanges for ten bushels of corn?' This problem of exchange rates is easily solved when all other commodities are valued in terms of a single commodity which then acts as a standard of value. Money now serves as such a standard and when all economic goods are given money values (i.e. prices), we know, immediately, the value of one commodity in terms of any other commodity.

3 A store of value

Once a commodity becomes universally acceptable in exchange for goods and services, it is possible to store wealth by holding a stock of this commodity. It is a great convenience to hold wealth in the form of money. (The advantages of money as an asset are discussed on p. 271.) Consider the problems of holding wealth in the form of some other commodity, say wheat. It may deteriorate, it is costly to store, it must be insured, and there will be significant handling costs in accumulating and distributing it. In addition, its *money value* may fall while it is being stored. The great disadvantage of holding wealth in the form of money has become very apparent in recent years – during periods of inflation its *exchange value* falls.

4 A means of making deferred payments

An important function of money in the modern world, where so much business is conducted on the basis of credit, is to serve as a means of deferred payment. When goods are supplied on credit, the buyer has immediate use of the goods, but she does not have to make an immediate payment. She can pay for them 3, or perhaps 6, months after delivery. In the case of hire purchase contracts, the buyer takes immediate delivery but pays by means of instalments spread over 1, 2, or 3 years.

A complex trading organisation based upon a system of credit can only operate in a monetary economy. A seller would be most unlikely to accept any promise to pay in the future which was expressed in terms of a commodity other than money. She will have no idea how much of that commodity she will need in the future and if she does not want it she will be faced with the trouble and risks involved in selling it. She is prepared to accept promises to pay expressed in terms of money, because, whatever the pattern of her future wants, they can be satisfied if she has money.

The development of money

If the commodity chosen to serve as money is to carry out its functions efficiently it must possess certain characteristics. Except in the most developed societies the commodity used as money must be desired for its own sake. People will only accept as a medium of exchange something which they know will be acceptable to others, and the best guarantee of that *acceptability* is that the money should have an intrinsic value. So for a very long period in the history of money the currency had to have a commodity value which was related to its monetary value. Gold met such a requirement admirably.

An efficient medium of exchange must be *portable* by having a high ratio of value to bulk and weight. It would be very inconvenient to use large, heavy, and bulky objects as money.

The commodity must also be *divisible*, that is, capable of subdivision into smaller units without any loss in value. Suppose hides are being used as money and two sheep are worth one hide. How does one buy one sheep? When the hide is cut into two equal parts, the value of the two halves is less than the value of the whole hide.

A most essential characteristic of whatever is to serve as money is *durability*. People will not accept anything which is subject to rapid deterioration and hence loses value while it is in their possession.

Finally the commodity must be *limited in supply*. Unless there is some limitation on supply, either natural or artificial, people will have no confidence in the value of the commodity.

Precious metals

This list of desirable qualities enables us to see why, at all times and in all places, people have adopted the precious metals, gold and silver, as the commodities to serve as money. Gold and silver are portable since they have a very high commodity value and it is very easy to produce them of uniform fineness. They are divisible without loss in value and they are easily recognisable. These metals can be stored without risk of deterioration and, most important, they are limited in supply. Gold especially is difficult and costly to extract. Since the annual additions to the existing world stocks are relatively very small there is virtually no risk of a large increase in supply destroying the value of gold.

Coins

The precious metals were first used as money on the basis of weight. We read in the Bible, 'And Abraham weighed unto Ephron the silver' (Gen. 23:16). The shekel and the pound are units of currency and also units of weight. The inconvenience of weighing out the metals each time a transaction took place led to the introduction of coins. It was appreciated that exchange would be greatly facilitated if the pieces of metal to be used as money carried some clear indication of their weight and fineness. Coins are shaped pieces of metal bearing some authoritative imprint which certifies their money value.

There is, however, always a temptation for rulers to enrich themselves by reducing the commodity value of the coinage below its declared money value. They do this by reducing the precious metal content and adding some metal of lower money value. By this means any given weight of gold and silver can be used to produce more coins. The declared money value of the coins is not changed and the additional coins can be used to swell the royal coffers. In the middle of the sixteenth century the debasement of the coinage, which was seriously affecting the acceptability of money, led to the formulation of *Gresham's Law* which stated that *bad money drives out good*. Where a variety of coins are circulating some of which have a higher gold or silver content than others (of the same money value), people will hoard the coins with a higher commodity value and try to use the debased coins.

Bank-notes

Development

The next great step forward in the history of money was the introduction of paper money. Bank-notes first came into use in Britain during the seventeenth century. The essential feature of the new development was that people began to use *claims* to precious metal as money instead of the metal itself. The dangers of theft and the lack of security in the average home meant that gold and silver were deposited in goldsmiths' vaults – the depositors receiving some written acknowledgement of their ownership. If these receipts were stolen no loss was suffered because the gold and silver would not be withdrawn without the depositor's signature. It became a common practice for a person to pay his debts by endorsing his receipts with an instruction to the goldsmith (the embryonic banker) to transfer his deposit to some other person. Thus, bankers' receipts were endorsed and passed from hand to hand in settlement of debts. A further and important step forward came when bankers made out the deposit receipts, or 'promises to pay', as *payable to bearer* instead of to some named person. These claims to gold and silver could now be transferred without endorsement and the person in possession had a full legal claim to the amount of money specified on the receipt. These notes came to be issued in convenient denominations (e.g. £1, £5, or £10) instead of being a single receipt for the full deposit. Bearer notes were the first fully-fledged bank-notes.

Fractional Backing

Initially the bank-note would be accepted as a claim to gold or silver, used for one transaction and then 'cashed'. But, in time, the bank-note itself came to be regarded as money and was passed from hand to hand financing numerous transactions. As long as people were absolutely certain that they could, at any time, convert the notes into gold (or silver) they would be quite happy to accept them in payment for goods and services. In the early stages of banking the value of the notes issued was exactly equal to the value of precious metals held in the strongrooms. In other words the bank-notes had a *100 per cent backing* in the form of precious metals.

As the public gradually acquired more confidence in them, bank-notes began to circulate more and more freely and it became apparent to the bankers that the greater part of their holdings of precious metal (specie) was lying idle. Every day some notes would be presented for conversion into gold or silver, but at the same time other people would be depositing specie. Only a small proportion of the metallic 'backing' would be required to meet any daily *net* demand for precious metal. It became fairly obvious that bankers could issue notes to a total value well in excess of the value of the gold and silver they were holding, and still meet all the likely demands from those who wished to convert their notes. Suppose a banker found by experience that over a period of time the maximum net withdrawal of gold and silver was equal to 20 per cent of the average value of his stock of these metals. This would indicate that his stock of specie would support a note issue equal to five times its own value. The cautious banker would be aware of the fact that he might at some time be called upon to meet unexpectedly heavy demands for conversion of his notes and he might allow for this by issuing notes equal to twice the value of his stock of precious metals.

When bankers began to issue notes in excess of their holdings of gold and silver they were, in fact, creating money. When notes are backed 100 per cent by specie, no money has been created – the public have merely changed the form in which they are holding money, but *fractional backing* implies the creation of money since the value of banknotes issued exceeds the value of the precious metal supporting them. Bankers issued these additional notes as loans on which the borrower had to pay interest. It was a profitable exercise and banks were tempted to over-issue by reducing the size of the backing. During the seventeenth and eighteenth centuries there was a series of crises and bank failures when bankers' reserves of gold and silver were found inadequate to meet demands for conversion. Failure to meet these demands destroyed confidence in banks, holders rushed to convert their notes, banks were forced into liquidation and heavy losses were incurred by depositors. Bank-notes fell into disrepute and after 1833 the state was obliged to regulate the note issue.

Regulation and token money

The Bank Charter Act of 1844 followed a long dispute about the control of the money supply and whether the value of the note issue should be allowed to exceed the stock of gold [1] available to support it. The Act placed a statutory limit on the *fiduciary issue* (that part of the note issue which was not backed by gold) and restrictions were placed on the issue of notes by joint stock banks other than the Bank of England. In fact, these regulations were framed so that the passage of time would eventually leave the Bank of England as the sole note-issuing authority in England and Wales. The last private bank of issue in England surrendered its rights in 1921.

Apart from relatively short periods of emergency when conversion was suspended, all bank-notes, until 1914, were convertible into gold. Convertibility on a restricted basis was restored in 1925, but finally

---

[1] In 1816 gold became the single standard of value.

abandoned in 1931. Since that time Bank of England notes have been wholly inconvertible and we have now reached the stage where our bank-notes, while still carrying a 'promise to pay' printed on their faces, are no more than *token money*. This is also true of the coinage; the commodity value of the coins is but a tiny fraction of their money value. Nevertheless the notes and coins are universally acceptable; the fact that they have no real commodity value, and are not backed by gold, in no way affects their ability to serve as money.

Bank deposits

Bank-notes and coins are not the most important form of money in developed economies. In the UK about 90 per cent, by value, of all transactions are settled by means of cheques. But cheques themselves are not money, they are merely orders to bankers to transfer money from one person to another. The money so transferred consists of bank deposits. If there is no money in the form of a bank deposit then any cheques drawn on that account will be worthless.

Cheques were used as early as the second half of the seventeenth century, but they did not come into general use until the second half of the nineteenth century. The Bank Charter Act of 1844 put strict limitations on the note issue at a time when the output of goods and services was expanding rapidly. The need for an expansion of the money supply to keep pace with increasing output greatly stimulated the use of bank deposits.

This most developed form of money (i.e. bank deposits) consists of entries in the banks' ledgers, or more likely nowadays, of records on computer tapes. The greater part, in value terms, of the payments made each day are carried out by adjustments made to the totals in different bank deposits. A payment from one person to another merely requires that the banker reduces the amount in one deposit and increases it in another. Transferring money, therefore, has become little more than a kind of bookkeeping exercise; the money itself does not consist of some physical tangible commodity.

Table 18 The UK money supply in August 1982

	£ million
Notes and coins in circulation	10 741
Bank deposits[1] held by UK residents	77 902
	88 643

[1] Includes deposits held on current account (known as sight deposits) and time deposits.

The creation of bank deposits

Bank deposits are created by the banks and not by the state, although the state, as we shall see later, has various ways of controlling the commercial banks' ability to create deposits. Bank deposits come into being in three ways:

1 When a bank receives a deposit of cash (notes and coin).
2 When a bank makes a loan.
3 When a bank buys securities with cheques drawn on itself.

1 When a person deposits cash (say £1 000) in his bank he receives a bank deposit of the same money value. The value of his personal supply of money has not changed, it has simply changed its form; he now has a bank deposit whereas he previously held notes and coin. The effect of this transaction in the bank's accounts may be represented as follows:

Liabilities	*Assets*
Deposits £1 000	Notes and coin £1 000

The bank's assets and liabilities have increased by equal amounts. A bank's liabilities consist of claims against the bank. The banker's deposits are liabilities because he is committed to meet all his depositors' demands for cash and to honour all cheques drawn on these deposits. The cash (notes and coin) is an asset because it is a claim against the central bank.

2 The second and more important method by which bank deposits come into being is by means of a bank's lending operations. Lending is the most profitable of a bank's activities (it charges interest on its loans). When a bank makes a loan, say £1 000, it credits the account of the borrower with the amount of the loan. In this case the bank has created a bank deposit without any prior deposit of cash. The effect on the bank's accounts will be as follows.

Liabilities	*Assets*
Deposits £1 000	Loans £1 000

The money supply in this case *has* increased. What has taken place, in fact, is an exchange of claims. The banker has exchanged a claim against himself (i.e. a deposit of £1 000) for a claim against the borrower (i.e. a loan of £1 000). If you lend me £10, then I acquire an asset together with an equal and opposite liability to repay you the £10. The bankers' loans represent assets because they are claims against the borrowers and banks usually safeguard themselves as far as possible by requiring borrowers to provide some kind of security to cover the value of the loan. This security may take the form of a legal charge against the borrower's property or some good evidence of his ability to repay.

3 Banks may also create deposits by purchasing securities (usually government bonds) with cheques drawn on themselves. The seller of the security will pay the cheque into his bank account and his deposit will increase by the amount he has been paid for his security, say, £1 000. There has been no transfer of funds from any other depositor – the total of bank deposits will increase by the amount paid by the bank for the securities. In the bank's books the transaction will have the following effect:

Liabilities	*Assets*
Deposits £1 000	Securities £1 000

Again, the bank's assets and liabilities have increased by equal amounts.

Cash and liquid assets ratios

The banks cannot create deposits to an unlimited extent. Bank deposits are convertible into cash either immediately (in the case of current accounts) or at relatively short notice (in the case of most time deposits). Banks, therefore, must always be in a position to meet depositors' demands for cash (notes and coin). Deposit banking is based on the principle that all depositors will not simultaneously exercise their rights to withdraw their funds in the form of cash.

Just as the goldsmith-bankers discovered that only a small part of their note issue was likely to be converted into gold on any one day, so modern deposit-bankers realise that, on any one day, only a small part of their total deposits is likely to be 'cashed'. Every day a large number of people will be withdrawing cash from the banks, but it is likely that, at the same time, many other people will be depositing cash. It is the possible *net* withdrawal of cash which concerns the bankers.

Although confidence in modern banks is so great that by far the greater part of total payments (by value) takes the form of transferring deposits by means of cheques, bankers must maintain some safe ratio between their cash reserves and total deposits. In a developed country where cash payments account for a very small percentage of the total value of all transactions, this ratio will be very small and banks will be able to create deposits to a much greater money value than the amount of cash they are holding.

For example, if the banks decide that a 5 per cent cash ratio is more than adequate to meet all likely demands for cash and they adopt this particular ratio, then total deposits could be expanded to a value twenty times as great as the banks' holdings of cash. In other words, cash reserves of £10 million will support bank deposits to a value of £200 million. We assume that banks will always try to expand their deposits to a maximum since lending is the banks' most profitable activity. Thus, if banks decide to maintain some strict cash ratio either by agreement, or because it is a legal requirement, then the maximum level of bank deposits is automatically regulated by the amount of cash they hold.

$$\text{Maximum level of bank deposits} = \frac{1}{\text{Cash ratio}} \times \text{Cash reserves}$$

Thus if the cash ratio is 5 per cent,

$$\text{Maximum level of bank deposits} = \frac{1}{\frac{5}{100}} \times \text{Cash reserves}$$
$$= 20 \times \text{Cash reserves}$$

In the developed countries one of the main reasons why the banks can operate with such very small cash reserves is the availability of very liquid assets which the banks are able to hold as secondary reserves (see page 315). Unexpectedly heavy demands for cash can be met by converting these liquid (or reserve) assets into cash. Under these conditions, therefore, the amount of cash held by the banks is not the strict regulator of the total value of banks deposits. Banks can always replace any net outflow of cash by converting some of their liquid assets. It does not follow, therefore, that a loss of cash will force the banks to reduce their total lending (i.e. deposit creation). What is critical for the banks is their ability to obtain liquid or reserve assets.

If there is a conventional or legal ratio between the value of the banks' liquid assets and the level of bank deposits, it is the availability of liquid assets which determines the total value of bank deposits. Thus, if the banks are obliged to maintain a supply of specified liquid assets equal to *at least* 10 per cent of total deposits, then bank deposits cannot exceed ten times the value of the liquid assets. More formally we can say that under this system,

$$\text{Maximum value of bank deposits} = \frac{1}{\text{Liquid assets ratio}} \times \frac{\text{Value of}}{\text{liquid assets}}$$

Thus, if the liquid assets ratio is 10 per cent

$$\text{Maximum value of bank deposits} = \frac{1}{\frac{10}{100}} \times \frac{\text{Value of}}{\text{liquid assets}}$$
$$= 10 \times \text{Value of liquid assets}$$

23 Banking and Monetary Policy

The structure of banking

The main functions of a bank are:
1 The provision of a safe deposit for money and valuables. This is the oldest banking function, but by no means the most important.
2 The lending of money. This is the most profitable banking activity and the major source of the bank's income.
3 The issuing of bank-notes. This, as we have noted, was one of the earliest functions of a bank. In England and Wales this right is now restricted to the Bank of England.
4 The provision, by means of bank deposits subject to movement by cheque, of a very efficient means of settling debts.

In addition to these basic functions, modern banks provide a wide range of financial services; most of these services will be mentioned later in the chapter.

The Bank of England

Most countries now have a central bank which stands at the apex of, and is responsible for, the operation of the banking system. In the UK the central bank is the Bank of England which was taken into public ownership in 1946. It has many responsibilities, the more important of which are summarised below. Many of them are discussed in more detail later in the chapter.
a It is the government's bank. It handles the income and expenditure of the Exchequer and other government departments.
b It manages the National Debt. This is a large responsibility and involves making repayments on government securities when they mature, floating new issues of long-term securities, making regular payments of interest to existing holders of securities, and handling the weekly issues of Treasury Bills (see p. 308). The management of the National Debt, as we shall see later, has important effects on the supply and price of money (i.e. the rate of interest).
c It is the bankers' bank. The clearing banks (see p. 302) maintain accounts at the Bank of England and the balances they hold in these current accounts are counted as part of their cash reserves. It is through these accounts that the banks settle their mutual indebtedness. The Bank is also banker to about 100 overseas central banks and monetary institutions.
d It is the central note-issuing authority for the UK and the sole

note-issuing authority for England and Wales. Some banks in Scotland and Northern Ireland still issue notes but they are largely backed by Bank of England notes.

e It is the lender of last resort: The Bank of England stands ready to come to the assistance of the banking system when a shortage of cash threatents to create difficulties which, in turn, could lead to a loss of the public's confidence in banks.

f It acts as the government's agent in the foreign exchange market.

g It has the responsibility for carrying out the government's monetary policy.

Although the Governor of the Bank of England has a certain amount of independence and is free to express his views, the Bank is subordinate to the Treasury which may at any time give instructions to the Governor. In practice the Bank's advice is sought when policy decisions are being made.

The commercial banks

The vast majority of ordinary banking business is handled by the clearing banks (members of the London Clearing House, see page 303). The business is dominated by the London clearing banks, Barclays, Lloyds, Midland, National Westminster (the 'Big Four'), Coutts and Co., and Williams and Glyn's together with three Scottish clearing banks, The Bank of Scotland, Clydesdale Bank, and the Royal Bank of Scotland. Between them these banks have some 12 000 branches. The Bank of England, the Cooperative Bank and the Central Trustee Savings Bank are also members of the Clearing House. There is a large number of non-clearing banks in the money market.

The strength of the large bank with numerous branches derives from its ability to obtain economies of scale. With a very large number of depositors no single depositor can embarrass the bank by withdrawing his funds. With many branches, the bank has a geographical spread of risks which enables it to withstand losses due a slump in any one industry or region.

The functions of the commercial banks

Deposits. The banks attract deposits from the public in three main forms:

Current accounts (sight deposits): these are deposits which can be withdrawn on demand and are subject to movement by cheque. Traditionally current accounts do not earn interest and, in some cases, the banks make a charge for the services rendered in providing current account facilities.

Deposit accounts (time deposits): these are deposits which cannot be transferred by cheque and they earn interest. Normally some period of notice of withdrawal is required, but subject to some loss of interest, banks may waive this requirement.

Large-term deposits: banks compete for these large deposits and offer more attractive rates of interest to attract large sums. *Certificates of deposit* are issued in respect of large amounts of money deposited for a fixed term (3 months to 5 years). These certificates carry fixed rates of interest, but they are a marketable security so that the yield will vary with the market price.

Lending. The commercial banks are profit-seeking enterprises and their major source of income in the interest they charge on bank loans. The commercial banks lend to all types of enterprise in all types of industry as well as to the government and other public authorities. Traditionally the banks make short-term loans of the type required for working capital (e.g. loans to buy seeds, raw materials, or stocks of finished goods), but in recent years they have become more flexible in their lending policy and longer term loans are increasingly available to households and firms. In recent years, the banks have greatly increased their lending for purposes of house purchase and have engaged in strong competition with the building societies.

Cheques. The clearing banks provide the country's main payments mechanism. Each year hundreds of millions of cheques are handled by the banks.

Other services. The banks provide a wide range of financial services such as; the provision of foreign exchange, investment advice and the management of funds, executor and trustee services, taxation advice, insurance services, and the provision of credit and cheque cards.

The Bankers' Clearing House

The procedure for making payments by cheque creates problems when the person making the payment keeps his account in a different bank from that which holds the account of the person receiving the payment. The final settlement of the debt will require a movement of funds from one bank to another. In any one day there will be many thousands of such inter-bank transactions to be carried out; many of them will offset each other. There will be a large number of cheques drawn on accounts in Bank A payable to accounts in Bank B, but there will also be many cheques requiring a transfer of funds in the opposite direction.

Each separate bank in a multi-bank system will find itself in this kind of situation at the end of the day. It is an obvious solution for each bank to pay (or receive) the net amount owing after the banks have totalled their claims against each other. This is the function of the Bankers' Clearing House. Cheques drawn on one bank but payable to another are sent to the clearing house where the mutual claims are offset and the banks merely settle the outstanding amounts. These payments from one bank to another are carried out by means of cheques drawn on the bankers' deposits at the Bank of England. It is important to note, however, that when one bank makes a payment to another bank, one bank loses cash and the other gains cash. The reason for this, of course, is that the deposits at the central bank are part of the banks' cash reserves.

The merchant banks

Many merchant banks date back to the nineteenth century when they were simply merchant houses trading in various parts of the world. Some of these houses grew in reputation and turned to the finance of trade as a specialised business. While the finance of international trade remains an important function of merchant banks other functions have tended to become rather more important. The main activities of the merchant banks are summarised below.

Acceptance business. The principal merchant banks are members of the Acceptance Houses Committee and their work consists of accepting (i.e. guaranteeing) certain promises to pay issued by merchants engaged in home and overseas trade. In other words they are providing a form of trade credit. This activity is explained more fully on p. 308.

Financial advice to companies. Their best-known activity is the handling of mergers and take-overs. Merchant banks advise and act for the parties concerned, but they will also advise on any aspect of a company's financial affairs.

Share issues. Merchant banks act as Issuing Houses. As well as advising on the method of raising funds they will usually carry out all the work involved in floating a new issue.

Investment managers. In addition to their advisory role, merchant banks will take over the active management of investments on behalf of other institutions and they also operate a number of investment and unit trusts.

Wholesale banking. These banks operate extensively in the Eurocurrency market (see p. 311), and in wholesale banking (dealings in very large deposits for periods of one year or more).

The discount houses — not necessary for exam

The London discount market is an important part of the financial structure of the City of London and is basically concerned with dealings in short and very short-term loans. The business is in the hands of the members of the London Discount Market Association (12 discount houses). As the name implies, the main function of a discount house is to 'discount' a variety of IOU's or 'promises to pay' which are issued by the government, local authorities, banks, and industrial and commercial companies. These promises to pay or securities are described in the next section.

Discounting is quite simply the procedure of buying a security for less than its face value (or redeemable value). For example, if a security carrying a promise to pay £100 in 3 months time is bought (i.e. discounted) for £99, the discount house has, in effect, made a loan of £99 for 3 months. By holding the security until it matures, the discount house will receive £100 from the person who is liable to pay the promised amount. It has, therefore, charged £1 for making a loan of £99 for 3 months. In other words, it has charged *a rate of interest* equal to,

$$\frac{1}{99} \times \frac{100}{1} \times \frac{4}{1} = 4\cdot04 \text{ per cent per annum}$$

Although this is the true rate of interest (i.e. the yield), the rate of discount is normally worked on the face value of the security. In the above example, the *rate of discount* would be,

$$\frac{1}{100} \times \frac{100}{1} \times \frac{4}{1} = 4 \text{ per cent per annum}$$

The discount houses borrow money on a very short term basis, much of it *at call* (i.e. repayable on demand), or borrowed overnight, from the various banks in the City of London. These funds are used to discount a variety of securities, and profits (or losses) are made from the differences between the rates paid on the borrowed funds and the rates charged for discounting the securities. The role of the discount houses in the money market is described on pages 313–14.

Foreign banks

The number of foreign banks in London has expanded rapidly in recent years and there are now more than 200 of them. United States and Japanese banks are the most numerous. One reason why banks establish foreign networks is to meet the requirements of their customers' international operations and this is particularly important in these days of large multinational companies. There has also been a large increase in the practice of raising loans abroad by governments, nationalised industries, and large joint stock companies. Large sums of money now move from one international financial centre to another seeking either higher interest rates or greater security against the loss in real value which occurs when a currency depreciates against other currencies. Foreign banks play an important part in the London Money Market.

Finance houses

Finance houses operate in a similar manner to banks by taking deposits from the public and employing them in loans, but they tend to specialise in providing hire purchase and other types of instalment credit. A large part of the finance houses' funds comes from the banking system but they also borrow substantial sums from companies and households. These borrowed funds are often term deposits (3 months being typical). Although the bulk of their assets are hire purchase loans an increasing proportion of their business takes the form of ordinary loans. Since the default risks are greater than those associated with ordinary bank lending, interest rates on loans by finance houses are higher than those on the traditional bank loan. Several of the leading finance houses are subsidiaries of the clearing banks.

Savings banks and the National Giro

There are two major savings banks, the National Savings Bank which is operated by the Post Office on behalf of the Department for National Savings and the Trustee Savings Bank. Both banks provide deposit facilities for small savers and these are collected at 21 000 post offices (in the case of the NSB) and at 1 500 branches of the Trustees Saving Bank. The Trustees Savings Bank now provides a current account service (i.e. payments may be made by cheque); the National Savings Bank does not provide such a service, but the National Giro provides money transmission services. All of the assets of the National Savings Bank and the greater part of the assets of the Trustees Savings Bank consist of government securities (i.e. loans to the government).

The National Giro is managed by the Post Office and commenced operations in 1968. Its aim is to provide a cheap, simple and quick money transmission service by making use of the existing network of post offices. All the records are kept, and the processing is carried out, at the computerised centre at Bootle. People holding giro accounts are provided with three basic services:

1 Transfers to other account holders. These are carried out by posting giro transfer forms to the computer centre. These transfers are free although there is a small charge for stationery.

2. Deposits. Deposits can be made in cash at any post office or by cheque. Deposits into one's own account are free, but a charge is made when people pay into some other person's account.

3 Payments. An account holder can draw cash through post offices or he can make payment to a non-account holder by means of a postal cheque. In each case, as long as the account is in credit, no charge is made for these services.

The giro system is not new, most western European countries have been running such systems for many years. In the UK the system started slowly and losses were made in the early years. It has since broadened its services to include deposit accounts, personal loans and limited overdraft facilities and cheque guarantee cards. It is now operating profitably and is widely used for local authority rent payments and for the payments of social security benefits.

The London Money Market

The London Money Market is the market for short-term and very short-term loans. It centres round the activities of the discount houses, the merchant banks, the head offices of the commercial banks, the Bank of England, and the London branches of overseas banks. The market deals in a variety of credit instruments – the more important of which are described below.

The bill of exchange

The bill of exchange is an important means of financing trade credit. It is a kind of post-dated cheque; that is, a cheque made out as payment for goods received but payable at some future date, usually 3 months after the date on which it is signed. It is used in the finance of domestic and international trade. It works something like this: when a trader sells goods he draws up a bill of exchange and sends it to the buyer (see Fig. 65). The bill is in the form of a promise to pay and specifies the sum of money owed and the due time for payment. It bears a stamp which makes it legally acceptable. The purchaser of the goods duly signs the bill and returns it to the seller who now has a legal acknowledgement of the buyer's indebtedness. Bills of exchange normally mature in 3 months so that the purchaser of the goods has been granted 3 months' credit. But the seller does not want to wait 3 months for his money. If the credit standing of the buyer is very good,

Introductory Economics

the seller may be able to persuade his bank to purchase, or more
accurately, discount his bill of exchange. The bank will hold the bill
until it matures and then present it to the buyer of the goods for
payment. In this way the banking system provides a kind of 'bridging'
finance – the buyer has 3 months to pay and the seller receives immediate payment.

LONDON   20th December 1982

£50,000

At 3 months *after* sight *pay to the Order
of* The Exporting Company Ltd, *the sum of*
Fifty Thousand Pounds *Value received.*

Drawn against the shipment of four knitting
machines from the UK to Rio de Janeiro

To: The X.Y.Z. Co.   *for the Exporting Co.*
Rio de Janeiro   J. Smith
                             Director

*Payable at the current rate of exchange for all sight
drafts on London plus all charges and stamps*

Fig. 65 A specimen Bill of Exchange

In order to make a bill of exchange more acceptable to financial
institutions, especially to the discount houses, it is usually necessary
to get it *accepted* by one of the Acceptance Houses which tend to specialise in certain branches of trade. They are, therefore, able to check
the creditworthiness of the person signing the bill and in return for a
commission they will accept the bill by endorsing it with the name of
the acceptance house. Such an endorsement guarantees payment of
the bill, by the acceptance house, should the drawee default. Discount
houses will readily discount bills bearing the name of one of the well-
known acceptance houses. After declining in importance for many
years, the 1960s saw a substantial revival of the commercial bill of
exchange and it has continued to be an important instrument in the
money market.

The Treasury Bill

As the bill of exchange declined in importance during the inter-war
period, another instrument of credit, the Treasury Bill, was becoming

Fig. 66 Treasury Bills are issued in denominations of £5 000, £10 000, £25 000, £100 000, £500 000 and £1 000 000

increasingly important in the work of the London Money Market. Treasury Bills (see Fig. 66) are government securities with a life of 91 days and are the instruments by which the government carries out its short-term borrowing. Each week the government borrows large sums of money by offering Treasury Bills for sale in the money market. They are government promises to pay which do not carry a fixed rate of interest. The system used is one of tendering and each week various financial institutions (e.g. discount houses, branches of overseas banks) are invited to submit bids for the following week's offer of Treasury Bills. The higher the bid price, the lower the rate of interest which the government has to pay for its borrowed funds. For example, if the bid price is £97½ (per £100 face value), the government is paying slightly more than 10 per cent per annum for a 3-month loan.

The discount houses obtain only a part of the weekly issue although they guarantee to take up the total issue at the prices they offer. Other financial institutions usually outbid them for part of the total issue.

Short-dated bonds

Since the money market is concerned with short-term loans it does not deal in the longer-term government securities, but as these securities approach maturity, they become, in effect, typical money market assets. Government securities with less than 1 year to run are accepted as liquid assets by the banking system because changes in the rate of interest will have relatively little effect on their market values. They are, therefore, assets which can be readily sold in order to replenish depleted cash reserves. The discount houses provide an active market in short-dated bonds and the commercial banks are substantial holders because short-dated government bonds are attractive liquid assets.

Local authority bills

In the 1950s local authorities became large-scale borrowers of short-term funds in the open market. They issue bonds (1 year being the popular maturity) and bills which are similar to Treasury bills. Local authority securities are dealt in by the discount houses and are held by the commercial banks as part of their liquid assets. Merchant banks and overseas banks are also important suppliers of very short-term loans to the local authorities.

Certificates of deposit

These are securities, payable to bearer, which entitle the holder to a given sum of money with interest on a particular date. Banks issue these certificates when someone deposits a sum of money (usually a large sum) for a fixed period of time (from 3 months to 5 years). The certificate of deposit has an advantage over the ordinary bank deposit in that it is a marketable asset (i.e. it can be bought and sold). Thus, there is a market in certificates of deposit and this is provided by the discount houses and other institutions in the money market. The holder of a certificate of deposit may convert it into cash before the certificate matures by selling it to a discount house, a merchant bank, a commercial bank or one of the overseas banks.

The Euro-dollar market

In the early 1960s the London money market became a major centre for dealings in Euro-dollars, that is, dollars held on deposit by non-US citizens. The market in Euro-dollars has grown very rapidly and London remains the main centre of business. Originally Euro-dollars came into being when the owner of a dollar deposit with an American bank (earned perhaps by exporting goods to the USA), transferred the title to that deposit to a London bank. He now had a dollar claim on a London bank and the London bank had a claim on a New York bank. At this stage the Euro-dollar is simply an indirect way of holding a deposit in a US bank. But when a London bank starts to re-lend its Euro-dollar assets we have the beginning of an important new money market.

The amounts dealt with in this market are very large; the basic unit is $1 m., and funds are loaned for periods ranging from 24 hours to upwards of 5 years. The merchant banks and the London offices of foreign banks are very active in the Euro-dollar market. Dollar certificates of deposit are used in this market in the same way as the sterling certificates of deposit described earlier. Funds borrowed in the Euro-dollar market are used by multinational companies to finance international trade and investment, but they are also converted into other currencies for domestic financing. Some nationalised industries in the UK have recently raised loans in the Euro-dollar market. Although the dollar is by far the most important currency, similar business is done in other currencies which are held outside their country of origin, notably the Deutschmark and the Swiss franc. For this reason the market is often referred to as the *Euro-currency market.*

The banking mechanism

The Central Bank

The Bank of England is divided into two departments, the Issue Department and the Banking Department. The Issue Department is responsible for the note issue and the Banking Department carries out all the other functions. The Bank publishes a weekly return which

Table 19 Bank of England weekly return (£ million)   18 August 1982

Issue Department

Liabilities		Assets	
Notes in circulation	10 880	Government securities	2 991
Notes in banking department	20	Other securities	7 909
	10 900		10 900

Banking Department

Public deposits	45	Government securities	485
Special deposits	—	Advances/Discounts	1 509
Bankers' deposits	514	Other assets	430
Reserves and other accounts	1 870	Notes and coin	20
Capital	15		2 444
	2 444		

Source: Bank of England Quarterly Bulletin

gives details of the assets and liabilities of the two departments. Table 19 is a copy of such a return.

At this stage we will merely define the separate items. Their relevance will become clearer as we explain the various operations in the money market.

Issue Department

Notes issued. These are the currency notes with which we are all familiar. Most of them are in circulation; that is, held outside the central bank. A small quantity is held in the Banking Department to meet demands for notes from the commercial banks.

Government securities. These are gilt-edged securities and Treasury Bills.

Other securities. These are securities of any other sort (e.g. securities issued by commonwealth and foreign governments and commercial bills).

Note that the UK note issue is wholly fiduciary.

Banking Department

Public deposits: This is the government's account. The published balance of £45 million has little meaning. The inflow and outflow of funds in this account is very large, amounting to hundreds of millions of pounds each week. The balance is always kept to a minimum and any temporary surplus is used to reduce the government's borrowing.

Special deposits. These are deposits which are called from the commercial banks when the monetary authorities (the Treasury and the Bank of England) wish to reduce the liquid (or reserve) assets of the banking sector. They are held in a special account because they are not part of the banks' current assets – they are 'frozen' assets. The function of special deposits is explained later.

Bankers' deposits. These are the deposits of the commercial banks, discount houses, etc. (See footnote to Table 20.)

Reserves and other accounts. This item comprises the accounts of overseas central banks and international monetary institutions, and the accounts of a small number of private customers. It also includes the Bank's reserve (retained profits).

Capital. A vestigial item – it is the share capital taken over when the Bank was converted from a joint stock company to a publicly-owned enterprise.

Govt. Stock see D.O.E.

Government securities. As was the case with the Issue Department, these are securities, both short and long term, issued by the British government.

Advances and discounts. These are short-term loans made to the discount houses (and some other customers). They are made against the security of first-class bills, or the Bank may buy (i.e. re-discount) such bills.

Other assets. These include a variety of securities such as foreign government securities, local authority bills, shares held in financial institutions such as Finance For Industry Ltd, and the value of premises and equipment owned by the Bank.

Notes and coin are issued to the commercial banks on demand. The central bank does not attempt to control the money supply by restricting the issue of currency. When a commercial bank wishes to obtain further supplies of notes it simply withdraws part of its deposit in cash – in exactly the same way as would a customer of a commercial bank. The effect of such a transaction, say the withdrawal of £10 m., would be:

In the Banking Department's account
a Notes and coin in the Banking Department would fall by £10 m.
b Bankers' deposits would fall by £10 m.

In the Issue Department's account
a Notes in circulation would rise by £10 m.
b Notes in the Banking Department would fall by £10 m.

Operations in the discount market

The discount houses borrow funds from the commercial banks (including the branches of the overseas banks) on a very short-term basis. Since these loans are secured (the discount houses pledge assets against their borrowings) and are taken up for such short periods of time, the rate of interest charged on them is low. These borrowed funds are used to discount commercial bills and Treasury bills and to buy certificates of deposit and short-dated bonds.

As the bills near maturity the discount houses sell parcels of them to the commercial banks which will hold them until they mature. Like the discount houses, the banks will earn interest on these bills. For example, the discount houses may buy newly-issued 3-month bills for £97 (per £100) and sell them to the banks after 6 weeks for £98½. Both the banks and the discount houses will earn approximately 12 per cent per annum on these bills.

In order to make a profit, the discount houses are obliged to take the risks involved in borrowing 'short' and lending 'long'. They lend

313

money on a longer term basis than that on which they borrow it. For example, call money may be used to discount 91-day bills. If the commercial banks are running short of cash they will normally react by calling back some of their loans to the discount houses, and the discount houses must honour their promises to repay these loans.

Since these funds are 'locked up' in bills and bonds, the discount houses must find some way of obtaining a new loan in order to repay the banks. If only one bank is 'calling', the problem may be solved fairly easily by obtaining a new loan from another bank which has funds to spare. If, however, all the banks are short of cash and making calls on the market, the discount houses will be forced to approach the *lender of last resort* – the Bank of England. The central bank will always come to the aid of the discount houses by buying some of their bills or providing loans against the security of such bills, but it will only deal in eligible bills.[1] Although the Bank of England will always meet the discount houses' demands for cash it is free to set its own terms for these loans and for discounting eligible bills. The rate of interest it charges (i.e. its discount rate[2]) depends upon its current monetary policy. If it wishes to bring about an upward movement in interest rates, it will tend to charge a rate of interest above the current market rate. Under these circumstances, the discount houses will be making losses because, in order to repay the loans being recalled by the commercial banks, they will have to pay a higher rate of interest to the central bank than they have been earning on their own lending. If the discount houses are being forced to borrow from the Bank of England at penal rates of interest (i.e. higher than market rates) they will act to eliminate their losses by raising their own discount rates and correspondingly other short-term rates of interest will tend to rise (e.g. banks will raise the rates for money at call).

If, however, the market is short of cash and the Bank of England does not wish to exert any upward pressure on interest rates, it will lend to the discount houses at the current market rate of interest.

The discount houses are useful to the banks in several ways. Their borrowings at call and short notice provide the banks with an extremely liquid income-earning asset. If these assets were not available the banks would have to maintain a higher ratio of cash to deposits. The discount houses sell the banks packages of bills of varying maturities to meet the banks' particular requirements. As the bills mature, the banks will have an inflow of cash and they can vary this inflow to suit their needs by buying assortments of bills which provide them with the required amounts of cash at the required times.

---

[1] Eligible bills are Treasury bills, certain local authority bills and commercial bills which have been accepted by eligible banks (see p. 318).

[2] Originally known as Bank Rate and then later as Minimum Lending Rate.

The commercial banks

Liquidity and profitability

The commercial banks are profit-seeking enterprises and, since lending is the most profitable of their activities, they have every incentive to maximise their loans. These loans are their income-earning assets. In addition to this obligation to their shareholders, however, the banks have obligations to their depositors which require them to meet all depositors' demands for cash (notes and coin). The banks' assets, therefore, must contain some adequate supply of cash to meet all normal and expected net withdrawals and, additionally, some extremely liquid assets to deal with unexpectedly heavy demands for cash. Table 20 shows the structure of the banks' assets.

These different obligations present the banker with a dilemma, because the need for liquidity conflicts with the objective of profitability. The more liquid the asset, the lower its earning power. Short-term loans usually carry lower interest rates than longer-term loans. Banks must maintain a supply of cash (i.e. notes and coin, plus balances at the central bank and other banks) which will meet the day-to-day demands for notes and coin, but they will want to keep this cash reserve to the absolute minimum because cash earns them no income. Just how small this cash reserve can be depends upon the supply of suitable liquid assets. British banks are able to obtain supplies of income-earning assets which can very quickly be converted into cash. Loans to the discount houses, brokers in the money market, and dealers on the Stock Exchange, can be recalled immediately or at very short notice. The banks also hold Treasury bills, commercial bills, and Government securities nearing maturity which can be sold to money market institutions or to the Bank of England at any time with little risk of capital loss.

Cash, money market loans, and bills are the traditional liquid assets of the British banking system. Until 1971, the UK banks maintained cash reserves equal to at least 8 per cent, and liquid assets equal to at least 28 per cent of their total deposits.

The most profitable but least liquid assets held by the banks are investments and advances. *Investments* comprise longer term government securities although the banks do not normally buy such securities until they have 5 years or less to run. These securities earn a more favourable rate of interest than the short-term loans within the money market and they can be sold at any time on the Stock Exchange. Heavy sales of such securities, however, would depress their market prices and cause the banks to suffer capital losses. They are, therefore, not classed as liquid assets. *Advances* are the most profitable asset. These bank loans provide a most valuable source of working capital to industry and commerce and there is a large business in personal loans. Interest rates on these loans vary according to the duration of

Table 20 London clearing banks combined balance sheet at 18th August 1982 (£ million)

Liabilities		Assets	
Sterling Deposits:		Notes and coin	862
Sight deposits	19 628	Balances at Bank of	
Time deposits	34 506	England:	
Certificates of deposit	2 755	Operational deposits	105
Other Currency Deposits:		Cash ratio deposits	201
Sight and time deposits	20 963	Special deposits	—
Certificates of deposit	1 502	Bills:	
Capital and other liabilities	11 044	Treasury bills	132
		Eligible bank bills	590
		Other bills	240
		Market Loans:	
		Secured money with	
		LDMA	2 611
		Certificates of deposit	376
		Other money market	
		loans	7 156
		Investments	4 679
		Advances	42 594
		Other currency assets	23 038
		Miscellaneous assets	7 814
	90 398		90 398

Eligible liabilities   46 241

Source: Bank of England Quarterly Bulletin September 1982

Notes on Table 20
Most of the items in this balance sheet have been explained earlier. The liabilities consist of deposits in sterling and other currencies together with the certificates of deposit issued by the banks. Balances at the Bank of England comprise (i) the operational or 'working' balances of the clearing banks, (ii) the obligatory non-operational balances equal to $\frac{1}{2}$ per cent of each bank's eligible liabilities and (iii) any special deposits which may have been called from the banks.

The Treasury bills and other bills are bought from the discount houses and bill brokers when they have about one half or less of their life to run. Eligible bills are explained in the footnote on page 314. Market loans is a large item and reflects the growth in the importance of the inter-bank market explained on page 318. The certificates of deposit on the assets side of the balance sheet are those which the banks have purchased (i.e. discounted). Other currency assets comprise the loans made in other currencies; they are claims on borrowers which are denominated in foreign currencies.

the loan and the creditworthiness of the borrower. Until 1971, the banks operated a cartel agreement whereby they all charged the same rate of interest to the most creditworthy borrowers (i.e. *the base rate*). Each bank is now free to set its own base rate, and rates for other borrowers normally range from 1 to 5 per cent above base rate.

Liquidity ratios

In 1971 the Bank of England introduced its 'Competition on Credit Control' measures for controlling and influencing the operations of the banking sector. Recognised banks were obliged to maintain, day by day, assets equal to a minimum of $12\frac{1}{2}$ per cent of eligible liabilities in the form of specified *reserve assets*. These reserve assets comprised public sector debt (e.g. Treasury bills, local authority bills and government securities with less than one year to run) together with money at call and commercial bills.

Eligible liabilities comprise, in broad terms, the sterling deposit liabilities of the banks except deposits made for terms of over two years. For the individual bank this sum is reduced by offsetting the following assets:

i the bank's loans to other banks and the sterling certificates of deposits which it has purchased as assets;

ii its operational balances held at the Bank of England (see below);

iii secured money at call loaned to the discount houses and to certain money brokers (the loans are secured because the banks have claims against gilt-edged stocks, Treasury bills, local authority bills and eligible bank bills held by the borrowers).

The 1981 monetary measures

The reserve assets ratio was reduced to 10 per cent in January 1981 and abolished in August 1981. At this time the Bank of England introduced new measures designed to influence the assets structure of the banking system.

1 All the institutions recognised by the Bank of England as banks (and licensed deposit takers) are obliged to hold non-operational and non-interest bearing deposits at the central bank. This non-operational requirement will be $\frac{1}{2}$ per cent of each bank's eligible liabilities and will apply to all banks which hold eligible liabilities of £10 million or more.

Note that these non-operational deposits are additional to the current 'working' balances which commercial banks maintain at the Bank of England.

2 The special deposits scheme (see page 324) remains in force.
3 The Bank of England now issues a list of 'approved' banks whose acceptances (of commercial bills) are eligible for rediscount at the Bank. This means that the Bank of England will not refuse to discount or lend against the security of the bills which these banks have accepted. These banks are described as *eligible banks*.
4 All eligible banks must maintain loans (e.g. call money) with members of the London Discount Market Association and with certain money brokers and gilt-edged jobbers such that the total funds so held average at least 6 per cent of the bank's eligible liabilities. Two-thirds of this amount (i.e. 4% of ELs) must be placed as secured call money with members of the LDMA.
5 The monetary sector for purposes of calculating the money supply is now defined as comprising,
a all recognised banks and licensed deposit-takers
b the National Giro Bank
c the Trustee Savings Bank
d The Banking Department of the Bank of England
e any banks in the Channel Islands and the Isle of Man which opt to join the cash ratio scheme

6 The Bank of England has dropped the practice of announcing its discount rate (i.e. minimum lending rate).

Note:
a The purpose of provisions 3 and 4 above is to ensure that there is an adequate supply of funds and bills in the money market. This is necessary because the Bank of England is to make greater use of open market operations (see page 324) in its attempt to control the money supply.
b Although the $12\frac{1}{2}$ per cent reserve assets ratio no longer applies, the Bank of England has announced that banks are still required to maintain certain ratios between liquid assets and total deposits. The purpose of this requirement is to protect depositors by making sure that banks always have sufficient liquid assets to meet depositors' demands for cash.

The inter-bank market

The inter-bank market is the main channel through which the London banks lend to or borrow from each other and the number of banks now participating in it is over 200. The sums transferred are in the form of drawings on balances held in the clearing banks. Nearly all the lending in this market is unsecured (no assets are pledged) and the deals are arranged by firms of brokers. Transactions normally range in amount from a minimum of £250 000 to sums of £10 m. or more, but the typical transaction is about £500 000. The funds are borrowed for any period from 'overnight' up to 5 years, but the great majority of the deals are for a short term (less than 1 year). Sterling certificates of deposit have become an important instrument in the inter-bank market. These are issued in multiples of £10 000, with a minimum of £50 000 and a maximum of £500 000.

The rapid growth of this market stems from the relaxation of controls on bank lending and the greater competition between banks resulting from the changes introduced in 1971. Banks use the inter-bank market to adjust their liquidity positions. When a bank finds its ability to lend is restricted by a shortage of liquid assets it may borrow directly from another bank which has a surplus of such assets. In other words it is a direct and efficient way of spreading funds within the banking system.

The structure of the money supply

One of the most important issues in present-day economics is whether or not the level of activity and especially the rate of inflation can be effectively influenced by measures which attempt to control the supply of money. This controversy has led to a further controversy on what exactly constitutes the supply of money. In terms of the four functions of money described on pages 292–293 we find that a large number of assets fulfil some but not all these functions. There are plenty of assets which serve as a store of value, but this does not make them money. Some assets act as a medium of exchange (e.g. luncheon vouchers), but they do not serve as a unit of account. A large volume of financial assets (e.g. deposits in building societies and time deposits in banks) are not media of exchange because they are not immediately 'spendable'. Nevertheless they can quickly and easily be converted into cash. There is no group of assets which would command unanimous agreement as constituting the stock of money.

If one is concerned with money as a medium of exchange then clearly the definition must be restricted to notes, coin and bank deposits on current account. If, however, one is concerned with the potential spending power in the economy, then a much wider definition is appropriate. In the UK there are three definitions which are widely used by the authorities, namely, M1, Sterling M3 and M3.

M1 is a narrow measure and consists of notes and coin in circulation plus sight (or demand) deposits held by the UK private sector.

Sterling M3 consists of all the items in M1 plus the time deposits held by the private sector and all the deposits held by the public sector. M1 and Sterling M3 refer only to the money held in the form of sterling.

M3 consists of all the items included in Sterling M3 plus UK residents' deposits in other currencies.

In the operation of its monetary policy the UK government has tended to use Sterling M3 as its target, but it does take account of movements in other measures.[1]

Private sector liquidity

Since 1979 the Bank of England has published a series of financial data entitled *The Components of Private Sector Liquidity* (PSL) which embrace both those items regarded as money in the narrow sense and assets generally described as *near money*. This data (i.e. PSL) is an attempt to measure the private sector's ability to mobilise extremely liquid financial assets and it clearly has relevance to an analysis of people's willingness and ability to spend and lend.

PSL 1 includes the private sector's deposits in M3 (excluding deposits with a maturity of more than two years) plus private holdings of money market instruments (Treasury bills and bank bills), deposits with local authorities and finance houses and holdings of certificates of tax deposits.

PSL 2 includes all the items in PSL 1 plus deposits in building societies (excluding money deposited for more than one year), deposits in the National Savings Bank and National Savings Certificates.

Monetary policy

Aims and objectives

We have now discussed two important aspects of money, namely its price (the rate of interest) and its supply. Monetary policy refers to the attempts to manipulate these two variables so as to bring about desired changes in the economy. The aims of monetary policy are the same as those of economic policy generally. They are the maintenance of full employment, price stability, a satisfactory rate of economic growth, and a balance of payments equilibrium. In its attempts to control the economy the government until fairly recent times has

---

[1] In June 1982 the Bank of England introduced a new monetary aggregate, M2, which is designed to provide a better measure of the *transactions* balances held by the private sector. In other words it attempts to measure the private sector's holdings of balances which are either immediately spendable or are subject to a very short notice of withdrawal. M2 will include:

a notes and coin in circulation with the public;

b non-interest bearing sight deposits held by the private sector;

c all other deposits on which cheques can be drawn or from which standing orders or other payments may be made;

d other deposits of less than £100 000 which are subject to less than one month's notice of withdrawal.

sterling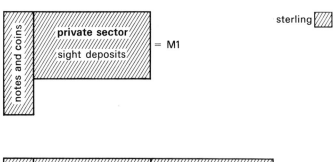

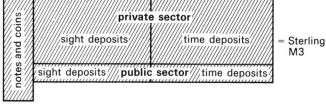

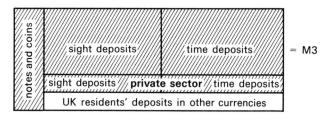

Fig. 67 UK money supply

tended to give the major role to fiscal or budgetary policy which is concerned with changes in taxation and government spending. In the last few years, however, far more attention has been paid to the use of monetary policy and many economists believe that the control of the money supply is probably the most important instrument for regulating total demand in an economy. There is no doubt that changes in the supply of money and in the rate of interest can have important effects on output, employment and prices.

We have seen that the greater part of the money supply consists of bank deposits and that a large part of these deposits come into being as a result of bank lending. Total spending is very much influenced by the spender's ability to borrow from the banks either directly through loans or overdrafts, or indirectly through hire purchase schemes. Any attempt to control the money supply therefore must be directed at controlling the banks' ability to lend, or to influencing firms' and households' willingness to borrow. We have already shown that the banks' ability to lend depends upon their supplies of liquid assets and some instruments of monetary policy are designed to act directly on the banks' supplies of these assets. But the willingness and ability to spend does not depend solely on the availability of bank credit – the price of that credit is also important. Even if the banks are willing and able to provide loans, some potential borrowers may not be persuaded to take up the bank loans if the rate of interest is so high that the prospective profits from the use of the loan, or the satisfactions from spending it on consumption, are scarcely higher than its cost.

The targets of monetary policy

The supply of money and the rate of interest are not independent variables. The monetary authorities cannot fix both the quantity *and* the price of money. If we refer back to Fig. 62 we see that if the demand for money (liquidity preference) does not change, any changes in the supply of money will alter the rate of interest (except at very low levels). Alternatively, if the supply of money remains fixed, any change in the demand for money will bring about changes in the rate of interest. Since the monetary authorities cannot determine demand they are in the same position as a monopolist; they can determine the quantity or the price – not both.

If the government chooses to fix a particular rate of interest then it must supply whatever quantity of money will be demanded at that rate. As the demand for money changes, so must the supply; otherwise the rate of interest must change. If the authorities decide to fix the supply of money, the rate of interest will vary as the demand for money varies. The authorities are thus presented with a dilemma – should they try to influence demand by manipulating the rate of interest or control the supply of money by more direct means?

There are very divergent views on the effectiveness of the rate of interest as a policy instrument. There seems no doubt that by raising the rate high enough it will reach a level which is a deterrent to borrowing and hence spending. But in times of boom when business people are very optimistic this level may be very high indeed, and such high interest rates may well conflict with other objectives of government policy. As the largest borrower in the country the government will be seriously affected by the greatly increased interest burden of the national debt. High interest rates will also be very unpopular in the politically sensitive housing market where interest charges are a major cost item. At the opposite extreme low interest rates are not likely to be very effective as a stimulant when the economy is depressed. Reducing interest rates to very low levels is not likely to encourage borrowing and spending when new investment offers little or no prospect of reasonable profits. When there is heavy unemployment lower interest charges are not likely to lead to any significant increase in hire purchase borrowing in the markets for consumer goods.

Nevertheless changes in the rate of interest can be used in conjunction with other measures and the policy has the advantage that it is a flexible instrument which can be applied fairly quickly. In between the extremes of boom and slump it has effects on costs of production which can lead to changes in investment, especially in the holdings of stocks, which will, in turn, affect output and employment. Changes in the rate of interest also, it is believed, have important psychological effects on business people's expectations. They are also an important influence on the balance of payments position. It may be necessary at times to encourage an inflow of short-term capital or alternatively to ensure that there is not a large-scale withdrawal of balances by foreign depositors. This may be achieved by raising interest rates in the domestic market to levels which are more attractive than those in foreign money markets.

In order to minimise the costs of the large-scale borrowing by governments, nationalised industries, and local authorities, and to hold down the costs of industrial investment and house purchase, the government for many years tended to concentrate on an interest rate policy which held down the rate of interest below its true market level. This was known as the 'cheap money' policy. It meant, of course, that the money supply had to be expanded according to demand, or some kind of physical controls (rationing) had to be applied to bank credit.

In more recent times the authorities have given more attention to the control of the money supply and allowed interest rates to move more freely according to the demand for funds. This change in policy has been due to the growing influence of a group of economists known as the Monetarists who believe that changes in the money supply have a much more direct influence on the level of the total spending than existing Keynesian theory indicates (see p. 337).

The instruments of monetary policy

The central bank's discount rate

This is the rate at which the central bank is prepared to lend to the banking system when the institutions are short of funds, either by re-discounting first class bills or lending against the security of such bills. In the UK, this assistance is supplied via the discount houses. The rate of interest charged by the Bank of England was, until 1981, known as the minimum lending rate and this rate was publicly announced so as to give the money market a clear signal of the Bank's intentions. This is no longer the case. The idea now is that the central bank will operate as a buyer and seller in the money market so as to influence the price of bills. By increasing the demand for bills, it will raise their prices and hence cause interest rates to fall. By selling bills it will increase the supply and lower the prices of the bills and hence cause interest rates to rise (see page 273). In other words it will use open market operations (see below) to bring about the desired changes in the rate of interest.

Open market operations

In addition to setting the terms on which it is prepared to lend, the central bank can act directly on the supply of financial assets in the banking system by means of its activities in the markets for securities. The Bank of England through its brokers buys and sells securities (Treasury Bills and other government securities) in the open market. If it wishes to restrict bank lending, it will instruct its broker to sell securities. The buyers will pay for these securities with cheques drawn on their accounts in the commercial banks. These cheques will be payable to the Bank of England which will then hold claims on the commercial banks. The debts will be settled by a reduction of the bankers' deposits at the Bank of England. A fall in these deposits represents a reduction in the banks' liquid assets ratio and they will be obliged to reduce the level of their total deposits in order to restore the required ratio of liquid assets to deposits. We should note, however, that this action will only force the banks to reduce their lending if they are operating with the minimum level of liquid assets. If the banks have a surplus of liquid assets, a reduction of their deposits at the central bank might still leave them with an adequate total supply of liquid assets and they will not be obliged to reduce their total deposits.

When the central bank wishes to see an expansion of bank lending it will enter the market and buy securities, making payment for them with cheques drawn on itself. The sellers of these securities pay the central banks' cheques into accounts at the commercial banks. The banks now hold claims on the central bank which will settle its indebtedness by crediting the outstanding amounts to the bankers' deposits. An increase in bankers' deposits at the central bank amounts to an increase in the liquid assets ratio. The banks will be able to expand their total lending by a multiple of the increase in their liquid assets.

Special deposits

This particular instrument of monetary policy is fairly new – it was first used in 1960. It is now regarded as a most important means of controlling the money supply. The payment of special deposits (see p. 312) deprives the banks of some of their liquid assets since they have been instructed that the funds for such payments should not be obtained from the sale of longer term securities. A call for special deposits, therefore, has the same effect as open market sales of securities, but it is a much more direct instrument. If the monetary authorities wish to encourage bank lending they can release any special deposits they are holding and thus increase the banks' supply of liquid assets. Note also the supplementary special deposits mentioned under Quantitative controls, below.

Funding

Although open market operations and calls for special deposits may be successful in changing the banks' liquid assets ratio, they will not be effective instruments for restraining bank lending when the banks are holding surplus liquid assets. Funding is a way of reducing the supplies of liquid assets available to the banking system. The policy requires the Bank of England to change the structure of the national debt by issuing more long-term securities and fewer short-term securities (Treasury Bills). This operation would make the banks more vulnerable to open market operations and calls for special deposits.

Quantitative controls

In recent years the Bank of England has supplemented its controls over the money supply by making increasing use of direct requests to the banks. Each bank has been asked to limit the amount of its lending (total deposits) to some specified figure. These *ceilings* have not been confined to the clearing banks but have been applied to a wide range of financial institutions. Quantitative directives have usually been accompanied by qualitative guidance as when banks have been asked not to restrict loans to exporters or to firms in development areas, but to be much more selective with requests for loans to finance consumption or speculation. Ceilings applied to advances became the most important direct control during the 1960s, but the new policy measures introduced in 1971 indicated that the Bank of England intended to make little use of such ceilings and would place far more reliance on special deposits and open market operations.

In December 1973 the Bank of England made a partial return to more direct forms of control when it introduced a *Supplementary Special Deposits* scheme. Under this scheme the banks were obliged to limit the growth of total interest-bearing eligible liabilities to some stated figure. For the first 6 months the rate of growth permitted was 8 per cent. If the actual rate of growth exceeded this figure a percentage of the excess amount had to be placed in a special deposit which did not bear interest. The penalties were arranged on a sliding scale. For example, if deposits were allowed to grow by more than 1 per cent but less than 3 per cent, of the permitted figure, 25 per cent of the excess was taken; if over 3 per cent, 50 per cent of the excess had to be placed with the Bank of England. This scheme was abolished in June 1980.

Hire purchase controls

Although this is a more direct and physical type of control, it is usually included in the list of instruments of monetary policy. The government has the power to change, at any time, the terms of hire purchase contracts. By increasing the minimum deposit and reducing the period allowed for repayment, the government has a quick-acting method of reducing the demands for consumer durables such as cars, furniture, electrical appliances, and so on. Relaxing the terms of hire purchase agreements is a fairly effective way of stimulating consumer expenditure.

Monetary policy and the national debt

In addition to its responsibility for operating the government's monetary policy the Bank of England has the responsibility for the management of the national debt. These two responsibilities may present the central bank with conflicting objectives. As manager of the national debt the Bank of England has the task of raising large sums of money for the government every year. It must float new issues of securities to finance current government spending and to repay the loans which are maturing. The money and capital markets will only take up large issues of government securities if they are attractively priced, the risk of capital losses are not too great, and the yield is satisfactory. The central bank must· operate in the open market by buying and selling securities in such a way as to maintain security prices and yields at attractive levels. The current rate of interest is a very important consideration because it influences the rate of interest which must be offered on new issues of securities, and with such a large national debt, it is desirable to minimise the interest burden.

But the central bank, as we have seen, is obliged to carry out open market operations with a view to controlling the lending activities of the commercial banks. It is very likely, therefore, that situations will arise where the objectives of debt management will conflict with those of monetary policy. For example, the central bank may be obliged to conduct open market sales of securities in order to reduce the banks' liquid assets. Heavy sales of securities, however, will depress security prices and the lowering of security prices has the effect of raising interest rates. Existing holders of government securities will suffer capital losses and this will not make the market very receptive to any new issue of securities which the central bank may be trying to float in order to finance government expenditure. There may also be occasions when monetary policy calls for a fall in interest rates (to stimulate private spending). If this occurs at the same time as the central bank has the responsibility for putting a large new issue of securities on the market, the Bank of England would be frustrating its debt policy objective since increasing the supply of securities would raise interest rates instead of lowering them.

The public sector borrowing requirement

In recent years government have tended to run relatively large budget deficits; public expenditure has exceeded income from taxes, rates, rents, profits and interest. This excess expenditure has to be financed by borrowing. The extent to which the public sector as a whole borrows from other sectors of the economy in order to finance its expenditure is known as the public sector borrowing requirement and it has important implications for monetary policy.

The public sector comprises central government, local authorities and public corporations and it may borrow,

a by selling securities to the public outside the banking sector,
b from overseas' residents, and
c from the banking sector.

If the government borrows from the banking system, then, other things being equal, there will be an increase in the money supply as bank deposits are created to supply the government with the necessary funds.

If the government borrows from the non-bank public, the money supply may be unaffected because deposits are transferred from the private sector to the public sector. But heavy sales of government securities will tend to lower their prices and hence increase interest rates. This may reduce the private sector's demand for bank loans.

If the government borrows from overseas' residents and the country is operating a system of floating exchange rates, the inflow of foreign currency will tend to raise the exchange rate (see page 374). This will make imports relatively cheaper and may reduce the demand for transactions balances.

24 The Value of Money

The exchange value of money

The functions of money have been dealt with in some detail, but one very important aspect of money remains to be discussed: namely, its value. The intrinsic value of money may be negligible; the £1 note regarded as a piece of paper is practically worthless, and its only value arises from its acceptability in exchange. Units of money exchange for goods and services, and the rates at which money exchanges for these things are known as prices. In the modern world we are doing exactly what is done under a barter system: exchanging goods and services for goods and services. Money serves to facilitate these exchanges. If the price of a loaf of bread is 20p this only has meaning to the buyers and sellers if they know the amounts of other things which 20p will buy. The value of the loaf is the goods and services for which it can be exchanged and the money price gives us an indication of the exchange value of the loaf. In the same way the rewards for our labour are expressed in terms of money, but what we are really interested in is the rate at which our hours of labour will exchange for goods and services. A system of money prices helps us to understand this rate.

But prices are always changing and so the rate at which one good exchanges for another is always changing. If all prices were to double, the exchange values of different goods would not change. A tonne of coal would be worth exactly the same number of pounds of meat. The only value which would change would be the value of money itself; the exchange value of a £1 note would have halved. If the expression *the value of money* has any meaning, it can only be expressed in terms of what the unit of money will buy, and this is determined by the prices of the various goods and services. When prices rise, the value of money falls and likewise falling prices indicate an increase in the value of money. This is all very well, but the question now arises – 'What prices?'.

When the person in the street thinks about the value of money, he is considering the value of *his* money and this can only be measured in terms of the prices of the goods which *he* buys. If the prices of beer and cigarettes increase, but no other prices are changed, then the value of the money spent by the teetotaller and non-smoker will not have changed, but this would not be true of the money spent by the man who smokes and drinks. Changes in the prices of raw wool and raw cotton will affect the value of money used by the importer, the merchant, and the manufacturer far more than the value of the money spent by other groups.

Thus if we wish to speak of the value of money in precise terms, then we have to admit that there are as many different values of money as there are spenders of money, for it is unlikely that any two individuals will spend their money in exactly the same manner. In spite of this difficulty it is necessary to attempt some assessment of the extent to which the value of money is changing. People want to know what is happening to the real values of wages, pensions, the National Income, and other important economic variables.

Measuring changes in the value of money

This task would be easy if all prices moved proportionately and in the same direction, but prices do not move in this way. In any given period of time some prices will rise, others will fall and others remain unchanged, and those prices which do move in the same direction will not all move to the same extent. As we have already indicated, different groups of buyers and sellers are interested in different groups of prices. Statisticians deal with this problem by providing measurements of movements in export prices, import prices, commodity prices, wholesale prices, and so on. In what follows we shall be concentrating on the value of money as reflected in changes in retail prices. Before proceeding further it is necessary to point out that we cannot, in fact, measure the value of money at any given moment in time. It is impossible to give a meaningful answer to the question 'What is the value of £1?'. The only possible answer would be an almost endless list of the quantities of the various goods and services for which £1 may be exchanged. We can, however, measure *changes* in the value of money and for this purpose we make use of a statistical device known as index numbers.

Index numbers

Index numbers deal with *percentage changes* rather than with absolute changes. The price change of each commodity is expressed in percentage terms and the average of these percentage changes is then calculated. The index number 100 is given to each price in the year on which we base our comparisons. Subsequent price changes are expressed as movements from 100 and then averaged. In Table 21, a simple arithmetic average of the percentage changes in prices indicates that prices in Year 2 are 31·6 per cent higher than they were in Year 1. Prices in subsequent years would be expressed as percentages of those in Year 1 (the base year) and averaged in a similar manner.

Example:

Commodity	Year 1 Price	Index	Year 2 Price	Index
A	5p	100	10p	200
B	12½p	100	15p	120
C	100p	100	75p	75

	3)300		3)395
	Price Index = 100		Price Index = 131·6

The index numbers resulting from these calculations would be misleading since each of the commodities is assumed to be of equal importance. In other words a 10 per cent change in the price of Commodity A would have exactly the same impact on the index as a 10 per cent change in the price of Commodity C or Commodity B. In the real world we know that the prices of those things on which we spend a large proportion of our income are far more important to us than the prices of those things we rarely purchase. Changes in the price of bread are of much greater relevance to the mass of consumers than changes in the prices of fur coats. It is possible to overcome this particular difficulty by using a system of weights whereby each commodity is given a weight proportional to its importance in the general pattern of consumer spending. Referring back to the example above, let us suppose that 50 per cent of total consumer spending is devoted to Commodity A, 30 per cent to Commodity B, and 20 per cent to Commodity C. Weights are now allocated in the proportions 5:3:2. The price indices for each year are multiplied by the appropriate weights and the average is obtained by dividing the total of these weighted indices by the total of the weights.

Table 21 Calculating price indices by weighting commodities according to how important they are in consumer spending

Commodity	Weights	Year 1 Price	Index	Weighted index	Year 2 Price	Index	Weighted index
A	5	5p	100	500	10p	200	1 000
B	3	12½p	100	300	15p	120	360
C	2	£1	100	200	75p	75	150
	10			10)1 000			10)1 510
				Price index = 100			Price index = 151

The weighting of the commodities has produced a different result from that obtained in the earlier calculation. The average price movement is now revealed as an increase of 51 per cent, as against 31·6 per cent in the earlier example. This is due to the fact that Commodity A, which had the largest percentage price increase, is the commodity which is most heavily weighted.

The index of retail prices

In the United Kingdom official attempts to measure movements in the cost of living began in 1914 with the Cost of Living Index. This was restricted in its coverage since its construction was based on a sample of 2 000 'typical working class' households. It was compiled on the same basis until 1947 when the name was changed to the *Index of Retail Prices*. Subsequently the index has been revised and rebased in 1952, 1956, 1962, and 1974. The basic features of the construction of this index are as follows:

1 A representative sample of the population is selected and asked to maintain a careful budget of their expenditure over some period of time, usually 1 month.

2 These budgets are analysed to provide information on the pattern of consumer spending. From this information we derive a picture of the spending patterns of the 'average family'.

3 In the light of the data derived from the expenditure surveys decisions are taken on the range of goods and services to be included in the index and on the weights to be allocated to each class of goods.

4 Some particular date is now chosen as the base date and the prices at this date are expressed as 100.

5 The prices of the selected commodities are checked each month and the new prices are expressed as percentages of those ruling at the base date.

6 The price index is then calculated as shown in Table 21.

The earlier indices had weights which were based upon some single prior sample survey of consumer spending. The current index has weights which are revised every year and which are based upon a continuous survey of family spending. The sample of households used for this purpose was recently increased from 3 000 to 6 000 households. As time has gone by the samples used in the surveys have become more and more representative of the entire population and it is held that the current index is based upon an expenditure survey which is representative of 88 per cent of the whole population. Likewise the list of goods and services included in the index has been gradually extended and now includes more than 350 separate items for many of which information is collected for several different varieties.

The Department of Employment, which is responsible for the calculations, carries out, through its local offices, price checks in some 200 towns of different sizes, distributed geographically according to population densities. Prices are collected from the whole range of retail outlets – small shops, supermarkets, chain stores, department stores, cooperative societies, mail order firms, and so on. The Index of Retail Prices divides the goods and services covered into eleven main groups each of which contains a number of sub-sections. In addition to the index for all items, indices are calculated for each of the main groups. Table 22 shows the main groups, the weighting applied to each group, and some recent movements in price indices.

Table 22 UK index of retail prices

	Weights 1982	1974 Index (Jan 1974 = 100) April 1982
Food	206	302·6
Alcoholic drink	77	338·8
Tobacco	41	404·4
Housing	144	364·9
Fuel and light	62	416·2
Durable household goods	64	243·4
Clothing and footwear	77	210·2
Transport and vehicles	154	341·1
Miscellaneous goods	72	322·1
Services	65	331·4
Meals bought and consumed outside the home	38	336·4
	1 000 All items	319·7

Source: Department of Employment Gazette HMSO

The Index of Retail Prices is published monthly and has come to be regarded as one of the most important economic indicators. Changes in the index form the basis of many wage claims, and official incomes policies have sometimes used the index as the guideline for permissible increases in money incomes (e.g. the threshold agreements in 1974). The index, however, should be used with some caution and we must be careful not to read into the index a degree of accuracy which it cannot possibly possess. Some of the problems associated with its use are discussed below.

1 The index only attempts to measure changes in retail prices as they affect the *average* family, but are there any such families?
2 The pattern of consumer spending is always changing. As incomes, tastes, and fashions change, so do the demands for various goods and services. This raises problems with regard to weighting and it is for

this reason that the current index allows for a frequent adjustment of the weights.

3 Many commodities are subject to frequent changes in design, or quality, or performance. Where a price change accompanies the introduction of a new model or an improved design, it is extremely difficult to assess the real nature of the price change. Can we really say what has happened to the prices of furniture, washing machines, television sets, or motor cars over the past 10 years? The price comparisons would not be related to the same products. If the price of a particular make of car increases by 10 per cent, but the quality and performance of the new model is much superior to that of the older model, has the exchange value of the car increased or decreased?

4 New materials and new products are continually coming into use and causing significant shifts in consumer demand. The introduction of television changed the patterns of spending on entertainment and thousands of cinemas closed down in the 1950s and 1960s. In recent years a whole new range of plastics has transformed the nature of household appliances and fittings available to the great majority of households. These changes call for frequent modifications of the weighting structure.

5 Consumers' shopping habits change. In recent years there has been something of a revolution in the retail trade with the introduction and rapid growth of supermarkets. Families with deep-freezers now undertake bulk-buying of many foodstuffs. The abolition of resale price maintenance has led to price competition at the retail stage and price differences (for the same product) as between different retail outlets. This has made the task of measuring price changes more difficult. Nowadays a greater weight must be given to the prices of goods sold in the supermarkets and chain stores and a smaller weight to the prices in the small independent shops.

Price movements

We have seen that it is possible, by means of index numbers, to obtain some approximate idea of the extent of the changes in the value of money. The forces which change prices tend to change *all* prices although there will be deviations from the general pattern (e.g. a change of fashion leading to a temporary surplus and hence a lower price when other prices are moving upwards). There are great differences in the flexibility of different prices. The most variable prices are those of raw materials and other primary products which are traded on world markets. A glance at any table of commodity prices (mining and agricultural products) will reveal just how extensive the price variations can be over relatively short periods of time. The explanation lies in the fact that both the demands for and the supplies of these commodities tend to be inelastic. Quite small changes in demand or supply lead to relatively large changes in price. It is significant that most major government schemes to stabilise prices are concerned with primary products.

The prices of manufactured goods tend to be much more stable. The prices of many of these goods are controlled by very large firms and stability of price is important from the point of view of advertising campaigns and production planning. There is also the point that the supplies of manufactured goods tend to be fairly elastic and output can be more easily adjusted to changes in demand.

The long-term tendency is for prices to rise. Over the past seven centuries the average trend of British prices has been an increase of about 1½ per cent per annum. But it would be misleading to interpret this statement as indicating a smooth steady upward movement in prices. There have been periods when prices have been falling and several periods of comparative price stability. The general picture seems to be one of a series of periods when there was a strong upward movement in the price level followed by periods of stable prices or periods when price were falling – the upwards movements being closely associated with wars except for the most recent experience of inflation. Figure 68 shows how rising prices have reduced the internal purchasing power of the dollar, the mark, and the pound sterling.

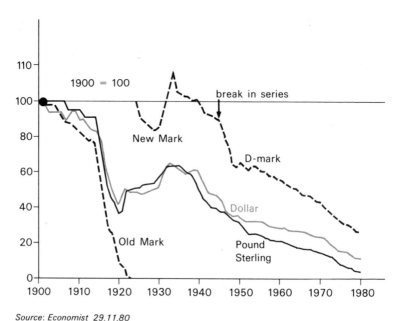

Source: Economist 29.11.80

Fig. 68 The purchasing power of money

The quantity theory of money

In the chapter on prices we saw that the value of a commodity was determined by the forces of demand and supply. The earliest formulation of the Quantity Theory of money held that changes in the value of money could be explained by changes in the supply of money. It assumed that the spending habits of the population and the output of goods and services were fairly stable so that the demand for money was also stable. In this situation changes in the value of money could be explained by changes in the quantity available. If we represent the quantity of money by the symbol M and the general price level by the symbol P, the older quantity theory may be expressed in the form,

$$M \propto P$$

It holds that price changes are directly proportional to changes in the quantity of money. A 10 per cent increase in the money supply would cause a 10 per cent increase in prices.

It should be obvious, however, that changes in the quantity of money may or may not have an influence on prices. It is the act of *spending* which influences prices and, if any increase in the money supply is not spent, it will not influence the prices of goods and services. In this early theory M is seen as the actual stock of money, in the form of coin, notes, and bank deposits. There is, however, another aspect of the supply of money which is much more relevant; namely, the rate at which the supply is used over a given period of time, say 1 year. During a period of 1 year each unit of money may be used several times. The term the *Velocity of Circulation* (V) is used to describe the rate at which money changes hands.

If the total value of all transactions during one year was £20 000 m. and the stock of money was £5 000 m., then the velocity of circulation must have been 4 since, on average, each £1 of money purchased £4 worth of goods and services, and each £1 must on average have changed hands 4 times. Although the stock of money was only £5 000 m., the total purchasing power was equal to £20 000 m. If the velocity of circulation increased to 5, the same stock of money would purchase £25 000 m. worth of commodities in 1 year.

We have, therefore, two views of the quantity of money. It may be regarded as a stock (M) or as a flow, that is, as a stock of money moving at some given rate. It is the latter view which is important since it is this flow of money which determines the level of spending. The flow of spending will be equal to MV; that is, the quantity of money multiplied by the number of times each unit changes hands.

The value of total expenditure (MV) must be equal to the value of goods and services sold by businesses. If we designate P to stand for the average price level and T to represent the total volume of transactions, then PT will represent the value of goods and services bought and sold. It should be clear therefore, that

$$MV = PT$$

This *Equation of Exchange* represents a refinement of the older Quantity Theory. $MV = PT$ is not a theory but a statement of fact and, as shown, it must by definition be true. It is not a theory because it tells us nothing about the causes of changes in the various quantities. The value of the Equation of Exchange lies in the fact that it identifies and calls our attention to the different factors which influence the value of money.

It draws our attention to the importance of V. If V were constant then a change in M would lead to a change in P or T or both. If full employment conditions existed, an increase in T is not possible in the short run, so that if V were constant, an increase in M would cause an increase in P. It was this kind of direct relationship between M and P, based on the assumption that V and T were constant, which was the basis of the crude Quantity Theory.

If, however, unemployed resources were available, an increase in M, V remaining constant, would lead to an increase in output (and hence in T) so that P might remain unchanged.

But V is not constant and there is evidence to show that it has increased very much in the years since the Second World War. If an increase in M is accompanied by an increase in V, as is very likely in inflationary periods, then, if T is constant, an increase in M will lead to a more than proportionate increase in P. An increase in V is one of the causal factors in a situation of hyperinflation. When prices begin to rise fairly rapidly people will be reluctant to hold money because it is losing its value and they will exchange it for goods and services as quickly as possible.

In the 1930s during the Great Depression, fears of unemployment and possible business losses greatly reduced the spending of consumers and businessmen. In other words there was a reduction in V. An increase in M in such circumstances would be offset by a fall in V and would have little effect on output or prices.[1]

The idea that changes in the value of money can be explained simply in terms of changes in the supply of money is very much disputed. Modern thinking has tended to lay more emphasis on changes in incomes as determinants of the price level and has regarded changes in the quantity of money as a consequence rather than a cause. According to these ideas, changes in output and income give rise to changes in the demand for money and the monetary authorities merely supply, quite passively, the quantities of money demanded.

---

[1] The increase in M would find its way into idle balances.

But the Quantity Theory has survived remarkably well. Certain long-term trends can be partially explained in terms of this theory. The major changes in the price level during the nineteenth century bear a close correlation to the movements in the supply of gold to which the supply of money at that time was linked. The large increases in the level of prices during the two world wars was accompanied by very large increases in the supply of money, and the great inflations in Germany during the early 1920s and in Hungary in the 1940s were both characterised by massive increases in the supply of money.

The revival of the quantity theory

In the 1960s there was a great revival of interest in the role of changes in the quantity of money as a determinant of changes in output and prices. The 'new' Quantity Theory is associated with Professor Friedman of Chicago who is mainly responsible for the empirical and analytical work. It is a very complex subject and we can only outline in very simple terms the main ideas. Studies by the Chicago School have shown that fluctuations in the level of national income appear to follow quite closely the fluctuations in the rate of growth of the money supply. Monetarists believe that the relationship is causal; that is, the changes in the money supply cause the changes in the level of income. As we have already mentioned, opponents of this view believe that increases in the level of economic activity lead to an increased demand for money which is duly supplied.

An essential difference between the Keynesian viewpoint and the Friedman theory is the role ascribed to the rate of interest. According to Keynesian theories, as explained in Chapter 19, a change in the quantity of money will cause people to buy or sell securities as they adjust their holdings of cash and other assets. If an increase in the money supply leaves them with surplus holdings of money they will buy securities; a reduction in the money supply will, other things being equal, leave them with inadequate cash balances and they will attempt to sell securities. The increased demand for, or supply of, financial assets will alter their market prices and so change the market rates of interest. It is these changes in the rate of interest which will affect the demands for capital and consumer goods. Briefly, then, changes in the quantity of money affect the national income via their effects on the rate of interest.

Now the Chicago School take a much broader view of 'the rate of interest'. It is no longer confined to the rate of return on financial assets. Interest is a flow of returns over a period of time. On financial assets this flow is clearly defined and can be stated in terms of money. But most durable goods yield a flow of returns over time; a house yields the services of shelter and accommodation and the value of these services can be related to the cost of the house in the form of a 'rate of interest'. The same can be said for cars, television sets, washing machines, furniture, and so on. The flow of income is real enough in these latter examples although it may not be possible to express it accurately in numerical terms.

According to the Monetarists, people are just as likely to use excess money balances to buy real goods as to buy financial assets. When the money supply increases, the demand for real goods as well as the demand for securities will rise. A person may find the 'yield' on a new car more attractive than the yield on a bond. The Monetarists, therefore, see changes in the money supply as having a direct impact on aggregate demand. (See also pages 458–9.)

25 Inflation

Types of inflation

There are several ways of defining inflation. In some contexts it refers to a steady increase in the supply of money. In others it is seen as a situation where demand persistently exceeds supply. It seems best, however, to define inflation in terms of its basic symptom – rising prices. Inflation is a situation in which the general price level is persistently moving upwards. The excess demand definition hardly fits the recent British experience when prices were rising quite sharply and unemployment was increasing.

In an extreme form of inflation, prices rise at a phenomenal rate and terms such as *hyperinflation*, runaway inflation, or galloping inflation have been used to describe these conditions. Germany experienced this kind of inflation in 1923 and by the end of that year prices were one million million times greater than their pre-war level. Towards the end of 1923, paper money was losing half or more of its value in one hour, and wages were fixed and paid daily. The price of a newspaper rose to 200 000 000 000 marks (one mark had been worth about one shilling in 1914). In 1924 the currency was withdrawn and new marks were issued at the rate of 1 Reichsmark = 1 000 000 000 000 old marks. In 1944 Hungary experienced an even more severe inflation, the note circulation reaching a figure with 27 noughts.

Under conditions of hyperinflation people lose confidence in the currency's ability to carry out its functions. It becomes unacceptable as a medium of exchange and other commodities, such as cigarettes, are used as money. When things have become as bad as this the only possible course of action is to withdraw the currency and issue new monetary units. So great was the loss of confidence in Hungary that the new currency had to be given a new name, the Forint replacing the Pengo.

Another type of inflation is described as *suppressed inflation*. This refers to a situation where demand exceeds supply, but the effect on prices is minimised by the use of such devices as price controls and rationing. We should note that price controls do not deal with the causes of inflation, they merely attempt to suppress the symptoms. The excess demand still exists and it will tend to show itself in the form of waiting lists, queues, and almost inevitably, in the form of black markets.

The most common type of inflation is that experienced since the war in Britain and most other developed countries. This is *creeping inflation* where the general price level rises at an annual rate between 1 and 6 per cent. In Britain the average rate for the period 1939–67 was about 4 per cent per annum, but in more recent years the rate of inflation has increased quite sharply.

The causes of inflation are usually classified as demand-pull or cost-push.

Demand inflation

Demand inflation may be defined as a situation where aggregate demand persistently exceeds aggregate supply at current prices so that prices are being 'pulled' upwards. This type of inflation is usually associated with conditions of full employment. If there are unemployed resources available an increase in demand can be met by bringing these resources into employment. Supply will increase and the increase in demand will have little or no effect on the general price level. If the total demand for goods and services continues to increase, however, a full employment situation will eventually be reached and no further increases in output are possible (i.e. in the short run). Once the nation's resources are fully employed, an increase in demand must lead to an upward movement of prices.

Conditions of excess demand when there is full employment can arise in several different ways. Wartime conditions provide a good example. War brings full employment, a large increase in the numbers at work, and a great deal of overtime working. The net result is a large increase in total income and hence in potential demand. On the other hand, the supply of consumer goods and services will fall as resources are diverted to meet military demands. In the markets for consumer goods, demand will be much greater than supply at current price levels. During wartime the excess demand is not allowed to exert its full effect on the price level. The government imposes price controls on essential commodities and supports these price controls with a system of rationing. Large-scale savings campaigns and heavy taxation are also used to remove some of the excess demand.

The dangers of inflation are probably at their greatest in the immediate post-war years. After years of austerity and rationing, people will be very anxious to return to the greater freedoms of peace-time conditions and to spend the savings accumulated during the war. They will have a strong desire, supported by a great ability to spend, but the supplies of consumer goods will still be severely restricted since a large proportion of economic resources will have to be devoted to reconstruction. Restraints on demand will have to be imposed but they will not be accepted so willingly as they were when the nation was at war.

A situation of excess demand may arise when a country is trying to achieve an export surplus, in order, perhaps, to pay off some overseas debt. Exports are inflationary because they generate income at home, but reduce home supplies. Imports, of course, can make good this deficiency of home supplies, but if exports are greater than imports there will be excess demand in the home market unless taxes and savings are increased to absorb the excess purchasing power.

Demand inflation might develop when, with full employment, a country tries to increase its rate of economic growth. In order to increase the rate of capital accumulation, resources will have to be transferred from the production of consumer goods to the production of capital goods. Incomes will not fall since the factors of production are still fully employed, but the supply of the things on which these incomes may be spent will fall. Unless taxation and/or savings increase there will be excess demand and rising prices.

Another possible cause of inflation under conditions of full employment is an expansion of government spending financed by borrowing from the banking system. In this case the expenditure is being financed by an increase in the money supply. Even where the additional government spending is financed from taxation the effect may still be inflationary since the additional taxes might reduce private saving rather than private spending.

The inflationary process

We have shown how excess total demand might arise at the full employment level of national output. Prices will rise, but why should they continue to rise? An inflationary process of the demand-induced type is usually explained in terms of the conditions in the markets for the factors of production, especially those in the labour market.

When firms can sell more goods and services than they are producing, they will increase their demands for the factors of production and since these are already fully employed their prices will rise. For example, firms will have to bid up wages in order to tempt workers away from their existing jobs. If, as is most likely, the rise in wages exceeds any increase in productivity, costs will rise and business people will pass on these higher costs in the form of higher prices. Where demand persistently exceeds supply, firms will have little fear that the higher prices will reduce the demands for their products. But the increases in wages, salaries, and other factor incomes will mean that aggregate demand will also rise, so that once again we have excess demand – and so the process will go on. Prices in the markets for goods and in the markets for factors of production are being pulled upwards.

More recent experience of inflation, however, provides evidence of the pressures on prices coming from 'below' rather than 'above'. Prices have continued to rise under conditions where there has been excess supply rather than excess demand in the labour markets.

Cost-push inflation

Initiating factors

Cost-push inflation describes a situation where the process of rising prices is initiated and sustained by rising costs which push up prices. It must not be confused with a situation where excess demand is causing entrepreneurs, faced with shortages, to bid up the prices of factors of production. In such cases the passing on of the higher costs in the form of higher prices is a feature of demand inflation.

Cost inflation occurs when prices are forced upwards by increases in factor prices (i.e. costs) which are *not* caused by excess demand. There are several ways in which costs may rise independently of the state of demand. In the 1970s a major contributor to British inflation was the *rising prices of imported materials*, especially the price of oil. Under these circumstances domestic costs, and hence prices, are increased whatever the level of domestic demand. *An increase in indirect taxation* (i.e. taxes on goods and services) is another way of giving the general price level an inflationary 'push'. Again prices would rise regardless of the state of demand. Possibly the most common cause of cost-push inflation, however, is an *increase in wages which exceeds any increase in productivity*. Any of these events may initiate a rise in prices – we have to explain why that rise continues.

The inflationary process

An increase in indirect taxes will lead to a once-and-for-all rise in prices. Import prices may rise for several months, but eventually they level out or begin to fall. The 1967 devaluation raised British import prices by about 15 per cent, but like taxation, it was a once-and-for-all effect. These things cause prices to rise, but they do not explain the continuous process of rising prices.

It is the wage-price spiral which is the most common feature of cost inflation. An increase in wages which is designed to compensate for an increase in prices will generate a further increase in prices which in turn leads to another round of wage increases and so it goes on. The compensating wage rise which exceeds the growth in productivity appears to be the main explanation for the persistent rise in prices which is the feature of cost inflation.

Cost inflation continues of course because the increases in costs which lead to price increases are also increases in income. Factor prices are costs to the entrepreneur, but incomes to the factors of production, so that although prices increase so does the ability to pay these higher prices. An increase in costs is followed by an increase in demand.

It can be shown that if wages were to increase by no more than the amount strictly necessary to compensate for the increase in the price level, the inflationary sequence would gradually peter out. Wages make up only part of total costs so that an increase in wages would not lead to a corresponding increase in prices. For example, if wages make up 70 per cent of total costs, a 10 per cent increase in wages (no change in productivity) would cause prices to rise by 7 per cent. A compensating wage increase (an attempt to maintain real income) would now lead to a price increase of 4·9 per cent and so on. There must be other elements contributing to the price increases if the inflationary process is to continue. Either wages must be increasing by far more than is necessary to offset the price increases or the other elements in prices (e.g. profits) must be increasing proportionately with wages.

Cost inflation and unemployment

Whereas demand-pull inflation is invariably associated with full employment conditions, this is not usually the case with cost-push inflation. In recent years, in Western Europe and North America, prices have continued to rise even when unemployment has been at relatively high levels. This particular development has led to some readjustment of views regarding the bargaining powers of organised labour. For a long time economists held the view that wage pressures and the level of unemployment were inversely related. High levels of unemployment, it was believed, would seriously weaken the bargaining strength of the unions; the fear of increasing the numbers out of work would cause them to moderate their wage claims. This was certainly not the case in the later 1960s and early 1970s when rising unemployment in no way diminished the pressures for higher wages.

Many factors have contributed to the changed circumstances in the labour market. Firm government commitments to policies of full employment have probably relieved the unions of fears that higher wage claims might result in unacceptable levels of unemployment. Although unemployment might rise above the very low levels of the 1950s and 1960s, unions believed, it seemed, that governments would not allow unemployment to reach intolerable levels, Improved unemployment and social security benefits and the introduction of redundancy payments have alleviated the hardships formerly associated with unemployment; it is not the nightmare prospect it was in the inter-war period. We have already noted that, as industry becomes more specialised and capital-intensive, so the strike weapon becomes more effective and labour has tended to make greater use of this instrument. The bargaining power of organised labour has undoubtedly increased and we must expect the unions to use this power in the interest of their members, especially in a society based on the principles of free enterprise.

These and other factors created a situation where trade unions could force through wage increases substantially greater than any current increases in productivity, even under conditions when there were labour surpluses rather than labour shortages. The high unemployment levels of the late 1970s and early 1980s, however, did seriously diminish the strength of union pressures for higher wages.

Differentials

An important element in the wage-price spiral is the strong attachment to existing wage differentials. An increase in pay in one sector of the economy leads to a chain reaction of wage increases elsewhere as other groups try to restore the previous pattern of wage differentials. It may be that the originating wage increase was granted in an industry where productivity had also increased so that the increase in wages did not increase labour costs. It is most likely, however, that wage increases in many other sectors, based on comparability arguments, will lead to average increases in wages which are significantly greater than the average increase in productivity. Costs will rise and entrepreneurs, in order to protect their profit margins, will raise prices. These price increases will provoke further wage claims.

One feature of cost-push inflation which seriously increases social tensions is the fact that existing wage and salary differentials are *not* maintained. Groups with more powerful bargaining positions will gain relative to those in weaker positions. How to restrain the stronger groups and how to protect the weaker groups are, of course, major problems in the operation of incomes policies. This subject is discussed in Chapter 33.

The distinction between the two types of inflation is important from the point of view of the appropriate policies to deal with inflation. Where the cause is excess demand, measures to reduce aggregate demand are called for. But very different policies are required to deal with cost inflation which is often associated with rising unemployment. It would seem to be inappropriate to reduce aggregate demand when unemployment is increasing. These policy questions are dealt with in Chapter 33.

The effects of inflation

Inflation is regarded as undesirable because it produces some serious economic and social problems.

The effects on the distribution of income

Inflation leads to an arbitrary redistribution of real income. Although a rise in the general price level produces a corresponding rise in money incomes, all prices do not rise to the same extent and different income groups will be affected in different ways. There will be some 'gainers' and some 'losers'.

The losers are those whose incomes are fixed, or relatively fixed, in money terms. This group will include people whose income is derived from fixed interest securities, controlled rents, or some private pension schemes. Income recipients in this category will experience a fall in their real incomes.

When incomes are directly related to prices, real income will remain relatively unchanged. The incomes of sales people, and professional groups such as architects, surveyors, and estate agents whose fees are expressed as a percentage of the value of the work undertaken, fall into this category. A large number of wage earners also come into this group since many workers have agreements which link their money wages to the Retail Price Index.

The effects on incomes derived from profits depend largely upon the kind of inflation being experienced. During demand-pull inflation, profits tend to rise. The prices of final goods and services tend to be more flexible in an upwards direction than many factor prices, some of which are fixed on fairly long-term contracts. The margins between the two price levels tends to widen because of this time lag. When there is cost-push inflation, profits may be squeezed. Since there is no excess demand some firms may find it rather difficult to pass on the full effects of rising costs in the form of higher prices.

Wage earners generally more than hold their own when the price level is rising. In the UK and most other industrial countries wages in most years have risen faster than prices, but, as already mentioned, there tends to be some redistribution effect as those with superior bargaining power gain at the expense of the weaker groups.

Inflation tends to encourage borrowing and discourage lending because debtors 'gain' and creditors 'lose'. Debtors repay in monetary units which have less purchasing power than those which they borrowed. If a person borrows a sum of money for 2 years during which time inflation is running at 10 per cent per annum, the same sum repayable at the end of the term will be worth about 17 per cent less in real purchasing power than the sum of money borrowed.

Effects on production

Demand-pull inflation is associated with buoyant trading conditions and sellers' markets where the risks of trading are greatly reduced. These easy market conditions might give rise to complacency and inefficiency since the competitive pressures to improve both product and performance will be greatly weakened. This is not likely to be the case in a cost-push inflation where trading conditions are likely to place a premium on greater efficiency. Where firms cannot absorb some of the higher factor prices by improving productivity they may find it difficult to survive. It is possible that employers seeking to hold down costs will react to rapidly rising wage costs by devising means of economising in their use of labour and hence raise the level of unemployment.

Demand inflation, it is sometimes argued, is conducive to a faster rate of economic growth since the excess demand and favourable market conditions will stimulate investment and expansion. The falling value of money, however, may encourage spending rather than saving and so reduce the funds available for investment. It may also lead to higher interest rates as creditors demand some additional return to compensate for the falling value of money. Nevertheless relatively high nominal rates of interest may not be a deterrent to investment. If the nominal rate of interest is 10 per cent, but the rate of inflation is 8 per cent, the 'real' rate of interest is only 2 per cent.

Effects on the balance of payments

In economies such as the UK which are dependent upon a high level of exports and imports, inflation often leads to balance of payments difficulties. If other countries are not inflating to the same extent, home-produced goods will become less competitive in foreign markets and foreign goods will become more competitive in the home market. Exports will be depressed and imports will rise. If this process continues it must lead to a balance of payments deficit on the current account. The problem will be a particularly difficult one where inflation is of the demand-pull type, because in addition to the price effects the excess demand at home will tend to 'draw in' more imports. These balance of payments effects apply particularly where a country is operating a fixed rate of exchange. As we shall see in Chapter 28, a floating rate of exchange means that the rise in home prices does not have such an unfavourable effect on the volumes of exports and imports.

Counter-inflationary policies are discussed in Chapter 33.

Part Nine: International Trade, Finance and Cooperation

26 International Trade

The basis of trade

In the earlier chapters of this book we saw how specialisation increases productivity and raises the standard of living. Within a country individuals specialise, factories specialise, and whole regions specialise. In Coventry, for example, workers specialise on some tiny part of the production of a motor car, factories specialise in the production of components for the motor car, and the whole area specialises to a very great extent in motor car production.

The exchange of goods and services across international boundaries has enabled this principle of the division of labour to be extended to the international sphere. International trade originated on the basis of nations exchanging their products for others which they could not produce for themselves (or which they could only produce at exorbitant cost). The obvious examples are the exchanges of commodities between Europe and the tropics. Europeans exchange manufactures for foodstuffs, timber, and minerals from Africa, India, South East Asia and South America. Adam Smith pointed out that Scotland might well produce its own wine by creating artificial hothouse conditions for the vine, but that this would be a most inefficient use of resources. Scotland could obtain her wine more cheaply by using her resources to produce engineering products and then exchanging these for the wine produced in Mediterranean countries.

International trade arises because:

a The production of different kinds of goods requires different kinds of resources used in different proportions.

b The various types of economic resources are unevenly distributed throughout the world.

c The international mobility of resources is extremely limited.

Land is obviously immobile in the geographical sense. The international movement of labour is restricted by barriers of language and custom and most nations now impose restrictions on immigration. Capital is more mobile geographically but it only crosses international boundaries when particularly favourable conditions exist (e.g. political stability, no threats of confiscation, no barriers to taking profits out of the country, etc.).

Since it is very difficult to move resources between nations, the goods which 'embody' the resources must move. Nations which have an abundance of land relative to labour will concentrate on 'land-intensive' commodities such as wheat and meat. They will exchange these goods for 'labour-intensive' products such as manufactures made by countries which have an abundance of labour and capital relative to land. Just as our individual abilities and aptitudes fit us for different occupations, so the different resources and the historical development of nations equip them for the production of different products. Unlike individuals, nations do not specialise completely in one process or in one product. They tend to concentrate on certain types of activity, but even the greatest importers of food grow some of their own requirements, and importers of manufactured goods carry out some manufacturing.

The gains from international trade

We know that in the real world international trade is carried on by a large number of countries in a vast range of goods and services. This is a very complex situation but it is possible to gain an understanding of the principles which underlie this complicated economic structure by using a very simplified model. For this purpose we assume that;
a There are two countries, Country A and Country B.
b Only two commodities are produced, tractors and wool.
c There are no barriers to trade and no transport costs.
d Resources within each country are easily transferred from one in-dustry to another.
Within the limits set by this model we can consider three possibilities.
1 Each country can produce only one of the commodities.
2 Each country can produce both commodities, but tractors can be produced more efficiently in one country and wool more efficiently in the other.
3 Each country can produce both commodities, but one of the coun-tries can produce both commodities more efficiently than the other.

Each country can produce only one commodity

We need not spend much time discussing this first possibility because the gains from trade are self-evident. International trade greatly in-creases the variety of goods available to each country. These particular circumstances were the basis for most of the earlier examples of inter-national trade and they still explain a great deal of present-day trade. Britain, for example, must rely on foreign trade for most of her raw materials and a substantial part of her food supply. It does not, how-ever, explain the major part of international trade, because this takes place between countries which could well produce for themselves the goods which they import. The greatest producer of cars, the USA, is also the greater importer of cars.

Each country has an absolute advantage

This is the fairly realistic situation where each country is more effici-
ent than the other in the production of one of the commodities.
Country B, we will assume, produces wool more efficiently than
Country A, while Country A has the advantage in producing tractors.
We can use a simple arithmetical example to illustrate the potential
gains from trade.

	Tractors		*Wool (bales)*
With x resources Country A			
can produce (per annum)	20	or	100
With x resources Country B			
can produce (per annum)	10	or	150

It is fairly easy to show that greater specialisation will increase total
output. Suppose Country A moves 2x resources from wool production
to tractor production and Country B moves 2x resources from tractors
to wool. The effect on total output would be,

	Tractors	*Wool*
In Country A	+40	−200
In Country B	−20	+300
Net gain	+20	+100

Let us now suppose that each of these countries has 10x resources and
in the absence of international trade each country devotes half its
resources to each industry.

	Tractors		*Wool*
Country A will produce	100	and	500
Country B will produce	50	and	750
Total output	150	and	1 250

Now if international trade were possible these countries would tend to
specialise. We shall assume that they specialise completely.

	Tractors		Wool
Country A now produces	200	and	0
Country B now produces	0	and	1 500
Total output	200	and	1 500

As one would expect, total output is much greater when the countries specialise. In order to obtain the benefits of specialisation these countries must exchange some part of their individual outputs, but the rate at which they exchange wool for tractors must be beneficial to *both* countries. We cannot specify the exact rate of exchange, but we can identify the limits within which the exchange rate must lie. It will be somewhere between the *domestic opportunity cost ratios* of the two countries.

In Country A the 'cost' of 1 tractor is 5 bales of wool since this is the output of wool which must be forgone in order to produce 1 tractor. Country A, therefore, will not accept less than 5 bales of wool for each tractor since she can obtain wool on these terms by transferring resources at home. Similarly, Country B will not offer more than 15 bales of wool for 1 tractor since she can obtain tractors at this 'price' by using her own resources. The domestic opportunity costs ratios are,

	Tractors		Wool
In Country A	1	:	5
In Country B	1	:	15

In order to be favourable to both countries, the terms of trade must lie between these ratios. Let us suppose that it settles at 1 tractor for 10 bales of wool and 70 tractors are exchanged for 700 bales of wool. After trade, therefore, the position is as follows.

	Tractors		Wool
Country A now has annual supply of	130	and	700
Country B now has annual supply of	70	and	800
Total	200	and	1 500

Both countries are clearly better off[1] than when they were operating on a basis of self-sufficiency. In Fig. 69 we have used the figures from the above example to provide a diagrammatic representation of the situation in Country B before and after specialisation and trade.

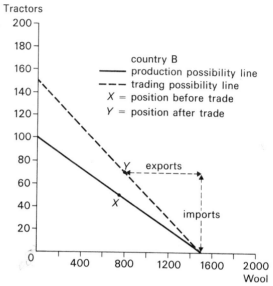

Country B can produce any combination of tractors (T) and wool (W) on the line joining 100 tractors and 1500 wool. She chooses the combination represented by (50T and 750W) when trading possibilities are not available. When trading opportunities arise, Country B specialises in wool which exchanges internationally at the rate of 10W for 1T. She now chooses position Y.

Fig. 69

Each country has a comparative advantage

We now turn to the third of the possibilities mentioned earlier. One country is more efficient than the other in the production of both commodities. We shall assume that Country A is the more efficient country; it has an *absolute advantage* over Country B in both industries. It can be shown that even in these circumstances it is possible for specialisation and trade to benefit both countries. The principle involved is known as the *Principle of Comparative Costs*. This states that even where one country has an absolute advantage over the other in both industries, specialisation and trade can benefit both countries

---

[1] A now has 30 more tractors and 200 more bales of wool. B now has 20 more tractors and 50 more bales of wool.

providing each country has a *comparative cost advantage*. Comparative cost relates to the opportunity costs of producing the commodities and not the absolute costs. The best way of explaining the idea is to make use of a simple arithmetical example.

	Tractors		*Wool* (*bales*)
With x resources Country A can produce either	20	or	200
With x resources Country B can produce either	10	or	150

Quite clearly in terms of resources used, the costs of production in both industries are lower in Country A. If we look at the opportunity costs, however, the picture is rather different. In Country A the 'cost' of 1 tractor is 10 bales of wool, while in Country B it is 15 bales of wool. Country A has a *comparative advantage* in tractors. In Country A the cost of a bale of wool is 1/10 of a tractor, while in Country B the cost is 1/15 of a tractor. In terms of the output of tractors forgone, wool is cheaper in Country B than in Country A. Country B has a *comparative advantage* in wool.

Let us now assume that each country has 10x resources and in the absence of international trade devotes half its resources to each industry.

	Tractors		*Wool*
Country A produces	100	and	1 000
Country B produces	50	and	750
Total output	150	and	1 750

If trading possibilities arise, each country will tend to specialise, but in this case if they specialise completely, we find that the total output of tractors increases, but the output of wool falls. Each country will specialise in that industry in which it has a comparative advantage so that complete specialisation would give us, 200 tractors and 1 500 bales of wool. It is possible to show that the increase in the output of tractors, in value terms, more than offsets the fall in the output of wool, but this is not really necessary because by partially specialising the more efficient country we can have more of both commodities. Thus if Country A devotes 2x resources to wool and 8x resources to tractors while Country B specialises completely in wool we have the following situation.

	Tractors		Wool
Country A produces	160	and	400
Country B produces	0	and	1 500
Total output	160	and	1 900

We now have a greater total output of both commodities than that which obtained when both countries were producing only for domestic consumption. As explained earlier the fact that the opportunity cost ratios are different in the two countries means that beneficial trade is possible.

Some qualifications

1 The gains from trade are modified by the existence of transport costs and tariffs. The economic effects of these are very similar since in both cases the cost of moving the goods is increased. In the case of transport costs the increase in price is unavoidable, whereas in the case of tariffs the cost increase is 'artificial' because it is the result of a policy decision and, therefore, reversible.
2 The theory outlined above is based on the unrealistic assumption that the opportunity cost ratios remain unchanged as resources are moved from one industry to another. In the last example we assumed that every time Country A moved x resources from wool production to tractor production, the output of wool fell by 200 bales and the output of tractors increased by 20 units. This is not very likely since some resources will be more efficient in one industry than the other. In other words, as the degree of specialisation increases we are likely to encounter the law of diminishing returns.
3 As opposed to the preceding point it is very possible that increasing specialisation will yield advantages in the form of economies of scale. This is most likely in the manufacturing industries.
4 Comparative cost advantages are always changing. New methods of production, the use of newer types of raw materials, improvements in transport, and changes in market conditions will change the relative efficiencies of different countries in different types of economic activity. In the nineteenth century a substantial world lead in technology gave the UK a very great comparative advantage in the production of cotton cloth. In the later twentieth century she has become a net importer of cotton cloth.

5 The shifting nature of comparative cost advantages points to a major danger of over-specialisation and of too great a dependence on foreign trade. A country which concentrates most of its resources on a very narrow range of industries is very vulnerable to economic change.

6 International trade leads to greatly enlarged markets and increases the extent of competition. It should, therefore, stimulate efficiency.

The terms of trade

The rate at which one nation's goods exchange against those of other countries is referred to as the Terms of Trade. In the examples used earlier the concept can be seen very clearly because the terms of trade could be expressed as 'so many bales of wool per tractor'. In the real world things are more complex. Countries import and export a great variety of goods and services and it is not possible to express the terms of trade as a simple ratio between physical units of commodities. Although the reality of international trade is the exchange of goods and services for other goods and services, all these items have money prices and it is possible to measure their exchange values in terms of these prices. The method adopted makes use of two important index numbers – the Index of Import Prices and the Index of Export Prices.

The terms of trade are given a numerical value which is equal to:

$$\frac{\text{Index of Export Prices}}{\text{Index of Import Prices}} \times 100$$

In the base year each of the two index numbers will be 100 so that the terms of trade will be 100. If, subsequently, export prices rise relative to import prices the numerical value of the terms of trade will rise. The terms of trade index will fall if import prices rise relative to export prices. There are a number of ways in which such changes might come about.

a Export prices and import prices could be moving in opposite directions.

b One set of prices could be stable while the other is changing.

c Export and import prices could be moving in the same direction but one of them could be rising or falling faster than the other.

A rise in the numerical value of the terms of trade is described as a *favourable* movement since it indicates that any given volume of exports is now exchanging for a greater volume of imports. Similarly a fall in the terms of trade index is said to be *unfavourable* because any given volume of exports now exchanges for a smaller volume of imports.

The terms of trade and the balance of payments

We must be careful not to interpret the words 'favourable' and 'unfavourable' too literally when talking about movements in the terms of trade. While the price movements may be favourable the movements in the values of exports and imports may be unfavourable because these depend upon quantity changes as well as price changes. Likewise an unfavourable movement in the terms of trade may well have a favourable effect on the balance of payments.

For example, if the prices of UK exports rise by 5 per cent she will earn more foreign currency only if the quantities sold remain unchanged or fall by less than 5 per cent (i.e. if demand is inelastic). If the foreign prices of her imports fall by 5 per cent she will spend less foreign currency only if the quantities imported expand by less than 5 per cent (i.e. if demand is inelastic). If the demands for exports and imports were elastic, the 'favourable' movement in the terms of trade would *worsen* the balance of payments because expenditures on foreign commodities would rise while revenues from exports would fall.[1]

Table 23 The terms of trade in the UK (1975 = 100)

Year	Export Prices	Import Prices	Terms of Trade
1975	100·0	100·0	100·0
1976	119·6	122·2	97·9
1977	141·5	141·3	100·2
1978	155·5	146·8	105·9
1979	171·7	161·6	106·3
1980	192·8	185·8	103.7
1981[1]	217·1	216·2	100·4
1982[2]	220·2	218·6	100·7

[1] December
[2] May

Source: Economic Trends HMSO *July 1982*

There is also the income effect to consider. Lower prices for imports could mean that foreign countries are earning less from *their* exports and hence their abilities to buy from other countries will be correspondingly reduced. In the case cited above, the UK might find that she is selling less abroad because the prices of her imports have fallen.

For countries which engage in world trade on an extensive scale, as the UK does, movements in the terms of trade are of great significance.

---

[1] Not true in every case; e.g., a rise in export prices might be due to an increase in demand for exports.

When the volumes of imports and exports are very large, quite small changes in the terms of trade can make a large impact on the balance of payments. With imports running at about £48 000 million per annum (1981), even a 1 per cent fall in import prices could mean, for the UK, a saving of some £480 million in foreign currency, or alternatively, the existing level of exports could buy additional imports worth £480 million.

Restrictions on international trade

Our theoretical account of the gains to be obtained from international trade seemed to be fairly conclusive yet the fact is that every major trading nation operates some form of restriction on its trade with the rest of the world. It is true that the years since the Second World War have seen a very substantial reduction in the barriers to trade, but those that remain are still formidable. Before examining the reasons for these restraints on trade, it is necessary to describe the types of restriction most commonly used.

Quotas

A quota is the most serious kind of restriction since it takes the form of a physical limitation on the quantity of the commodity which is allowed to enter the country in a given year. Quotas bring in no revenue to the state, and foreign producers cannot overcome them by reducing prices, as they might do in the case of a tariff.

Tariffs

The tariff is the most common barrier to trade. It acts in exactly the same way as a tax by artificially raising the price of the foreign product as it enters the country. Tariffs may be *ad valorem*, that is, a percentage of the monetary value of the import, or *specific*, that is, a tax per unit of weight or physical quantity.

Exchange control

Importers require foreign currencies in order to buy goods abroad. American firms will require payment in dollars, German firms in marks and so on. A country obtains its supplies of foreign currencies by means of the efforts of its exporters. A thorough-going system of exchange control will require the foreign currencies earned by exporters to be surrendered to the central bank which will pay for them in the home currency. Importers requiring foreign currency must apply to the central bank which can thus, very effectively, control the variety and volume of imports by controlling the issue of foreign currency.

Subsidies

A nation may decide to subsidise certain domestic industries as a means of protecting them from the competition of lower-priced foreign goods. The subsidy will reduce the price of the domestic product and hence make it more difficult for the foreign producer to sell a similar product in the home market. There will be a redistribution of income towards the producers and consumers of the subsidised good because the cost of the subsidy will fall on taxpayers.

The next question to be answered is 'Why are such restrictions on trade so commonplace?' The reasons advanced for protecting home industries from foreign competition are often classed as economic and non-economic, but this can be misleading because they will all have economic effects.

Arguments advanced for protection

For revenue purposes

The use of customs duties as a means of providing the state with revenue has a long history (more than 300 years in Britain). The budget statement on p. 421 reveals that such duties are not a major source of revenue as far as the UK is concerned. (See page 426.) Although not primarily intended to be protective, revenue duties will have some such effect unless the articles subject to duty are not produced at home.

To counter the effect of a general depression

During the Great Depression of the 1930s, most countries resorted to increased protection of home industries in an attempt to maintain employment at home by diverting expenditure from foreign to domestic products. The philosophy is simple enough – money spent on home-produced goods creates employment at home while that spent on imports does not. But the imports of one country are the exports of another and restrictions on imports create unemployment and distress in other countries. They are very likely to retaliate by protecting their own industries. A cumulative effect is inevitable; the barriers to trade become higher and higher and more and more widespread. As world exports decline all trading nations must, to some extent, be worse off.

To protect particular industries

1 The best-known argument for the tariff or the quota is the 'infant industry' argument. A nation may be relatively late in developing a particular industry and yet be favourably endowed with the basic economic requirements for the effective operation of such an industry. If the industry were to be established on a small scale in conditions of free trade, it would not survive the competition from fully-developed large scale producers abroad who would be operating at much lower costs. It is necessary, therefore, to protect the infant industry until it reaches a scale of production large enough to allow its costs to fall to a level which is competitive with its foreign rivals. Many developing countries have had to resort to severe protectionist policies in order to establish domestic industries. Unfortunately, once imposed, these tariffs are difficult to remove. Even when they have achieved large-scale production, industries do not welcome the removal of the protective barrier – there is always strong pressure on governments to retain the tariff.

2 As mentioned earlier, the comparative advantages enjoyed by different countries in the production of different commodities are always changing. The country which was the first to establish a major cotton industry may find eventually that a faster rate of technical progress in other countries has moved the advantages in this industry to other parts of the world. Other producers may be nearer the source of the raw materials, or to the major markets, or they may have much cheaper supplies of labour.

These changes in the comparative costs of production will mean that particular industries will be declining in some countries and expanding in others. Ideally, a country should be moving its resources from those industries where it is losing its cost advantages to those newer industries where it is enjoying cost advantages, but economic resources are usually not sufficiently mobile for this transfer to take place without some hardship. Capital and labour cannot be moved quickly and easily from say the cotton industry to the computer industry; specialised labour and capital are very immobile. When industries come under pressure from the lower-priced goods of the more efficient foreign competitors there is usually a strong political demand for some measure of protection. Tariffs or quotas are advocated as a means of protecting an industry while some adjustment to the new situation takes place. Lancashire asked for protection from the low-priced cotton goods from India, Pakistan, and Hong Kong while the industry was being scaled down in size and the remaining firms modernised and merged into larger units. Without some degree of protection it is unlikely that private investment would be forthcoming for projects such as these.

To safeguard the interests of workers

The basis of this particular argument is that imports from countries where wages are relatively low represent 'unfair' competition and threaten the standard of living of the more highly paid workers in the home industries. But a policy of restricting imports from low-wage countries will simply reduce the demand for these products, increase unemployment in these countries and drive wages there even lower. It will also increase the cost of living at home and lessen the incentives to move resources out of the industries which have lost their cost advantages. It is an argument which could well be used against the country imposing the restrictions. For example, the USA might use such an argument to restrict the entry of British goods, since, relative to the USA, Britain is a low-wage country.

For strategic reasons

Some industries such as iron and steel, agriculture, chemicals, and scientific instruments are regarded as strategic industries which are absolutely essential to a nation at war. It is regarded as most desirable that such industries should be maintained so as to reduce a nation's dependence on foreign supplies of strategic materials. Where they have not been competitive in world markets these industries have normally been protected by means of tariffs or quotas.

To prevent or eliminate a balance of payments deficit

A country may find that it is persistently spending more on foreign goods and services than it is earning from the sale of its exports. When it has made every effort, without success, to eliminate this deficit by increasing its exports and substituting home products for imported goods, it has little alternative to the use of import controls. We shall see later that a major trading nation would only use protection as a last resort in dealing with a balance of payments problem.

On purely economic grounds it is difficult to support most of the arguments for the restriction of international trade. Tariffs distort the true cost relationships and reduce the differences in comparative costs. The extent of international specialisation is reduced and so is the potential level of world output. Consumers in the home country are obliged to pay higher prices for the protected home-produced goods and for the imported goods. The erection of trade barriers also invites retaliation and increases the probability of a general reduction in world trade. Industries operating behind tariff walls are protected from foreign competition and this could lead to a lower level of efficiency.

On the other hand we can be too enthusiastic in advocating any move towards freer trade, particularly where the gains are heavily weighted in favour of a particular group of countries. It seems that liberalisation of world trade has generally benefited the wealthier industrialised countries and done little to narrow the gap between the rich and poor countries. Some limitation on free trade may be necessary in order to assist the developing countries. They could be allowed, for example, to impose restrictions on imports to protect their infant industries while being granted access to markets in the developed world on very favourable terms. We must also remember the point made earlier about the vulnerability to change which results from over-specialisation.

General Agreement on Tariffs and Trade

In 1947 some 23 major trading nations made an agreement on certain rules in respect of international trade and began a series of conferences with a view to reducing tariffs and dismantling other barriers to trade. This arrangement has survived and is known as the *General Agreement on Tariffs and Trade* (GATT). Member nations meet at regular intervals and negotiate agreements to reduce quotas, tariffs, and other restrictions. There are now some 80 members of GATT and it includes most of the trading nations of the non-communist world. At the heart of the GATT agreement is the 'most favoured nation clause' which provides that every tariff concession agreed between any group of countries must be extended to all members of GATT. There is a problem here, however, because a nation which is prepared to strike bargains with some other nation might be dissuaded from doing so because it is obliged to allow any concessions agreed upon to apply to all other member nations.

Although the work of the organisation has increased, the rate of progress is relatively slow. There are many difficulties to be overcome. The GATT rules forbid any discrimination among members, but countries are allowed to use quotas when they are in serious balance of payments difficulties and developing nations are granted preferential treatment both in respect of the trade restrictions they can apply to imports and in respect of their exports to developing countries. GATT also permits members to establish free trade areas and customs unions (such as the EEC), although such economic integration involves discrimination against imports from countries that are not parties to the arrangement.

A major achievement of GATT was the sixth round of trade negotiations conducted during 1964–7 and popularly known as the Kennedy Round. This resulted in across-the-board tariff cuts averaging more than 35 per cent on a wide range of goods. For industrial products the tariff cuts ranged between 35 and 50 per cent. Another major round of negotiations got under way in 1975 (the Tokyo Round). When the Tokyo Round tariff cuts are implemented during the 1980s, industrial countries' tariffs will average only 5 or 6 per cent in ad valorem terms. They will, however, be much higher on labour-intensive products which are of prime importance to developing countries. In addition to the problems of quotas and tariff barriers, GATT is increasingly interested in reducing a wide range of non-tariff barriers to trade (e.g. a country may insist on particular technical specifications which favour home producers).

27 International Payments

Foreign exchange

Different countries use different currencies. In Britain the unit of currency is the pound sterling, in the USA it is the dollar, and in Germany it is the mark. These different currencies circulate freely within the different national boundaries, but they are generally unacceptable in another country. A French firm selling equipment to the USA will require payment in francs and not in dollars. Thus an international transaction gives rise to two exchanges. First there is an exchange of one currency for another and then an exchange of currency for goods and services. The American firm will ask its bank to supply francs and pay for them with dollars drawn from its account at the bank.

There is a highly organised foreign exchange market which deals in this business of exchanging currencies. Most of the commercial banks have foreign exchange departments and the merchant banks, branches of overseas banks, and foreign exchange brokers all deal in the foreign exchange market buying and selling foreign currencies in response to the needs of traders and travellers. The great financial centres such as New York, London, and Zurich are all linked directly by modern electronic communications equipment.

A demand for foreign goods is represented in the foreign exchange market by a supply of the home currency and a demand for foreign currency. The British firm seeking German goods creates a supply of pounds and a demand for marks. Similarly exports create a demand for the home currency and a supply of foreign currency. Fig. 70 shows the directions in which currencies will move. Dollars and pounds will not move in the physical sense – the transactions will take the form of movements in bank deposits held in the great financial centres.

The balance of payments

A country engaging in foreign trade will be making payments to foreign countries and receiving payments from them. Each nation keeps an account of its transactions with the rest of the world which it presents in the form of a balance sheet described as the *balance of payments*.

In the UK full details of these transactions are given in the annual balance of payments statement, while estimates of the overseas payments position are provided quarterly. International payments arise from a variety of transactions.

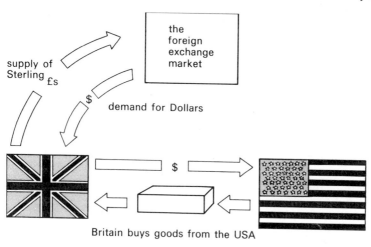

the
foreign
exchange
market

supply of
Sterling £s

$ demand for Dollars

$

Britain buys goods from the USA

Fig. 70

The purchase and sale of goods (visible trade)

The export and import of goods is referred to as visible trade and the differences between the values of exports and imports of physical items is known as the balance of visible trade. Estimates of this particular balance are provided on a monthly basis.

The purchase and sales of services (invisible trade)

In addition to the international trade in visible items there is a considerable trade in services. London, New York, and Zurich, for example, provide financial services for countries all over the world. Some countries have large merchant navies which earn foreign currencies by providing shipping services for other countries. British insurance companies insure property and people all over the world. Countries such as Italy, Switzerland, Spain, and Greece have very large tourist industries which sell a variety of holiday services to foreigners. A company providing services to foreign households and firms is earning foreign currency just as effectively as the firm selling machinery or motor cars to foreigners. Capital invested abroad earns foreign currency in the form of interest, profits, and dividends. Britain, like most developed countries, earns a great deal of foreign currency by selling services to overseas residents,[1] but she also spends a great deal in buying such services from foreign residents. Britain also spends large sums in pur-

[1] i.e. private individuals, firms, and public authorities.

chasing local services for the armed forces stationed overseas. This international trade in services is described as *invisible trade*.

Capital movements

International payments also arise from the movements of capital from one country to another. These capital transactions are usefully distinguished as long-term and short-term.

Long-term capital movements are those which arise from overseas investments in shares or long-term securities, or from the establishment of factories in foreign countries. If an American firm decided to build a plant in Britain, there is a movement of foreign currency to the UK. Britain receives dollars which she exchanges for the pounds necessary to carry out the work. Typical long-term capital movements are:

a Long-term lending between governments or between governments and international institutions.

b The purchase of stocks and shares in foreign companies or the purchase by foreign residents of shares in home-based companies.

c The setting up of plantations, mines, or factories abroad, or the establishment of similar enterprises by foreign companies in the home country.

Short-term capital movements reflect the transfer of liquid assets from one country to another. These funds are held in bank accounts or in very short-term securities such as Treasury Bills or local authority bills. They can, therefore, be withdrawn at very short notice. As an international banker the UK holds a very large amount of money on short-term deposit for foreigners. Since sterling is a *key currency* and is used to finance a relatively large share of world trade, many nations maintain working balances in London, and some part of the large surpluses accumulated by the Arab oil states is held in London. In recent years a large volume of short-term capital or 'hot money' has been moving from one country to another seeking greater security (e.g. against depreciation) or higher interest rates. A movement of short-term capital to a country represents an inflow of foreign currency and there is a corresponding outflow when such funds are withdrawn by foreign holders of domestic financial assets.

Balancing the Balance of Payments

When all transactions between residents of one country and the rest of the world, during the course of one year, have been recorded we have that country's balance of payments. Like all balance sheets it must balance. All those transactions which lead to an inflow of foreign currency are placed on the credit side (or given a plus sign) and those transactions which give rise to an outflow of foreign currency are placed on the debit side (or given a minus sign). It is, perhaps, rather puzzling to read that the balance of payments always balances, because we are always hearing about countries having deficits or surpluses on their balance of payments. There is no contradiction here, because the deficit or surplus refers to the way in which the accounting balance was achieved. If the total payments made for foreign goods and services plus the outflow of capital exceeds the receipts from exports plus any inflow of capital the difference must have been made up in some way. A family can only spend more than it earns by borrowing, drawing on savings, receiving gifts, or selling some of its assets. A country in its relationships with the rest of the world is in exactly the same position and if it has a deficit on its balance of payments, the account will be balanced by an item similar to those mentioned above (e.g. a loan from abroad). A balance of payments surplus indicates that the account is balanced by a net addition to the foreign currency reserves or by net lending abroad.

The figures in the balance of payments statement will be expressed in terms of the home currency, but it must be remembered that the transactions referred to involve income and expenditures in foreign currency.

The balance of payments account

Countries present their balance of payments in different ways, but the British presentation is very much in line with recommended international practice. The following summary (Table 24) shows the main

Table 24 Summary of the UK balance of payments in 1981 (£ million)

Current Account:	
Visible trade	+3 013
Invisible trade	+3 023
Current Balance	+6 036
Investment and other capital transactions	−7 209
Balancing item	+328
Balance for official financing	−845
Allocation of SDRs	+158
Official financing:	
Changes in reserves, additions (−), drawings (+),	+2 419
Official borrowing (+), repayments (−)	−1 732

sections of the balance of payments account. Table 25 on page 368 gives a more detailed picture of the UK balance of payments.

The current account

The first section of the summary comprises the sum of all the visible and invisible transactions. The current balance is of great importance because it shows the nation's net deficit or surplus on its day-to-day trading with the rest of the world. Since the current account is made up of a very large number of independent decisions to buy and sell, it is very unlikely that it will balance. If there is a surplus, the country has acquired foreign assets in the form of claims on other countries. These may be used to augment the foreign currency reserves, to acquire property abroad, to make foreign loans, or to repay any existing loans. A deficit on current account implies some borrowing abroad, the sale of overseas assets, or a running down of the foreign currency reserves. A surplus or deficit in the current account must be offset in some way by movements in the other sections of the balance of payments.

Investment and other capital flows

This section is made up of a variety of capital movements, both long-term and short-term, carried out by governments, firms, and households. We have already noted the type of transaction recorded in this section.

The balancing item

It is impossible to get a completely accurate record of the millions of transactions which affect the balance of payments. Since the Bank of England knows the net effect of all transactions from movements in foreign currency balances, the actual discrepancy in the records can be calculated. The balancing item represents the sum of all errors and omissions. If it is positive, it means that there have been unrecorded net exports; if it is negative, there are some unrecorded net imports.

Balance for official financing

The sum of the current balance, capital movements and the balancing item gives the overall net balance or total currency flow. If this balance is negative there has been a net outflow of foreign currency; if it is positive there has been a net inflow. A positive balance, however, can be misleading; it does not necessarily indicate that a country has been earning a surplus on its trading transactions. Net borrowings on capital account may more than offset a deficit on current account so that the overall balance is positive.

SDRs are a specialised form of international money created by the IMF. They are treated as a credit item because they add to the official reserves of the UK. SDRs are discussed on page 388.

Official financing

This final section of the balance of payments account shows how the monetary authorities have dealt with the net currency flow (i.e. the balance for official financing). If the overall balance has a negative sign (i.e. a net outflow), the authorities must (i) draw upon the official foreign currency reserves and/or (ii) borrow from the IMF and/or (iii) borrow from foreign central banks. If the balance for official financing is positive, the authorities may (i) increase the official foreign currency reserves, and/or (ii) repay borrowings from the IMF and/or (iii) make repayments or loans to foreign central banks.

The use of the plus and minus signs in this account is sometimes a source of confusion. An addition to the reserves is given a minus sign and so is the repayment of a short-term loan. Drawings on the reserves and borrowings from the IMF and other monetary institutions are given plus signs. The explanation lies in the fact that since the account must balance, the sum of all the credit items ($+$ signs) must equal the sum of all the debit items ($-$ signs). If it is necessary to balance a deficit currency flow of, say, 100, then the item which effects the balance (e.g. a reduction in the reserves) must appear as $+100$. If there is a positive balance for official financing, then the disposal of the surplus (e.g. an addition to the reserves) must be given a minus sign.

Equilibrium in the balance of payments

Although the balance of payments always balances this does not mean that it is always in equilibrium. It is a commonly held belief that the balance of payments situation is satisfactory when it shows a surplus. But it should be clear that *world* exports and *world* imports must be identically equal. If one nation is in surplus there must be a corresponding deficit somewhere in the world, assuming, that is, other things remain equal. All nations cannot achieve a surplus simultaneously.

A country can only run a persistent deficit on current account if it has unlimited reserves of gold and foreign currencies or if it can persistently borrow these resources from the rest of the world. Neither of these possibilities is very realistic. A country may, however, run a deficit on current account for several years if it is being balanced by

Table 25 UK balance of payments in 1981 (£ million)

Visible trade				
Exports	51 100		Visible balance	+3 013
Imports	48 087			
Invisible trade				
Shipping	+3 772			
	−3 870	−98		
Civil aviation	+2 359			
	−1 922	+437		
Travel	+2 999			
	−3 285	−286		
Interest and profit	+10 082			
	−9 078	+1 004		
Other services	+7 160			
	−2 463	+4 697		
Private transfers	+844			
	−1 119	−275		
Government	+2 122			
	−4 578	−2 456	Invisible balance	+3 023
			Current balance	+6 036

Investment and Other Capital Flows

UK private investment abroad	−10 637		
Foreign investment in UK private sector	+3 168		
Foreign investment in UK public sector	+188		
Official long-term capital	−334		
UK Banks' foreign currency trans-actions (net)	+1 404		
Other capital flows	−998	Total capital	−7 209

Balancing Item	+328
	Balance for official financing −845
Allocation of SDRs	+158

Official Financing

Changes in reserves; additions (−), drawings (+)	+2 419
Foreign currency borrowings (+) or repayments (−) by UK government	−1 732

Source: UK Balance of Payments 1981 HMSO

long-term capital inflows (loans or grants) which are financing new productive capacity in industry or agriculture. This new capacity hopefully will in time generate additional exports to earn the foreign currency required to repay the loans. Where there are no such loans, and the foreign currency reserves and temporary borrowing facilities are strictly limited, the existence of a persistent deficit means that the balance of payments is in disequilibrium. A country faced with this situation must introduce policy measures to restore equilibrium. We shall deal with these measures later when discussing foreign exchange because they depend very much on whether the country is operating a floating or fixed exchange rate.

But the idea of an equilibrium situation in the balance of payments being considered solely in terms of external balance is probably much too limited. For example, a low level of exports may be balanced by a low level of imports simply because the country is experiencing heavy unemployment. If the country moved to a full employment level of output there would probably be a sharp rise in imports (raw materials, fuel, and finished goods) which would put the balance of payments in deficit. Imports may be in balance with exports because the country has imposed severe trade restrictions in the form of tariffs, quotas, and exchange control. Equilibrium in the balance of payments can only be considered in relation to the other objectives of economic policy. If full employment and trade liberalisation are objectives of that policy neither of the situations cited above could be considered

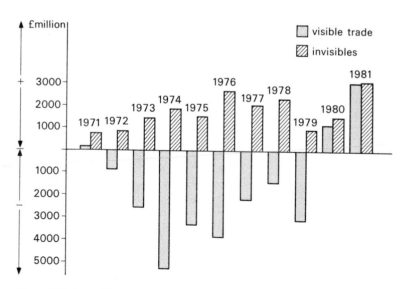

Source: UK Balance of Payments 1981 HMSO.

Fig. 71 UK visible and invisible balances

satisfactory because the equilibrium in the balance of payments is being achieved (a) at the cost of heavy unemployment and (b) by imposing severe trade restrictions.

Recent developments in the UK balance of payments

In the 1950s the UK balance of payments maintained a fairly small surplus on current account because the traditional surplus on invisibles more than offset the deficit on visible trade. In the 1960s, the position deteriorated into one of fundamental disequilibrium. One major factor in this worsening situation was the large deficit on government account in the invisibles. This situation eventually led to a cutback in the country's overseas military commitments.

During the same period the visible trade balance also deteriorated as imports grew faster than exports. After trying to remedy the situation by strong deflationary measures and the imposition of a temporary import surcharge supported by massive borrowings from the IMF and other overseas monetary authorities, the government finally resorted to devaluation (November 1967). The immediate effect of devaluation was a worsening of the deficit. This is explained by the fact that while devaluation has immediate effects on relative prices (exports cheaper abroad, imports dearer at home), the volume changes take time. The favourable effects of devaluation appeared in 1969, 1970, and 1971, as the increased demand for the lower-priced exports led to an increased volume of exports. The surpluses of these years enabled the government to repay the major part of the short-term loans which had been obtained to deal with the problems of the late 1960s. In the early 1970s the terms of trade moved unfavourably as the prices of oil and other imported commodities rose much faster than the prices of exports. The pound was floated (see page 389) in 1972 and this was followed by a significant depreciation of sterling. This was another factor causing a deterioration in the terms of trade and it also helped to generate serious cost-push pressures in the British economy.

In the period 1976–79 there was an improvement in the current account situation, due mainly to the increasing output of North Sea oil. In this period, as explained later, there was also a substantial inflow of short-term capital. In 1979 there was a sharp reduction in the surplus on invisibles. This was brought about by (i) the increased UK contributions to the EEC Budget, (ii) increased profits accruing to foreign-based companies operating in the North Sea and (iii) higher interest payments on overseas debt.

In 1980 the visible trade of the UK moved into surplus. This was due mainly to the effects of the recession which led to a substantial fall in imports, although the balance of trade in oil also improved. The invisible surplus also increased because the UK government had negotiated a reduction in its contributions to the EEC Budget. The current accounts for 1980 and 1981 therefore, were in substantial surplus (see Fig. 71). It is anticipated (i.e. in 1982) that this account might remain in surplus although much depends upon the extent and pace of any recovery from the recession. An increase in economic activity in the UK will certainly bring about a substantial increase in imports.

The fairly persistent adverse imbalance in Britain's overseas trade is a complex subject and many possible explanations have been put forward. Attempts to raise the rate of economic growth have contributed to some of the deficits. A growth in national output must invariably be preceded by a substantial increase in the imports of raw materials and machinery. This puts the balance of payments in deficit and if there are inadequate foreign currency reserves to deal with the situation, the government may be obliged to take measures which restrict demand before the level of exports can be increased to offset the increase in imports.

Another factor was the recovery of Germany and Japan during the 1950s and 1960s. The successes of these countries in foreign markets undoubtedly had some adverse effect on the UK's export performance. Although British exports have continued to increase, the country's share of world trade has been falling.

Some part of the explanation for the country's recent balance of payments problems may lie in the fact that the rate of inflation in the UK has tended to be much higher than the rates in the major competitor countries so that UK prices have become relatively unfavourable. To a large extent this has been due to the fact that unit labour costs have risen much faster in the UK than in most other industrialised countries.

The progressive liberalisation of world trade has revealed some lack of competitiveness in the UK performance because foreign suppliers have been rather more successful in penetrating UK markets than British firms have been in penetrating foreign markets. Other factors often mentioned in studies of this problem are certain inadequacies in respect of designs, delivery dates, after-sales service, market research, and salesmanship. It is, of course, extremely difficult to measure the extent to which these factors affect exports and imports. Many authorities would say that, in the case of the UK, such inadequacies as may exist are only of marginal importance. The lack of competitiveness in world markets seems to be especially marked in finished manufactures. In 1955, finished manufactures accounted for 5 per cent of UK imports while in 1981 the share was more than 30 per cent. The UK share of world exports of manufactures over the same period fell from 20 per cent to about 10 per cent.

As an international banker the UK holds large balances for nonresidents and is, therefore, particularly vulnerable to events which may cause these balances to be withdrawn from the country. When a foreign resident withdraws funds from London it has the same effect on the balance of payments as an increase in imports; the UK holdings of foreign currencies are reduced.

A substantial deficit on current account, or a series of such deficits, may cause a large net withdrawal of funds because overseas holders of deposits in London will fear a devaluation or substantial depreciation in the value of the pound relative to other currencies. Such a movement is described as 'a speculative outflow' or 'flight from the pound'. Thus, a deficit on current account may lead to a deterioration in the capital account. The UK has experienced several such heavy withdrawals of short-term capital in recent years particularly in the period immediately preceding the floating of the pound in 1972. On the other hand the exploitation of the North Sea oilfields increased the attractiveness of sterling as an international financial asset and together with the relatively high UK interest rates in the late 1970s brought about a large inflow of short-term capital.

North Sea oil

The exploitation of the UK's North Sea oilfields is having a substantial impact on the balance of payments. The UK became a net exporter of oil in 1981 and is likely to continue to be a net exporter of fuel for a number of years. But the UK is still a relatively large importer of oil from the Middle East. This is because North Sea oil is lighter than the typical Middle East crude oil and UK refineries are most economically run on a mix of crude oil. The UK, therefore, is a large exporter and a large importer of oil but she now has a favourable trade balance in this commodity.

Assessments of the recoverable reserves of oil in the North Sea are subject to much uncertainty. To some extent these assessments depend upon the future movements in the market price of oil. A significant rise in the real price of oil would tend to increase the estimates of recoverable reserves because some fields which were uneconomic to operate at the lower price would now become economically workable.

At the same time as the North Sea oilfields were being developed, in the early 1970s, the real price of oil more than doubled. It remained fairly steady from 1974 until it doubled again in 1979–1980. The extraction of oil from the North Sea is a relatively high cost operation and prior to the first OPEC price rise (1974) the cost of producing North Sea oil was very close to the world price of oil. Since the early 1970s, however, the world oil price has exceeded this cost by a large margin. In other words, a substantial part of the income from North Sea oil is in the form of economic rent.

A very large part of the development costs in the North Sea was financed by overseas investment. This led to a favourable movement in the balance of payments in the form of capital inflows. In the early years this favourable effect was largely offset by the fact that much of the specialised equipment and expertise had to be purchased overseas. The sales revenues from North Sea oil did not begin to cover the current and capital costs until the late 1970s. This surplus has rapidly increased and is expected to exceed £10 billion (in 1980 prices) by 1985. Much of this surplus is taken in taxation (see pages 421 and 423) but a sizeable proportion of the revenue net of tax accrues to foreign investors in the form of interest, profits and dividends and appears as a debit item in the invisible account of the balance of payments.

The major balance of payments effect of the extraction of North Sea oil is on the balance of invisible trade where, in a matter of seven years, a substantial deficit on oil ($-$£8·8 billion in 1974) has changed to a small surplus ($+$£1·8 billion in 1981).

The fact that the UK is now a major oil producer has serious implications for the external value of sterling and hence for the terms of trade. When the price of oil is rising and world demand is strong, the value of sterling in the foreign exchange markets will rise and affect the competitiveness of UK goods in foreign markets. In 1982 fears of an oil glut and forecasts of falling prices in the oil markets caused a sharp depreciation of the pound in the foreign exchange markets.

28 The Rate of Exchange

Currencies are exchanged in the foreign exchange market, but what determines the rates at which they exchange for one another? This is really a question of prices – we are asking what determines the price of one currency in terms of another. The key issue which dominates the debate on this subject is whether currencies should stand in a fixed relation to each other or whether their values should be allowed to fluctuate in response to the free operation of the forces of supply and demand. We shall look at the extreme possibilities and then at the compromise system which has operated for most of the post-war period.

Free, fluctuating or floating exchange rates

In principle, this means the existence of a free or competitive foreign exchange market where the price of one currency in terms of another is determined by the forces of supply and demand operating without any official interference. In this type of market the value of the pound in terms of the dollar would depend upon the demand for pounds from holders of dollars and the supply of pounds from holders of sterling who are wanting to buy dollars. British residents trying to buy foreign goods and services will be *supplying pounds* to the foreign exchange market (and demanding foreign currencies) while overseas residents wishing to buy British goods and services will be *demanding pounds* (and supplying foreign currencies). There will be some equilibrium price (i.e. exchange rate) which equates these two forces. The price of pounds, of course, will be expressed in terms of foreign currencies.

Thus, the foreign exchange value of a national currency will be closely related to that country's balance between exports and imports. It will also be influenced by the capital transactions between that country and the rest of the world. In addition to the normal commercial transactions, however, there are the activities of speculators to consider. Speculators buy and sell foreign currencies with a view to making a capital gain. They buy when the value of a currency is expected to rise and sell when it is expected to fall. If the exchange value of the pound is expected to rise and in fact does rise from, say, £1 = $2 to £1 = $2·5, then someone who transfers $10 000 into pounds at the lower rate and moves back into dollars at the higher rate will make a profit of $2 500. These transactions, when carried out on a large scale, can have a very significant influence on exchange rates. The great attraction of the floating rate is that it provides a kind of automatic mechanism for keeping the balance of payments in equilibrium. Suppose the pound sterling is floating and Britain is importing goods and services of greater value than her exports. At the current exchange rate the supply of pounds will exceed the demand for them and the exchange value of the pound will fall. Let us suppose it falls from £1 = $2·5 to £1 = $2. British goods now become cheaper in foreign markets (a £1 000 machine will fall in price from $2 500 to $2 000) and the volume of exports will rise. In the home market foreign goods will become more expensive *in terms of pounds*, because the pound will buy less foreign currency, and the volume of imports will fall. What happens, of course, in that the changes in the exchange rate alter the terms of trade, but whether these relative price changes can bring about the necessary changes in the volumes and values of exports and imports quickly and smoothly depends upon the elasticities of the demand for and supply of exports and imports. Nevertheless it is clear that movements in the exchange rate will tend to bring the balance of payments back into equilibrium. The reader should reason out for himself the sequence which results from a surplus balance of payments position.

A major disadvantage of free or floating rates is that they add a further element of uncertainty to international trading. The world prices of many commodities are far from stable (look at the indices of world commodity prices) and traders are obliged to accept a high degree of risk on this account. A system of floating rates, however, injects another variable element into the cost structure of firms buying goods from abroad. Buyers now have two price levels to watch – the foreign price of the commodity, *and* the price of the foreign currency. For example, it would be possible for the dollar price of cotton to be falling while the price of cotton to the Lancashire importer is rising. This would be the case where the value of the pound falls proportionately more than the dollar price of cotton. Some authorities believe that this added element of uncertainty is a major deterrent to the growth of world trade and in particular it discourages long-term contracts.

The type of speculation mentioned above is a further cause of instability. There is however a type of speculation which reduces the risks of trading. Some foreign currency dealers provide a *forward market* whereby they will quote fixed prices for foreign currencies for future delivery. Importers buying raw materials from abroad, for which payment is due several months hence, can be certain of the prices they must pay by buying 'future' dollars, marks, francs, etc., in the forward market. They will, on average, pay prices rather higher than those which will be ruling at the time their payments are due but the differential may be regarded as a kind of insurance premium for the risks taken by speculators who could, of course, lose heavily if they seriously misjudge the future course of exchange rates. The current prices quoted in the foreign exchange market are known as *spot* prices.

Critics of floating rates say that the *external* prices of home-produced goods will be subject to constant change and this will lead to a very unstable pattern of demand. This makes production planning very difficult because economic resources are not sufficiently mobile to cope with this type of situation without imposing some kind of hardship (e.g. a much greater uncertainty about employment prospects).

Under a system of floating exchange rates, a balance of payments surplus or deficit is automatically adjusted by movements in the exchange rate. This is very attractive to governments who are relieved of the unpleasant task of dealing with a deficit by using tariffs or quotas, or by taking measures to restrict home demand. But there are dangers in this greater freedom. If a country is suffering from inflation, a floating rate may remove some of the pressure on the government to deal with the problem, because the higher prices of home produced goods will not prejudice exports (the rate of exchange will fall and the *foreign prices* of exports will not rise). But the depreciation of the currency in the foreign exchange market will make imports dearer and this could well lead to cost-push inflation. A floating exchange rate cannot insulate the home economy from external forces.

Fixed exchange rates

The great advantage of a fixed exchange rate is that it removes the uncertainty associated with floating rates. The negotiation of long-term contracts, the granting of long-term credits, and the undertaking of long-term investment overseas are less risky when there is some confidence in the stability of the exchange rate.

In a typical fixed exchange rate system the countries must fix the values of their currencies in terms of some common standard. In the past this common standard has invariably been gold and a *Gold Standard* system operated for much of the nineteenth century and for a short time in the years between the wars. Nations on the gold standard had to obey certain rules. Their currencies were all given a fixed value in terms of gold and were freely convertible into gold at this fixed parity. The export and import of gold was not subject to any restrictions. Since each currency had a fixed value in terms of gold, the exchange rate between any two currencies was automatically established. For example, if the dollar were equal in value to 0·01 ounces of gold and the pound to 0·04 ounces, the rate of exchange would be £1 = \$4. Exchange rates could only vary within very narrow limits on each side of the fixed rate otherwise it became cheaper to use gold rather than foreign currencies to pay foreign debts. Since the currencies were fully convertible into gold the domestic money supplies were linked to the domestic supplies of gold. Nations receiving inflows of gold would expand their money supplies; when gold was flowing out of the country the money supply would be reduced.

The gold standard, like floating exchange rates, provided a self-correcting mechanism for balance of payments disequilibria. If a country had a balance of payments surplus, gold would flow into the country as payment for the excess exports. This would lead to an expansion of the money supply and an increased level of demand which, in turn, would lead to higher prices. Exports would become less competitive and imports more competitive. Thus, exports would fall and imports rise until the surplus was eliminated. The reader should have little difficulty in reasoning out the processes which eliminate a deficit.

But the gold standard proved difficult to work in the twentieth century. It requires a great flexibility of prices for the adjustment of exports and imports, but in modern conditions prices are extremely inflexible in a downward direction. A fall in demand leads to a fall in output and employment rather than a fall in prices. Governments with deficits will not allow prices to fall, as the gold standard rules require, if it requires a massive increase in unemployment in order to achieve the objective of lower prices. Likewise countries enjoying balance of payments surpluses will be very reluctant to carry out the required policy of inflation. As we have seen, this causes all kinds of problems in relation to income distribution, borrowing and lending, investment and saving. Quite simply, governments are no longer prepared to surrender control over the money supply, the domestic price level, and employment to external market forces.

For most of the post-war period the non-communist world has operated on *a dollar standard* with the values of currencies being quoted in terms of dollars. Since, until 1971, dollars were convertible into gold, the system was, in fact, a gold-exchange standard.

In order to maintain a currency at a fixed value, the monetary authorities of a country must stand ready to buy and sell the currency at the fixed price. This means that they must have large supplies of their own currency, gold, and convertible foreign currencies in order to remove any excess demand or supply at the fixed price. Figure 72 helps to explain this problem.

We assume that the UK authorities have agreed to maintain a fixed exchange rate of £1 = $2. Initially the market is in equilibrium at this price. Imports now increase and the supply curve moves from SS to S^1S^1. In the absence of any intervention by the authorities the price would fall to £1 = $1·5. The authorities, however, enter the market and buy pounds raising demand from DD to D^1D^1 and maintaining the exchange rate at £1 = $2.

When the authorities are intervening, as in the case above, to buy the domestic currency, they are, of course, spending the official reserves of foreign currency and gold. In the example above the Bank of England would be buying pounds with gold, or dollars, or marks, or some other convertible currencies. Thus, when we read that 'the pound had to be supported' we know that the official reserves have been depleted. Similarly when the demand for the currency exceeds its supply at the fixed price, the monetary authorities will be selling the home currency on the foreign exchange market and hence replenishing the reserves of foreign currency.

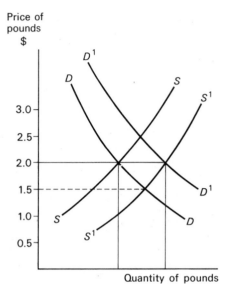

Fig. 72

This brings us to the major disadvantage of fixed exchange rates. Whereas with the floating rate the burden of adjusting a balance of payments disequilibrium falls on the exchange rate itself, under a fixed rate system this burden tends to fall on the domestic economy. A country with a persistent deficit would soon exhaust its foreign currency reserves and indeed any temporary borrowing facilities in trying to hold up the exchange value of its currency. It must take steps to remove the cause of the deficit. The necessary measures to reduce imports and stimulate exports will inevitably have some adverse effects on the home economy. Monetary and fiscal measures will be used to reduce home demand so that the demands for both home-produced goods and imports will fall. The use of tariffs and quotas will inevitably raise home prices. The reduction of demand in the home market will provide domestic firms with more resources and more incentive to increase their export sales. Higher interest rates may be used to attract short-term capital from abroad. This will improve the balance of payments, but it will also raise home costs and discourage investment. It is because the fixed exchange rate puts the official reserves at risk and hence puts the burden of adjustment on the home economy that most governments favour some more flexible system.

Revaluation and devaluation

Situations arise when the exchange rate cannot be held. A persistent surplus or deficit indicates that the fixed rate is being held at well below or well above its true market rate of exchange. A persistent surplus might be dealt with by measures which increase home demand so as to encourage more imports and, perhaps, raise home prices making exports less competitive. A reduction in the restrictions on imports would also help to reduce the surplus. A persistent deficit might be eliminated by measures to reduce home demand and/or increase the restrictions on imports. When these measures prove ineffective, or, more likely, when governments are not prepared to impose them on the domestic economy, the only solution is to change the rate of exchange. Countries with surpluses would revalue by moving the exchange values of their currencies to higher parities. Countries with deficits would devalue by lowering the exchange value of their currencies in terms of other currencies.

Revaluation makes exports relatively dearer (in terms of foreign currencies) and imports relatively cheaper in terms of the home currency. Since a balance of payments surplus is widely regarded as a sign of success, surplus countries are usually reluctant to revalue,[1] but if they do not, they are perpetuating the imbalance of world trade and other countries in persistent deficit may be forced to resort to the use of trade restrictions.

Devaluation

The immediate effect of devaluation is to change the relative prices of imports and exports. Exports become cheaper *in terms of foreign currency*, while imports become dearer *in terms of the home currency*.

Example: *Before devaluation* £1 = $2·5
A British car, price £5 000, costs $12 500 in the USA
An American machine, price $20 000, costs £8 000 in the UK
          After devaluation   £1 = $2
A British car, price £5 000, costs $10 000 in the USA
An American machine price $20 000 costs £10 000 in the UK

The analysis from here on, of course is exactly the same as that for the depreciation of a currency on a floating exchange rate. Export volume will increase and the volume of imports will fall. But export *earnings* will only increase if the demand for exports is elastic, that is, if the volume of exports increases by a greater percentage than the

[1] See p. 387.

percentage fall in their external prices. Since the foreign prices of imports do not change, any fall in the volume of imports must lead to a reduction in foreign currency expenditures.

There are several other factors which influence the effectiveness of devaluation as a remedy for a balance of payments deficit. It can only lead to favourable price movements if major trading rivals do not devalue their own currencies. The situation with regard to the supply of exports must also be considered. The full benefits of the increased demand for exports can only be realised if additional supplies of exports can be made available. If the devaluing country is operating at full employment, more goods can only be supplied to export markets by reducing supplies to the home market. It may be necessary, therefore, to increase taxation and restrict bank credit to reduce home demand in order to free supplies for foreign markets.

In present circumstances devaluation is very likely to initiate or worsen a cost-push inflation. Import prices will rise and, if the demand for these goods is inelastic (e.g. foodstuffs and raw materials), this will raise the domestic price level and provoke claims for compensating wage increases. A further effect of devaluation is to increase the burden of overseas indebtedness. Since foreign debts are usually expressed in terms of foreign currency, the repayment of any given loan will now require a greater volume of exports in order to earn that given amount of foreign currency. There may also be adverse income effects. If devaluation succeeds in reducing imports by a substantial amount, other countries must be suffering a corresponding fall in their exports. This loss of income will reduce their ability to buy foreign goods and the devaluing country may find the beneficial price effects somewhat offset by this unfavourable income effect.

The adjustable peg system

This type of system was operated by member countries of the IMF throughout the 1950s and 1960s. The essential features are that countries should adopt fixed par values and agree to maintain the exchange values of their currencies within some agreed limits around this fixed rate of exchange. For example, the UK might declare that the value of the pound is to be fixed at £1 = $2·5 and then guarantee to maintain its exchange value within a range of 1 per cent of the declared parity. There is, therefore, a narrow band within which currencies may fluctuate. In order to maintain the par values central banks must use stabilisation funds of currencies and gold to intervene in the foreign exchange markets. In the UK, this stabilisation fund is the *Exchange Equalisation Account*[1] which holds the official reserves of

---

[1] Controlled by the Bank of England.

gold and foreign currencies. These reserves can if necessary be supplemented by borrowing from foreign central banks and international monetary institutions.

In the event of a fundamental disequilibrium, countries are allowed to adjust the prices at which their currencies are pegged, that is, they can revalue or devalue. The system is designed to obtain most of the benefits of stability associated with fixed exchange rates without imposing the unacceptable disciplines required to maintain rigidly fixed rates. The adjustable peg system worked reasonably well until the late 1960s, but it had some inherent weaknesses. It depended upon devaluations and revaluations being sufficiently infrequent to provide the advantages of exchange rate certainty yet taking place promptly whenever countries got into fundamental disequilibrium. The conditions of the late 1960s and early 1970s, as we shall see later in this chapter, placed strain on the system which it could not carry.

International liquidity

The adjustable peg system and, indeed, all the proposed alternatives envisage some degree of intervention by central banks in the foreign exchange market. International liquidity is the name given to the assets which central banks use to influence the external value of their currencies. There are four main types of international liquidity.
1 Gold.
2 Convertible national currencies.
3 Borrowing facilities.
4 International reserve assets.

Gold has a long history of use as a money commodity and has almost universal acceptability. The great advantage of gold as an international currency is the confidence people have in its ability to maintain its exchange value. This stems mainly from the knowledge that world supplies of gold cannot easily and quickly be augmented. Nevertheless it is clearly wasteful to employ vast resources of men and capital to produce gold merely in order to store it away in central banks.

There are several advantages in using *a particular national currency* as an international standard of value and as an international reserve asset. Unlike gold, its costs of production and storage are negligible and the reserve asset is in the same form as the currency used by traders and investors. The supply can easily be increased or diminished to meet the needs of world trade. There are however some serious disadvantages in using the currency of a particular country as a form international liquidity. Other countries can only build up their official reserves if the reserve-currency country is running a large and persist-ent deficit. But a prolonged deficit will cast doubt on the ability of that country to maintain the exchange value of its currency. The de-valuation of a reserve currency imposes a financial penalty on foreign holders of that currency since the purchasing power of their reserves will fall, and the attempt to avoid such a devaluation will impose a heavy burden on the domestic economy of the reserve-currency country.

Borrowing facilities are rather different from gold and reserve cur-rencies because they are conditional – they have to be repaid. Bor-rowing facilities as a source of liquidity have the advantage that they can be expanded to meet growing demands, but the drawback is that lenders can dictate terms to the borrowers.

Because of the disadvantages of using gold and national currencies and the objections raised to conditional borrowings there has been a growing awareness that the world's need for liquidity can best be met by the creation of an *international reserve asset* which would be costless to create, and whose supply and acceptability can be internationally controlled and enforced. Progress towards this objective has been rather slow because the creation of money is regarded as a matter for *national* governments and they are very reluctant to surrender this right. Nevertheless we now have such an international reserve asset in the form of the Special Drawing Rights issued by the IMF (see p. 388).

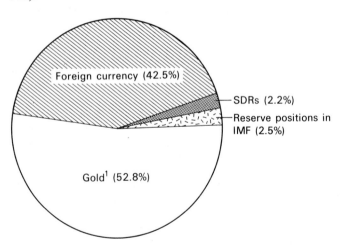

¹Valued as at London market price

Source: IMF Annual Report 1981

Fig. 73 Composition of world reserves (May 1981)

The International Monetary Fund

Establishment and aims

In 1944 the representatives of the allied nations met at Bretton Woods in the USA to discuss plans for promoting world recovery after the Second World War. This conference led to the establishment of two very important institutions, The International Monetary Fund (the IMF) and the International Bank for Reconstruction and Development (the World Bank).

The IMF began operations in 1947 with 40 members; there are now 141 member countries.

The aims of the IMF were to encourage the growth of world trade by, (i) working for the full convertibility of national currencies, (ii) promoting stability of exchange rates and (iii) providing short-term financial assistance to members in balance of payments difficulties. These are still the main purposes of the IMF.

i Convertibility

Currencies are convertible when holders can freely exchange them for other currencies. Convertibility is an important requirement for the full development of multilateral trade because it means that a country does not have to strike a trading balance with each of its trading partners. A deficit with one country can be offset by a surplus with another country. Figure 74 provides a simple arithmetic example to illustrate this important point.

The aim of convertibility proved difficult to achieve, because, for many years after the Second World War, the only currency in strong demand was the US dollar. The USA was the only major source of foodstuffs, raw materials and machinery and all countries were desperately short of dollars. Any movement towards general convertibility would have soon exhausted the other members' meagre supplies of dollars. Not until 1958 was there any real progress. In this year some 15 Western European countries made their currencies fully convertible for current transactions. By 1965 all the major currencies were convertible and some progress had been made towards reducing exchange controls on capital transactions.

ii Stability of exchange rates

The architects of the IMF were looking for a system which would give the advantages of stability but would be more flexible than the gold

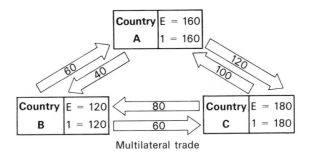

Multilateral trade

Each country's trade is in balance (exports = imports), but no pair of countries have balanced trade. Balance is achieved because currencies are convertible, e.g. Country B will exchange her surplus of Country A's currency for that of Country C in order to finance her deficit with C.

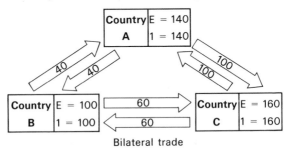

Bilateral trade

Currencies are not convertible – the lower of the two demands will determine the volume of trade between any pair of countries, e.g. Country C can only purchase 100 from Country A, because Country A only wishes to purchase 100 from Country C.

Fig. 74

standard. They opted for the *adjustable peg system* as described earlier. Members were obliged to define the values of their currencies in terms of gold and this, as under the gold standard, automatically determined the exchange rates between members' currencies. In fact the values of currencies were expressed in terms of the US dollar and since this currency was convertible into gold, other currencies were also convertible into gold via the dollar.

Exchange rates were to be held within 1 per cent of the declared parities. The system was not rigid, however, because the IMF rules permitted devaluation and revaluation. The external value of a currency could be adjusted upwards or downwards by up to 10 per cent without prior IMF permission; devaluations and revaluations of more than 10 per cent required the permission of the Fund. This system was in operation from 1947 to 1971 although it came under severe pressure in the 1960s.

iii Financial assistance

All members contribute to a large pool of foreign currencies. The size of each member's contribution (i.e. its quota) is determined by the size of its national income and its share of world trade. The original arrangement was that a quota was payable 75 per cent in the member's own currency and 25 per cent in gold. This smaller proportion is no longer payable in gold; it may be paid in foreign currency or SDRs and may, in fact, be less than 25 per cent.

The purpose of this pool of currencies is to assist members in balance of payments difficulties. When a member country draws currencies from the IMF, it pays for them with an equivalent amount of its own currency. Members, therefore, do not 'borrow', they 'purchase'; conversely they do not 'repay', but 'repurchase'. When a country makes a drawing on the Fund, therefore, the Fund's holdings of that member's currency increase.

Drawings on the Fund are split into *tranches*. The reserve tranche equals the amount by which a member's quota exceeds the Fund's holdings of its currency. Purchases of currencies in the reserve tranche can be made automatically. For example, if the UK's quota was £2 000 million and the IMF was holding £1 700 million of sterling, the UK could purchase £300 million of foreign currencies without any conditions being attached to the transaction. In addition to the reserve tranche, there are four credit tranches, each equal to 25 per cent of the quota. Drawings in the credit tranches are conditional. In considering an application for drawings in the credit tranches the IMF will take into account the country's economic position and its likely ability to overcome its problems within a short period. The country must reach agreement with the IMF on the suitability of the policies it proposes to put into effect. A member is expected normally to repurchase as its balance of payments and reserve position improves; it will of course repurchase its own currency with foreign currencies. IMF assistance is essentially short-term and members are expected to repurchase within 3 to 5 years.

A member's drawing rights expire when the IMF is holding, in that member's currency, an amount equal to twice the value of its quota. There are, however, as explained later, special facilities available which allow drawings in excess of this amount.

Early achievements

The main function of the Fund is to provide temporary financial assistance. A nation experiencing a serious balance of payments deficit might, in the absence of such help, be forced to impose restrictions on its imports. This could lead to retaliation and a general increase in the barriers to trade. In the two decades following the end of the Second

World War, there was an enormous expansion of world trade and the world experienced unprecedented rates of economic growth and unparalleled levels of prosperity and consumption. The work of the IMF (together with GATT) in helping to reduce the barriers to trade (e.g. exchange control and the use of quotas and tariffs) and in promoting international cooperation in the monetary and financial fields undoubtedly made an important contribution to these developments.

Emergence of problems

By the mid-1960s there were signs of serious trouble with the Bretton Woods system. The steady growth of world trade and generally rising prices meant that the monetary value of surpluses and deficits increased substantially even when they remained about the same proportion of a nation's exports and imports. There was growing concern that the size of the nationally held reserves of gold and foreign currencies and the short-term facilities available from the IMF would prove inadequate to support the growing volume of trade. Remember that adequate supplies of international liquidity are absolutely vital for the effective operation of a fixed rate of exchange.

The policy of keeping the official price of gold pegged at the 1934 price of $35 per ounce meant that very little of any new output found its way into monetary reserves. At this time, too, the industrial and speculative demands for gold were increasing.

The dollar problem

The main reserve currency was the dollar and the supply of this currency as a reserve asset is dependent upon the size of the balance of payments deficits experienced by the USA. If the USA runs a deficit then other countries' holdings of dollars will increase. The very large US deficits in the 1960s undermined confidence in that country's ability to maintain the exchange value of the dollar. At this time the dollar was convertible into gold (for official holders) and the volume of dollars held outside the USA began to exceed the size of the US gold reserve. There were real fears that foreign holders would exercise their right to convert their dollars into gold on a large scale and force the USA to suspend the convertibility of the dollar into gold as eventually happened in 1971; this convertibility was the basis of the IMF system of stable exchange rates.

Parity adjustments

Although the IMF system allowed for the adjustments of parities (revaluation and devaluation), governments displayed a reluctance to use these measures. Devaluation, especially for countries such as the UK whose currencies were important reserve assets, was regarded as an admission of economic weakness and political failure which would further weaken confidence in the currency, act as a deterrent to foreign investment and encourage further speculation against the currency. Under an adjustable peg system, speculators have what amounts to a one-way option. The balance of payments figures over a period of time provide a fairly clear indication of whether a currency is over-valued or under-valued. A series of deficits would indicate over-valuation and if the exchange rate is to be moved it will be in a downward direction. Speculators, therefore, face little risk of loss. They sell the currency; if devaluation does take place, they make a profit (by buying back the currency at a lower rate); if devaluation does not take place, their losses will be limited to the costs of the currency transactions. Countries running balance of payments surpluses were reluctant to revalue because it would have been politically unpopular with the successful exporting industries and with producers who would have to face competition from cheaper imports. It was also argued that any falling off in the level of exports would reduce the rate of economic growth.

This unwillingness of governments to revalue or devalue meant that currencies were often over-valued and under-valued in the foreign exchange markets. This is a situation which can rapidly lead to a crisis as speculators and investors move their short-term balances from one currency to another in anticipation of changes which seem more and more inevitable the longer they are delayed.

Movements of short-term capital

There has been a progressive internationalisation of banking operations in the post-war years. This together with the removal of restrictions on convertibility means that the working balances of multinational corporations and other short-term balances can now be switched from one currency to another easily and quickly. The flow of funds in the international money markets has been massively augmented by the huge surpluses accumulated by the oil-exporting states. The size of these mobile funds and the speed with which they can be switched from one currency to another in response to interest rate differentials or anticipated changes in exchange rates means that individual nations are extremely vulnerable. In the 1960s and 1970s many governments found it extremely difficult to defend fixed exchange rates when massive flows of short-term capital could so quickly transform the balance of payments situation.

Measures to deal with the liquidity problem

Against the background outlined above several steps were taken to supplement the supplies of world liquidity.

a Increased quotas. Members' quotas in the IMF were increased on several occasions.

b Stand-by credits. These allow a member country the right to draw on a stated amount of foreign currency from the IMF and they are valid for a limited period of time. The availability of these resources (which it may not be necessary to use) helps to restore confidence in a member's currency when it has a deficit and is under severe pressure from speculators.

c Currency swaps. These involve the direct exchange of national currencies between central banks under an agreement to reverse the transactions at the same exchange rate at some future date (usually 3 months). Normally swap arrangements are used to restore confidence in a currency which is under heavy speculative pressures.

d The General Arrangement to Borrow (GAB). This arrangement was set up by ten of the larger and richer IMF members after a currency crisis in 1961. These ten countries agreed to lend their currencies to the IMF should the latter run short of one of their respective currencies. This assistance does not become available automatically; its use requires the prior approval of the lending country and the aid is likely to be conditional.

e Special Drawing Rights (SDRs). These represent an entirely new form of reserve asset. Their supply, their value and the interest payable on them are all determined by the IMF. SDRs are issued by the IMF to member countries in proportion to their quotas and represent claims or rights which are honoured by other members and by the IMF itself. By joining the scheme a member accepts an obligation to provide currency, when designated by the Fund, to other participants in exchange for SDRs. It cannot, however, be obliged to accept SDRs to a greater total value than three times its own allocation. Participants whose SDR holdings are less than their allocation pay interest on the difference between their allocation and their actual holdings and members holding SDRs in excess of their allocation receive interest.

The value of the SDR is calculated daily as a weighted average of the exchange values of five major currencies (the US dollar, the Deutschmark, the French franc, the Japanese yen and the pound sterling). The value obtained is then expressed in dollars. SDRs are increasingly used as a unit of account by official organisations and in financial markets.

f Special facilities. In addition to the drawing rights on the reserve and credit tranches the IMF has made further funds available to meet special circumstances. Compensatory facilities allow drawings mainly by primary producing countries whose exports are adversely affected by factors beyond their control. Buffer stock facilities allow members to obtain financing for their contributions to international buffer stocks of primary products.

The collapse of the adjustable peg system

The eventual collapse of the IMF system of exchange rates came about as a result of an intensification of the pressures which developed during the 1960s. The USA experienced larger and larger balance of payments deficits and in 1971 suspended the convertibility of the dollar into gold. An attempt to rescue the par value system was made at a meeting in Washington in December 1971, when new parities for the major currencies were agreed and the permitted band of deviation from agreed parities was increased from 1 per cent to $2\frac{1}{4}$ per cent. But this experiment was short-lived. The pound sterling was floated in 1972 and by 1975 all the major currencies were floating. Exchange rates, however, were not set perfectly free; most central banks intervened in the market to smooth out fluctuations and to counter some speculative pressures. The present system is better described as one of *managed flexibility*. The huge increases in oil prices in 1973 dealt a very severe blow to the stability of the international monetary system. This initial price rise and subsequent increases in the price of oil resulted in a massive imbalance in world payments because the major oil exporters (as a group) have not been able to increase their imports on a scale which matches the increase in their revenues. There is, therefore, the serious problem of 'recycling' the oil exporters' surpluses back to countries suffering serious balance of payments deficits, in ways which will not cause instability (as would happen if funds were frequently switched from one country to another). The IMF has played some part in this process by borrowing from oil exporting countries, but most of the recycling has been carried out by the international banking system.

Recent developments

Recent years have seen continuing rises in the price of oil with consequent large imbalances in international payments, intractable inflation, rising unemployment and growing protection. The IMF has responded to these conditions in a variety of ways.

1 It has accepted the fact that member countries should be free to adopt floating exchange rates if they so desire. The IMF, however,

has laid down principles and practices which member states should follow in managing floating rates. It has been given authority to act as a watchdog to ensure that countries are not managing their exchange rates to the disadvantage of other countries.

2 Lending policies have been liberalised by increasing the resources available to members and extending the periods for which assistance is available. The annual access to the Fund's resources has been increased to 150 per cent of a country's quota, extending over a period of three years to 450 per cent. Two more special facilities have been introduced to provide assistance to members with balance of payments deficits which are large in relation to the size of their quotas.

3 The IMF has increased its resources by undertaking more direct borrowing from countries with strong balance of payments positions.

4 Attempts have been made to increase the attractiveness of SDRs as financial assets by removing several restrictions on their use and increasing the rate of interest payable on them.

5 The IMF has broken the links with gold. Member countries do not have to pay part of their quota (or increase in their quota) in gold and they cannot use gold in transactions with the IMF.

29 International Economic Cooperation

The European Economic Communities

Origins

At the end of the Second World War there was a strong desire to speed up the tasks of reconstruction by cooperation and collaboration. A number of international organisations such as the IMF, the World Bank, and GATT were established for this purpose. In Europe, the Organisation of European Economic Cooperation (OEEC) was set up to administer the aid provided under the Marshall Plan. When the Marshal Plan came to an end, OEEC was replaced by the Organisation for European Cooperation and Development with the USA, Canada, and Japan as full members. Encouraged by the success of these co-operative ventures, Belgium, Holland, Luxembourg, Italy, France, and Germany (the *Six*) joined together to establish the *European Coal and Steel Community* (ECSC) in 1952. Its aim was to promote industrial expansion by creating a common market in coal and steel by removing all discrimination and restrictions on the production and distribution of these commodities between member states. This venture was successful and encouraged further plans for economic integration. These led to the six countries signing the *Treaty of Rome* in 1957. This treaty established two more communities – The *European Economic Community* (EEC), which aimed to create a much wider common market, and the *European Atomic Energy Commission* (Euratom) which was designed to coordinate nuclear research and power projects within the community. EEC and Euratom came into operation in January 1958.

Aims

As set out in the Rome Treaty the basic aims of the EEC are as follows.

1 The elimination, as between member states, of customs duties and quantitative restrictions (quotas) in regard to the import and export of goods.

2 The establishment of a common customs tariff and a common commercial policy towards third countries.

3 The abolition between member states of obstacles to the free movements of persons, services, and capital.

4 The establishment of common policies for agriculture and transport.
5 Ensuring that competition within the common market is not distorted.
6 The association of overseas countries and territories with the community.

The abolition of internal tariffs and the acceptance of a common external tariff creates what is known as *a customs union*. But the implications of membership went much further than this. Economic union is expected to provide a basis for much closer political integration.

Size

Britain, Denmark, and Ireland became members on 1 January 1973 while Greece joined the Community on 1 January 1981. At the end of 1981, the EEC represented a common market with a population of about 270 million and it is the world's largest trading bloc. Spain and Portugal are currently negotiating for membership.

Institutions

The present position is that there are four main institutions serving all three communities – the Council of Ministers, the Commission, the Court of Justice, and the European Parliament.

The council of ministers

This is the body which takes policy decisions and is the only Community institution whose members, one from each country, directly represent the national governments. Different ministers attend depending on the subject matter under discussion. Thus, finance ministers attend when economic and financial matters are being discussed, agriculture ministers when farm policies are the subject matter, and so on. Decisions on 'essential' matters must be taken unanimously. For other matters, the Rome Treaty generally prescribes majority voting, but there are some issues for which voting is weighted. For this purpose, Germany, France, Italy, and the UK have 10 votes each, Belgium, Greece, and the Netherlands 5 votes each, Denmark and Ireland 3 votes each, and Luxembourg 2 votes.

The commission

At present (1982) the Commission consists of 14 members appointed by agreement between national governments. The commissioners, who are appointed for 4 years, are independent in the sense that they are not in Brussels to represent the particular interests of their own national governments – they are committed to European policies. The role of the Commission is to draft policies and present them to the Council of Ministers for decision. It has the task of seeing that approved policies are carried out and for this purpose it has important executive powers.

The court of justice

The Court consists of 10 judges, one from each Community country and is completely independent of the other Community institutions. It is the only court with jurisdiction over matters of Community law. Individuals, institutions, and member governments may appeal to it. Its function is to settle disputes about the interpretation of the treaties which established the communities.

The European parliament

This now consists of 434 members who are elected directly by the citizens of the Community and who serve for a period of 5 years. Decisions made by this Parliament are influential but not binding. It must be consulted by the Commission on important matters and it has the right to question the Commission and the Council on their activities.

Other community institutions

There is an important *Economic and Social Committee* whose members represent trade unions, employers' associations, and other interests. This committee must be consulted by the Council and the Commission before action is taken on all major economic and social matters.

The European Investment Bank obtains its funds from two sources – the capital subscribed by member countries, and the issue of securities in the capital markets. Its aims are to assist projects of common interest to several members, to finance regional development, and help with modernisation programmes.

The European Regional Development Fund draws its resources directly from the Community's revenues. Its main purpose is to provide additional aid for projects mounted by national governments for regional development. In other words it boosts member states' own efforts to assist their less prosperous areas.

The European Social Fund draws its resources from contributions by member governments and directly from the Community's revenues. It is particularly concerned with the problems of redundancy caused by the reallocation of resources brought about by the development of the Community. Most of its financial aid is devoted to the promotion of schemes to help with the retraining and rehousing of displaced workers.

The European Agricultural Guidance and Guarantee Fund. This is the main instrument of the common agricultural policy (the CAP) and accounts for the greater part of the Community's expenditure. The funds come directly from the Community's budget (see below).

The Guidance section of the Fund provides financial assistance (e.g. grants) for the structural reform of agriculture such as farm modernisation, the consolidation of holdings into larger units, and long-term improvements such as drainage and reafforestation. The basic aims of the CAP are to increase productivity in agriculture, to ensure a fair standard of living for farmers, to guarantee regular supplies of food and to ensure reasonable prices for consumers. To help achieve these aims, the CAP protects the Community's internal agricultural markets from outside competition through a system of import taxes and it maintains prices at annually adjusted minimum levels by intervening in the market.

Subsidies are paid on exports so as to move surpluses out of the Community when internal prices are likely to be depressed. The authorities in member states buy up produce when the average market price falls below the 'intervention' price. A shortage in the Community may be relieved by lowering the protective barriers against non-EEC producers. The increasing productivity in agriculture and the fairly stable demands for foodstuffs have led to large surpluses in some farm products (e.g. cereals, dairy products, and sugar). It has proved difficult to eliminate these surpluses by lowering intervention prices. Although the CAP has ensured adequate supplies of good quality foodstuffs, there is widespread dissatisfaction with the way it is operated. It is extremely costly, it has led to some large surpluses and the problem of setting suitable common prices against a background of widely differing productivity levels in different countries is proving a major difficulty.

The Community's Budget

The EEC Budget is financed by,
a all import duties and agricultural levies on trade with non-EEC sources,
b a proportion of the revenue from Value Added Tax (not exceeding 1 per cent of a VAT levied on a uniform basis in the Community)

In the late 1970s, the UK sought ways of reducing its net budget contribution. Although in terms of GNP per head the UK was one of the poorer members of the Community, her budget contribution calculated on the existing basis meant that she would be making the largest contribution per head. This situation came about because the UK is heavily dependent on imports from non-EEC sources and hence makes a large contribution to the EEC budget in the form of import duties and agricultural levies. The small size of the UK agricultural sector and its relatively high efficiency means that its receipts from the CAP are small (and most of the budgetary payments at this time were devoted to the CAP). In 1980 the UK successfully negotiated a substantial reduction in its net contribution to the EEC budget.

Table 26 EEC budget estimates in 1982

Income	% of total	Expenditure	% of total
VAT	55	Agriculture	65·0
Customs duties	31	Special support for	
Agricultural levies	12	UK	7·4
Other income	2	Overseas aid and	
		development	5·1
		Regional policy	5·0
		Administration	5·0
		Social policy	4·6
		Repayments to	
		member countries	4·3
		Research, energy,	
		industry and transport	2·1
		Other expenditure	1·5
	100·0		100·0

Source: Europe 81 (EEC) Numbers 8 and 9

The economic arguments

Greater specialisation and economies of scale

Supporters of the idea of a customs union argue that the creation of a greatly enlarged 'home' market enables the more efficient producers to achieve a much larger scale of production and hence produce at lower costs. Within the EEC, industries can operate on a Community rather than a national scale. It is also pointed out by the supporters of

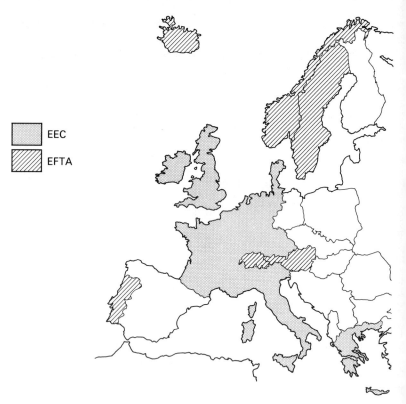

Fig. 75 West European trading blocs

EEC

EFTA

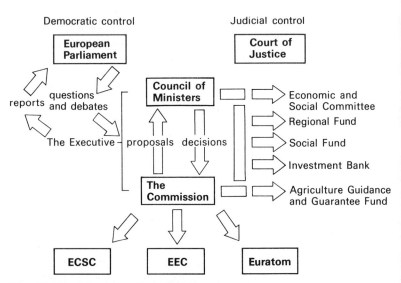

Fig. 76 The European Communities

the EEC that the exploitation of the results of technological development and research in areas such as nuclear energy, space, aviation, and computers is extremely costly and probably beyond the resources of any single European country. If such industries are to be efficient and capable of competing with those of the industrial giants such as the USA, the USSR, and Japan, smaller countries will have to collaborate, pool their research facilities and operate joint development programmes. Economic integration in the form of a customs union makes it much easier to operate joint industrial programmes of this sort.

Greater competition

The removal of trade barriers allows more scope for the application of the principle of comparative advantage. Regional cost differentials will reveal themselves as differences in market prices and these differences will enable the more efficient firms to expand at the expense of the less efficient who will no longer enjoy the protection afforded by tariffs and quotas. The allocation of resources will be determined by the relative efficiencies of producers within the Community as a whole. This argument assumes, of course, that competition within the Community will not be distorted by the formation of monopolies and cartels.

Increased exports

The increased efficiency of producers within the Community brought about by more competition and larger-scale production will, it is believed, enable them to compete more effectively in world markets.

More investment

If the formation of a customs union does generate a faster rate of economic growth then the rising prosperity of the group as whole will make it possible to provide more funds to help the less developed parts of the Community, and to provide more aid to developing countries in other parts of the world.

The dynamic effects

Many economists believe that one important advantage of forming a customs union is the dynamic effect. Economic activity is influenced very much by the expectations of entrepreneurs. The prospects of a much larger potential market and of increased competition could well act as a stimulant to investment both for purposes of modernisation and expansion. Actions based on the expectations of economic growth will help to bring about that growth.

Possible disadvantages

A trading bloc might pursue an inward-looking policy, concentrating on its own problems while operating behind a protective common tariff. It might, therefore, show little interest in the liberalisation of world trade. If this is so, a customs union would lead to trade diversion rather than trade expansion. If the common tariff is seriously protective, more efficient producers outside the Common Market will suffer while relatively less efficient producers inside the customs union will expand.

The economies of scale argument can be overemphasised. In many industries the national markets in countries such as the UK, France, and Western Germany should be large enough to achieve substantial economies of scale. Recent studies have shown that higher productivity may owe more to managerial skills than to the scale of production. The argument for the enlarged 'home' market may also be exaggerated, especially where consumption patterns have strong national characteristics. In the 1975 debate on Britain's continuing membership those who wished to see a withdrawal from the Community pointed to the loss of sovereignty as the major disadvantage of Community membership.

EEC – Progress

Since it came into being, the EEC has made substantial progress. Whether this progress results directly from the formation of the EEC or whether the member countries would have made the same economic progress as independent economies cannot be proved one way or the other. Nevertheless the record is favourable.

By July 1968 trade between the original members had been freed of all customs duties on industrial goods and the common external tariff had replaced the national tariffs on imports from the rest of the world. The three newer members, Denmark, Ireland, and the UK had abolished tariffs against EEC members by 1977 and a customs union between the nine countries became a reality on 1 July 1978.

The common tariff itself has been progressively reduced. In 1980 the EEC average tariff was 6 per cent against the USA's 7·1 per cent and Japan's 9·7 per cent.

Although progress has been made towards establishing a common market in agriculture, there have, as mentioned earlier, been many difficulties. The CAP ran into a serious problem when exchange rates were floated in in the 1970s. With fixed exchange rates it is relatively easy to establish a common price for a commodity in different countries, but when exchange rates are floating great difficulties arise.

There has been good progress towards the free movement of labour, services, and, to a lesser extent, capital. The free movement of labour has already been achieved – no work permits are required by EEC citizens and all are treated equally in each country in respect of social security rights, trade union rights, and residential qualifications. Many services have been freed from restrictions, but for some professions progress has been delayed by failure to achieve a general recognition of different national qualifications. Capital movements have been freed in respect of direct investment, the acquisition of real estate, and capital movements of a personal nature. Other capital movements are still subject to restrictions.

Perhaps the most publicised aspect of the EEC has been the improvement in the living standards in member countries. Between 1958 and 1972, in the Community as a whole, real wages doubled. The rate of economic growth within the original Community (i.e. the Six) was very much faster than that achieved by the UK before its entry (roughly twice as fast). But the economic performance of some European countries outside the Community was quite as good and sometimes better. As one would expect trade between the member countries has grown exceptionally fast. Between 1958 and 1980 exports among the EEC countries rose by 3 000 per cent (in dollar terms) in a period when their exports to the rest of the world rose by a mere 1 300 per cent.

The economic buoyancy of the Community which had been such a feature of its earlier years began to falter after the oil crisis of 1973 and economic recession was fully apparent at the beginning of 1976. Rates of economic growth and investment fell and large scale unemployment began to appear in several EEC countries. At the beginning of 1982 unemployment in the EEC was still rising.

Britain and Europe (EEC and EFTA)

The formation of the European Communities presented a number of problems for other European countries. They had to consider the effect on their trade and the possibility of a serious division of interests arising within Europe. Many of them, although conscious of the possible economic benefits arising from membership of a large common market, hesitated to take the decisive step of joining because of the political implications. The existence of the Community's supranational institutions appeared to call for a substantial sacrifice of political independence by the governments of member countries. This view was widely held in Britain, and although she was invited to take part in the negotiations which led to the signing of the Rome Treaty she declined. Britain in Europe, it was argued, would not be free to adjust her tariffs independently – this would be a matter for the Commission; harmonisation of taxation policies would reduce her freedom to operate an independent fiscal policy; Britain's policy on agriculture was fundamentally different to that proposed for the Community, and, most important, membership would mean the end of Britain's special relationship with the Commonwealth. The objections to the EEC policy on agriculture were based on the fact that food prices in the Community were, at that time, substantially higher than those in the UK. This was due to the fundamentally different systems used for assisting agriculture. Food entered Britain duty free and sold on the British market at world prices which were then substantially below European costs of production. British farmers received subsidies from the government which raised their incomes above those earned from the sales of foodstuffs at market prices. In the EEC, farmers are protected from low-cost food imports by means of tariffs or levies. These levies are adjusted to current world prices so that imported food sells in the EEC at prices which do not undercut the prices of domestically produced food. Thus, in the 1950s and 1960s, food prices in the EEC were considerably higher than world prices and, hence, British prices.

The Commonwealth trading links have become much less important in recent years but Britain was very reluctant to break them. Under the Commonwealth Preference system most Commonwealth goods entered Britain duty free or were subject to tariffs at lower rates than goods from other areas. In return Britain enjoyed preferences in some parts of the Commonwealth. Some Commonwealth countries at this time were particularly dependent upon access to the British market (e.g. New Zealand for her lamb and dairy produce). Entry to the EEC would have meant the end of this preferential system and on these grounds many people opposed such a step. In fact, Britain succeeded in getting special treatment within the EEC for some of the most affected Commonwealth products.

The European Free Trade Area (EFTA)

Arguments such as those outlined above persuaded the UK to seek alternative arrangements when the EEC was formed. Before the Treaty of Rome was signed she attempted to form a large European Free Trade Area in industrial goods embracing all the members of OEEC, but the venture was not successful. Nevertheless a small European Free Trade Area (EFTA) in industrial goods, was brought into being in 1959 and began operations in 1960. The original members were the UK, Norway, Sweden, Denmark, Austria, Portugal, and Switzerland (Iceland and Finland joined later).

A free trade area is a different concept from that of a customs union. It is a much more flexible organisation and it has no supra-national institutions. Member states retain the right to determine their own tariffs against non-members – there is no common external tariff. There is no loss of political sovereignty because a free trade area amounts to little more than an agreement between nations to establish free trade among themselves. Critics point out that because it is so easily formed and lacks any strong legal and political bonds, it can easily be broken up – it is a relatively unstable arrangement.

When EFTA was formed the programme of tariff reductions was deliberately planned to keep in step with the EEC programme since it was hoped that, in time, some links might be arranged between the two associations. In fact, this did come about in 1972 when the EEC concluded free trade agreements with those countries which had decided not to join the Community (Austria, Norway, Sweden, Portugal, Finland, Iceland, and Switzerland).

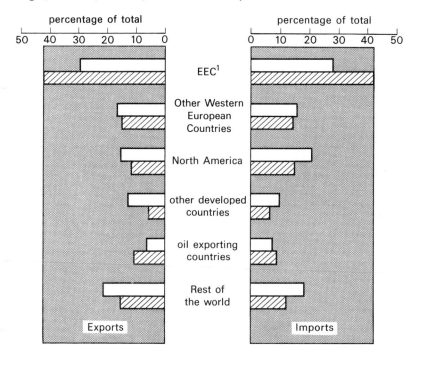

UK Balance of Payment 1981 C.S.O.

[1]Nine members (excluding Greece)

Fig. 77 UK visible trade

401

Britain's trade with Europe

One reason for Britain's decision to enter the EEC was the increasing importance of her trade links with Europe. The interests of Britain as a mercantile nation are increasingly European and this trend was apparent long before the EEC treaties were signed. In the years immediately following entry into the EEC, UK trade with the Community moved adversely, especially in manufactured goods, and Britain's lack of competitiveness in this field was clearly revealed. The economic advantages which had been forecast by the pro-EEC commentators did not materialise. It was perhaps unfortunate that the UK joined the EEC at a period of economic disarray in Western industrialised countries exacerbated by the oil crisis. On the other hand it has been argued that membership of the EEC shielded the UK from a worse impact on her economy. The UK has received substantial loans from the Community to help in restructuring industry in poorer areas and in the retraining of redundant workers.

Nevertheless, since joining the EEC, Britain's exports to the Community by 1980 had risen by 560 per cent (in dollar terms) while its exports to the rest of the world has risen by only 290 per cent. As Figure 77 shows, more than two-fifths of British exports now go to the EEC. In 1980, Britain achieved a surplus on her trade with the EEC countries.

The European Monetary System (the EMS)

The EMS was introduced in 1979 in an attempt to obtain a greater degree of stability in the exchange rates between member countries of the EEC. There are three separate aspects of the scheme:

1 The European Currency Unit (the ECU)

This is a unit of account (or numéraire) made up of a basket of fixed amounts of EEC currencies weighted according to the importance of the economies they represent (the Deutschmark accounts for about one-third of the total weights). When the dollar equivalents of all the components of the basket have been calculated, they are added together to give the dollar value of the ECU.

2 The exchange rates and intervention mechanism

The value of each member's currency is declared in terms of the ECU and this automatically gives the parity between any pair of currencies. Each participating central bank is required to intervene in the foreign exchange market to keep the rate for its own currency against every other participating currency within 2¼ per cent of the agreed parity or central rate. The Italian lira was made an exceptional case and a 6 per cent deviation was permitted. Although the currencies of countries which are members of the EMS are thus linked together, as a block they are floating against third currencies.

In order to ensure that a country whose currency is divergent takes action at an early stage there is a kind of early warning system known as 'the divergence indicator' which signals the fact that the value of a currency is getting out of line. This second mechanism is based on a currency's value in terms of the ECU, not in terms of other participating currencies. Each currency has a given permitted percentage divergence from its central value in terms of the ECU; these limits are described as 'divergence thresholds'. If a currency crosses its divergence threshold, it is presumed that the central bank will take steps to correct the situation (i.e. it will buy or sell the currency in the foreign exchange market).

3 Credit arrangements

The ECU is used as a denominator for expressing debts and claims between central banks. It is also an instrument for settlement between Community central banks; in this role the ECU functions as an asset. All members of the EMS have deposited 20 per cent of their reserves of gold and foreign currency with the European Monetary Co-operation Fund in return for ECUs. These ECUs can be used to settle debts of all kinds between central banks. The eventual aim is to set up a European Monetary Fund to help members in ways similar to those used by the IMF. At the moment (1982) credit is available to members of the EMS on the basis of loans from one member to another.

The UK did not join the EMS on its foundation although sterling is one of the currencies in the basket which determines the value of the ECU.

Other international groupings

Although this chapter has tended to concentrate on the EEC it must be noted that there are now quite a number of examples of regional economic integration in different parts of the world. Some of these have met with considerable success, while others have found it difficult to make progress. It is possible to provide only very brief details of some of these regional trading blocs.

The Council for Mutual Economic Assistance

The CMEA or *COMECON* (the common English abbreviation) is an important economic association of the USSR and the communist countries of Eastern Europe. It was founded in 1949 with the aim of establishing 'wider economic cooperation between countries of people's democracy and the USSR'. Initially the CMEA had only political functions but as the establishment of the EEC progressed, more importance was attached to economic cooperation. The original member states were Bulgaria, Czechoslovakia, Hungary, Poland, Romania, and the USSR. East Germany joined later and several other communist countries have been admitted as observers.

Unlike the EEC, this organisation has no supranational powers – it is based on the principle of full national sovereignty. Recommendations are made on matters of economic, scientific, and technical cooperation and are implemented by decisions of member governments. The administrative framework of the CMEA consists of a Council Session, an Executive Committee, several Standing Commissions, and a Secretariat. These bodies have functions similar to those of the EEC institutions, but they do not have any supranational authority.

The CMEA appears to have been particularly successful in stimulating the exchange of technical information between members, in encouraging the standardisation of technical products and in extending the degree of specialisation within the group. It has also played an important part in some ambitious joint investment projects such as a common electricity grid and the construction of oil and natural gas pipe lines linking the USSR, Poland, East Germany, Czechoslovakia, and Hungary. Trade between members is still largely on a bilateral basis and the expansion of this trade is restricted to some extent because prices in communist countries do not necessarily reflect costs of production. It is difficult, therefore, to establish realistic terms of trade. Additionally, exchange rates do not bear any close relationship to the relative domestic purchasing powers of the currencies. Nevertheless, trade between members has continued to expand and there are plans to adopt pricing policies more appropriate to multilateral trading and to develop a multilateral payments scheme. Under this scheme each member country will balance its payments with the CMEA area as a whole instead of with each member individually. Transactions will be carried out in 'transferable roubles' through the International Cooperative Bank in Moscow.

The Latin American Free Trade Area (LAFTA)

The treaty establishing LAFTA came into effect in 1961. The member countries are Argentina, Brazil, Chile, Mexico, Paraguay, Peru, Uruguay, Colombia, Ecuador, Venezuela, and Bolivia. The aim of the association is the gradual removal of restrictions on trade flows between members and it was hoped that a free trade area would be fully established by 1980. Progress has been slow because of the wide discrepancies in the levels of economic development within the group. The poorer countries are ill equipped to face the growing competition from the industrially more advanced countries such as Argentina, Brazil, and Mexico.

The Central American Common Market (CACM)

This association came into existence as the result of a treaty signed, in 1960, by El Salvador, Guatemala, Honduras, and Nicaragua – Costa Rica joined in 1962. By 1969 the common market had become a reality – tariffs between members had been abolished and the common external tariff was operational.

There are also free trade associations or common markets in the Caribbean, Central Africa, and West Africa.

Commodity agreements

A further important example of international economic cooperation is provided by international agreements on the supply of certain primary products. The aim of such agreements is to stabilise world prices of commodities in the interests of both producers and consumers. Commodity agreements take various forms.

1 The multilateral contract system, where buyers and sellers undertake to buy and supply certain quantities at agreed prices.

2 The quota method, where the quantity which any country can export in any one year is fixed. It is often necessary to support the export quota by fixing production quotas for each country.

3 The buffer stock system, where the countries concerned establish an international agency to intervene in the market when the price moves outside some agreed range. The agency will buy (for stock) when the price nears the minimum price limit and sell its stocks when the price moves towards its maximum limit. There are important commodity agreements for Wheat (multilateral contract system), Sugar (quota system), Coffee (quota system) and Tin (quota and buffer stock system). Commodity agreements are difficult to operate. They can only be really successful if all major producers are parties to the agreement. If an important supplier remains outside the agreement it will threaten the ability of the other suppliers to hold up price by restricting their supplies. It is also difficult to reach international agreement on the price ranges. More efficient producers will tend to demand relatively low prices so that they can expand their share of the market.

Effective supervision of the agreement is a major problem especially where there are a large number of producer countries operating a quota system. The setting of the quotas for each country is another obvious possible cause of disagreement.

The best known international commodity agreement is undoubtedly that operated by the oil-producing states. The 13 members of the Organisation for Petroleum Exporting Countries (OPEC) are Algeria, Ecuador, Gabon, Indonesia, Iran, Iraq, Kuwait, Libya, Nigeria, Qatar, Saudi Arabia, The United Arab Emirates, and Venezuela. Between them they account for about 60 per cent of the world's crude petroleum production and some 90 per cent of the world's petroleum exports (because the other large producers, the USA and the USSR, are not large exporters). The OPEC countries have been able, by concerted action on the supplies of oil, to bring about a massive increase in world prices.

Aid to developing countries

Extent of the problem

Developing countries are those where the real income per head and the general standard of living are much lower than in the developed countries of North America, Western Europe, Australia, and New Zealand. There is no completely satisfactory way of measuring the level of economic development. National income per head is normally taken as the indicator for official purposes, but, as pointed out in Chapter 17, this may be misleading. There is, however, no doubt about the very great differences between living standards in the developed world and standards in the developing world. In 1979 the Gross National Product per capita in the USA was about $10 800 while in India it was about $190. Africa, Asia, and Latin America contain 70 per cent of the world's peoples yet have only 20 per cent of the world's income. The USA has only 6 per cent of the world's peoples, but 30 per cent of the world's income. About two-thirds of the world's population lives in regions which are seriously underdeveloped and which make up the greater part of the inhabited areas of the world. The developing world comprises most of Asia, the greater part of Africa, much of the Middle East, parts of Southern Europe, and most of South and Central America. Table 27 provides some indication of the extent of the divergencies in G.N.P. per capita between different regions.

Some common characteristics of developing countries

Every country has its special problems and rates of progress vary widely as between different countries, but there are some features

Table 27 Income per head in 1979

	GNP per capita (US$)	Population (millions)
North America	10 500	247
Japan	8 730	116
Oceania	7 000	22
Europe (excluding USSR)	6 760	524
USSR	4 040	264
Middle East	4 310	48
South America	1 730	233
Central America	1 620	106
Africa	700	456
Asia (excluding Japan and Middle East)	310	2 165

Source: World Bank Atlas 1981

which are common to the majority of the developing countries.

1 High birth rates, relatively high death rates and a low expectancy of life. The application of Western medicine has tended to reduce death rates while birth rates remain high. Most of these countries are experiencing a rapid growth of population.

2 Concentration on agriculture. It is common to find 70 per cent or more of the labour force engaged in agriculture, but, in spite of this high degree of 'specialisation', productivity is extremely low.

3 A very low capital to labour ratio. All developing countries are suffering from a grave deficiency in the supply of capital.

4 A poor natural resource endowment. Many of the developing countries are in tropical and sub-tropical regions where soils are fragile and climatic conditions unfavourable to many agricultural activities. Massive investment in programmes for soil conservation, irrigation, the control of pests and the use of fertilisers are needed in order to raise the productivity of the land.

5 Massive underemployment. Most people do some work but most are underemployed. Peasant holdings are very small and the system of land tenure often means that all the members of the peasant's family work on the family plot. Under these conditions the marginal productivity of labour is probably zero. There is often little activity between planting and harvesting.

6 Social, religious, and cultural patterns of life often act as serious barriers to change and development. Where people are strongly attached to customary ways of doing things, it is extremely difficult to improve the mobility of labour and introduce new techniques.

7 A low-quality labour force. Workers are lacking in education and technical skills and the relatively low standards of health often mean a low level of physical performance.

8 A heavy dependency on one or two export products (invariably primary products). Foreign currency earnings will be subject to large variations because the world prices of primary products are notoriously unstable.

9 A totally inadequate industrial and social infrastructure. Rapid economic development needs a basis in the form of good communications, adequate power and water supplies, an educated and trained labour force, and so on. The returns on this type of investment are of a very long term nature so that private investors are not likely to supply the resources for social overhead capital (or infrastructure). This is a task for public enterprise.

Four Key Issues

1 Raising the rate of investment. These countries are caught in 'the vicious circle of poverty'. The rate of capital accumulation can only be increased if there is an increase in the rate of saving, but an increase in savings requires an increase in income and an increase in income requires an increase in investment! The current levels of income cannot possibly provide the necessary savings. One alternative is to raise the necessary funds by means of taxation (i.e. forced savings), but taxes are difficult to collect in most developing countries and, in any case, the tax base is very narrow. There is a temptation for governments to finance investment by expanding the money supply, but this would only lead to inflation which is simply another form of taxation (real incomes are reduced by rising prices). Some part of the capital needs of developing countries must be provided in the form of foreign aid. But the type of investment is also important. High technology capital equipment is probably inappropriate in most cases, because it needs an educated and trained labour force to operate it, and because it does not generate any large demand for labour.

2 Agriculture v. industry. If the developing countries concentrate on increasing their effiencies in primary production, they face the problem that most of these products have very inelastic demands. A large increase in world supplies might well reduce the incomes of the poorer countries. On the other hand, improvements in agricultural productivity are necessary if labour is to be released from the land in order to develop industrial production, and to provide the raw material inputs for manufacturing industry. It has been demonstrated that small doses of capital generally bring greater returns in agriculture than in industry.

3 Population policy. The rapid increase in population being experienced in developing countries is creating serious problems. Developing countries must either accept the growth of population as inevitable and try to do something about the consequences, or make some attempt to limit the growth of population. The first alternative means giving priority to increasing the output of food and to job creation by concentrating on labour-intensive industries. It will be extremely difficult to raise real income per head because any increase in output must be devoted to feeding and housing the increasing numbers of people rather than to increasing the productivity of labour. The second alternative calls for a massive campaign to encourage family limitation, but this policy may run into strong religious and ideological resistance.

4 Foreign trade. Once the developing countries have established some industrial capacity they need overseas markets for the products of these industries. They must increase their exports to earn the foreign currencies they need to buy capital equipment from the advanced countries, to pay interest on their foreign loans and to make repayments of these loans. This point is developed further in the next section.

Motives for giving aid

There are three motives for providing economic aid to the developing world.

1 Humanitarian motives

The plight of hundreds of millions of people living in abject poverty must strike the consciences of those whose lot is so much better. Humanitarianism demands that the fortunate minority should give some of their income to those who have so little.

2 Political motives

Both the communist and non-communist worlds have given some economic aid in the hope that it will help to win the political allegiance of the recipients.

3 Economic motives

If the developing countries succeed in escaping from 'the poverty trap' and achieve faster rates of economic growth, they will be able to enter more fully into international trade and provide growing markets for the outputs of other countries.

Forms of aid

The United Nations considers that economic aid consists of outright grants and long-term loans for non-military purposes. The chief aid-giving countries, however, take a much broader view and include private capital investment and export credits. In fact the term 'aid' is being increasingly replaced by the term 'development assistance'. Economic aid may take several forms.

Gifts of consumer goods

This form of aid has consisted mainly of the free distribution of American stockpiles of foodstuffs (e.g. wheat). There are several problems associated with this type of aid. The type of food stockpiled in the West may not be suitable for people living in the East and the large-scale release of such commodities may upset world prices and affect the earnings of other producers. In the early 1970s a series of poor harvests and the rapid growth of world population led to a severe shortage of foodstuffs and this form of aid was seriously curtailed.

Loans and grants

Loans may be arranged on commercial terms (i.e. at market rates of interest) or on concessionary terms (i.e. at interest rates well below market rates). Grants and loans may be allocated to a specific project, or 'tied' to exports from the donor country, or without any such conditions. Grants and concessionary loans tend to take the form of *official assistance*, that is, they are supplied on a government to government basis (bilaterally) or via multilateral organisations. The main multilateral agencies are the World Bank and its two affiliates, the IDA and the IFC (explained later); the IMF; the regional development banks related to areas such as Latin America, Asia and Africa; the United Nations; the EEC institutions, and the Arab/OPEC funds.

In the 1970s commercial bank lending to the developing countries rose very sharply, due, in part, to the recycling of the surpluses of the oil exporting countries. This heavy borrowing on commercial terms has meant that many developing countries are now burdened with severe debt-servicing problems. For some of them about one half of their annual export earnings are used to meet interest payments and repayments of capital.

Direct investment

This as the name implies, consists of the establishment of factories, mines, plantations, hotels, etc., in developing countries by firms which are based in developed industrialised countries. In some cases direct investment takes the form of a joint venture, the government of the developing country acquiring part ownership of the new installations.

Technical and direct assistance

The advanced nations provide technical experts to advise and assist the developing countries in their efforts to achieve growth. In many cases the industrial nations have undertaken the building of such projects as steelworks and power stations as a direct form of aid. They also provide technical training programmes for students from developing countries.

Education

Most of the wealthier nations provide facilities for overseas students to attend universities and colleges and provide them with scholarships. In addition they send teachers and instructors overseas.

Specialist services

The World Bank, The IMF, and the United Nations as well as individual countries carry out economic surveys for, and offer a variety of financial, technical, and advisory services to, developing countries.

Trade

Efforts to increase the productive capacity of the poorer nations will only be effective if these nations are able to increase their exports. It does not make much sense for the advanced nations to assist the economic development of the poorer countries and then to exclude their exports on the grounds that they are the products of low-wage labour. If these countries are to 'earn their way out of poverty' rather than become permanent recipients of aid, they must be granted wider opportunities to sell their products in overseas markets. There is a strong case, on economic grounds, for granting them preferential treatment in world markets. Such policies run into trouble when exports from developing countries cause redundancies in the developed countries. As we have already indicated earlier (p. 359), these are difficulties arising from the immobilities of resources.

411

The International Bank for Reconstruction and Development

The IBRD or *World Bank*, as it is commonly known, was established as a result of the Bretton Woods conference and is a sister institution of the IMF. While the purpose of the IMF is to provide short-term assistance to nations in balance of payments difficulties, that of the World Bank is to provide long-term assistance for reconstruction and development purposes. The IBRD has grown steadily since its establishment and there are now some 124 members. It is the world's largest multilateral source of development finance. Member nations are required to subscribe to the capital stock of the Bank, each being given a quota which is related to the member's national income and position in world trade. This capital stock, however, is not the major source of the Bank's lending ability. Each member is only called upon to pay a small part of the amount it has agreed to pay. For example, if the member countries are only called upon to pay 10 per cent of their agreed subscription, the remaining 90 per cent constitutes a guarantee fund; the Bank has the right to request payment of the outstanding amount. The existence of this guarantee fund provides the Bank with a security which enables it to borrow the majority of its funds in the world's capital markets.

The IBRD tends to set fairly stringent conditions on its lending, but because it has a reputation for investing only in soundly conceived projects and because its securities are backed by the capital subscribed (or guaranteed) by its members, it is able to attract investors who might otherwise have never become involved in the financing of projects in developing countries. Interest is charged on the loans, but the interest rate is set as low as is compatible with the Bank's ability to borrow.

In the early years of the Bank's existence, the major part of its lending was to European countries for purposes of reconstruction. Since the early post-war years, World Bank loans have gone increasingly to the developing nations. Its main purpose, nowadays, is to finance projects which help economic development such as road systems, electric plants, railways, irrigation, water supply, and industrial undertakings. Loans are made to member governments, government agencies, or to private enterprise providing the latter can obtain a government guarantee.

The borrower's application for a loan is carefully examined by World Bank experts who must be satisfied that the project is designed to strengthen the economy and forms part of a sound economic development plan. One of the most valuable services rendered by the Bank is the advice it makes available to member countries from its teams of experts who have great experience of, and maintain a continuous research into, the problems of economic development. Technical assistance is an important part of the Bank's operations. It runs a staff college which trains personnel from developing countries.

The Bank will generally finance only part of the cost of project, insisting that the borrowing country should have some financial stake in the enterprise.

A general feeling that finance on somewhat easier terms should be made available to the poorer areas of the less-developed world led to the formation of the *International Development Association* (IDA). This is an affiliate of the World Bank. The Bank and the IDA operate with the same staff and the same standards, but the IDA makes funds available on very much easier terms. Loans by the IDA are free of interest although they carry a service charge. The repayment period is longer than that for IBRD loans. A country's economic condition determines whether it qualifies for World Bank or IDA loans, the weaker countries qualifying for IDA loans. Whereas the World Bank borrows most of its funds in the capital markets, the IDA is almost entirely dependent on the contributions of 18 of its wealthier members.

Another member of the World Bank Group is the *International Finance Corporation* (IFC), which operates on more commercial lines. Its main function is to encourage the flow of domestic and foreign funds into productive private investment in developing countries. It can supply capital in any form – long-term loans, equity subscriptions, or both, and it can invest without government guarantee of repayment. Its capital is subscribed by member countries and these resources are supported by the income on its investments and by the revolving of its funds. It sells off its successful investments and reinvests the funds in other projects.

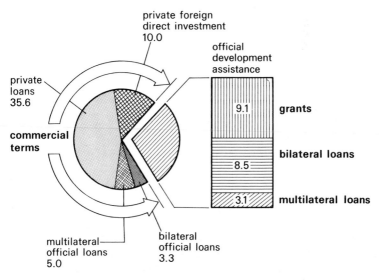

Total net 1980 inflow 74.6

private foreign direct investment 10.0

official development assistance

private loans 35.6

9.1 **grants**

commercial terms

8.5 **bilateral loans**

3.1 **multilateral loans**

multilateral official loans 5.0

bilateral official loans 3.3

Source: Finance and Development (World Bank and IMF) September 1980

Fig. 78 Financial flows to developing countries (billions US dollars)

Part Ten: Public Finance

30 Income and Expenditure of Public Authorities

The public sector

Public and private spending

How much of the national income should be at the disposal of the state and how much at the disposal of the individual citizens? This is a question about the optimum allocation of resources – that particular allocation which maximises total utility. Resources may be said to be allocated in an optimal manner when the value of the marginal product of each factor of production is the same in all its different uses. If this could be achieved, total utility could not be increased by transferring units of a factor of production from one activity to another. On this basis the optimum distribution of resources between the public and private sectors would be obtained when the marginal social benefit from expenditure is the same in both fields; society, then, would gain no benefit by transferring money from public to private use or vice versa.

This principle is easily stated and quite easy to understand, but it is virtually impossible to apply it in the real world. How do we measure the social benefits arising from economic activities? In an imperfectly competitive world the prices of the goods and services produced may not be good indicators of the social benefits derived from them nor good indicators of the social costs incurred in producing them (see p. 22). In the public sector we have the problem that most of the services are not sold in the open market so that there is no way of comparing revenue with cost. It is also impossible to measure the indirect or *external* effects of public expenditures. How does one measure the benefits of a flood-control scheme, or a scheme which reduces traffic congestion? How does one assess the social costs of rehousing families to allow the construction of a motorway?

In any case we cannot consider the effects of public expenditure in isolation, we must take account of the manner in which the money is raised. The imposition of taxation deprives people of utility. This has led to the formulation of the principle of maximum social advantage which states that government should spend money until the marginal utility of public spending is just equal to the marginal disutility of taxpaying.

There is, in fact, no objective way of deciding whether the present

414

balance between public and private spending is or is not the optimum situation. The increasing use of *cost-benefit analysis*, which attempts to place money values on social costs and benefits, is improving our knowledge in this field, but a view of what constitutes the 'right' size of the public sector must be based on a value judgement and the decision is a political one.

Public expenditure

In the UK, public expenditure is officially defined as that expenditure which has to be financed from taxation (including local rates), national insurance contributions, and government borrowing. This expenditure will include the current and capital expenditures of central and local government and any loans and grants to the nationalised industries. It does not include the trading expenditures of the nationalised industries nor any of their investment which is financed from internal sources. The exception to this generalisation is that for some public corporations such as the water authorities, the Civil Aviation Authority and New Town Corporations; the whole of their capital expenditure is included in the figure for total public expenditure.

The present century has seen an enormous growth in total public spending. In 1981–82 total planned public expenditure in the UK was £117 billion, equal to about one half of the Gross Domestic Product. Public spending consists of two distinct types of outlay:
1 The expenditure by central and local government on goods and services. This will include the wages and salaries of civil servants, nurses, teachers, policemen etc., and the direct purchases of goods (both consumer and capital goods).
2 The second type of 'expenditure' consists of transfers of purchasing power from one section of the community to another. These transfer payments comprise such items as social security benefits, subsidies, grants and interest payments on the debts of central and local government.

Only with the first type of expenditure does the state make a direct claim on the national resources. Changes in this type of public spending will have a direct effect on the levels of output, employment and prices. To the extent that they are financed by taxation, transfer payments represent a redistribution of income. Although they appear as items of public spending, the money is really spent by households and firms in the private sector. In 1981, transfer payments accounted for about 48 per cent of total public expenditure in the UK.

Broad functions of public expenditure

To a certain extent both the total and pattern of public expenditure will depend upon the political philosophy of the government, but it is possible to identify the major functions of public spending.

1 The provision of public goods and services

These are goods and services for which there is clearly a demand but which must be provided on a collective basis. They are characterised by two important features, (a) non-rivalry in consumption and (b) non-excludability.

The first feature simply means that consumption by Mrs Brown does not in any way reduce the consumption of Mrs Green or any other individual. The second feature (non-excludability) refers to the fact that consumption of a public good cannot be confined to those who have paid for it.

These features obviously apply to such things as national defence, law and order, lighthouses, flood control schemes, and street lighting. Public goods and services will not be provided by the price mechanism because producers cannot withhold the goods and services for non-payment and, since there is no way of measuring how much a person consumes, there is no basis for establishing a market price. Public goods, therefore, must be supplied by the state and financed by compulsory levies known as taxation.

2 Subsidising the production of goods and services

The state is concerned to increase or maximise the consumption of certain goods which it considers to be highly desirable for the welfare of the citizens. Such goods are described as *merit goods* and the best known examples are the public health and education services which are supplied free or at nominal prices. In a market system, private spending on education and health would be determined by the private benefits derived from these services. It is generally accepted, however, that the social benefits from education and health services are much greater than the private benefits. There seems to be a valid argument for state intervention to ensure a greater provision of these services than would be supplied under the operation of a price mechanism in free markets. The policy of subsidising goods and services such as health, education, housing and food is also likely to assist in the redistribution of income because the subsidies are met out of taxation and if the tax system is progressive (see page 430), the benefits accruing to the lower income groups will be much greater than the contributions they make to the subsidies.

3 Social security

The largest single category of public expenditure in the UK is the

416

spending on social services. Under this heading it is usual to include, education, health and social security benefits and these three items account for about one half of total public expenditure.

Social security is the largest single item of public spending in the UK. It embraces a wide range of benefits in the form of money grants (i.e. transfer payments), including old age pensions, unemployment benefits, child allowances, sickness benefits and widow's pensions. The state also provides a range of personal social services to assist the elderly and the disabled.

The aim of the social security schemes is clearly to carry out a redistribution of income. The market economy provides opportunities for people to earn an income and to acquire wealth. But the opportunities for earning an income are not equally distributed. Some people are limited in their capacity to learn or they may have acquired a skill only to find the demand for that skill is declining. People are also subject to illness and incapacity and people also grow old. The market system does not guarantee that everyone will have the same opportunity to accumulate wealth and once an inequality in the distribution of wealth arises it tends to be self-perpetuating because wealth can be inherited.

People generally have come to expect the state to use its powers to reduce the inequalities in the distribution of income and wealth by levying higher rates of taxation on the higher income groups and distributing benefits in cash or in kind to the poorer groups in society. The broad objectives of the system of social security are to ensure that everyone is guaranteed some adequate minimum level of income and to prevent families from suffering undue hardship when their incomes fall due to some misfortune.

4 The regulation of economic activities

The state intervenes extensively in the economic activities of the private sector. It has set up a variety of supervisory and enforcement agencies to ensure that industrial and commercial activities are not conducted in ways which adversely affect the public interest. The Factories and Offices Acts lay down minimum standards for working conditions; The Public Health and Clean Food Acts control standards of hygiene in public and private premises; Town and Country Planning Acts regulate the development of land; Companies Acts enforce certain standards of commercial behaviour and the Monopolies and Restrictive Practices Acts regulate trading practices in the business world. This list could be greatly extended.

5 Influencing resource allocation and industrial efficiency

The state uses public funds and the instruments of fiscal policy such as taxes, tariffs, grants and subsidies to influence the structure, performance and location of privately-owned industry. It also goes into business for itself and, in the UK and many other countries, several of the 'essential' or 'basic' industries have been taken into public owner-ship. Many of these points have been discussed earlier (see Chapter 12) and there is a section on public ownership later in the book.

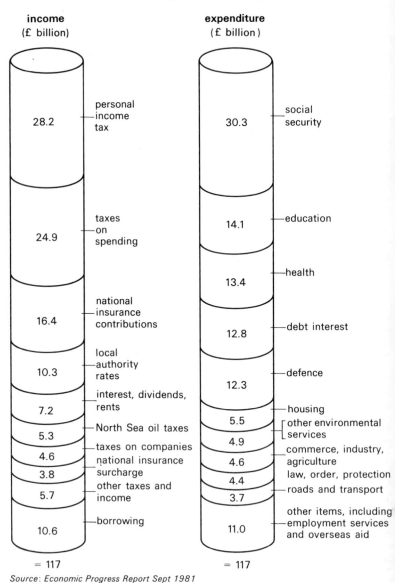

income
(£ billion)

28.2	personal income tax
24.9	taxes on spending
16.4	national insurance contributions
10.3	local authority rates
7.2	interest, dividends, rents
5.3	North Sea oil taxes
4.6	taxes on companies
3.8	national insurance surcharge
5.7	other taxes and income
10.6	borrowing

= 117

expenditure
(£ billion)

30.3	social security
14.1	education
13.4	health
12.8	debt interest
12.3	defence
5.5	housing
4.9	other environmental services
4.6	commerce, industry, agriculture
4.4	law, order, protection
3.7	roads and transport
11.0	other items, including employment services and overseas aid

= 117

Source: Economic Progress Report Sept 1981

Fig. 79 UK public income and expenditure 1981–1982

6 Influencing the level of economic activity

The income and expenditures of the public authorities are now so large that any changes in these variables have a great influence on the levels of output, employment, and prices. The use of taxation and public expenditure as regulators to move the economy in the direction in which the government wants it to go is the most important single instrument of economic policy although, in more recent years, the control of the money supply has been strongly advocated as a more effective instrument. Much more is said about this subject in subsequent chapters.

In the UK, in 1981–82 about 72 per cent of public spending was undertaken by the central government, about 25 per cent by local authorities, about 2 per cent by the nationalised industries (only that part financed externally) and about 1 per cent by other public corporations.

The budget

The Budget is the main occasion each year when the Exchequer Accounts are reviewed. The Chancellor presents a financial statement which forecasts government income and expenditure for the year ahead and reports on the actual income and expenditure during the

Notes on Figure 79
1 More than 90 per cent of the government sector's revenue is derived from various forms of taxation (including national insurance contributions and local rates). Total revenue in 1981–82 fell well short of total spending leaving a substantial amount of public spending to be financed by borrowing.
2 The different types of taxes are explained later in this chapter.
3 National insurance contributions may be regarded as a form of taxation since they are compulsory levies on employers, the self-employed and employees. These contributions do not appear in the Budget accounts because they are paid directly into the National Insurance Fund and are earmarked for the financing of social security benefits and the health service.
4 Local authority rates are also a form of taxation. They are levied on the owners of property and the basis of taxation is the rateable value of the property which is assessed by Inland Revenue valuation officers.
5 The National Insurance surcharge is a tax and the revenue appears in the Budget accounts. It is levied on employers and is a type of payroll tax.
6 Under the heading of Social Security by far the largest item of expenditure is the pensions for the elderly. Other important items of expenditure are child allowances, unemployment benefits and sickness benefits.
7 The debt interest item represents the annual interest payments on the debt of the government sector (£10 billion on central government debt and £2·8 billion on local authority debt).
8 The expenditure on housing covers the capital costs of new council houses and subsidies on the rents of existing houses.
9 Other environmental services include, water supply, sewerage, refuse collection and grants for the improvement of local amenities.

year just ended. Budget Day is usually between 1 April and 5 May because the powers to collect income tax and corporation tax have to be renewed by Parliament within one month of the end of the financial year on 5 April. In normal times there is only one Budget each year, but in recent years the economic difficulties of the UK have led to the presentation of 'mini-Budgets' in the autumn or winter. The Chancellor has a certain amount of freedom to act between Budgets in the form of the 'regulator' which gives him or her power to vary excise duties by up to 10 per cent either way, and VAT by up to 25 per cent.

Until relatively recent times the Budget was regarded as little more than a balance sheet showing how the government proposed to raise the least possible revenue to meet expenses which must be kept to a minimum. Nowadays the Budget is the most powerful single instrument of economic policy. The Chancellor does not simply aim to 'balance the budget' in the sense that current outgoings must be matched by current revenue – he or she will deliberately unbalance the Budget (i.e. aim at a deficit or surplus) in order to influence the direction of economic activity.

The accounts of the central government are centred on two funds, the *Consolidated Fund*, which handles the revenues from taxation and other miscellaneous receipts such as broadcasting licence fees, interest, and dividends, and the *National Loans Fund*, which conducts the bulk of the government's domestic borrowing and lending. Most of the expenditure from the Consolidated Fund is devoted to *Supply Services* which are itemised in the Budget Statement (Table 28). Estimates of these expenditures have to be submitted to and voted by Parliament annually. In addition to the supply services there are items of expenditure which come under the heading *Consolidated Fund Standing Services* and which do not require an annual parliamentary vote. They include the appropriation of funds to meet interest on the national debt, salaries and pensions of judges, and payments to members of the Royal Family.

The National Loans Fund receives income in the form of interest on government loans, repayments of past loans, the standing charge on the Consolidated Fund to cover interest on the national debt, and any surplus from the Consolidated Fund. Outgoings include interest on the national debt, loans to the nationalised industries and local authorities, and loans to private industry. Where receipts exceed payments, the balances of the NLF may be used to repay part of the national debt; if payments exceed receipts the government will have to borrow.

When the expenditure from the Consolidated Fund is set against revenue there will be a surplus or a deficit. If a surplus arises it will be paid into the National Loans Fund and serve to reduce any borrowing requirement. If there is a deficit, it will be financed by a loan from the NLF and this will increase the amount of the government's borrowing requirement.

Table 28 UK budget estimates (1982–1983) £ million

The Consolidated Fund

Revenue		Expenditure	
Inland revenue		*Supply services*	
Income tax	30 775	Defence	13 945
Corporation tax	4 850	Overseas services	1 605
Capital gains tax	600	Support for industry	6 660
Petroleum revenue tax	4 330	Roads and transport	2 019
Capital transfer tax	465	Housing	2 318
Stamp duties	810	Law, order, protection	2 475
Other taxes	50	Education, science, arts	2 850
		Health and personal	
Total inland revenue	41 880	social services	10 260
		Social security	11 768
		Rate support grant	16 087
Customs and Excise		Scotland[1]	2 988
VAT	14 750	Wales[1]	1 168
Oil	5 100	Northern Ireland[1]	1 103
Tobacco	3 525	Other services	6 128
Spirits, wine, beer	3 275		
Betting and gaming	550	Total supply services	81 374
Car tax	600		
Other excise duties	20		
Customs duties and levies	1 330	*Standing services*	
		Payment towards interest	
Total customs and excise	29 150	on national debt	5 175
		Payments to EEC	2 820
Vehicle excise duties	1 854	Other standing services	1 522
National insurance			
surcharge	3 443	Total standing services	9 517
Total taxation	76 327		
Broadcast receiving			
licences	754		
Interest and dividends	321		
Other revenue	5 493		
Total revenue	82 895	*Total expenditure*	90 891

(Deficit on Consolidated Fund = 7 996)

[1] These figures include only the expenditures which are within the responsibilities of the Secretaries of State for Scotland, Wales, and Northern Ireland.

continued overleaf

Table 28 continued

The National Loans Fund

Receipts		*Payments*	
Consolidated Fund		National Debt:	
contribution to interest		Interest	11 467
on national debt	5 175	Management	133
Interest on loans and		Consolidated fund deficit	7 996
profit on the note issue	6 425	Loans to:	
Borrowing by National		nationalised industry	721
Loans Fund	9 632	other public	
		corporations	1 242
		local authorities	− 300
		others	− 27
Total receipts	21 232	*Total payments*	21 232

Source: Financial Statement and Budget Report 1982–83

Note on Table 28
The major items of expenditure are either self-explanatory or have been mentioned earlier in the text. We must take note of the fact that whereas Figure 79 deals with *total* public spending, the Budget deals only with the income and expenditure of the central government excluding National Insurance Fund items. The item Education in this table refers to the direct financing of education (e.g. grants to the universities); most of the funds for education are contained within the Rate Support Grant to local authorities.

The structure of taxation in the UK

The Inland Revenue department

The taxes collected by this department are sometimes described as *direct taxes*. They are levied on income and capital and the burden of such taxes is borne by the person or company responsible for paying the taxes. Direct taxes are not usually passed on in the form of higher prices as is the case with indirect taxes (i.e. taxes on expenditure).

Personal income tax

The present system is a single graduated personal tax. The tax is not chargeable on a person's gross income because certain expenditures known as allowances can be offset against tax liabilities and there are also allowances according to a person's marital status. Thus
Gross Income − Allowances = Taxable Income.

In 1982 − 83 the rates of personal income tax in the UK were as follows:

Taxable Income (£s)	Rate of Tax
0–12 800	30%
12 801–15 100	40%
15 101–19 100	45%
19 101–25 300	50%
25 301–31 500	55%
over 31 500	60%

Corporation tax

This tax is levied on the profits of all companies resident in the UK whether the profits are earned at home or abroad. The tax is charged after allowances for such things as interest on loans and depreciation of capital. In 1982–3 the basic rate was 52 per cent with lower rates for small companies. Corporation tax is levied on all profits whether paid out as dividends or not. Dividends are subject to personal income tax but it is assumed that the basic rate of income tax has been applied to dividends before they are paid out (part of the corporation tax paid by a company is imputed to its shareholders). Corporation tax may encourage firms to raise funds in the form of loan capital rather than by an issue of shares, because interest on loan capital can be offset against corporation tax as a cost of production whereas dividends cannot.

Petroleum taxes

The taxation levied on the increasing flow of gas and oil from the North Sea is becoming a most important source of government revenue. Income from the extraction of oil and gas from Britain's continental shelf is subject to three charges:

a A royalty of $12\frac{1}{2}$ per cent of the value of the oil and gas extracted:

b A Petroleum Revenue Tax (PRT) which is levied on the net revenue from each field. In 1982–3, PRT was levied at 70 per cent although a supplementary duty had been introduced in the 1981 Budget. It is proposed to terminate the supplementary duty and raise PRT to 75 per cent from December 1982;

c Corporation tax is levied at 52 per cent after the deduction of PRT and royalties.

Capital gains tax

This particular tax is levied on the increase in the value of certain

423

assets between the time of their purchase and the time of their sale. Any increase in the value of most assets is taxable when the assets are disposed of. In 1982–3 capital gains tax was levied at a rate of 30 per cent. There are important exemptions for such things as personal private residences, private motor cars, life assurance policies, winnings from gambling and capital gains on government securities. The first £5 000 of an individual's gains in a year is also exempt.

Capital transfer tax

The UK introduced a capital transfer tax in 1975 as a replacement for estate duty. It is generally referred to as a *gift tax* since it applies to gifts made during life and to transfers of wealth on death. It is chargeable on a person's lifetime transfers as they occur and it is cumulative, that is, in calculating the tax on any gift or transfer of wealth the previous gifts are taken into account. In other words it is not an annual tax. The tax is generally payable by the donor, but it may be recovered from the beneficiary. Lower rates are applied to transfers made during life than to transfers on death. In both cases the rates are progressive increasing from 15% (lifetime transfers) and 30% (transfers on death) to 75% on transfers on death of more than £2½ million.

The first £55 000 of transfers is not chargeable and transfers between husband and wife are not chargeable. Certain other types of gift (e.g. donations to charities) are also given special treatment.

Stamp duties

Many kinds of legal and commercial documents are required to be stamped. Among the more common of these documents are those which transfer the ownership of property (including stocks and shares).

The Customs and Excise Department

The taxes collected by this department are usually described as *indirect taxes* since the person who actually makes the tax payment to the authorities may pass on the burden of the tax to some other person. For example, the excise duties on petrol and beer are invariably passed on as higher prices although they are collected from manufacturers and distributors. The main indirect taxes or taxes on expenditure consist of, excise duties on home produced goods and services and on goods imported from abroad, the value added tax and car tax, and the protective or import duties.

424

The excise duties

Most of the revenue from these duties is derived from three sources, tobacco, alcoholic drinks and hydrocarbon oil.

Tobacco. Cigarettes are subject to an ad valorem duty based on the recommended retail price and a specific duty based on quantity. Other smoking products are charged by reference to their weight.

Alcoholic drinks. The duties on spirits, wines and beer are specific duties which vary according to the alcoholic strength of the liquids.

Hydrocarbon oil. These duties are also specific (i.e. related to quantity) and are levied mainly on petrol and diesel oils used in transport.

Betting and gaming. Most forms of betting and gaming in the UK are now liable to taxation. A proportional tax is levied on pool betting; casino gambling is taxed by means of licences and a similar system is applied to gaming machines.

Matches and mechanical lighters are also subject to an excise duty.

Value added tax (VAT)

VAT is a general sales tax which applies to a wide range of goods and services. The tax is charged to the sellers of output and their tax liability amounts to a percentage (15 per cent in 1982–3) of the value added at that particular stage of production. The firms engaged in the production of a commodity add VAT to the value of their outputs, but they deduct from this figure the amount of VAT already paid on their inputs. In other words they pay VAT only on the value added by their particular activities.

Certain goods and services are given special treatment; they are either exempt or zero rated. When goods and services are exempt the trader does not charge his customer any output tax, but he cannot claim back any VAT already paid on his inputs. Exemption from VAT applies to land (including rents), insurance, postage, betting and gaming, finance, education, health services, burial and cremation.

Zero-rating means complete relief from VAT. A trader does not charge VAT on the goods and services he sells and he can reclaim any VAT which has been paid on his inputs. Zero-rating applies to exports, food (except meals out), childrens' clothing and footwear, books, newspapers, fuel (except road fuel), construction, passenger transport, drugs, and medicines on prescription and certain supplies to charities.

A major reason for the introduction of VAT in the UK was that it is a necessary condition of EEC membership. Since VAT is not levied on exports (i.e. exporters can reclaim any VAT already paid on the goods) it should provide some incentive to exporters.

Car tax is a special tax on motor cars and motor caravans which is levied in addition to VAT. It applies to domestically manufactured and imported vehicles.

Protective duties are levied on imports into the UK from non-EEC countries. The rates of duty are those which apply throughout the EEC since membership of the EEC obliges the UK to apply the common tariffs. Revenues raised by these duties are payable to the EEC.

Motor vehicle excise duty. All motor vehicles in use in the UK have to be registered and licensed. The rates of motor vehicle duties vary according to the type of vehicle, heavier vehicles paying much higher duties.

Miscellaneous licences. Central government revenue is obtained from the issue of a variety of licences of which much the most important is the television licence.

Local taxation

In the UK, the principal local taxes are the 'rates'. These are taxes levied by local authorities on the occupiers of property. The basis of this local tax is the rateable value of the property which is based on an assessment of the rent which the property would command if it were let on the open market. The rate is then fixed as 'a poundage'.

For example, if, in a particular year, the local rate is fixed at 80p in the £, the occupier of a house with a rateable value of £300 would be liable to pay $300 \times 80p = £240$ in rates for that year.

The rate poundage is determined by the planned expenditure of the local authority, the amount of the grant it receives from the central government and the rateable value of the property in its area. Thus, if a local authority after taking into account the funds it expects to receive from central government, decides that it has to raise £600 million by local taxation and the total rateable value of the property in its area is £800 million, it will levy a rate of $\frac{£600 \text{ million}}{£800 \text{ million}}$ pence in the pound. It will announce a rate of 75p in the £.

A system of rate rebates now tends to reduce the rate burden on low income households.

The national debt

The budget statement (Table 28) shows a central government borrowing requirement of more than £9 billion. The national debt is the accumulation of such government borrowings over past years. It is *not* the debt of the whole public sector; it is the debt of the central government. Until fairly recent years, the national debt grew most rapidly during the wars when governments found it impossible to finance all wartime expenditures from taxation. The very large increases in the debt which resulted from the First and Second World Wars can be clearly seen in Table 29.

Table 29 The growth of the sterling national debt

Year	£ million
1800	200
1815	800
1914	640
1918	8 000
1945	26 000
1965	29 000
1974	39 500
1981	113 260

Wartime borrowing results in what is sometimes described as 'deadweight debt' since the assets created by the borrowed funds are largely destroyed; the debt literally 'goes up in smoke'. Some people, however, would regard these expenditures as an investment in the preservation of freedom which yields very high returns even though these returns cannot be measured in money terms.

Since the Second World War, much of the borrowing has been used to finance the creation of assets such as houses, power stations, motorways, gas pipe lines, telephone exchanges etc. A series of large Budget deficits in the 1970s and early 1980s has led to a fairly sharp increase in the national debt. In 1981 it amounted to about £2 000 per head of the population and in Table 28 we can see that the interest payments on the national debt is now a major item of government expenditure.

Composition of the national debt

The government borrows by issuing a wide range of different securities in an attempt to satisfy the requirements of different types of lenders (or 'savers'). An important distinction is that between marketable and non-marketable debt. Marketable debt consists of those government securities which can be bought and sold before the final maturity date. Such securities can change hands many times before the final date for repayment. Government stocks can be traded on the Stock Exchange and Treasury bills can be bought and sold in the money market. Marketability makes these securities liquid assets but, as explained earlier (page 273), their market values will depend upon the current rate of interest. Non-marketable debt consists of securities which must be held by the original purchaser until they are repaid. A major part of the non-marketable debt consists of National Savings Certificates.

Table 30 Composition of the UK national debt

		£ million
Official holdings (marketable and non-marketable)		18 277
Sterling marketable debt;		
Government and government-guaranteed securities		75 536
Treasury bills		1 209
Sterling non-marketable debt;		
National savings		11 556
Other securities		3 599
	Total Sterling Debt	110 177
Foreign currency debt		3 083
	Total Debt	113 260

Source: Bank of England Quarterly Bulletin December 1981

Marketable debt represents about 78 per cent of the total debt and consists mainly of Government stocks (gilt-edged) which may be classified as follows:

Short-dated stocks. These are repayable by the government at some specified date within 5 years.

Medium-dated stocks. The government redeems these stocks at some specified date within 5 to 15 years.

Long-dated stocks. These securities mature at some specified date, but the securities have more than 15 years to run before that maturity date is reached.

Undated stocks. The government is under no obligation to pay back the money borrowed on undated stocks unless it so wishes. In other words there is no redemption date.

The majority of these securities carry a fixed rate of interest although in 1977 the government issued stocks with a variable rate of interest which is linked to the market rate of interest on Treasury bills.

That part of the debt which consists of Treasury bills is often referred to as the *floating debt* because it represents short-term borrowing which has to be continually re-financed.

National savings securities include national savings certificates, defence bonds, premium bonds, national savings stamps, the index-linked saving certificates and the Save-As-You-Earn scheme.

The holders of the national debt

Official holdings account for about 16 per cent of the national debt. This part of the debt is held by government departments and the Bank of England. The relatively large holdings of the central bank consist of government securities held as a backing for the note issue and for the Bank's operations in the open market (see page 324). Another large slice of official holdings is held by the National Debt Commissioners who are responsible for the investments of the National Insurance Fund and the deposits of the National Savings Bank. A large proportion of the debt is held by financial institutions such as insurance companies, pension funds, building societies, and banks. Individuals and private trusts also hold a significant proportion of the national debt.

About 10 per cent of the UK national debt is held by overseas residents. As explained later, this external debt has important implications for the balance of payments.

The burden of the debt

Although the absolute size of the national debt has shown a striking increase in the years since the Second World War, taken by itself, the figure has little meaning. It must be judged in relation to the means of supporting the debt, that is, the ability to meet the interest payments to the holders of the debt. In 1946 the national debt was equal to about 290 per cent of the Gross Domestic Product whereas in 1981 this proportion had fallen to about 54 per cent. Like all major borrowers the government has gained substantially from inflation. If the *money values* of the sums owed and the interest payments due on the debt remain unchanged, the *real values* of these liabilities will be substantially reduced by inflation.

It is often said that the practice of financing government spending by means of borrowed funds is 'unfair' because it transfers the liability for present spending to future generations who will be called upon to meet the interest payments and to repay the debt. This is not true. The financing of war by borrowings does not transfer the real burden of war. This has to be borne by the generation engaged in the war. It is they who have to go without the consumer goods, houses and so on so that war materials can be produced. We could not have increased the output of tanks in 1943 by reducing the output of motor cars in 1980. The same argument applies to the interest payments and the capital repayments in the years after the money was borrowed, because these transactions amount to a redistribution of income at the time when the payments are made. The generation making these payments is the same generation which is receiving them. Over the community as a whole the taxes are cancelled out by the interest received; the whole community does not experience any net gain or loss.

Since the national debt is simply a debt owed by the people collectively (i.e. the state) to the people individually, the community is neither richer nor poorer. If one brother borrows from another brother, the wealth of the family remains unchanged. If, however, the national debt were narrowly held (i.e. by relatively few rich people), the annual interest payments would amount to a fairly large redistribution of income from the taxpayers (most of the people) to the security holders (a small percentage of the people). The nation, however, is poorer to the extent of the debt held overseas. This is a real burden on the community because the interest payments and the repayments of capital must be made in foreign currencies and these, in turn, must be earned by exporting goods and services. The servicing and repayment of foreign debt involves a sacrifice of real output, that is, exports which do not exchange for imports.

The economics of taxation

The structure of taxes

Progressive taxes

A tax is progressive when the marginal rate of taxation is greater than the average rate. The higher income groups and the more wealthy individuals not only pay more tax than the less well off, they pay a greater proportion of their income and wealth in taxation. For example, a person earning £5 000 per annum may be taxed at a rate of 20 per cent while a person earning £15 000 per annum may be taxed at a rate of 45 per cent. The British income tax and capital transfer tax are examples of progressive taxes.

Proportional taxes

A tax is proportional when all taxpayers pay the same percentage of their income or wealth. In the UK, corporation tax is an example of a proportional tax.

Regressive taxes

Taxes are regressive when the poor are called upon to make greater sacrifices than the rich. If the first £1 000 of income were taxed at 40p in the £, and the second £1 000 at 30p in the £, the tax would be regressive. Flat rate taxes such as the excise duties on tobacoo, beer, and petrol act regressively since the amount of tax included in the prices of these goods represents a greater percentage of the incomes of the lower paid groups.

We may summarise by saying that a tax is progressive, proportional, or regressive according to whether it takes from the higher income groups a larger fraction of income, the same fraction of income, or a smaller fraction of income than it takes from the lower income groups.

Canons of taxation

Adam Smith laid down certain canons of taxation which are still generally acceptable as basic principles for a system of taxation.

Equity

There must be equality of sacrifice. This implies that the burden of taxation should be distributed according to people's ability to pay. Smith thought that proportional taxes would satisfy this criterion, but nowadays it is generally accepted that progressive taxes are the most equitable type of tax. The argument is based on the idea that the principle of diminishing marginal utility applies to income. On this basis it might be argued that taking £20 per week away from the man earning £150 per week only deprives him of the same amount of satisfaction as would the removal of £5 from the wage packet of the man earning £60 per week.

The capital gains tax was introduced on grounds of equity. It was felt that a capital gain obtained by speculation in share or commodity markets should be subject to taxation in the same way as income earned on the factory floor.

431

Certainty

The taxpayer should know how much tax he has to pay, when it must be paid, and how it must be paid. He should be able to assess his tax liability from information provided and should not be subject to tax demands made in an arbitrary fashion. In theory, the British system of taxation satisfies these requirements – all the necessary information is available to taxpayers, but the tax laws have become so complex and extensive that it is sometimes difficult for the average man to be certain of all his rights and responsibilities.

Convenience

Taxes must be collected in a convenient form and at a convenient time. The Pay As You Earn (PAYE) system of tax collection is probably the most convenient method in general use. Under the previous system income tax was paid in arrears – the tax on the income earned in one period was payable in the following period. This system laid the onus of building up a tax reserve fund on each individual taxpayer. Taxes are paid in money and generally speaking this is the most convenient form of making tax payments. Some difficulties arise, however, when taxes are levied on wealth, the majority of which will not be held in the form of money. Problems arise in making accurate valuations of different assets and sometimes in realising these assets so that payments can be made in money. When wealth is held in the form of shares in a private company, for example, there might be difficulties in disposing of them – they cannot be offered for sale to the general public.

Economy

The costs of collection and administration should be small in relation to the total revenue. This requirement often conflicts with that of equity. The 'fairest' system of taxation would involve casting the net so widely and so carefully that collection costs would be disproportionately high.

The economic effects of taxation

On the distribution of income

Taxes will reduce the disposable income of firms and households. When the tax is progressive, the incomes remaining after tax must be less unequally distributed than incomes before tax. Only a proportional tax would leave the distribution of income unchanged. Indirect taxes also affect the distribution of income. The commodities which are subject to heavy taxation are widely consumed and have demands which are inelastic with respect to price. Since the lower income groups tend to spend a greater proportion of their incomes on some of these commodities the effect of the taxes can be regressive. For example, there is evidence that the tax on tobacco is regressive; it takes a higher proportion of the income of the poor than the rich. It appears, in fact, to be getting more regressive because tobacco consumption has fallen among the higher income groups. On the other hand the tax on alcohol seems to act progressively. The higher income groups consume relatively more wines and spirits which are subject to higher rates of tax.

On consumption

Direct and indirect taxes will affect both the total and the pattern of consumer spending. Direct taxes reduce disposable income, but the effect on consumption will depend upon the propensity to consume and the level of saving. If there is very little saving, direct taxes must reduce consumption. If, however, taxpayers are enjoying a relatively high standard of living which enables them to save, an increase in direct taxes may have relatively little effect on consumption. People may resist any cut in their living standards by reducing saving rather than spending.

Indirect taxes will also reduce the total demand for goods and services, especially where they are imposed on commodities with inelastic demands. Consumers will tend to maintain their consumption of these goods and so they will have less to spend on other goods and services. Again, much depends upon the propensity to consume and the existing levels of saving.

On incentives

Each time the Chancellor increases taxation voices are raised to proclaim the fact that the new levels of taxation will result in less effort, less investment, and less risk-taking, because taxation has now reached levels which make the *net* rewards for extra work and responsibility seem very unattractive. This argument applies particularly to progressive taxation where *additional* income is taxed at higher rates. There is obviously some level of taxation at which these disincentive effects will come into operation, but it is very difficult to determine that level. It might be argued that additional taxation will increase the workers' efforts. A person becomes accustomed to a certain standard of living and he might well react to an increase in taxes by working harder or longer hours in order to maintain the same disposable income.

433

On saving and investment

Heavy and steeply progressive taxation will reduce the ability to save; it might also reduce the willingness to save. As noted above, an increase in taxes might lead to a fall in saving rather than spending. Capital transfer and wealth taxes might also reduce the willingness to save because one of the incentives to accumulate wealth is the desire to pass on some of the results of one's efforts to one's children and grandchildren. It is difficult to determine the strength of these effects since so many factors influence the level of savings.

Private investment is determined largely by expected profitability so that we must expect the taxation of profits to have some disincentive effects. Much will depend upon the particular level of the tax, but the heavy taxation of profits will probably act as a disincentive as far as the more risky projects are concerned. Let us take as an example two projects, one fairly safe, one very risky, and assume a profits tax at the rate of 50 per cent.

| | *Estimated profits* | |
	Before Tax	*After Tax*
Project A (fairly safe)	£10 000 p.a.	£5 000 p.a
Project B (very risky)	£30 000 p.a.	£15 000 p.a.

After tax, Project B still holds out the prospect of profits three times as great as those expected on Project A, but the absolute difference has fallen from £20 000 to £10 000. Is it worthwhile taking the much greater risks for a possible net gain of £10 000 as against the £20 000 which might be forthcoming without the tax?

On prices

Direct taxes fall on income and have no direct influence on the price level, but indirect taxes have an immediate impact on prices. An increase in direct taxes which led to a significant fall in demand could, of course, lead to a fall in prices, but in present-day conditions it is more likely to reduce output rather than prices.

It was pointed out in Chapter 25 that an increase in indirect taxes is a potentially powerful generator of cost-push inflation. Much depends upon the weighting of the taxed commodities in the Retail Price Index. It is also possible that increases in direct taxes could stimulate wage demands and so lead to cost-push inflation.

Public finance and equity

One very important objective of government policy is to create a more equal distribution of income and wealth than that which would result from the uncontrolled exercise of market forces. Taxation which falls more heavily on the better-off groups is one policy instrument used for this purpose. The other aspect of the policy is the redistribution of this revenue in a manner which gives proportionately greater benefits to the poorer classes. This subject is discussed more fully in Chapter 36.

Fiscal policy

We have defined fiscal policy as the deliberate manipulation of government income and expenditure so as to achieve desired economic and social objectives. These objectives and the role of fiscal policy in economic management are discussed more fully in later chapters, but it seems appropriate, at this stage, to make some general comments about fiscal, or budgetary policy.

The instruments of fiscal policy (taxation and government spending) act directly on the major economic variables (e.g. output, employment, prices); they are very powerful instruments. A budget surplus will remove purchasing power from the economy and reduce aggregate demand – a budget deficit will inject purchasing power and raise aggregate demand. But fiscal policy can be used in a discriminating manner to change the allocation of resources both industrially and regionally. The products of some industries can be taxed while other industries receive subsidies. Some industries may be selected for protection by means of tariffs while others may be allowed to compete with unrestricted imports. Some types of investment may be encouraged with investment grants or preferential tax treatment of profits. If the government wishes to encourage economic growth in particular regions it can apply such measures as investment grants, employment premiums, training grants, and so on, on a strictly regional basis. It may also deliberately bias its own spending by placing a disproportionate share of its own orders with firms in the selected regions.

A major disadvantage of fiscal policy is its relative inflexibility. Major changes in taxation and public expenditure cannot be carried out at frequent intervals – there is a great deal of administrative work involved. Changes in income tax, for example, involve the calculation and distribution of millions of new codes. Changes in public spending on goods and services take a long time to become effective. Much of this expenditure is tied to long-term contracts (e.g. the building of roads, power-stations, hospitals) which cannot be switched on and off as short-term regulators. There is often a serious time lag between the identification of the problem to be dealt with and the time when the fiscal measures begin to take effect. In this respect monetary policy may be a more efficient short-term regulator because it can be operated on a day to day basis.

Most fiscal arrangements have some features built into them which are known as *automatic stabilisers*. For example, as money incomes rise, a progressive system of income tax will automatically remove an increasing proportion of those incomes in taxation. Providing government spending remains unchanged there will be some restraining effects on inflationary tendencies. When incomes are falling the opposite effect occurs, proportionately less is taken in taxation, and if government spending is unchanged total demand will not fall as fast as gross money incomes.

Unemployment and other social security benefits also act as automatic stabilisers. When unemployment rises and incomes fall, unemployment benefits increase and the opposite effect applies when unemployment is falling. Thus, a reduction in wages and salaries due to rising unemployment will not lead to a proportionate fall in aggregate demand.

31 The Economic Mechanism

Economic policy

The overall performance of the economy is now generally accepted as a major responsibility of government. That branch of economics which deals with the economy as a whole (the subject matter of this section of the book) is known as *macro-economics*, while the study of the 'parts' of the economy is known as *micro-economics*. Thus, an examination of the forces which determine the price of beef, or the wages of miners, or the size of the firm, would be an example of micro-economic analysis, whereas a study of the forces determining the general price level, or the general level of wages, or the balance of payments would be classified as macro-economic analysis.

Economic analysis is concerned with the means of achieving particular economic objectives. The choice of the objectives – how people want economic resources to be used in order to satisfy their wants – is a matter for political decision. While governments will differ in the emphasis they give to particular objectives and in the ways in which they try to achieve them, there seems to be broad general agreement on the main aims. They are:

1 A high and stable level of employment.
2 Price stability.
3 A satisfactory balance of payments position.
4 An acceptable rate of economic growth.
5 An equitable distribution of income and wealth.

Each of these objectives is discussed in more detail later, but it is important to note that governments have found that some of these objectives may be incompatible. In order to achieve one goal governments have often been obliged to sacrifice another. Policies designed to bring about full employment have sometimes generated unacceptable levels of inflation; policies aimed at eradicating a balance of payments deficit have restricted the rate of economic growth, and so on. Policy-makers, therefore, are obliged to establish some scale of priorities. If the choice is, or seems to be, between a higher rate of inflation or a higher rate of unemployment, then the issue must be solved by the value judgements of the people concerned (i.e. through the political system).

The framework of economic policy

The first task is determine the *objectives*. The next task is choose the *instruments* of policy to be used in pursuit of the objectives and these instruments are based upon some available range of *measures*. For example, the government might decide that its immediate objective is to reduce the level of unemployment. For this purpose it might choose to use the instruments of taxation and government spending. The particular measures adopted might be a reduction in income tax and an increase in public spending on housing and roads. But the essential link between the desired objective and the appropriate means of achieving it is economic *analysis*. The role of analysis is to provide some understanding of how the economic system works. We cannot choose realistic objectives or design appropriate measures for attaining those objectives unless we have some knowledge of how the economy works. In the preceding chapters of this book we have used economic analysis to explain the structure and operation of different sectors of the economy and although we have discussed many of the inter-relationships between these sectors we have not looked at the functioning of the economy as a whole.

A model of the economy

The circular flow of income

In order to understand how the measures of economic policy operate on the macro-economic variables (prices, output, employment, the balance of payments and so on), we have to make use of a fairly simple model of the economy. We begin with an economy in which there is no government and no foreign trade. There are only two sectors, *firms* and *households*. Firms are the producing units which hire services provided by the people from the households. For these services firms pay wages (for labour), rent (for land), interest and dividends (for the services of loan and risk capital). There is, therefore, a flow of factor services from households to firms and a flow of income from firms to households. These flows are represented by the upper pipes in Fig. 80.

But in this model, households are also the purchasers of the national output. There is a flow of spending from households to firms and a flow of goods and services from firms to households. These flows are represented by the lower pipes in Fig. 80. This economy would remain in equilibrium since firms are selling their goods at prices which are made up of their various costs (including profits) and these costs represent the incomes paid to households. Thus, incomes received by households are always sufficient to buy the total output of firms. We are assuming that the economy has unemployed resources so that any

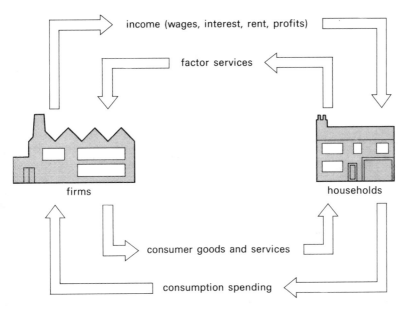

Fig. 80

change in planned spending leads to changes in output and employment.

Leakages and injections

The model as it stands is very unrealistic because even in the simplest economy all the income received by households is not spent – some of it is saved. *Saving represents a leakage* from the circular flow of income because it is part of the income paid out by firms which is not returned to them through the spending of households. When saving takes place, firms' expenses will be greater than their receipts and some of their output will remain unsold. They will react by reducing output so that income and employment will fall. If we assume that households always save some fraction of their income and there are no other expenditures to offset this leakage, income must eventually fall to zero.

Fortunately there is an offsetting expenditure in the form of investment. Our first model of the economy assumed that firms only produced consumer goods and services which were in turn bought by households. In fact, some firms produce capital goods for sale to other firms. This expenditure on capital goods adds to the circular flow of income; it has the opposite effect to a leakage and causes output and income to expand. We can say, therefore, that *investment is an injection*. Fig. 81 shows a more realistic model of the economy which incorporates the saving leakage and the investment injection. This dia-

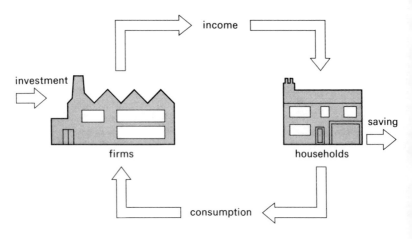

Fig. 81

gram concentrates on money flows; for purposes of simplification the real flows (i.e. goods and services) have been omitted.

Saving and investment

It is fairly obvious from the diagram that a stable or equilibrium level of income will only be achieved when the rate of saving is equal to the rate of investment. The amount which people plan to save in any time period, however, is not likely to match the amount which firms plan to invest. By and large the decisions to save and the decisions to invest are taken by different groups of people who have different objectives. There will be some limited amount of overlapping because firms both save (i.e. they retain some profits) and invest.

The consequences of any discrepancy between saving and investment are far-reaching. When the rate of saving out of current income exceeds the rate of investment, the total demand for goods and services is less than the value of the firms' current output. Fig. 81 should help us to see why this is so. Firms are paying out expenses in the form of incomes which are equal in value to their total output. These incomes are either consumed or saved. Thus,

Income (= Output) = Consumption + Saving

Firms will be receiving back the consumption spending by households and the spending by firms on investment goods. Thus,

Demand = Consumption + Investment

It should be clear, therefore, that when saving exceeds investment, aggregate demand will be insufficient to buy total output. Stocks will pile up and firms will react by cutting back production. Employment and income will fall.

When investment exceeds saving, aggregate demand will exceed the value of current output. Stocks will run down and firms will be obliged to increase production. Employment and income will rise. Only when saving is equal to investment will aggregate demand be just sufficient to purchase the firms' total output. This is the equilibrium condition. We can summarise as follows:

When Planned I > Planned S, Income will rise
When Planned I < Planned S, Income will fall
When Planned I = Planned S, Income will not change

For a long time economists held the view that market forces would tend to bring about an equality between saving and investment via movements in the rate of interest. A brief outline of these views is given in Chapter 19. Furthermore they believed that these same market forces would bring about a full employment equilibrium because the rate of interest would always rise or fall until the amount saved out of a full employment level of income was fully invested. For example, suppose that a fully employed community was planning to save more than firms were prepared to invest. The rate of interest would fall. This would lead to a fall in saving and an increase in investment and the changes would continue until saving and investment were equated. Likewise an excess of investment over saving at full employment levels of output would cause the rate of interest to rise until equilibrium was restored.

Keynes attacked this particular theory on the grounds that what people *plan to save* and what in fact they *do save* are quite different things. An increased desire to save does not necessarily result in a higher level of saving. It could, indeed, cause the total level of saving to fall! The immediate effect of an increased desire to save is a fall in consumption. A fall in consumption spending reduces the incomes of those who produce and sell consumer goods and this fall in incomes, as explained in the next section, develops into a cumulative process. The fall in the propensity to consume will lead to an eventual fall in total income much greater than the initial fall in consumption spending. It could be so great in fact that although people are *trying to save* more, the ability to save is reduced to such an extent that total savings actually fall. This effect is known as the *paradox of thrift*.

Keynes demonstrated that saving and investment are brought into equality by changes in income rather than changes in the rate of interest, and market forces do not guarantee an equilibrium with all resources fully employed. For purposes of subsequent analysis we shall continue to assume that the economy is not fully employed.

From here on we shall make some use of the common abbreviations: Y = National Income. C = Consumption. S = Saving. I = Investment. G = Government spending on goods and services. T = Taxation. X = Exports. M = Imports.

The multiplier

Discrepancies between the rate of leakage and the rate of injection cause movements in income, but these upward and downward movements will not continue for ever. The expansions or contractions of income will gradually peter out because there are forces at work which tend to bring the economy into equilibrium. Changes in income bring about changes in saving and investment until the plans to save and the plans to invest are made compatible. This adjustment process is explained by the theory of the multiplier.

Let us assume that initially an economy is in equilibrium when Y = £10 000 m., S = £4 000 m., and I = £4 000 m. Now suppose that investment increases to £5 000 m. due to an increase in housebuilding. The income received by those engaged in the building industry will rise by £1 000 m., but this is not the end of the matter. If the saving habits of the community remain unchanged (i.e. they continue to save 0·4 of their income), then £600 m. of this additional income will be spent and £400 m. will be saved. The recipients of this extra spending will have additional income equal to £600 m. They will spend £360 m. of this income and save £240 m., and so it will go on. The increase in the rate of investment will set up a series of rounds of spending and saving. The total income and total saving will gradually increase, but at each stage the increments are getting smaller and smaller until they become immeasurably small. The series looks like this:

Increase in Income = £1 000 m. + £600 m. + £360 m. + £216 m. + + +
Increase in Saving =   £400 m. + £240 m. + £144 m. + + +

Series of this type can be summed by using the very simple formula

$S = \dfrac{a}{1 - r}$ where S = the sum of the series, a = the first term, and

r = the common ratio (i.e. the fraction by which we multiply each term in order to get the next term).

Using this formula we get the following results:

Increase in Income = £2 500 m.   Increase in Saving = £1 000 m.

The value of the multiplier must be $2\frac{1}{2}$, because an increase in investment has caused income to rise by an amount equal to $2\frac{1}{2}$ times the increase in investment.

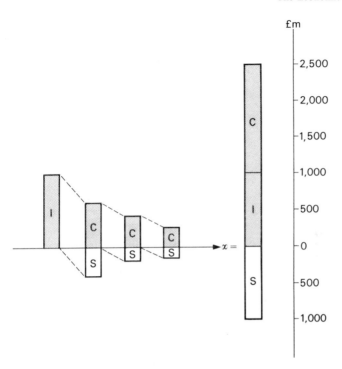

Fig. 82 The multiplier

In the two-sector economy, the multiplier is equal to the eventual change in income divided by the initiating change in investment.
Note that the economy is once again in equilibrium.

Income = £12 500 m. Saving = £5 000 m., and Investment = £5 000 m.

The increase in investment causes income to rise until the level of saving is once again equal to the level of investment. This arithmetical example of the multiplier is illustrated in diagrammatic form in Fig. 82.

The multiplier, however, works both ways. A fall in investment has downward multiplier effects and income falls until saving is equal to the new and lower level of investment. We use the same formula and series to calculate the effects of a cut in investment spending. The only difference will be the signs in the spending and saving series; they will now be minus signs.

The determinants of the multiplier

The size of the multiplier depends upon the proportion of any increase in income which is spent (i.e. passed on within the circular flow). In the example above, 0·6 of each addition to income was spent and 0·4 was saved. Clearly if 0·8 of any additional income had been spent, the final increase in income would have been much larger. Another way of looking at it is to say that the size of the multiplier depends upon the proportion of any increase in income which leaks out of the system. Thus, the smaller the fraction saved, the larger the multiplier.

The Marginal Propensity to Consume (MPC)

The MPC is that fraction of any small increase in income which is spent on consumer goods and services. If an extra £1 of income leads to an increase of 70p in consumption spending, the MPC is 0·7. Empirical evidence indicates that the MPC declines as income increases. In other words, although consumption rises as income increases, *the rate of increase* of consumption tends to decline. As we become more affluent we spend more on consumer goods and services, but we spend a smaller proportion of our income on these things. It is the MPC which determines the size of the multiplier. This may be demonstrated by returning to the arithmetical example used a little earlier, where we assumed the MPC was 0.6.

Using the formula $S = \dfrac{a}{1-r}$ we have

$$\text{Increase in Income} = \frac{\text{Increase in Investment}}{1-r}$$
$$= \frac{£1\ 000\ m.}{1-r}$$
$$= \frac{£1\ 000\ m.}{1-0.6}$$
$$= £2\ 500\ m.$$

Now, $\dfrac{£1\ 000\ m.}{1-0·6}$ may be written as £1 000 m $\left(\dfrac{1}{1-0·6}\right)$ or, £1 000 m $\left(\dfrac{1}{1-\text{MPC}}\right)$.

The expression in the last bracket is the multiplier since this is the quantity by which we multiply the increase in investment in order to obtain the increase in income. Thus,

The Multiplier $= \dfrac{1}{1-\text{MPC}}$

The Marginal Propensity to Save (MPS)[1]

The MPS is that fraction of any small increase in income which is saved. In the simple model of the economy which we are now using, income can only be disposed of in two ways – it can be consumed or saved. Thus, if, of every extra £1 of income, 70p is spent and 30p is saved, the MPS will be 0·3. Since consumption rises more slowly than income, the MPS will increase as income increases. In a two-sector economy, MPC + MPS = 1, and 1 − MPC = MPS. We can, therefore, rewrite the formula for the multiplier *in a two-sector economy* as,

$$\text{The Multiplier} = \frac{1}{\text{MPS}}$$

A worked example

In a two-sector economy, MPS = 0·2, I = £5 000 m., and
Y = £25 000 m.
a Assuming investment remains constant,
 i What is the equilibrium level of saving?
 ii What is the value of the multiplier?
b If investment were to increase by £1 000m. what would be the new equilibrium level of income?

a i In equilibrium $S = I$, so that if Investment remains constant at £5 000m., the economy will settle in equilibrium where S = £5 000m.
 ii If MPS = 0·2, then MPC = 0·8

$$\text{The Multiplier} = \frac{1}{1-\text{MPC}} \text{ or } \frac{1}{\text{MPS}}$$
$$= \frac{1}{1-0·8} \text{ or } \frac{1}{0·2}$$
$$= 5$$

b Increase in Income = The Multiplier × Increase in Investment
  = 5 × £1000 m.
  = £5 000 m.
 New level of Income = £25 000 m. + £5 000 m. = *£30 000 m.*

A more realistic model

In order to bring our model of the economy nearer to reality we must take account of the fact that governments play an important part in determining the level of economic activity and that all countries take

[1] The Average Propensity to Consume (APC) and the Average Propensity to Save (APS) are simply the proportions of *total* income which are consumed and saved.

some part in international trade. It is not difficult to introduce these additional sectors into the circular flow of income analysis.

Foreign trade

Some part of the expenditure of households does not flow back to domestic enterprises because households buy foreign goods as well as home-produced goods. These *imports are a leakage* from the circular flow because they represent income paid out by firms which does not flow back to them. *Exports are an injection* into the circular flow because this spending by foreigners on home-produced output is an additional source of income which is not generated within the domestic system. For purposes of this particular analysis, exports and imports may be treated in the same way as investment and saving. If exports exceed imports there will be an expansionary effect on income while an import surplus will have a depressing effect on income.

Government

Government spending takes several forms, but we are only concerned with that part of it which directly creates income for factors of production. *Public spending on goods and services is an injection* because it adds to real output and creates employment. Transfer payments do not, directly, generate output and income. When they are spent they will increase demand but this will show up as an increase in the propensity to consume. *Taxes are a leakage* because they remove purchasing power from the system. The importance of G and T lies in the fact that they can be deliberately manipulated by the authorities in order to influence the level of output and employment. A budget deficit will have an expansionary effect and a budget surplus a depressing effect on income.

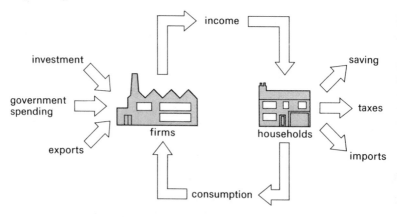

Fig. 83

Fig. 83 provides a highly simplified picture of the circular flow now that we have taken account of the government and international sectors. According to Fig. 83 all the leakages originate in the household sector. In the real world, of course, this is not the case, because the same leakages take place at different points in the circular flow. Firms pay taxes on their income, they save (i.e. they retain profits), and they buy foreign materials and machines. Taxes are levied on expenditures as well as incomes so that the tax leakage also applies to the streams of consumption and investment spending. Fig. 83 would become very complicated if we tried to show the locations of the injections and leakages more accurately – the important point is to identify the nature of these leakages and injections and to understand just how they affect the flow of income.

The multiplier in the more complex economy

The multiplier is still governed by the proportion of any marginal change in income which consumers spend on domestic output. The expression $\frac{1}{1 - \text{MPC}}$ still gives us the value of the multiplier, but the proportion of any additional income which is 'passed on' within the system is now reduced by three leakages, namely, saving, imports and taxation. This means that $1 - \text{MPC}$ is no longer equal to MPS. In fact $1 - \text{MPC}$ is equal to that proportion of any increase in income which leaks out of the circular flow. As a fraction of additional income this leakage is equal to $\text{MPS} + \text{MPM} + \text{MPT}$, where $\text{MPM} = $ the marginal propensity to import, and $\text{MPT} = $ marginal rate of taxation. We can now rewrite the formula for the multiplier in an economy with government activity and foreign trade,

$$\text{The Multiplier} = \frac{1}{1 - \text{MPC}} \text{ or } \frac{1}{\text{MPS} + \text{MPM} + \text{MPT}}$$

The multiplier takes effect whenever there is a change in the planned rate of spending. Thus a change in I, or G, or X will have multiplier effects on income. There will also be multiplier effects when there is a change in consumption spending which is independent of changes in income. A change in the *propensity to consume*, therefore, will have multiplier effects. We have illustrated the multiplier process by talking about increases in planned spending, but remember that the multiplier also applies when there are decreases in planned spending. Income will fall by a multiple of the fall in planned expenditure.

A worked example

Out of every extra £1 of income, a community saves 20p, spends 15p on foreign commodities, and the government takes 15p in taxation. What is the value of the multiplier?

Out of each extra £1 of income, consumption spending on domestic output accounts for £1 – (20p + 15p + 15p) = 50p.
Therefore, MPC = 0.5, MPS = 0·2, MPM = 0·15, and MPT = 0.15

$$\text{The Multiplier} = \frac{1}{1 - \text{MPC}} \text{ or } \frac{1}{\text{MPS} + \text{MPM} + \text{MPT}}$$
$$= \frac{1}{1 - 0\cdot5} \text{ or } \frac{1}{0\cdot2 + 0\cdot15 + 0\cdot15}$$
$$= 2 \qquad\qquad = 2$$

Equilibrium

The economy will be in equilibrium when planned leakages are equal to planned injections. In our more realistic model (Fig. 83) an equality between saving and investment is not a sufficient condition for equilibrium. Equilibrium does not require that S should be equal to I, or G equal to T, or X equal to M. The necessary condition for equilibrium is,

Planned Injections = Planned Leakages
i.e. I + G + X = S + T + M

Thus, an excess of saving over investment may be offset by a budget deficit, or an export surplus. A balance of payments surplus may be offset by a budget surplus, and so on. It must be pointed out at this stage that an equilibrium level of income is not, in itself, a desirable state of affairs. An economy can settle into an equilibrium position while there are still millions out of work. The great economic problem facing governments is to achieve an equilibrium level of income which is compatible with the objectives outlined at the beginning of this chapter, and, in particular, a full employment level of income. The problems associated with this task make up the subject of the rest of this chapter.

Economic management

The basic problem

Our elementary analysis of the workings of the capitalist system indicates that, in the absence of government intervention, the economy would be (i) subject to instability, and (ii) capable of settling down in equilibrium with a large proportion of the nation's resources unemployed.

In order to visualise the problem we need to eliminate the government sector from our model of the economy. For this purpose we can use Fig. 83 and omit G and T. In this free enterprise economy, instability is likely because the injections and leakages are determined by millions of independent decisions – they are not coordinated. There is no reason why changes in planned I or X should bring about corresponding changes in planned S or M, or why changes in the plans to save and import should lead to balancing changes in I or X. Changes in one or more of the injections and leakages will cause upward or downward movements in income and these income changes will be cumulative because of the multiplier effects. Thus the level of employment, the level of prices, the balance of payments, and the rate of economic growth will all be affected by this instability of income.

Full employment can only be maintained if aggregate money demand (i.e. planned spending) is equal to the value of output when all resources are employed. Now when there is no government sector, aggregate demand for home-produced output is equal to $C + I + X - M$.[1] It is equal to the total planned spending in the home market, minus imports, plus exports. There seems to be no good reason why market forces should maintain aggregate demand at the required level. To maintain full employment we must have a situation where, when all resources are working, that part of income which is saved and spent on imports (i.e. the leakages) is exactly balanced by investment and exports (i.e. the injections). But suppose that the amounts which people plan to save and spend on imports *out of a full employment level of income* are greater than the amounts which firms plan to invest and foreigners wish to spend on home output? Then output and income must fall until $S + M$ is equal to $I + X$. This will leave some resources unemployed.

This then is the case for government intervention. The public authorities must manage aggregate demand so as to remove these unacceptable features of the free market system and achieve the objectives of economic policy. The reintroduction of the government sector brings us back to the model illustrated in Fig. 83 where we can identify the components of the total spending which generates factor incomes in the home economy.

Aggregate Money Demand $= C + I + G + X - M$

If the government is to manage the economy effectively it must have instruments of policy which are capable of controlling the variables on the right-hand side of this equation. Clearly G and T will be its main instruments and by running budget deficits or surpluses it can try to offset any imbalances in the private sector (see Fig. 83). In earlier chapters we have seen how the use of fiscal policy and monetary policy can influence C and I and we also know that the government

[1] Where C represents total consumption spending (i.e. on home produced goods and imports).

can use exchange rate policies, fiscal measures, and direct controls to influence X and M. We must remember that government measures which act on these macro-economic variables will be reinforced with multiplier effects. Thus, if fiscal policy or monetary policy succeeds in increasing the rate of private investment from say £1 000 m. to £1 200 m. when the multiplier is 2, income will rise eventually by £400 m.

Some limitations of demand management

The Second World War was followed by a quarter of a century of unparalleled economic growth and prosperity in the non-communist industrialised nations. Unemployment remained extremely low by historical standards and rates of inflation, judged by subsequent experience, were also very low. In the UK, for example, unemployment averaged 1·6 per cent in the 1950s and 2·1 per cent in the 1960s, while inflation averaged 3·2 per cent in the 1950s and 3·8 per cent in the 1960s. The remarkable growth in world trade was an important factor in creating these conditions, but there is no doubt that the application of Keynesian demand management policies were also instrumental in preventing unemployment from returning to the intolerably high levels of the inter-war years. These policies have proved much less successful since the mid-1960s and this subject is discussed later, but we can note some of the limitations of demand management policies.

One great problem is the adequacy of the evidence on which government policies are based. Statistical information has greatly improved in recent years both in content and coverage, but there are still gaps and it takes time to collate and process the data. It has been said that we know everything about the economy except what is happening now. In other words, it is often difficult to judge what measures are appropriate at a particular time since the judgement must be based on information which is probably three months out of date. A similar problem arises with the timing of the measures. Some instruments of policy (e.g. a change in direct taxation) do not take immediate effect and it is difficult to assess just when they ought to be introduced.

The amount of change required is also difficult to predict. For example, the most recent statistics might show a downward turn in economic activity, but the Chancellor has to decide whether it is a temporary deviation from an upward trend or the beginning of a serious depression. Miscalculations on these matters have sometimes led to the Chancellor being accused (after the event!) of 'doing too little too late' or 'doing too much too soon'. The amount of stimulation or restriction to apply to aggregate demand is difficult to calculate because the multiplier is not capable of precise measurement. Its size depends upon the marginal propensity to consume and we cannot forecast exactly how people will react to a change in their disposable incomes.

Perhaps the greatest problem is the fact that in a democratic society many economic policies depend for their effectiveness on the voluntary cooperation of many different groups each of which demands a wide measure of freedom of choice and many of which exercise considerable economic and political power. Governments might be able to manage the economy more effectively if they had more power to impose their policies on the community, but whether they ought to have such powers is a matter of political judgement. It is certain, however, that if people continually demand more than the economy can produce, inflation will develop and policies which aim to reduce the rate of inflation have, in the past, cause unemployment to rise.

32 Full Employment

The reasons for pursuing a policy of full employment are self-evident. Bitter memories of the hardships and social distress of the 1930s virtually compel all policymakers to give it priority. From the strictly economic viewpoint, unemployment represents a waste of valuable resources and a permanent loss of potential output.

The meaning of full employment

Our first problem is to define full employment. It cannot mean a situation where everyone wanting to work and able to work is constantly employed. Labour is not perfectly mobile and in a world of changing demands there will always be some people temporarily unemployed while they are in the process of moving from one job to another. Unemployment which arises from immobilities in the labour force rather than from a lack of demand for labour is known as *frictional unemployment*. A particularly serious type of frictional unemployment arises when a major industry experiences a permanent decline in the demand for its products. This is described as *structural unemployment* and the nature of the problem is discussed in some detail on pages 133 and 456. In all societies there is also an element of *residual unemployment* because there will always be some people that are virtually unemployable on a permanent basis. These are people that find it difficult or impossible to cope with the demands of modern production methods and the disciplines of organised work. There will also be an element of *seasonal unemployment* in those industries which experience marked seasonal patterns of demand. Industries such as farming, building and tourism are affected in this way.

Unemployment which is not due to the causes described above must be accounted for by inadequate demand and is usually described as *demand-deficiency unemployment* or *cyclical unemployment* (because it is associated with the trade cycle). It was this type of unemployment to which Keynes directed his attention and which, it was believed, could be eradicated by demand management policies.

Full employment, then, cannot mean zero unemployment. There will always be some elements of frictional, structural, seasonal and residual unemployment. It is sometimes taken to mean a situation where the number of vacancies is at least equal to the numbers out of work. In this case aggregate demand is providing the right number of jobs, but they are not in the right place or of the right type to match the geographical distribution and occupational skills of the unemployed. This definition is not acceptable because it is possible to visualise a situation where there is a large number of unemployed and a correspondingly large number of vacancies. For this reason full employment is usually defined in terms of some politically acceptable level of unemployment. This level will vary according to the prevailing conditions and the experience of recent years. In the twenty five years which followed the end of the Second World War people became accustomed to unemployment rates of $1\frac{1}{2}$ per cent to 2 per cent. At this time a rate of unemployment of something less than $2\frac{1}{2}$ per cent would probably have been regarded as a situation of full employment. In recent years the rates of unemployment have been much higher. Early in 1982, with 3 million out of work, the UK unemployment rate was 12 per cent; about eight times the rate for 1960. It is likely, therefore, that, after several years of relatively high unemployment rates, a politically acceptable definition of full employment would specify an unemployment rate rather higher than $2\frac{1}{2}$ per cent.

The economic objective is a *full* and *stable* level of employment. The history of industrial capitalism is one of booms and slumps, generally described as the trade cycle. The government's aim is to achieve and *maintain* a high level of employment. The maintenance of full employment, however, does not imply a stable level of aggregate demand. Technological progress increases productive capacity so that, as time goes by, any given output can be produced by a progressively smaller labour force. If a country's productive potential is rising at a rate of 5 per cent per annum, then some given level of output could be maintained while employment is falling at 5 per cent per annum. If productivity is increasing, full employment can only be maintained if aggregate demand is increasing at the same rate as productivity.

In the short run, however, we can assume that techniques remain unchanged so that employment varies directly with output. Since we shall also assume that output, in the short run, is determined by demand we can relate changes in employment directly to changes in demand. Once full employment has been achieved, of course, any further increases in demand will simply raise prices.

Let us suppose that an economy is in equilibrium producing a less than full employment output. The task of government is to increase aggregate demand until all resources are employed. If the deficiency of income is estimated to be £10 000 million and the multiplier is believed to be 2, then one or more of the components of aggregate demand must be raised, in total, by £5 000 m. How can this be achieved?

Fiscal policy

The government might act in a direct manner by increasing its own expenditures on goods and services while leaving taxation unchanged. Alternatively it might decide to stimulate private spending (both C and I) by reducing taxation, but the effects here are more difficult to estimate because some of the increase in disposable income will be saved rather than spent. An increase in social security benefits will be an effective way of bringing about an increase in C because the MPCs of the recipients will be very large. Private investment might be encouraged by more generous investment grants. In other words the government will budget for a deficit, but we must remember the points made in Chapter 30 regarding the time lags associated with some fiscal measures. In an economy like the UK with a fairly large public sector, aggregate demand could be increased by stepping up the investment programmes of the nationalised industries, but, again, these measures could not take effect immediately.

Monetary policy

The appropriate monetary measures were discussed in Chapter 23. In this particular case, attempts will be made to encourage private investment and consumption spending by relaxing any restrictions on the commercial banks' lending activities and the authorities will take steps to bring about a fall in the rate of interest. Private spending may also be stimulated by a relaxation of any existing hire purchase restrictions. But, again, we must note the qualifications on the effectiveness of monetary policy which were explained in Chapter 23.

A worked example

In an economy, National Income = £1 000 m.
The injections are, G = £100 m., I = £80 m., X = £70 m.
The leakages are, M = 0·05 of income, S = 0·1 of income, and T = 0·1 of income and these proportions are constant.
The government considers that it is necessary to raise national income to £1 200 m. in order to achieve full employment. It decides to increase its own expenditure and leave the rate of taxation unchanged. By how much must G be raised?

a Since the consumption of home-produced goods is a constant proportion of income,
MPC = $1 - (0·05 + 0·1 + 0·1) = 0·75$

The Multiplier $= \dfrac{1}{1 - 0·75} = 4.$

In order to raise national income by £200 m., therefore, government spending must increase by £50 m. (i.e. to £150 m.)

b Alternatively,
In equilibrium,   Planned Injections = Planned Leakages
i.e.   I + G + X   = S + T + M
When the equilibrium level of income is £1 200 m.,
I(£80 m.) + G + X(£70 m.) = S(£120 m.) + T(£120 m.) + M(£60 m.)
                    G = £150 m.

The initial and final situations are illustrated in Fig. 84, where
(a) shows the original equilibrium and (b) the equilibrium situation after
the effects of the increase in G have worked themselves out.

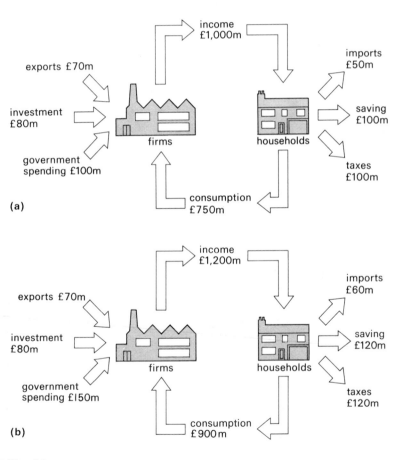

Fig. 84

The above examples have dealt with demand–deficiency unemployment. Demand-management policies were successful in dealing with
this type of unemployment for a considerable period following the

Second World War. Other types of unemployment, however, have also presented problems.

Frictional unemployment

Even when aggregate demand is at a level which creates sufficient jobs to absorb the entire labour force, there will be some unemployment of the frictional type. Although total spending may be raised to the required level, the patterns of spending within that total are always changing so that some industries will be expanding and others declining. Hence a fairly large number of people will always be changing their jobs and many of them will spend some time on the unemployment register 'in between' jobs. Frictional unemployment is essentially short-term unemployment. In the 1950s and 1960s it is probable that most of the unemployment in the UK was of the frictional type. In the early 1980s, however, there was a much greater element of the cyclical or general unemployment. For example, in 1980, half the people who became unemployed left the register within three to four months, compared with one month in the mid-1970s and only two weeks in the 1960s. In October 1981 some 800 000 people had been out of work for more than 12 months.

The policies for dealing with frictional unemployment aim to increase the mobility of labour and they are fully discussed on pp. 49–50 and 138.

Regional unemployment

Particularly acute unemployment problems arise when a major and heavily localised industry is in permanent decline. This gives rise to *structural unemployment*, so named because it is associated with a fundamental change in the structure of industry. The region dependent upon the industry will suffer particularly heavy unemployment because there will be local multiplier effects arising from the decline in the income generated by the major industry. This type of regional unemployment cannot be dealt with simply by increasing aggregate demand. Any additional spending created by the appropriate monetary and fiscal measures will probably increase the demands for the goods produced by the expanding industries and do little to help the declining industries. It might for example increase the demand for electrical appliances (when that industry is already fully employed) and do nothing to relieve unemployment in mining or shipbuilding. Raising aggregate demand when the problem is one of structural and regional unemployment is most likely to generate inflationary pressures in the prosperous areas while leaving the regional pockets of unemployment largely unaffected. The appropriate measures for dealing with this problem are discussed in Chapter 12.

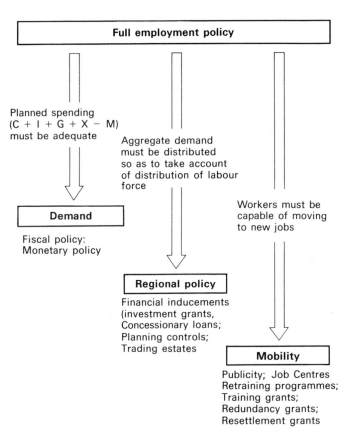

Full employment policy

Planned spending
(C + I + G + X − M)
must be adequate

Aggregate demand
must be distributed
so as to take account
of distribution of labour
force

Demand

Fiscal policy:
Monetary policy

Workers must be
capable of moving
to new jobs

Regional policy

Financial inducements
(investment grants,
Concessionary loans;
Planning controls;
Trading estates

Mobility

Publicity; Job Centres
Retraining programmes;
Training grants;
Redundancy grants;
Resettlement grants

Fig. 85

Unemployment and inflation

For much of the post-war period economists have discussed something
called a 'trade-off' between unemployment and inflation. In their
anxiety to achieve the major objective of full employment, governments – so many people believe – sometimes maintained demand at
excessively high levels. Due to the immobilities of the factors of production, this high level of demand led to shortages and bottlenecks in
some industries and these shortages led to rising prices. It was also
argued that high levels of demand greatly increase the bargaining
powers of the trade unions so that inflationary pressures also arose
from wage settlements in the labour market. When the government
tackled the problem of inflation by reducing aggregate demand, the
result was an increase in unemployment. Prices proved to be extremely
inflexible in a downward direction so that a reduction in demand

457

reduced output rather than prices. The idea that there is an inverse relationship between the level of unemployment and the rate of inflation seemed to be supported by experience in the UK in the 1950s and 1960s when a relatively small rise in unemployment was associated with a marked fall in the rate at which wages were increasing. It appeared reasonable to suppose that a little more unemployment would curb inflation. Any such inverse relationship seemed to disappear in the late 1960s. Since that time high rates of inflation have often been associated with high (and rising) levels of unemployment.

The natural rate of unemployment

When the apparent inverse relationship between the level of unemployment and the rate of inflation broke down in the 1960s and unemployment and inflation began to rise at the same time, many economists argued that economic behaviour had changed. Inflation was no longer caused by excess demand but by cost-push pressures. Monetarists, however, refute this argument and insist that inflation *is* a consequence of excess demand and that this excess demand is determined by the growth in the money supply.

A most important concept in the monetarist argument is that of the *natural rate of unemployment*. This level of unemployment is 'natural' in the sense that it represents an equilibrium situation where the supply of and demand for labour are equal and the average *real* wage is constant. The natural rate of unemployment is not unchangeable; its level depends upon the various frictions in the labour market. Many of these are discussed on pages 48 and 49; they also include such features as discrimination, the adequacy of retraining facilities, the rate of technical progress, the level of social security benefits relative to wage rates and the existence of minimum wage laws. Monetarists assert that attempts to reduce unemployment below the natural rate by increasing aggregate demand can only succeed in the short run and then only at the cost of increasing the rate of inflation. In very simplified terms the monetarists' argument runs as follows.

Assume that unemployment in the economy is at the natural rate. The average real wage will be constant and, given no change in productivity, the rate of change of prices (i.e. inflation) will also be constant. Let us assume that the rate of inflation is 3 per cent per annum and has been at 3 per cent for some considerable time. This will be *the expected rate* and wage claims will be linked to this rate because workers will attempt to maintain real wages. The government now decides that the existing level of unemployment is unacceptably high and decides to increase aggregate demand by running a Budget deficit. It will be reluctant to raise market rates of interest by borrowing heavily from the non-bank private sector and will, therefore, finance its deficit, to some extent at least, by borrowing from the banking sector. This, as noted earlier, will increase the money supply.

The increase in aggregate demand will increase the demand for labour, which, given the frictions in the labour market, will cause money wages to be bid upwards. Workers will believe that real wages have risen and unemployment will fall as more people are attracted into employment. But the increase in the money supply will lead to rising prices and the rate of inflation will increase to, say, 5 per cent per annum. The realisation that real wages have not increased will cause some workers to leave employment and 5 per cent will now become the expected rate of inflation. Wage claims will now be based on this rate and 5 per cent per annum will become the prevailing rate of inflation.

The end result of the increase in demand will be a higher level of inflation and no long term change in the level of employment; this will revert back to the natural rate. Any further attempts to reduce employment below the natural rate by expanding aggregate demand can only lead to even higher rates of inflation.

Special employment measures

The high and increasing rates of unemployment experienced by the UK (and other countries) in the later 1970s and early 1980s led the government to introduce measures to alleviate the problem in the form of (i) subsidies to employers to encourage them to retain labour or to provide jobs on a temporary basis and (ii) a great expansion of full-time training schemes.

Several of these measures are aimed at the younger age groups because of the relatively high rates of unemployment among young people. To some extent this was due to the very large increase in the number of school leavers in the late 1970s and early 1980s (reflecting the high birth rates during the 1960s). Early in 1982 it was estimated that some 700 000 young people were on special employment and training schemes. Brief details of some of the special employment measures are set out below.

1 The Temporary Short-Time Working Scheme offers financial assistance to employers who agree to withdraw a planned redundancy affecting at least 10 workers. If such employers are prepared to introduce short-time working instead of dismissing workers, the government pays a weekly subsidy for a limited period in respect of each worker affected.

2 The Youth Opportunities Programme helps unemployed young people by providing training courses and work experience. The state offers free allowances to those taking part in the scheme. These training and

459

work experience courses usually last for six months. In 1983 this scheme will be replaced by a Youth Training Scheme under which all those leaving school at age 16 and who fail to find a job will be guaranteed a year's training. This will take the form of a combination of college-based training and work experience.

3 The Young Workers' Scheme aims to encourage the employment of young people by offering employers a subsidy (£15 p.w. in 1982) for all young people under the age of 18 providing they are in their first year of work and their earnings are below £40 per week (in 1982).

4 The Job Release Scheme provides financial inducements for people nearing statutory retirement age to give up their jobs and make way for unemployed people.

5 The Community Enterprise Programme gives priority to those aged 18 to 24 who have been out of work for more than 6 months and those of 25 or over who have been unemployed for more than 12 months. The scheme aims to provide full-time temporary employment on projects which benefit the community directly.

33 Counter-Inflationary Policy

Recent experience seems to indicate that of all the objectives of economic policy price stability is probably the most difficult to achieve. The causes and effects of inflation have been discussed in Chapter 25. Although opinion is divided on whether a low rate of inflation (2 or 3 per cent per annum) is undesirable, there is little disagreement on the undesirability of higher rates of inflation (more than 10 per cent per annum). Inflation creates serious tensions because it tends to redistribute income in favour of the more militant groups with strong bargaining powers and penalises those on fixed incomes and those with weaker bargaining powers. It usually leads to a deterioration in the balance of payments, and favours debtors at the expense of creditors. The most serious problem is the tendency for inflation to escalate. It creates expectations of further price rises and these expectations lead unions and firms to raise wages and prices by amounts which take account not only of past and present, but of future price increases. Once inflation becomes firmly established, the most important and the most difficult objective of any policy to cure inflation is to change these expectations. People must be convinced that the proposed measures will be effective.

Demand inflation

Prices will rise and continue to rise if aggregate money demand persistently moves ahead of the value of current output. If price controls and rationing are to be avoided, there are two possible ways of achieving some degree of price stability. One is to increase supply and the other is to reduce demand (or some combination of both). Since excess demand is usually associated with full employment, there is little scope for any short-term increase in total output. Productivity can be raised by using better techniques and equipment, larger scale production, and the relaxation of restrictive labour practices, but such changes normally come about relatively slowly. The only other way of increasing home supplies in the short period is by means of a large increase in imports, but as far as the UK is concerned the balance of payments position has tended to rule out such a remedy.

Our model of the circular flow of income will help us to see how measures to reduce demand might be applied. The policy must aim to increase the leakages and/or reduce the injections. For example, an increase in saving or taxation will reduce the flow of consumption spending. A fall in C will reduce the profit expectations of entrepreneurs who will tend to cut back investment and this effect could be reinforced by an increase in corporation tax. The injections could be reduced directly by a cut in government spending, but as noted earlier, this is difficult to carry out in the short term. Saving might be stimulated by the introduction of more attractive national savings schemes (e.g. by linking the value of savings to the retail price index). The monetary measures will aim to restrict bank lending and raise interest rates. The effectiveness of an increase in interest rates depends very much on the state of business expectations. With a high rate of inflation, high interest rates may not be a serious deterrent to borrowers because the real rate of interest may be quite low; indeed, it may well be negative. Restrictions on hire purchase have proved to be an effective way of reducing demand although they discriminate heavily against certain industries (e.g. motor cars, furniture, and electrical goods).

Any reductions in C, I, or G will, of course, have downward multiplier effects and, unfortunately, they will tend to increase the rate of unemployment. They will also restrict the rate of economic growth because a reduction in the current rate of investment means a slower growth of productivity in the future. To many people, the obvious way to stop prices rising is to apply price controls. Such controls, however, attack the symptoms of inflation rather than the causes. Where the cause of inflation is excess demand, price controls will only lead to shortages and create a demand for a system of rationing. Another problem is that the size of the administrative task means that price controls and rationing can only be applied to a limited range of key commodities. Price controls, if maintained for any extended period, will distort the allocation of resources because price movements are the indicators which inform suppliers and purchasers of the extent and direction of the changes in supply and demand which are always taking place. Nevertheless, price controls may have a role to play in dealing with the problems of cost-push inflation.

Cost-push inflation

The causes of cost inflation are described in Chapter 25. Since it is not necessarily associated with excess demand, the policies described above are not appropriate for dealing with cost inflation. In recent years high rates of inflation have been experienced at times when the rate of unemployment was also high. Under these conditions, measures to reduce aggregate demand would only worsen the unemployment situation. Some of these measures (e.g. an increase in indirect taxation) might well increase the rate of inflation. Demand management policies if pushed far enough would certainly reduce the rate of inflation. Interest rates and direct taxes could be raised to very high levels, but it now seems that such measures would not begin to have any significant effect on inflation until unemployment had reached totally unacceptable levels. Under conditions of 'stagflation' (i.e. high unemployment *and* inflation) the traditional demand management policies are not only inappropriate as anti-inflationary weapons, they cannot be used to deal with the unemployment problem either, since attempts to increase aggregate demand will only worsen the inflationary problem.

Many economists now believe that inflation is essentially a monetary problem. They largely accept the Friedman view (see p. 337) that there is a causal relationship between changes in the money supply and changes in the level of economic activity; that is, changes in the money supply *cause* the changes in income (although there is a time lag). Critics of this theory accept the fact that movements in total spending and movements in the money supply are directly related, but they argue that the causal relationship runs the other way. They maintain that increasing economic activity creates a demand for more money and the money supply is increased to meet the growing demand for it. There seems to be increasing support for the view that governments have 'validated' inflation by increasing the money supply in order to prevent unemployment reaching unacceptable levels. When unions have succeeded in achieving wage increases which raise costs and prices, governments have increased the money supply to meet the rise in prices. The government, it is argued, have passively increased the money supply to maintain full employment at whatever wage levels unions and employers have agreed. Whether it is the wage pressures or the accommodating increases in the money supply which *cause* inflation is a subject of much dispute. Monetarists say that inflation can only be checked by exercising a tighter control over the money supply. This particular solution is resisted by those who maintain that an attempt to restrict the money supply while union leaders are still convinced of their power to raise money wages frequently and substantially, can only lead to large-scale unemployment. Unions would probably succeed in getting the wage increases and these would lead to prices increases, but the restrictions on the money supply would not allow demand to expand in order to maintain the volume of sales.

The lack of any convincing evidence on the role of changes in the money supply and doubts about the consequences if it were seriously restricted have led the authorities in the UK and several other countries to the view that the most practicable (and politically acceptable) policy for dealing with cost-push inflation is some kind of incomes policy.

Incomes policies

The main aim of an incomes policy is to link the growth of incomes to the growth of productivity so as to prevent the excessive rises in factor incomes which raise costs and hence prices. It also has the important objective of preventing a redistribution of income towards those groups with powerful bargaining positions. By focussing attention on the need to raise productivity in order to justify wage increases, an incomes policy may lead to a greater awareness of the need to increase industrial and commercial efficiency. Although an incomes policy must embrace all forms of income – wages, interest, rent, and profits – it will tend to concentrate largely on wages because these account for about two-thirds of the value of final output.

Structure

There are three fundamental steps in establishing and operating an effective incomes policy.

1 A decision must be taken on the permitted (or recommended) percentage increase in aggregate income for the period ahead (normally one year). This figure is referred to as the *norm* and is usually based on the anticipated increase in total output. In the sequence of incomes policies which have been tried in the UK from 1965 onwards, the norms have varied from zero to about 10 per cent.

2 The next step is to decide the manner in which the total increase in income is to be distributed among the various income groups.

3 The third and most difficult task is to give effect to these decisions by setting up some machinery for enforcement and supervision.

Major difficulties arise when the second stage is reached. Even if we assume that general agreement is reached on the *average* wage increase, it does not mean that all workers will receive the same percentage increase in wages. If this policy were adopted, existing wage differentials would be frozen and the major incentive to labour mobility would be removed. If the government is anxious to encourage labour mobility it will have to allow industries which are short of labour to offer something higher than the norm while industries trying to shed labour will pay something less than the norm. There will also be demands from other groups for 'exceptional' treatment. Workers who feel that they have been left behind in previous wage-price spirals will press for special treatment. It might also be necessary to allow some exceptions in order to encourage greater efficiency by permitting increases above the norm where workers have made a substantial contribution to increased productivity.

It is very difficult to introduce flexibility into an incomes policy without causing resentment among those who do not qualify for special treatment. When it comes to justifying a wage increase we all feel that we have a special case to plead. Movements away from existing differentials are often regarded as 'unfair'. Such feelings also arise because increases in productivity vary enormously as between different industries. Some industries, especially those which are science-based (e.g. chemicals) and those which can obtain important technical economies (e.g. the motor industry), are capable of achieving annual increase in productivity well above the national average. Workers in such industries may feel that their wage increases should be related to movements in productivity in their own industries and not to the national average.

Perhaps the most difficult task of all is that of enforcement and supervision. In a society where the traditional method of wage negotiation is that of freely conducted collective bargaining and where powerful trade unions are determined to retain their freedom to negotiate on behalf of their members, it is extremely doubtful whether the statutory enforcement of an incomes policy is a practical proposition, except perhaps for a very short period in a crisis situation. On the other hand, voluntary policies do not appear to have met with much success. Where there is a large number of trade unions each representing sectional interests, it is extremely difficult to obtain general agreement on the guidelines for an incomes policy. There are many thousands of separate wage settlements and the effective policing of these agreements to make sure that they conform with the general principles of the incomes policy is a formidable administrative task.

Profits and rent

What can be done to control the level of profits? Distributed profits may be limited by (i) legislation which places a ceiling on dividends, (ii) a form of price control which fixes prices on a cost-plus basis, and (iii) a variable profits tax which could be adjusted to keep profits to some agreed figure.

The great drawback to all these schemes is that they reduce the incentive to lower costs. In the case of (ii) it might be argued that there is a positive incentive to increase costs. The incentives to embark upon new projects, adopt new methods, introduce new products, and to develop new markets, all risky undertakings, would certainly be diminished under a regime of profit limitation. Another problem would be that differences in profitability would no longer serve as an indicator to potential investors. Capital normally flows to the more profitable industries or to those with the best prospects of profits, but when dividends are limited, the more successful firms would not be able to offer potential investors any better rewards than the less successful firms. In spite of these disadvantages, however, some limitation of profits is necessary if other income groups are to be persuaded to accept restrictions on their ability to increase their earnings.

The control of rents in the UK has usually taken the form of statutory rent control on privately-owned houses. Landlords have been able to raise rents only when they have been able to satisfy some public rent tribunal that they have carried out some improvement to their property, or when there has been some unavoidable increase in the costs of maintaining the property. There are some serious disadvantages to a system of rent control especially when rents are held down to levels which represent a relatively low return on the capital employed. In the UK it has led to a very substantial fall in the supply of privately-owned houses to rent. When a rented house has become vacant, landlords, in order to recover their capital for re-investment in some more profitable venture, have tended to sell the house to an owner-occupier.

Effectiveness of incomes policies

Incomes policies have sometimes taken the form of a complete freeze on wages and prices. It is difficult to maintain a wage and price standstill for more than a few months, because supply and demand conditions will continue to change and hence relative prices must be allowed to change if the price mechanism is to perform any useful function. In addition, trade unions will strongly oppose any protracted wage freeze. While they have been in force, wage and price freezes have certainly slowed down the pace of inflation, but their effect has been like that of a temporary dam. Once the policy is relaxed, there is a flood of wage claims and price increases which very soon bring wages and prices back on their former trend.

It is very difficult to assess the effectiveness of the incomes policies which have been tried in recent years. It is not sufficient to discover whether wages and prices have risen faster in periods of controls than in periods without them. Incomes policies are normally applied when inflationary pressures have become very intense. The effects of the policies should be judged by the difference between what actually happened and what might otherwise have happened in the absence of any controls. As far as British experience is concerned, it seems that wage and price controls when firmly applied can work for a time, but they break down when prices are forced upwards by non-wage factors. The increases in prices due to the 1949 devaluation, the 1967 devaluation, the heavy increases in taxes in 1968, and the massive increases in world commodity prices in 1972–4, were important factors leading to the breakdown of British incomes policies.

Incomes policies have been criticised because they bring the government into conflict with the unions and increase the extent of industrial unrest. For this reason the Labour government in 1974 introduced the idea of a *social contract* between unions and government whereby the government promised industrial and social legislation desired by the unions in return for union promises to moderate their wage claims. Incomes policies both statutory and voluntary were operated for 10 out of the 14 years between 1966 and 1979. These policies, however, did not reverse the trend to higher rates of inflation although, for short periods, they certainly reduced the rate of inflation. Although incomes policies are unpopular with the trade unions, the high cost of alternative anti-inflationary policies (e.g. demand-management and control of the money supply) in terms of unemployment have led many economists to the view that the government must give high priority to the task of devising an acceptable and workable incomes policy.

Indexation

As a means of removing some of the distortions caused by inflation and, perhaps, as a means of slowing down the rate of inflation, some countries have introduced a system of 'monetary correction' or 'indexing'. Very simply this means that the monetary values of assets, incomes, savings, pensions, interest on loans, tax payments, and other incomes are all adjusted upwards according to the rate of inflation so that their relative real values remain unchanged. The idea was introduced temporarily into British incomes policy in 1973 when workers automatically qualified for threshold payments equal to 40p per week for each 1 per cent increase in the Retail Price Index.

The main purposes of indexation is to prevent the arbitrary redistribution of real income described in Chapter 25. It would also eliminate the increase in the tax burden which is often a consequence of inflation. When tax rates are progressive, an increase in *money* incomes might put the recipient into a higher tax bracket so that he pays a greater proportion of his income in tax, although his real income might have remained unchanged. Indexation of tax allowances would remove this anomaly, which is a contributory factor in the escalation of wage claims. Inflation will be reduced by indexation if wage earners are prepared to accept smaller basic settlements because they know that their real incomes are being protected. On the other hand, because increases in prices are immediately reflected in higher money incomes, it might speed up the inflationary process.

34 Balance of Payments Policies

Chapter 27 dealt with the main features of a country's external financial relationships. For countries like the UK, which are heavily dependent on foreign trade (about 30 per cent of UK output is exported directly or indirectly), the foreign balance is a critical matter. While short-term deficits might be covered by the use of official reserves and overseas borrowing, in the longer run a country must pay its way in the world. But a satisfactory balance of payments position is not simply one in which income equals expenditure on foreign account. Equilibrium should not be achieved at the expense of the other objectives of economic policy.

Government policy in this area is subject to several limitations. While the manipulation of tariffs and other barriers to trade is a legitimate part of a balance of payments policy, the use of such measures is restricted by membership of bodies such as GATT and customs unions such as the EEC. Secondly, membership of the IMF puts some limitations on a country's freedom to use exchange rate adjustments as an instrument of policy. We must remember, of course, that membership of international institutions also confers substantial benefits. Thirdly, a country's balance of payments performance is determined by the economic policies adopted by other countries as well as by its own policies. An expansionary policy in the USA will lead to a marked improvement in the level of UK exports, while policies to protect infant industries in developing countries will have the opposite effect.

Remember that exports are an injection into the circular flow of income and imports are a leakage, so that any changes in the propensity to import or in exports will have multiplier effects on income.

Measures employed to influence the balance of payments will be determined to a large extent by the type of exchange rate system in use.

Policies under fixed exchange rates

When countries are operating fixed exchange rates, national economies are closely linked and economic changes in one country will transmit their effects fairly quickly to other countries. Thus, a country experiencing a higher rate of inflation than its competitors will find its balance of payments position deteriorating because imports are becoming more competitive on the home market and exports less competitive in world markets. With a fixed exchange rate the immediate effect of any deficit falls on the official reserves of gold and foreign currency. When there is a persistent deficit, these reserves (plus borrowing facilities) will soon be exhausted so that, if the exchange rate is to be held, the government must take steps to eliminate the deficit. The appropriate measures were explained in Chapter 28, but we can look at them again in the context of overall macro-economic policy. The authorities can make use of expenditure-reducing or expenditure-switching measures.

Expenditure-reducing measures are those which aim to reduce aggregate demand, and we are now familiar with the manner in which fiscal and monetary policies are used for this purpose. A fall in total planned spending must lead to a fall in the expenditures on foreign goods and services. It might also lead to an increase in exports as domestic firms find it more difficult to sell in the home market and make greater efforts to sell in overseas markets.

There might, however, be an unfavourable 'feed-back' effect from abroad, because a cut-back in one country's imports reduces other countries' exports and, hence, other countries' income. The country carrying out the expenditure-reducing policy, therefore, might find that, although it has favourable effects on its imports, it also has unfavourable effects on its exports. The other major problem with these measures is that they tend to increase unemployment. If the deficit is a substantial one, expenditure-reducing measures would be very unpopular because it would require a relatively large reduction in aggregate demand in order to achieve the required cut in import expenditures. In other words, the 'cost' in terms of unemployment would be politically unacceptable.

Expenditure-switching measures attempt to divert spending from foreign goods to home-produced goods. In order to deal with a deficit, steps might be taken to make imports relatively dearer in the home market and exports relatively cheaper in foreign markets. Devaluation would be the appropriate instrument for this purpose. Alternatively, such measures might take the form of direct controls on imports. Tariffs, quotas, and exchange control can all be used to limit imports and divert demand to home-produced goods. An incomes policy might also be regarded as an expenditure-switching policy. If it succeeds in holding down a country's rate of inflation below the rates being experienced in other countries, the prices of its products will be *falling* (i.e. rising more slowly) *relative* to those of its competitors' goods. Expenditure-switching measures will not be very effective where there is a high propensity to import and the demand for imports is very inelastic. In such circumstances the use of tariffs or devaluation could lead to cost-push inflation.

Policies with floating exchange rates

The main argument put forward in favour of floating rates is that they remove the burdens of policies to deal with deficits from the domestic economy. There is no need for a country to hold large reserves of foreign currency and no need to depress home demand when there is a deficit on the balance of payments. But floating rates do not remove balance of payments problems so neatly as the theory indicates, neither do they isolate the economy from external forces. Surpluses and deficits, it is true, will change the relative prices of imports and exports via changes in the exchange rate, and this movement will bring about an equilibrium in the foreign exchange market. It does not follow, however, that this will also bring about an equilibrium in the balance of payments. This latter situation will only come about if the volumes of imports and exports change by the correct amounts, and this, as we saw in Chapter 28, depends upon the elasticities of demand for, and supply of, exports and imports. In any case, changes in the volumes of exports and imports take time, and the time lag between the change in the exchange rate and the changes in the quantities of exports and imports could be long enough for adverse effects to be felt in the home economy.

Let us take a deficit situation as an example. The depreciation of the currency will make imports dearer, and if the demand for them is inelastic, this could give rise to cost-push inflation. This inflation will eventually remove any price advantage which the depreciation had given to exports. More seriously the cost-push pressures could reduce profitability, weaken confidence, and cause investment to fall. This is a sequence which leads to a rise in unemployment. A cost-push spiral, once set in motion, might lead to a sequence of currency depreciation – rising import prices – further cost-push pressures, and so on. If this did happen, the authorities would be obliged to intervene in the foreign exchange market, resort to foreign borrowing, and, perhaps, take some steps to limit imports by direct methods. But these are the same measures as would be taken with fixed exchange rates!

In other words the success of floating exchange rates in liberating domestic economic policies from the restraints of the balance of payments situation depend very much on the mobility of the factors of production. When the currency depreciates, the volume of exports must be capable of responding very quickly to the increased demand brought about by the lower prices, and home producers must also be able to substitute domestically manufactured products for the relatively dearer imports.

A further point is that the depreciation of a currency will only remedy a balance of payments deficit when the problem is one of relative prices. If the imports are largely essential goods which cannot be produced at home, and if exports are non-competitive in terms of quality, design or performance, then changing relative prices cannot really solve the problem.

35 Economic Growth

Insistent demands for higher standards of living have put great pressures on governments to achieve faster rates of economic growth. One of the most publicised aspects of economic activity in recent years has been the 'league table' showing the growth rates achieved by different countries. Table 31 is an example of this type of thing.

Table 31 Growth of real GNP

	Average 1970–80 (per cent per annum)
Japan	4·8
Canada	4·0
France	3·6
Italy	3·1
Western Germany	2·8
United States	3·0
United Kingdom	1·9

Source: Economic Outlook (OECD) July 1982

In the more affluent societies there has been some reaction against the pressures for more rapid growth. Opponents of growth maintain that the costs of growth in terms of damage to the environment and the 'quality of life' are disproportionately high. Nevertheless, the demands for more consumption *and* more leisure are strong enough to make growth a major objective of economic policy.

The meaning of economic growth

In general usage, economic growth is taken to mean any increase in the Gross National Product, but for several reasons this is a rather misleading use of the term. First of all, GNP is measured in terms of money values so that inflation will increase the figure from one year to another. If we are to use the concept of growth to indicate changes in real income, the annual GNP figures must be corrected for price changes before any valid comparisons can be made. Secondly, changes in real GNP do not necessarily indicate corresponding changes in economic welfare. These are more accurately indicated by changes in real income per head so that changes in GNP should be related to changes in population. We should also take account of the composition of total output when relating growth to living standards. A massive increase in defence spending would show up as a large increase in GNP, but it would be misleading to use this as an indication of an improvement in material living standards.

There is one further important distinction to be made. When an economy is functioning with excess capacity, GNP may be increased by putting the unemployed resources to work. Economists do not usually describe an increase in GNP which arises from a fall in unemployment as economic growth because the extra output is a once-and-for-all gain. The problem of economic growth is how to increase output when all resources are fully employed; it refers, therefore, to an increase in the country's productive potential. This means that economic growth can only be measured between periods when the utilisation of resources, or rates of unemployment, were very similar.

The desirability of economic growth

Growth is an important objective of economic policy because it is the key to higher standards of living. It is economic growth which has made it possible for millions of people to escape from the miseries of long hours of back-breaking toil, deplorable living conditions, a low expectancy of life, and other features of low income societies. Furthermore, people have come to expect economic growth – we expect our children to have a better life (in the material sense) than we have had.

From the government's point of view, economic growth is desirable because it brings in increasing revenues from a given structure of tax rates. It means that more and better schools, hospitals, and other social services can be provided without resorting to the politically unpopular measure of raising the rates of taxation. Economic growth also makes it easier (politically) to carry out policies of income distribution which favour the less well off. If real income per head is increasing, a more than proportionate share of the increment can be allocated to the lower income groups and a less than proportionate share to the higher income groups. No one need be worse off.

Of great importance is the cumulative nature of economic growth. We must use compound interest calculations to work out the longer term effects of particular growth rates. For example, a country which maintains a growth rate of 3 per cent per annum will achieve a doubling of real income in 24 years. It is this aspect of growth which explains why relatively small differences in national growth rates can, in a matter of 10 or 15 years, lead to large absolute differences in living standards. It also explains why the differences in real income between a rich country and a poor country can widen even when they are both experiencing the same rate of growth. A 3 per cent increase on £1 m. is a much greater increase in absolute terms than 3 per cent on £1 000.

The causes of growth

Economists have identified several factors which determine the rate of growth, but there is a lot of disagreement on the relative importance of these factors. It is fairly obvious that, on the supply side, economic growth will depend upon the increase in the quantity and quality of the factors of production and the efficiency with which they are combined. But the demand side is also important. The incentives to increase capacity and output will clearly depend upon the level of aggregate demand. The object of demand management is not merely to bring planned spending up to a certain level and hold it there, it must be steadily raised to take account of the desired or attainable rate of growth. More is said about this later. In the meantime, we can look at some of the ways in which a nation's productive potential can be increased.

1 Increased skills and education

Education and training are often described as 'investment in people' and there is no doubt that they have an important part to play in raising the productivity of the labour force. The lack of these facilities provides a serious barrier to more rapid economic progress in the developing countries.

2 Economies of scale

We have already explained how larger scale production can raise productivity (see Chapter 7). The scope for improved growth rates on this particular basis depends very much on the size and stage of development of the economy. There is obviously much more scope for growth through economies of scale in the developing world than in the larger industrialised societies.

3 Investment

In this context we are mainly concerned with net investment; that is, the additions to the national stock of capital. There are two ways in which the stock of capital may increase. When the labour force is increasing, an equivalent amount of investment is likely to be made otherwise the amount of capital per worker would be falling. This process is known as 'capital widening' and need not necessarily lead to any increase in output per worker. Increasing the amount of capital per worker is known as 'capital deepening' and this process should lead to increasing labour productivity.

Although investment is recognised as a factor in economic growth, there is much dispute as to the way in which the two are linked. While it is true that no country has achieved a very fast growth rate without a high rate of investment, there are several examples of countries which have invested heavily and failed to achieve high growth rates. Much depends on the type of investment being undertaken. The construction of schools, houses, hospitals, and other forms of social capital does not have a direct influence on productive efficiency in the same way as manufacturing, commercial, or agricultural investment. One must look at the type of investment as well as its volume when assessing the likely effects on economic growth. In this connection a piecemeal modernisation of industry is not likely to be so effective as a complete rebuilding. Countries like Japan and Germany, which suffered widespread destruction of industrial capacity during the Second World War, were able to plan and build fully integrated plants embodying the very latest techniques. British industrial investment has tended to take the form of a much more dispersed programme for modernising existing industrial structures.

The extent to which new capital is used efficiently is also an important consideration. When improved machinery is installed, fears of redundancy may cause unions to insist on unchanged manning schedules so that the full potential gains in labour productivity may not be realised. The average age of the capital stock is another important determinant of productivity. If one country *replaces* its capital more frequently than another, it will have better and more efficient equipment even though the *net* investment figures may be the same for both countries.

4 New technology

Many economists believe that the introduction of new techniques may be a more important cause of growth than an increasing stock of capital. 'New technology', however, is a rather vague term and it is taken to include such things as new inventions, new techniques of production, improvements in the design and performance of machinery, better organisation and management, more efficient factory layouts, better training facilities, and more efficient systems of transport and communication. It is unrealistic to separate technical progress and investment completely, because much of the new technology tends to be 'embodied' in new kinds of equipment. When an old lathe is replaced by a more efficient new model, there has been no increase in the volume of investment, but there has been an increase in the industry's productive potential.

5 Reallocation of resources

Changes in output per head are very much influenced by changes in the distribution of the labour force. As economic development takes place, there is a tendency for labour to shift first from primary production (agriculture, mining, etc.) to secondary production (manufacturing) and later to the service industries. Normally, output per worker tends to grow more rapidly in agriculture and manufacturing than in the service industries since it is more difficult for people such as doctors, teachers, and civil servants to raise their productivity. It is also the case that productivity has tended to rise more rapidly in manufacturing than in agriculture.

Thus, in Japan and continental Western Europe where, since the Second World War, there has been a substantial movement of labour from agriculture to manufacturing, there have also been some very high growth rates recorded. In Britain and the USA, on the other

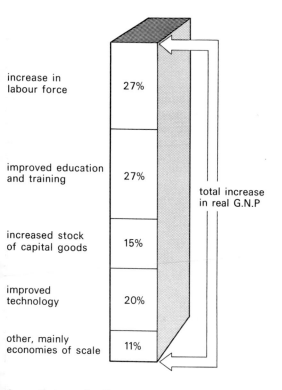

increase in labour force — 27%

improved education and training — 27%

increased stock of capital goods — 15%

improved technology — 20%

other, mainly economies of scale — 11%

total increase in real G.N.P

Source: Understanding Macro-economics
Prentice Hall

Fig. 86 USA sources of economic growth, 1929–1957

hand, the service sector has tended to grow much faster than the other sectors.

One particular estimate of the sources of economic growth in the USA is illustrated in Fig. 86.

The benefits and costs of economic growth

There are a variety of ways in which the benefits of economic growth may be enjoyed. By maintaining the same labour force working the same number of hours, the community may enjoy the gains from its increasing ability to produce in the form of higher levels of consumption. Alternatively, since any given output can now be produced with a small labour input, workers may decide to take part of their improved living standards in terms of increased leisure. It would also be possible to maintain consumption levels *and* reduce the proportion of the population at work by extending the provisions for full-time further education and/or reducing the age of retirement. Economic growth, as pointed out earlier, also makes it possible to devote more resources to the social services without having to cut private consumption.

Nevertheless, in whatever form society chooses to take the future benefits, economic growth imposes a sacrifice in terms of current living standards. In a fully employed economy a higher rate of investment can only be carried out by allocating more resources to the production of capital goods; the current output of consumption goods, therefore, will be less than it might otherwise be. It is true that a much greater annual output of consumer goods will be forthcoming in the future, but it may be many years before there is any *net* gain. Is it worth it?

Economic growth also gives rise to a variety of social costs. Rising incomes make it possible for more people to own cars, but this could lead to problems of pollution and traffic congestion. Huge modern steel plants, chemical works, oil refineries, and generating stations may be very efficient on the basis of purely commercial assessments, but they could impose costs on society by destroying natural beauty and other amenities. Modern methods of agriculture may greatly increase yields per acre, but they could have damaging effects on wild life. On the other hand we must remember that it is economic growth which makes it possible to devote more resources to the search for safer and cleaner methods of production.

Perhaps the most disturbing social costs are those associated with a rapid pace of economic change. The technical progress which makes machines and production methods obsolete also makes people redundant. Labour will have to learn new skills, adopt new methods of working, and accept more frequent changes of occupation. While programmes of retraining with adequate financial grants can deal with the problem to some extent, there still remains the social cost in terms of the disruption of a career and the unpleasant breaks in the patterns of a person's working life. The benefits of economic growth may not be evenly spread; instead of everyone reducing his working week by a small fraction, it is more likely that some individuals may find themselves completely redundant.

Economic policy and growth

The policy measures already discussed can be used to influence the various factors which determine growth. Fiscal and monetary measures can be used to stimulate private investment and public investment, research and development may be encouraged by grants and tax allowances, and the government can enlarge and improve educational and training facilities. It also has the ability to maintain demand at levels which will encourage firms to expand their capacities.

If growth were the only objective of economic policy, there is little doubt that it could be achieved. But we know that governments are faced with the problem of conflicting objectives. In the UK, these conflicts have been particularly acute and for much of the post-war period aggregate demand has been managed with a view to dealing with balance of payments problems and escalating inflation. In fact, for much of this period output has grown at a slower rate than the country's productive potential.

The use of demand management techniques to deal with inflation and external deficits resulted in a series of 'stop-go' phases. Deflationary measures were applied to slow down the rate of inflation or to reduce the level of imports and they were relaxed when unemployment rose to politically unacceptable levels. Stop-go policies however are not likely to encourage those attitudes and expectations which are conducive to economic growth. If business people become convinced that any expansionary phase will be short-lived, they will not undertake the longer term investment projects which would increase the nation's productive capacity. When there is a lack of confidence in the ability of the government to carry out a sustained programme of expansion, any increase in aggregate demand is likely to increase short-term speculation in shares and property rather than industrial investment.

Workers too are unlikely to be receptive to changing practices and techniques, many of which cause redundancies, unless they are convinced that sustained growth will generate new job opportunities.

The government may also find it difficult to persuade people to accept the sacrifices which a faster rate of economic growth demands. If people have a very strong time preference it will require very high rates of interest to persuade them to forgo current consumption (i.e. to save and lend more). Likewise a movement of resources from the creation of social capital to the production of more industrial capital may be strongly resisted. If the economy is fully employed, any attempt to raise the rate of economic growth must entail some sacrifice in terms of present living standards, otherwise measures designed to increase investment will simply give rise to inflation.

Countries like the UK, which are heavily dependent on imported materials, face another serious problem when trying to raise the rate of economic growth. An expansion of investment brings about an immediate increase in imports (materials and machinery) and since there is unlikely to be an immediate increase in exports, then, unless the country is enjoying an export surplus, the likely effect is a deficit on the balance of payments. If a deficit does arise and the foreign currency reserves are inadequate to deal with it, or the government is not prepared to allow the necessary depreciation of the currency, imports will have to be cut and the growth objective abandoned.

36 Inequalities of Income and Wealth

The distribution of wealth

Comprehensive details of the distribution of income and wealth in the UK became available for the first time in 1975 when a Royal Commission,[1] set up to examine this subject, presented its report. It shows that the distribution of wealth is very unequal, but that the degree of inequality has been declining. Fig. 87 provides some relevant details. The figures are derived from the Inland Revenue's estate duty records where wealth is taken to mean assets such as property, land, shares, works of art, jewellery, and bank deposits. The Royal Commission, however, carried out an adjustment to the 1972 figures by including people's accumulated pension rights as part of their wealth. It is true that pension rights are not *marketable* wealth, but the Commission thought that they represented personal wealth all the same. If these accumulated pension rights are taken into account (below the line in Fig. 87), the extent of the inequality is sharply reduced.

More recent figures giving the picture for 1979 show that from 1974 to 1979 there was relatively little change in the pattern of ownership of marketable wealth. The trend for marketable wealth plus pension rights, however, shows a fairly continuous movement towards greater equality illustrating the continuing growth in the significance of pension rights as a component of total wealth.

Wealth is distributed unequally for many reasons. Two obvious reasons are the inequality in the distribution of income which affects people's ability to save, and the fact that people have different propensities to save. Age, too, is a factor. Older people generally hold more wealth than younger people because they have had more years to accumulate wealth. One factor emerging from the report is that about one half of all corporate dividends, and one half of interest payments to individuals, go to pensioners. The fact that wealth can be inherited and earns income also helps to explain why, over a period of years, vast fortunes can be built up. Another source of wealth is private enterprise. A man who starts a business and builds it up into a successful enterprise not only increases his income, he also creates a marketable asset (the firm itself), the value of which will be greater than his financial investment in the business.

Royal Commission on Distribution of Income and Wealth. Cmnd. 6171.

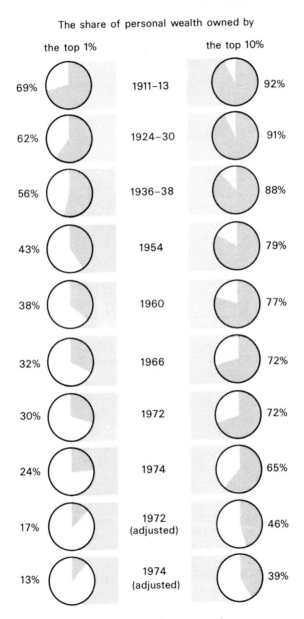

The share of personal wealth owned by

the top 1%   the top 10%

69%	1911–13	92%
62%	1924–30	91%
56%	1936–38	88%
43%	1954	79%
38%	1960	77%
32%	1966	72%
30%	1972	72%
24%	1974	65%
17%	1972 (adjusted)	46%
13%	1974 (adjusted)	39%

Source: Sunday Times 3 August 1975

Fig. 87 UK personal wealth

The distribution of income

There are estimates available for many countries which give details of the proportion of total income received by the top 5 per cent of households. These estimates show that income is more unequally distributed in poor countries than in rich countries. In many developing countries, the top 5 per cent of households receive about 30 per cent of total pre-tax income whereas for much of Western Europe (excluding Scandinavia) the top 5 per cent receive about 20 per cent of total pre-tax income. For the USA, Australia and Scandinavia the proportion is about 15 per cent.

If the distribution of income is to be used as a means of assessing economic welfare, it is necessary to use a wider definition of income than that used by the Inland Revenue, which includes wages, salaries, rent, interest and profits. The income referred to in Table 32 includes income from employment, self-employment, investment, cash benefits and income in kind. This table refers to income received by taxable units which broadly consist of either married couples or unmarried persons.

Table 32 Distribution of income in the UK

| | 1949 | | 1978–79 | |
Quantile groups	Pre-tax Share	Post-tax Share	Pre-tax Share	Post-tax Share
(tax units)				
Top 1 per cent	11·2	6·4	5·3	3·9
2–10 per cent	22·0	20·7	20·8	19·5
11–20 per cent	14·1	14·5	16·5	16·3
21–50 per cent	29·0	31·9	33·9	34·1
Bottom 50 per cent	23·7	26·5	23·5	26·2

Sources: Economic Trends May 1978; Social Trends 1982

Table 32 shows that the inequality in the distribution of income has been lessening mainly as a result of the fall in the share of total income received by the top 10 per cent of taxable units. The distribution of income is not so unequal as the distribution of wealth, but there are some wide discrepancies. Table 32 reveals that, in 1978–9, the top 10 per cent of taxable units received rather more income than the bottom 50 per cent. The effect of taxation (in this case, income tax and national insurance contributions) was less pronounced than might be expected. The share of total income going to the top 50 per cent of taxable units was reduced from 76·5 per cent to 73·8 per cent (in 1978–79) and the share going to the bottom 50 per cent was increased from 23·5 per cent to 26·2 per cent.

The reasons for the inequality in the distribution of income from

481

work have been discussed in Chapter 18 where the various barriers to labour mobility were examined. A study of the composition of income also throws some light on the causes of inequality. Major causes of low income are age and unemployment. Pensioners make up more than 80 per cent of the households in the bottom 20 per cent of the income range; in the top 20 per cent they account for only 1 per cent of the households. In the bottom quarter of the income range, state pensions and other social security benefits account for about 66 per cent of pre-tax income.

Investment income and self-employment income are important elements in the incomes of the top 1 per cent. They constitute nearly one half of the total pre-tax income of this group compared with an overall average of less than 11 per cent. The very unequal distribution of wealth, of course, leads to inequalities in the distribution of incomes which take the form of rent, interest and dividends.

How much inequality

Although economic analysis might *explain* the causes of economic inequalities, it does not *justify* them. Inequalities of income and wealth are still very great in absolute terms and there is no doubt that they generate widespread dissatisfaction. The economist must take note of these resentments because they have important effects on economic performance. The usual indicators of economic success such as the rate of economic growth, the stability of the price level, a balance of payments surplus, and even the level of employment, will not make much impact on, or excite a lot of interest from, the average citizen if he is convinced that the distributions of income and wealth are grossly inequitable. Such convictions can lead to serious social and economic stresses.

Gross inequalities in the distributions of income and wealth lead to feelings of 'unfairness' because, quite apart from creating inequalities in living standards, they lead to inequalities of opportunity. The wealthy can buy superior education and training for their children and there is no doubt that the possession of wealth confers certain social advantages. Inherited wealth provides an income to the recipient regardless of his abilities, aptitudes, or efforts.

In deciding what is an equitable distribution of income, the economist can offer no conclusive answers because it is a matter of personal judgement (i.e. a value judgement). On the assumption that the purpose of economic activity is to maximise the satisfaction of wants, it might be argued that an equal distribution of income would be the ideal. This conclusion is based on the notion that the Law of Diminishing Marginal Utility applies to income and that everyone derives the same utility from a given amount of income. Let us assume that satisfaction can be measured in some units called, say, 'utils'. If, for each person, the satisfaction derived from the first £5 of income is 8 utils and this diminishes by 1 util for each additional £5 of income, then the total utility or satisfaction to be derived from £30 distributed among 3 people is maximised when each receives £10.

But incomes are also incentives to production. In order to get people to work harder, accept greater responsibility, develop new ideas, undertake long and difficult training or to carry out unpleasant tasks, it is usually necessary to offer higher rewards. If these incentives are not forthcoming, the amount of real income available for distribution will probably be reduced. The problem is to weigh these considerations against each other. Equal distribution may give the highest level of satisfaction from any given income, but probably would cause total income to be less than it would be under an incentive system.

Purely economic arguments about the desirability of different patterns of income distribution will be inconclusive. In any case, the economist's criterion of desirability (i.e. the satisfaction of wants) is only one of several possible ways of judging what is 'best'. There are many people who think that rewards should be strictly related to effort, or risk, or responsibility. Others believe that people's needs (e.g. family responsibilities) should be the deciding factor.

Policies on redistribution

Whatever the disagreement on the criteria for deciding the most equitable distributions of income and wealth there seems to be fairly general agreement on the fact that existing distributions are inequitable so that virtually all governments have policies for reducing these inequalities.

In the UK, until very recent times, the main instrument for reducing the inequality in the distribution of wealth was a steeply progressive estate or death duty. This has had relatively little effect because avoidance of the duty, by transferring wealth before death, was a relatively simple matter. In 1975, the estate duty was replaced by a Capital Transfer Tax which taxes wealth whenever ownership is transferred. The Labour Party has proposed that this tax should be supplemented with a Wealth Tax which would take the form of an *annual* levy on wealth.

Redistributive effects of taxes and benefits

The Central Statistical Office carry out an annual study of the redistribution of income brought about by the effects of taxes and benefits. This analysis has three stages.

1 The starting point for the analysis is *original income*. This is the income in cash and kind of all members of the household before the

483

deduction of taxes or the addition of any state benefits. This first
stage looks at the redistributive effects of cash benefits. There is a
large number of such benefits including retirement pensions, child
allowances, unemployment benefit, supplementary benefits, widows'
benefit, sickness benefit and so on. When cash benefits are added to
original income we obtain the household's *gross income*.

2 Stage two deals with the effects of direct taxes on the distribution of
household income. As far as households are concerned the relevant
direct taxes are income tax and the employee's and self-employed
national insurance contributions. The deduction of direct taxes from
gross income gives us *disposable income*.

3 The third stage estimates the effects of indirect taxes and benefits in
kind. A wide range of indirect taxes have effects on household income.
These taxes include VAT, excise duties, motor vehicle duties, local
authority rates and employers' contributions to the national insurance
scheme. Taxes such as these are levied directly on consumers or are
assumed to be fully passed on to consumers. The more important
benefits in kind are the health and education services; school meals
and housing subsidies are other examples of benefits in kind. When
disposable income is adjusted to take account of indirect taxes and
benefits in kind we are left with households' *final income*. To summarise:

Original income *plus* benefits in cash = Gross income
Gross income *minus* direct taxes = Disposable income
Disposable income *minus* indirect taxes *plus* benefits in kind = Final
income

Figure 88 summarises the effects of taxes and benefits on the two
extremes of the income range in 1980, that is, the lowest 10 per cent of
households and the top 10 per cent of households (ranked according
to original income). The top 10 per cent of households had their original income cut from £17 580 to £12 360 while the bottom 10 per cent
had their income increased from £10 to £2 580. Thus the ratio between
the averages for the top and bottom groups was reduced from 1 758:1
to less than 5:1.

The most important measure in the policy for redistributing income
appears to be the payment of cash benefits since these go largely to
people who are not earning. We saw earlier that they make up the
larger part of the income of the lower income groups.

Direct taxes further increase *the share* of income going to the lower
income groups but the net effect on distribution is much less than that
due to cash benefits.

The effects of indirect taxation are less clear. These taxes take a
higher percentage of the disposable income of the middle-income
households than households at the extremes of the range. This is due
to the fact low-income households spend a large proportion of their

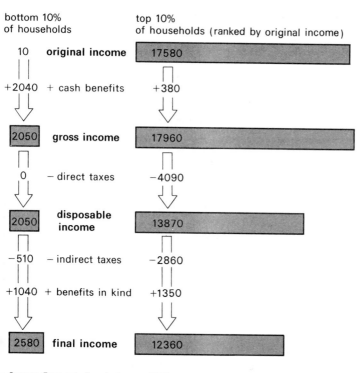

bottom 10% of households		top 10% of households (ranked by original income)

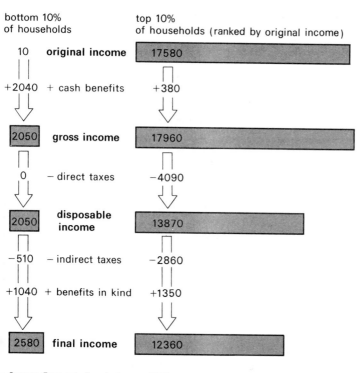

10 — **original income** — 17580

+2040 — + cash benefits — +380

2050 — **gross income** — 17960

0 — − direct taxes — −4090

2050 — **disposable income** — 13870

−510 — − indirect taxes — −2860

+1040 — + benefits in kind — +1350

2580 — **final income** — 12360

Source: Economic Trends January 1982

Fig. 88 UK redistribution of income 1980, showing annual average income per household (£).

income on food, fuel, and rent (which are exempt from indirect taxes) while high-income households tend to allocate more of their income to savings, mortgage interest and insurance premiums which attract little indirect tax. The regressive effects of indirect taxes are offset to some extent by the progressive nature of the subsidies on housing.

The higher paid tend to receive more benefit in kind mainly because of free education and subsidised school meals. Households at the bottom of the income range have a smaller number of children than those at the top. Better off parents tend to be older and have older children. They have fewer children under school age and more in the secondary school than less well off parents with the same number of children. They also obtain proportionately more benefits from the more costly further and higher education schemes.

The highest health benefits go to households with retired people and young children.

37 Public Ownership and Control

The proportion of the UK economy which is directly under state control is very large. It includes central and local government, the nationalised industries, other public corporations, defence and a number of government agencies such as the Forestry Commission. In 1981 the public sector accounted for about 30 per cent of the Gross Domestic Product and 30 per cent of total employment.

In addition to the nationalised industries listed in Table 33 and which are wholly state owned, the government also has a large stake in motor cars and several other industries. In Western Europe most countries have a large public sector and it is fairly general for the state to own and control electricity, gas, water, postal services, railways, broadcasting, and the national airlines.

Table 33 The Nationalised Industries 1982

British Airports Authority
British Airways Board
British Gas Corporation
British National Oil Corporation
British Railways Board
British Shipbuilders
British Steel Corporation
British Transport Docks Board
British Waterways Board
Electricity (England and Wales)
National Bus Company
National Coal Board
North of Scotland Hydro-Electric Board
Post Office
Telecom
Scottish Transport
South of Scotland Electricity Board

The size of the public sector is a much disputed political issue. In the UK some industries (e.g. steel and parts of road transport) have been both in and out of the public sector. The Conservative government elected in 1979 was pledged to reduce the extent of state ownership by returning certain publicly-owned enterprises to the private sector. By early 1982 British Aerospace and the National Freight Company had been sold to private enterprise and plans were being prepared to sell off parts of the British National Oil Corporation and British Gas.

Reasons for state ownership

1 'Natural' monopolies

In some industries the technical conditions of production make it impossible (or very wasteful) for more than one firm to operate (see p. 209). Such industries are often described as natural monopolies. The supply of electricity, gas, and water provide obvious examples. One argument advanced for public ownership of such industries is that the only certain way to guarantee that the monopoly power will not be used to exploit consumers (by charging prices which yield abnormal profits) is to take the industry out of the private sector. Furthermore, it may be argued that the full potential economies of scale can only be obtained by operating the industries on a national scale rather than as a number of smaller regional monopolies such as might arise under private ownership. Most of these industries are basic industries supplying services or products which are essential to the operation of all other industries. This has led to the argument that they should be run 'in the national interest' and not with a view to private profit, but, as recent events[1] have shown, it is very difficult to decide which particular policy measure best meets the national interest.

2 Adjustment to changing conditions

In the UK, one of the main arguments for nationalisation was the inability or reluctance of the private sector to provide the large injections of capital needed to re-structure and modernise certain capital-intensive industries which, due to declining demand, low profitability, or lack of capital replacement during wartime, were operating with excess capacity, out-of-date equipment, and, in some cases, on much too small a scale to meet modern demands. Only the state, it was felt, could provide investment on the scale need to revitalise these industries and bring about the necessary concentration, standardisation, and large-scale operation. These arguments were applied to the nationalisation of coal and the railways, and, to some extent, to the take-over of electricity, gas and steel. In the case of coal, the trade unions had also made it very clear that they were prepared to cooperate in plans for modernisation only if the industry were transferred to public ownership.

[1] e.g. problems associated with modernising the steel industry – the policy called for closures of uneconomic steel works.

3 To help to manage the economy

A further argument for having a substantial sector of the economy directly under government control is that it can be used as a powerful lever in controlling the economy. For example, the nationalised industries might be used to subsidise employment during a recession. Their investment programmes might be increased to produce multiplier effects during a depression, and slowed down during a boom in order to reduce aggregate demand. Governments have also used their powers to hold down prices charged by nationalised industries in order to slow down the rate of inflation. This particular use of government power, however, makes it difficult for nationalised industries to carry out long-term planning.

4 Social costs and benefits

We noted earlier (p. 22) that there are certain costs and benefits which are *external* to the firm in the sense that they do not appear in the costs incurred by, or the revenues received by, the firm. Private firms will generally ignore such costs (e.g. pollution or increased traffic congestion) and they will be unable to charge for the benefits (e.g. the amenity provided when an attractive building replaces derelict property). Nationalised industries charged with operating 'in the public interest' will be under strong political and social pressures to take account of these externalities. Thus, we find the railways under pressure to operate unremunerative lines because their abandonment would isolate certain communities or cause increased road congestion. The coal industry has been obliged to operate high-cost pits in areas where their closures would lead to heavy local unemployment. The question which arises is, 'Who should subsidise these loss-making activities, the consumers of railway services and coal, or the community generally through the tax system?'

5 Social and political arguments

The motives for nationalisation extend beyond the economic and into the social and political spheres. It is a central theme of socialist policy that the means of production should be owned by the people. Socialists believe that public ownership (i) enables the people to exercise full democratic control over the means whereby they earn their living and (ii) provides an effective means of redistributing income from property owners to the workers, or, to use the political terminology, 'to secure for the workers by hand and by brain, the full fruits of their labour'. More recent thoughts, however, raise doubts about the ability of the large state-owned corporation to meet these aspirations. Such corporations are, the critics maintain, too large and too bureaucratic to be subject to effective democratic control.

Ownership or control

It is possible that the purely economic objectives of state control may be achieved without resorting to complete public ownership (i.e. nationalisation). There are various ways in which a government can control the policy and performance of privately owned enterprise.

1 It may control the industry's prices, profits, and dividends.

2 It may take up shares in public companies and place its representatives on the board of directors.

3 It may exercise constant supervision of the costs and marketing policies of the firms in the industry.

4 It may take over the wholesale stage and hence control the prices received by the producers and those charged to distributors.

5 It may lay down technical specifications governing the quality and performance of the industry's products, or, through a system of licensing, control the nature of the services provided by the industry.

As for some of the other objectives, a redistribution of income may be achieved by subsidies on the prices of certain goods, or by a straight transfer of income to the poor, and social costs may be dealt with by taxing those who create the social burdens (e.g. 'taxing the polluters'). These alternatives would, of course, be unacceptable to those who are politically committed to public ownership. The organisational framework of public ownership was described on pp. 105–7.

Efficiency of public enterprise

Serious problems arise in trying to judge the efficiency of public enterprise. Efficiency is a measure of success in achieving a given objective, but if the objective includes such non-measurable elements as 'operating in the best interest of the public', then any single measure of efficiency is misleading.

The fact that a nationalised industry makes a profit cannot be taken as an indication of efficient operation because the industry may have used its monopoly powers to raise prices. Likewise a substantial loss does not necessarily imply inefficiency because a nationalised industry may be obliged, for social reasons, to operate unremunerative services, or its prices may be held down as part of the government's deflationary policy.

Movements in labour productivity are often used as a guide to changes in efficiency, but these too can be misleading. In fact, labour productivity in several of the British nationalised industries has risen faster than the rates for industry as a whole. This measurement how-ever does not take account of the degree of capital investment which has taken place and increases in output per unit of capital have often been relatively low.

It is also difficult to use performance elsewhere as a guide to effi-ciency since industries in the private sector do not offer any true basis for comparison. The performance of the industry relative to the per-formances of the same industries in other countries may be a better guide, but here again there are many special factors to take into ac-count. For example, in comparing productivities in coalmining the geological conditions may be very different in the countries being compared.

We must remember, too, that the performances of Britain's nationalised industries have been affected by the way in which they have sometimes been used as an instrument of economic policy. Al-though most of them are monopolies, they cannot be too complacent because they operate in a competitive framework to the extent that there are substitutes for their goods or services (e.g. coal *v.* oil, gas *v.* electricity, road *v.* rail).

Pricing policy

The Acts which established the nationalised industries merely said that prices should be related to costs but did not specify the nature of the relationship. The simplest method of ensuring that total revenue covers total cost is to make price equal to average cost. For many of these industries, however, the costs of supplying one group of consumers can be very different from those of supplying another group. For example, in the case of the railways, the cost per passenger mile on the busy inter-City routes is much less than that on suburban branch lines where trains are normally running with a lot of excess capacity. If fares on all lines were based on average costs for the whole network, passengers on busy lines would be subsidising those on other lines.

There has been much discussion on the subject of marginal cost pricing as a basis for fixing the prices of the commodities supplied by the nationalised industries. In theory, when price is equated with mar-ginal cost we have the optimum allocation of resources. If we assume that price is a good indicator of marginal utility and that marginal cost measures the opportunity cost of the resources used to supply the marginal unit, then output should be expanded up to the point where Price $= MC$ and no further. Additional units of output would yield satisfactions which were less than the value (in alternative uses) of the resources used to produce them, because the prices of these units would be less than their marginal costs. Unfortunately, it is very diffi-cult to obtain any precise measure of marginal cost. Another problem with this scheme is that when the industry is operating under conditions of increasing returns, marginal cost will be less than average cost so that, if Price = MC, the industry will be making losses. If it is operating under diminishing returns, marginal cost will be above average cost so that, if Price = MC, the industry will be making abnormal profits. Nevertheless there has been some movement towards marginal cost pricing for particular products and services (e.g. the two-part tariff for electricity).

In practice, the nationalised industries in the UK have not been given complete freedom in determining their pricing policies. For considerable periods they have been subject to restraint, either because the government wished to reduce inflationary pressures, or because the public has come to expect low prices in the public sector. This policy can lead to a misallocation of resources. If the private sector charges prices which yield profits while the public sector just breaks even or makes a loss, then public sector goods are underpriced, in terms of the resources used, compared with private sector goods. These 'artificially' lower prices will lead to larger quantities of public sector goods being demanded than would be the case if prices fully reflected costs in both sectors. More resources will be drawn into public sector production than consumers would 'vote' into that sector if the prices they paid were truly indicating the costs of production.

Financial objectives

Since the nationalised industries are state owned, the government is responsible for meeting any debts incurred by these industries. The nationalised industries do not borrow from the domestic market other than for short-term borrowing. Instead they borrow from the National Loans Fund and the government, in turn, borrows from the market. This means that the provision of external funds to meet the capital requirements of these industries has a direct effect on the borrowing of the public sector. In its attempt to control the growth of the money supply (and market rates of interest), the government is concerned to exercise strict control of public sector borrowing (see page 327).

The government has, therefore, introduced a system of external financial limits (EFLs) which control the amount of finance (grants and borrowing) which a nationalised industry can raise in any financial year from external sources. Further features of the financial framework which the government has created for the nationalised industries concern,

a some target for the industries' profits, and
b the basis on which investment decisions are made.

A government White Paper published in 1978 declared that an adequate level of profit was essential for the well-being of the nationalised industries; it would enable them to make contributions to their investment programmes and keep down their borrowing requirements on the economy. To this end the government established a financial target for each industry. This target takes the form of some given percentage return on the net assets employed by the industry, each industry being given a different target.

The second feature of financial control uses the idea of the opportunity cost of capital. Investment plans of the nationalised industries should only proceed if they are expected to earn a rate of return of 5 per cent in real terms. This figure was decided upon because it had been calculated that 5 per cent was the average real pre-tax return achieved by private investment. In other words it represented the opportunity cost of capital to the nationalised industries.

In setting financial targets as a measure of performance, the government has been obliged to allow the nationalised industries much greater freedom in setting their prices. In addition the government has agreed to compensate these industries for activities which are classified as 'public service obligations'. For example, the railways receive a grant towards the cost of keeping open lines (for social reasons) which they would otherwise choose to close.

Index